HARRY SINCLAIR LEWIS, the son of a country doctor, was born in Sauk Centre, Minnesota, in 1885. His childhood and early youth were spent in the Middle West and later he attended Yale University, where he was editor of the literary magazine. After being graduated in 1907, he went to New York, tried free-lance work for a time and then worked in a variety of editorial positions in various places from the East Coast to California. He was able to give this work up after a few of his stories had appeared in magazines and his first novel, *Our Mr. Wrenn* (1914), had been published. However, *Main Street* (1920) was his first really successful novel and his reputation was enhanced by the publication of *Babbitt* (1922). Lewis was awarded a Pulitzer Prize for *Arrowsmith* (1925) in 1926 but refused to accept this honor. However, he accepted the Nobel Prize which was awarded to him in 1930 and went to Stockholm to receive it formally. During the last part of his life he spent a great deal of time in Europe and continued to write both novels and plays. In 1950, after completing his last novel, *World So Wide* (1951), he intended to take an extended tour. He became ill, however, and was forced to settle in Rome, where he spent some months working on his poems. He died there in 1951.

Drawing based on photograph by MAN RAY

Sinclair Lewis

BABBITT

With an Afterword
by Mark Schorer

A SIGNET CLASSIC from
NEW AMERICAN LIBRARY
TIMES MIRROR
New York and Scarborough, Ontario

chapter **1**

THE towers of Zenith aspired above the morning mist; austere towers of steel and cement and limestone, sturdy as cliffs and delicate as silver rods. They were neither citadels nor churches, but frankly and beautifully office-buildings.

The mist took pity on the fretted structures of earlier generations: the Post Office with its shingle-tortured mansard, the red brick minarets of hulking old houses, factories with stingy and sooted windows, wooden tenements colored like mud. The city was full of such grotesqueries, but the clean towers were thrusting them from the business center, and on the farther hills were shining new houses, homes—they seemed—for laughter and tranquillity.

Over a concrete bridge fled a limousine of long sleek hood and noiseless engine. These people in evening clothes were returning from an all-night rehearsal of a Little Theater play, an artistic adventure considerably illuminated by champagne. Below the bridge curved a railroad, a maze of green and crimson lights. The New York Flyer boomed past, and twenty lines of polished steel leaped into the glare.

In one of the skyscrapers the wires of the Associated Press were closing down. The telegraph operators wearily raised their celluloid eye-shades after a night of talking with Paris and Peking. Through the building crawled the scrubwomen, yawning, their old shoes slapping. The dawn mist spun away. Cues of men with lunch-boxes clumped toward the immensity of new factories, sheets of glass and hollow tile, glittering shops where five thousand men worked beneath one roof, pouring out the honest wares that would be sold up the Euphrates and across the veldt. The whistles rolled out in

5

greeting a chorus cheerful as the April dawn; the song of labor in a city built—it seemed—for giants.

II

There was nothing of the giant in the aspect of the man who was beginning to awaken on the sleeping-porch of a Dutch Colonial house in that residential district of Zenith known as Floral Heights.

His name was George F. Babbitt. He was forty-six years old now, in April, 1920, and he made nothing in particular, neither butter nor shoes nor poetry, but he was nimble in the calling of selling houses for more than people could afford to pay.

His large head was pink, his brown hair thin and dry. His face was babyish in slumber, despite his wrinkles and the red spectacle-dents on the slopes of his nose. He was not fat but he was exceedingly well fed; his cheeks were pads, and the unroughened hand which lay helpless upon the khaki-colored blanket was slightly puffy. He seemed prosperous, extremely married and unromantic; and altogether unromantic appeared this sleeping-porch, which looked on one sizable elm, two respectable grass-plots, a cement driveway, and a corrugated iron garage. Yet Babbitt was again dreaming of the fairy child, a dream more romantic than scarlet pagodas by a silver sea.

For years the fairy child had come to him. Where others saw but Georgie Babbitt, she discerned gallant youth. She waited for him, in the darkness beyond mysterious groves. When at last he could slip away from the crowded house he darted to her. His wife, his clamoring friends, sought to follow, but he escaped, the girl fleet beside him, and they crouched together on a shadowy hillside. She was so slim, so white, so eager! She cried that he was gay and valiant, that she would wait for him, that they would sail—

Rumble and bang of the milk-truck.

Babbitt moaned, turned over, struggled back toward his dream. He could see only her face now, beyond misty waters. The furnace-man slammed the basement door. A dog barked in the next yard. As Babbitt sank blissfully into a dim warm tide, the paper-carrier went by whistling, and the rolled-up *Advocate* thumped the front door. Babbitt roused, his stomach constricted with alarm. As he relaxed, he was pierced by the familiar and irritating rattle of some one cranking a Ford:

snap-ah-ah, snap-ah-ah, snap-ah-ah. Himself a pious motorist, Babbitt cranked with the unseen driver, with him waited
through taut hours for the roar of the starting engine, with
him agonized as the roar ceased and again began the infernal
patient snap-ah-ah—a round, flat sound, a shivering cold-
morning sound, a sound infuriating and inescapable. Not till
the rising voice of the motor told him that the Ford was
moving was he released from the panting tension. He glanced
once at his favorite tree, elm twigs against the gold patina
of sky, and fumbled for sleep as for a drug. He who had
been a boy very credulous of life was no longer greatly interested in the possible and improbable adventures of each
new day.

He escaped from reality till the alarm-clock rang, at seven-
twenty.

III

It was the best of nationally advertised and quantitatively
produced alarm-clocks, with all modern attachments, including cathedral chime, intermittent alarm, and a phosphorescent
dial. Babbitt was proud of being awakened by such a rich
device. Socially it was almost as creditable as buying expensive cord tires.

He sulkily admitted now that there was no more escape,
but he lay and detested the grind of the real-estate business,
and disliked his family, and disliked himself for disliking
them. The evening before, he had played poker at Vergil
Gunch's till midnight, and after such holidays he was irritable before breakfast. It may have been the tremendous
home-brewed beer of the prohibition-era and the cigars to
which that beer enticed him; it may have been resentment
of return from this fine, bold man-world to a restricted region
of wives and stenographers, and of suggestions not to smoke
so much.

From the bedroom beside the sleeping-porch, his wife's de-
testably cheerful "Time to get up, Georgie boy," and the itchy
sound, the brisk and scratchy sound, of combing hairs out of
a stiff brush.

He grunted; he dragged his thick legs, in faded baby-blue
pajamas, from under the khaki blanket; he sat on the edge
of the cot, running his fingers through his wild hair, while his
plump feet mechanically felt for his slippers. He looked re-
gretfully at the blanket—forever a suggestion to him of free-

dom and heroism. He had bought it for a camping trip which
had never come off. It symbolized gorgeous loafing, gorgeous cursing, virile flannel shirts.

He creaked to his feet, groaning at the waves of pain which
passed behind his eyeballs. Though he waited for their scorching recurrence, he looked blurrily out at the yard. It delighted
him, as always; it was the neat yard of a successful business
man of Zenith, that is, it was perfection, and made him also
perfect. He regarded the corrugated iron garage. For the
three-hundred-and-sixty-fifth time in a year he reflected, "No
class to that tin shack. Have to build me a frame garage.
But by golly it's the only thing on the place that isn't up-to-
date!" While he stared he thought of a community garage for
his acreage development, Glen Oriole. He stopped puffing
and jiggling. His arms were akimbo. His petulant, sleep-
swollen face was set in harder lines. He suddenly seemed
capable, an official, a man to contrive, to direct, to get things
done.

On the vigor of his idea he was carried down the hard,
clean, unused-looking hall into the bathroom.

Though the house was not large it had, like all houses on
Floral Heights, an altogether royal bathroom of porcelain and
glazed tile and metal sleek as silver. The towel-rack was a
rod of clear glass set in nickel. The tub was long enough
for a Prussian Guard, and above the set bowl was a sensational exhibit of tooth-brush holder, shaving-brush holder,
soap-dish, sponge-dish, and medicine-cabinet, so glittering and
so ingenious that they resembled an electrical instrument-
board. But the Babbitt whose god was Modern Appliances
was not pleased. The air of the bathroom was thick with
the smell of a heathen toothpaste. "Verona been at it again!
'Stead of sticking to Lilidol, like I've re-peat-ed-ly asked her,
she's gone and gotten some confounded stinkum stuff that
makes you sick!"

The bath-mat was wrinkled and the floor was wet. (His
daughter Verona eccentrically took baths in the morning, now
and then.) He slipped on the mat, and slid against the tub.
He said "Damn!" Furiously he snatched up his tube of shaving-cream, furiously he lathered, with a belligerent slapping
of the unctuous brush, furiously he raked his plump cheeks
with a safety-razor. It pulled. The blade was dull. He said,
"Damn—oh—oh—damn it!"

He hunted through the medicine-cabinet for a packet of
new razor-blades (reflecting, as invariably, "Be cheaper to

buy one of these dinguses and strop your own blades,") and when he discovered the packet, behind the round box of bicarbonate of soda, he thought ill of his wife for putting it there and very well of himself for not saying "Damn." But he did say it, immediately afterward, when with wet and soap-slippery fingers he tried to remove the horrible little envelope and crisp clinging oiled paper from the new blade.

Then there was the problem, oft-pondered, never solved, of what to do with the old blade, which might imperil the fingers of his young. As usual, he tossed it on top of the medicine-cabinet, with a mental note that some day he must remove the fifty or sixty other blades that were also temporarily, piled up there. He finished his shaving in a growing testiness increased by his spinning headache and by the emptiness in his stomach. When he was done, his round face smooth and streamy and his eyes stinging from soapy water, he reached for a towel. The family towels were wet, wet and clammy and vile, all of them wet, he found, as he blindly snatched them—his own face-towel, his wife's, Verona's, Ted's, Tinka's, and the lone bath-towel with the huge welt of initial. Then George F Babbitt did a dismaying thing. He wiped his face on the guest-towel! It was a pansy-embroidered trifle which always hung there to indicate that the Babbitts were in the best Floral Heights society. No one had ever used it. No guest had ever dared to. Guests secretively took a corner of the nearest regular towel.

He was raging, "By golly, here they go and use up all the towels, every doggone one of 'em, and they use 'em and get 'em all wet and sopping, and never put out a dry one for me—of course, I'm the goat!—and then I want one and—I'm the only person in the doggone house that's got the slightest doggone bit of consideration for other people and thoughtfulness and consider there may be others that may want to use the doggone bathroom after me and consider—"

He was pitching the chill abominations into the bath-tub, pleased by the vindictiveness of that desolate flapping sound; and in the midst his wife serenely trotted in, observed serenely, "Why Georgie dear, what are you doing? Are you going to wash out the towels? Why, you needn't wash out the towels. Oh, Georgie, you didn't go and use the guest-towel, did you?"

It is not recorded that he was able to answer.

For the first time in weeks he was sufficiently roused by his wife to look at her.

IV

Myra Babbitt—Mrs. George F. Babbitt—was definitely mature. She had creases from the corners of her mouth to the bottom of her chin, and her plump neck bagged. But the thing that marked her as having passed the line was that she no longer had reticences before her husband, and no longer worried about not having reticences. She was in a petticoat now, and corsets which bulged, and unaware of being seen in bulgy corsets. She had become so dully habituated to married life that in her full matronliness she was as sexless as an anemic nun. She was a good woman, a kind woman, a diligent woman, but no one, save perhaps Tinka her ten-year-old, was at all interested in her or entirely aware that she was alive.

After a rather thorough discussion of all the domestic and social aspects of towels she apologized to Babbitt for his having an alcoholic headache; and he recovered enough to endure the search for a B.V.D. undershirt which had, he pointed out, malevolently been concealed among his clean pajamas.

He was fairly amiable in the conference on the brown suit.

"What do you think, Myra?" He pawed at the clothes hunched on a chair in their bedroom, while she moved about mysteriously adjusting and patting her petticoat and, to his jaundiced eye, never seeming to get on with her dressing. "How about it? Shall I wear the brown suit another day?"

"Well, it looks awfully nice on you."

"I know, but gosh, it needs pressing."

"That's so. Perhaps it does."

"It certainly could stand being pressed, all right."

"Yes, perhaps it wouldn't hurt it to be pressed."

"But gee, the coat doesn't need pressing. No sense in having the whole darn suit pressed, when the coat doesn't need it."

"That's so."

"But the pants certainly need it, all right. Look at them —look at those wrinkles—the pants certainly do need pressing."

"That's so. Oh, Georgie, why couldn't you wear the brown coat with the blue trousers we were wondering what we'd do with them?"

"Good Lord! Did you ever in all my life know me to wear

the coat of one suit and the pants of another? What do you think I am? A busted bookkeeper?"

"Well, why don't you put on the dark gray suit to-day, and stop in at the tailor and leave the brown trousers?"

"Well, they certainly need— Now where the devil is that gray suit? Oh, yes, here we are."

He was able to get through the other crises of dressing with comparative resoluteness and calm.

His first adornment was the sleeveless dimity B.V.D undershirt, in which he resembled a small boy humorlessly wearing a cheesecloth tabard at a civic pageant. He never put on B.V.D.'s without thanking the God of Progress that he didn't wear tight, long, old-fashioned undergarments, like his father-in-law and partner, Henry Thompson. His second embellishment was combing and slicking back his hair. It gave him a tremendous forehead, arching up two inches beyond the former hair-line. But most wonder-working of all was the donning of his spectacles.

There is character in spectacles—the pretentious tortoise-shell, the meek pince-nez of the school teacher, the twisted silver-framed glasses of the old villager. Babbitt's spectacles had huge, circular, frameless lenses of the very best glass; the ear-pieces were thin bars of gold. In them he was the modern business man; one who gave orders to clerks and drove a car and played occasional golf and was scholarly in regard to Salesmanship. His head suddenly appeared not babyish but weighty, and you noted his heavy, blunt nose, his straight mouth and thick, long upper lip, his chin overfleshy but strong; with respect you beheld him put on the rest of his uniform as a Solid Citizen.

The gray suit was well cut, well made, and completely undistinguished. It was a standard suit. White piping on the V of the vest added a flavor of law and learning. His shoes were black laced boots, good boots, honest boots, standard boots, extraordinarily uninteresting boots. The only frivolity was in his purple knitted scarf. With considerable comment on the matter to Mrs. Babbitt (who, acrobatically fastening the back of her blouse to her skirt with a safety-pin, did not hear a word he said), he chose between the purple scarf and a tapestry effect with stringless brown harps among blown palms, and into it he thrust a snake-head pin with opal eyes.

A sensational event was changing from the brown suit to the gray the contents of his pockets. He was earnest about these objects. They were of eternal importance, like baseball or the Republican Party. They included a fountain pen and a silver pencil (always lacking a supply of new leads) which belonged in the righthand upper vest pocket. Without them he would have felt naked. On his watch-chain were a gold penknife, silver cigar-cutter, seven keys (the use of two of which he had forgotten), and incidentally a good watch. Depending from the chain was a large, yellowish elk's-tooth—proclamation of his membership in the Brotherly and Protective Order of Elks. Most significant of all was his loose-leaf pocket note-book, that modern and efficient note-book which contained the addresses of people whom he had forgotten, prudent memoranda of postal money-orders which had reached their destinations months ago, stamps which had lost their mucilage, clippings of verses by T. Cholmondeley Frink and of the newspaper editorials from which Babbitt got his opinions and his polysyllables, notes to be sure and do things which he did not intend to do, and one curious inscription— D.S.S.D.M.Y.P.D.F.

But he had no cigarette-case. No one had ever happened to give him one, so he hadn't the habit, and people who carried cigarette-cases he regarded as effeminate.

Last, he stuck in his lapel the Boosters' Club button. With the conciseness of great art the button displayed two words: "Boosters—Pep!" It made Babbitt feel loyal and important. It associated him with Good Fellows, with men who were nice and human, and important in business circles. It was his V.C., his Legion of Honor ribbon, his Phi Beta Kappa key.

With the subtleties of dressing ran other complex worries. "I feel kind of punk this morning," he said. "I think I had too much dinner last evening. You oughtn't to serve those heavy banana fritters."

"But you asked me to have some."

"I know, but— I tell you, when a fellow gets past forty he has to look after his digestion. There's a lot of fellows that don't take proper care of themselves. I tell you at forty a man's a fool or his doctor— I mean, his own doctor. Folks don't give enough attention to this matter of dieting. Now I think— Course a man ought to have a good meal after the day's work, but it would be a good thing for both of us if we took lighter lunches."

"But Georgie, here at home I always do have a light lunch."

"Mean to imply I make a hog of myself, eating down-town? Yes, sure! You'd have a swell time if you had to eat the truck that new steward hands out to us at the Athletic Club! But I certainly do feel out of sorts, this morning. Funny, got a pain down here on the left side—but no, that wouldn't be appendicitis, would it? Last night, when I was driving over to Verg Gunch's, I felt a pain in my stomach, too. Right here it was—kind of a sharp shooting pain. I— Where'd that dime go to? Why don't you serve more prunes at breakfast? Of course I eat an apple every evening—an apple a day keeps the doctor away—but still, you ought to have more prunes, and not all these fancy doodads."

"The last time I had prunes you didn't eat them."

"Well, I didn't feel like eating 'em, I suppose. Matter of fact, I think I did eat some of 'em. Anyway— I tell you it's mighty important to— I was saying to Verg Gunch, just last evening, most people don't take sufficient care of their diges—"

"Shall we have the Gunches for our dinner, next week?"

"Why sure; you bet."

"Now see here, George: I want you to put on your nice dinner-jacket that evening."

"Rats! The rest of 'em won't want to dress."

"Of course they will. You remember when you didn't dress for the Littlefields' supper-party, and all the rest did, and how embarrassed you were."

"Embarrassed, hell! I wasn't embarrassed. Everybody knows I can put on as expensive a Tux. as anybody else, and I should worry if I don't happen to have it on sometimes. All a darn nuisance, anyway. All right for a woman, that stays around the house all the time, but when a fellow's worked like the dickens all day, he doesn't want to go and hustle his head off getting into the soup-and-fish for a lot of folks that he's seen in just reg'lar ordinary clothes that same day."

"You know you enjoy being seen in one. The other evening you admitted you were glad I'd insisted on your dressing. You said you felt a lot better for it. And oh, Georgie, I do wish you wouldn't say 'Tux.' It's 'dinner-jacket.'"

"Rats, what's the odds?"

"Well, it's what all the nice folks say. Suppose Lucile McKelvey heard you calling it a 'Tux.'"

"Well, that's all right now! Lucile McKelvey can't pull anything on me! Her folks are common as mud, even if her husband and her dad are millionaires! I suppose you're trying to rub in *your* exalted social position! Well, let me tell you

that your revered paternal ancestor, Henry T., doesn't even
call it a 'Tux.'! He calls it a 'bobtail jacket for a ringtail
monkey,' and you couldn't get him into one unless you chloro-
formed him!"

"Now don't be horrid, George."

"Well, I don't want to be horrid, but Lord! you're getting
as fussy as Verona. Ever since she got out of college she's
been too rambunctious to live with—doesn't know what she
wants—well, I know what she wants!—all she wants is to
marry a millionaire, and live in Europe, and hold some preacher's hand, and simultaneously at the same time stay right here
in Zenith and be some blooming kind of a socialist agitator
or boss charity-worker or some damn thing! Lord, and Ted
is just as bad! He wants to go to college, and he doesn't want
to go to college. Only one of the three that knows her own
mind is Tinka. Simply can't understand how I ever came to
have a pair of shillyshallying children like Rone and Ted.
I may not be any Rockefeller or James J. Shakespeare, but
I certainly do know my own mind, and I do keep right on
plugging along in the office and— Do you know the latest?
Far as I can figure out, Ted's new bee is he'd like to be a
movie actor and— And here I've told him a hundred times,
if he'll go to college and law-school and make good, I'll set
him up in business and— Verona just exactly as bad. Doesn't
know what she wants. Well, well, come on! Aren't you ready
yet? The girl rang the bell three minutes ago."

v

Before he followed his wife, Babbitt stood at the western-
most window of their room. This residential settlement, Floral
Heights, was on a rise; and though the center of the city was
three miles away—Zenith had between three and four hundred
thousand inhabitants now—he could see the top of the
Second National Tower, an Indiana limestone building of
thirty-five stories.

Its shining walls rose against April sky to a simple cornice
like a streak of white fire. Integrity was in the tower, and de-
cision. It bore its strength lightly as a tall soldier. As Babbitt
stared, the nervousness was soothed from his face, his slack
chin lifted in reverence. All he articulated was "That's one
lovely sight!" but he was inspired by the rhythm of the city;
his love of it renewed. He beheld the tower as a temple-

spire of the religion of business, a faith passionate, exalted, surpassing common men; and as he clumped down to breakfast he whistled the ballad "Oh, by gee, by gosh, by jingo" as though it were a hymn melancholy and noble.

chapter 2

RELIEVED of Babbitt's bumbling and the soft grunts with which his wife expressed the sympathy she was too experienced to feel and much too experienced not to show, their bedroom settled instantly into impersonality.

It gave on the sleeping-porch. It served both of them as dressing-room, and on the coldest nights Babbitt luxuriously gave up the duty of being manly and retreated to the bed inside, to curl his toes in the warmth and laugh at the January gale.

The room displayed a modest and pleasant color-scheme, after one of the best standard designs of the decorator who "did the interiors" for most of the speculative-builders' houses in Zenith. The walls were gray, the woodwork white, the rug a serene blue; and very much like mahogany was the furniture—the bureau with its great clear mirror, Mrs. Babbitt's dressing-table with toilet-articles of almost solid silver, the plain twin beds, between them a small table holding a standard electric bedside lamp, a glass for water, and a standard bedside book with colored illustrations—what particular book it was cannot be ascertained, since no one had ever opened it. The mattresses were firm but not hard, triumphant modern mattresses which had cost a great deal of money; the hot-water radiator was of exactly the proper scientific surface for the cubic contents of the room. The windows were large and easily opened, with the best catches and cords, and Holland roller-shades guaranteed not to crack. It was a masterpiece among bedrooms, right out of Cheerful Modern Houses for Medium Incomes. Only it had nothing to do with the Babbitts, nor with any one else. If people had ever lived and loved here, read thrillers at midnight and lain in beautiful indolence on a Sunday morning, there were no signs of it. It had the air of being a very good room in a very good hotel. One expected the chambermaid to come in and make it ready for people who would stay but one night, go without looking back, and never think of it again.

Every second house in Floral Heights had a bedroom precisely like this.

The Babbitts' house was five years old. It was all as competent and glossy as this bedroom. It had the best of taste, the best of inexpensive rugs, a simple and laudable architecture, and the latest conveniences. Throughout, electricity took the place of candles and slatternly hearth-fires. Along the bedroom baseboard were three plugs for electric lamps, concealed by little brass doors. In the halls were plugs for the vacuum cleaner, and in the living-room plugs for the piano lamp, for the electric fan. The trim dining-room (with its admirable oak buffet, its leaded-glass cupboard, its creamy plaster walls, its modest scene of a salmon expiring upon a pile of oysters) had plugs which supplied the electric percolator and the electric toaster.

In fact there was but one thing wrong with the Babbitt house: It was not a home.

II

Often of a morning Babbitt came bouncing and jesting in to breakfast. But things were mysteriously awry to-day. As he pontifically tread the upper hall he looked into Verona's bedroom and protested, "What's the use of giving the family a high-class house when they don't appreciate it and tend to business and get down to brass tacks?"

He marched upon them: Verona, a dumpy brown-haired girl of twenty-two, just out of Bryn Mawr, given to solicitudes about duty and sex and God and the unconquerable bagginess of the gray sports-suit she was now wearing. Ted—Theodore Roosevelt Babbitt—a decorative boy of seventeen. Tinka—Katherine—still a baby at ten, with radiant red hair and a thin skin which hinted of too much candy and too many ice cream sodas. Babbitt did not show his vague irritation as he tramped in. He really disliked being a family tyrant, and his nagging was as meaningless as it was frequent. He shouted at Tinka, "Well, kittiedoolie!" It was the only pet name in his vocabulary, except the "dear" and "hon." with which he recognized his wife, and he flung it at Tinka every morning.

He gulped a cup of coffee in the hope of pacifying his stomach and his soul. His stomach ceased to feel as though it did not belong to him, but Verona began to be conscientious and annoying, and abruptly there returned to Babbitt the doubts regarding life and families and business which had clawed at him when his dream-life and the slim fairy girl had fled.

Verona had for six months been filing-clerk at the Gruensberg Leather Company offices, with a prospect of becoming secretary to Mr. Gruensberg and thus, as Babbitt defined it, "getting some good out of your expensive college education till you're ready to marry and settle down."

But now said Verona: "Father! I was talking to a classmate of mine that's working for the Associated Charities—oh, Dad, there's the sweetest little babies that come to the milk-station there!—and I feel as though I ought to be doing something worth while like that."

"What do you mean 'worth while'? If you get to be Gruensberg's secretary—and maybe you would, if you kept up your shorthand and didn't go sneaking off to concerts and talk-fests every evening—I guess you'll find thirty-five or forty bones a week worth while!"

"I know, but—oh, I want to—contribute— I wish I were working in a settlement-house. I wonder if I could get one of the department-stores to let me put in a welfare-department with a nice rest-room and chintzes and wicker chairs and so on and so forth. Or I could—"

"Now you look here! The first thing you got to understand is that all this uplift and flipflop and settlement-work and recreation is nothing in God's world but the entering wedge for socialism. The sooner a man learns he isn't going to be coddled, and he needn't expect a lot of free grub and, uh, all these free classes and flipflop and doodads for his kids unless he earns 'em, why, the sooner he'll get on the job and produce—produce—produce! That's what the country needs, and not all this fancy stuff that just enfeebles the will-power of the working man and gives his kids a lot of notions above their class. And you—if you'd tend to business instead of fooling and fussing— All the time! When I was a young man I made up my mind what I wanted to do, and stuck to it through thick and thin, and that's why I'm where I am to-day, and—Myra! What do you let the girl chop the toast up into these dinky little chunks for? Can't get your fist onto 'em. Half cold, anyway!"

Ted Babbitt, junior in the great East Side High School, had been making hiccup-like sounds of interruption. He blurted now, "Say, Rone, you going to—"

Verona whirled. "Ted! Will you kindly not interrupt us when we're talking about serious matters!"

"Aw punk," said Ted judicially. "Ever since somebody slipped up and let you out of college, Ammonia, you been pulling these nut conversations about what-nots and so-on-and-so-forths. Are you going to— I want to use the car to-night."

Babbitt snorted, "Oh, you do! May want it myself!" Verona protested, "Oh, you do, Mr. Smarty! I'm going to take it myself!" Tinka wailed, "Oh, papa, you said maybe you'd drive 'us down to Rosedale!" and Mrs. Babbitt, "Careful, Tinka, your sleeve is in the butter." They glared, and Verona hurled, "Ted, you're a perfect pig about the car!"

"Course you're not! Not a-tall!" Ted could be maddeningly bland. "You just want to grab it off, right after dinner, and leave it in front of some skirt's house all evening while you sit and gas about lite'ature and the highbrows you're going to marry—if they only propose!"

"Well, Dad oughtn't to *ever* let you have it! You and those beastly Jones boys drive like maniacs. The idea of your taking the turn on Chautauqua Place at forty miles an hour!"

"Aw, where do you get that stuff! You're so darn scared of the car that you drive up-hill with the emergency brake on!"

"I do not! And you— Always talking about how much you know about motors, and Eunice Littlefield told me you said the battery fed the generator!"

"You—why, my good woman, you don't know a generator from a differential." Not unreasonably was Ted lofty with her. He was a natural mechanic, a maker and tinkerer of machines; he lisped in blueprints for the blueprints came.

"That'll do now!" Babbitt flung in mechanically, as he lighted the gloriously satisfying first cigar of the day and tasted the exhilarating drug of the *Advocate-Times* headlines.

Ted negotiated: "Gee, honest, Rone, I don't want to take the old boat, but I promised couple o' girls in my class I'd drive 'em down to the rehearsal of the school chorus, and, gee,

I don't want to, but a gentleman's got to keep his social engagements."

"Well, upon my word! You and your social engagements! In high school!"

"Oh, ain't we select since we went to that hen college! Let me tell you there isn't a private school in the state that's got as swell a bunch as we got in Gamma Digamma this year. There's two fellows that their dads are millionaires. Say, gee, I ought to have a car of my own, like lots of the fellows."

Babbitt almost rose. "A car of your own! Don't you want a yacht, and a house and lot? That pretty nearly takes the cake! A boy that can't pass his Latin examinations, like any other boy ought to, and he expects me to give him a motorcar, and I suppose a chauffeur, and an aeroplane maybe, as a reward for the hard work he puts in going to the movies with Eunice Littlefield! Well, when you see me giving you—"

Somewhat later, after diplomacies, Ted persuaded Verona to admit that she was merely going to the Armory, that evening, to see the dog and cat show. She was then, Ted planned, to park the car in front of the candy-store across from the Armory and he would pick it up. There were masterly arrangements regarding leaving the key, and having the gasoline tank filled; and passionately, devotees of the Great God Motor, they hymned the patch on the spare inner-tube, and the lost jack-handle.

Their truce dissolving, Ted observed that her friends were "a scream of a bunch—stuck-up gabby four-flushers." His friends, she indicated, were "disgusting imitation sports, and horrid little shrieking ignorant girls." Further: "It's disgusting of you to smoke cigarettes, and so on and so forth, and those clothes you've got on this morning, they're too utterly ridiculous—honestly, simply disgusting."

Ted balanced over to the low beveled mirror in the buffet, regarded his charms, and smirked. His suit, the latest thing in Old Eli Togs, was skin-tight, with skimpy trousers to the tops of his glaring tan boots, a chorus-man waistline, pattern of an agitated check, and across the back a belt which belted nothing. His scarf was an enormous black silk wad. His flaxen hair was ice-smooth, pasted back without parting. When he went to school he would add a cap with a long vizor like a shovel-blade. Proudest of all was his waistcoat, saved for, begged for, plotted for; a real Fancy Vest of fawn with polka dots of a decayed red, the points astoundingly long. On the lower edge of it he wore a high-school button, a class button, and a fraternity pin.

And none of it mattered. He was supple and swift and flushed; his eyes (which he believed to be cynical) were candidly eager. But he was not over-gentle. He waved his hand at poor dumpy Verona and drawled: "Yes, I guess we're pretty ridiculous and disgusticulus, and I rather guess our new necktie is some smear!"

Babbitt barked: "It is! And while you're admiring yourself, let me tell you it might add to your manly beauty if you wiped some of that egg off your mouth!"

Verona giggled, momentary victor in the greatest of Great Wars, which is the family war. Ted looked at her hopelessly, then shrieked at Tinka: "For the love o' Pete, quit pouring the whole sugar bowl on your corn flakes!"

When Verona and Ted were gone and Tinka upstairs, Babbitt groaned to his wife: "Nice family, I must say! I don't pretend to be any baa-lamb, and maybe I'm a little cross-grained at breakfast sometimes, but the way they go on jab-jab-jabbering, I simply can't stand it. I swear, I feel like going off some place where I can get a little peace. I do think after a man's spent his lifetime trying to give his kids a chance and a decent education, it's pretty discouraging to hear them all the time scrapping like a bunch of hyenas and never—and never— Curious; here in the paper it says— Never silent for one mom— Seen the morning paper yet?"

"No, dear." In twenty-three years of married life, Mrs. Babbitt had seen the paper before her husband just sixty-seven times.

"Lots of news. Terrible big tornado in the South. Hard luck, all right. But this, say, this is corking! Beginning of the end for those fellows! New York Assembly has passed some bills that ought to completely outlaw the socialists! And there's an elevator-runners' strike in New York and a lot of college boys are taking their places. That's the stuff! And a mass-meeting in Birmingham's demanded that this Mick agitator, this fellow De Valera, be deported. Dead right, by golly! All these agitators paid with German gold anyway. And we got no business interfering with the Irish or any other foreign government. Keep our hands strictly off. And there's another well-authenticated rumor from Russia that Lenin is dead. That's fine. It's beyond me why we don't just step in there and kick those Bolshevik cusses out."

"That's so," said Mrs. Babbitt.

"And it says here a fellow was inaugurated mayor in over-alls—a preacher, too! What do you think of that!"

"Humph! Well!"

He searched for an attitude, but neither as a Republican, a Presbyterian, an Elk, nor a real-estate broker did he have any doctrine about preacher-mayors laid down for him, so he grunted and went on. She looked sympathetic and did not hear a word. Later she would read the headlines, the society columns, and the department-store advertisements.

"What do you know about this! Charley McKelvey still doing the sassiety stunt as heavy as ever. Here's what that gushy woman reporter says about last night:

> Never is Society with the big, big S more flattered than when they are bidden to partake of good cheer at the distinguished and hospitable residence of Mr. and Mrs. Charles L. McKelvey as they were last night. Set in its spacious lawns and landscaping, one of the notable sights crowning Royal Ridge, but merry and homelike despite its mighty stone walls and its vast rooms famed for their decoration, their home was thrown open last night for a dance in honor of Mrs. McKelvey's notable guest, Miss J. Sneeth of Washington. The wide hall is so generous in its proportions that it made a perfect ballroom, its hardwood floor reflecting the charming pageant above its polished surface. Even the delights of dancing paled before the alluring opportunities for tête-à-têtes that invited the soul to loaf in the long library before the baronial fireplace, or in the drawing-room with its deep comfy armchairs, its shaded lamps just made for a sly whisper of pretty nothings all a deux; or even in the billiard room where one could take a cue and show a prowess at still another game than that sponsored by Cupid and Terpsichore.

There was more, a great deal more, in the best urban journalistic style of Miss Elnora Pearl Bates, the popular society editor of the *Advocate-Times*. But Babbitt could not abide it. He grunted. He wrinkled the newspaper. He protested: "Can you beat it! I'm willing to hand a lot of credit to Charley McKelvey. When we were in college together, he was just as hard up as any of us, and he's made a million good bucks out of contracting and hasn't been any dishonester or bought any more city councils than was necessary. And that's a good house of his—though it ain't any 'mighty stone walls' and it ain't worth the ninety thousand it cost him. But when it comes to talking as though Charley McKelvey and all that booze-hoisting set of his are any blooming bunch of of, of Vanderbilts, why, it makes me tired!"

Timidly from Mrs. Babbitt: "I would like to see the inside of their house though. It must be lovely. I've never been in-side."

"Well, I have! Lots of—couple of times. To see Chaz about business deals, in the evening. It's not so much. I wouldn't *want* to go there to dinner with that gang of, of high-binders. And I'll bet I make a whole lot more money than some of those tin-horns that spend all they got on dress-suits and haven't got a decent suit of underwear to their name! Hey! What do you think of this!"

Mrs. Babbitt was strangely unmoved by the tidings from the Real Estate and Building column of the *Advocate-Times*:

> Ashtabula Street, 496—J. K. Dawson to
> Thomas Mullally, April 17, 15.7 x 112.2,
> mtg. $4000 ....Nom.

And this morning Babbitt was too disquieted to entertain her with items from Mechanics' Liens, Mortgages Recorded, and Contracts Awarded. He rose. As he looked at her his eyebrows seemed shaggier than usual. Suddenly:

"Yes, maybe— Kind of shame to not keep in touch with folks like the McKelveys. We might try inviting them to din-ner, some evening. Oh, thunder, let's not waste our good time thinking about 'em! Our little bunch has a lot liver times than all those plutes. Just compare a real human like you with these neurotic birds like Lucile McKelvey—all high-brow talk and dressed up like a plush horse! You're a great old girl, hon.!"

He covered his betrayal of softness with a complaining: "Say, don't let Tinka go and eat any more of that poison nut-fudge. For Heaven's sake, try to keep her from ruining her digestion. I tell you, most folks don't appreciate how impor-tant it is to have a good digestion and regular habits. Be back 'bout usual time, I guess."

He kissed her—he didn't quite kiss her—he laid unmov-ing lips against her unflushing cheek. He hurried out to the garage, muttering: "Lord, what a family! And now Myra is going to get pathetic on me because we don't train with this millionaire outfit. Oh, Lord, sometimes I'd like to quit the whole game. And the office worry and detail just as bad. And I act cranky and— I don't mean to, but I get— So darn tired!"

chapter 3

TO George F. Babbitt, as to most prosperous citizens of Zenith, his motor car was poetry and tragedy, love and heroism. The office was his pirate ship but the car his perilous excursion ashore.

Among the tremendous crises of each day none was more dramatic than starting the engine. It was slow on cold mornings; there was the long, anxious whirr of the starter; and sometimes he had to drip ether into the cocks of the cylinders, which was so very interesting that at lunch he would chronicle it drop by drop, and orally calculate how much each drop had cost him.

This morning he was darkly prepared to find something wrong, and he felt belittled when the mixture exploded sweet and strong, and the car didn't even brush the door-jamb, gouged and splintery with many bruisings by fenders, as he backed out of the garage. He was confused. He shouted "Morning!" to Sam Doppelbrau with more cordiality than he had intended.

Babbitt's green and white Dutch Colonial house was one of three in that block on Chatham Road. To the left of-it was the residence of Mr. Samuel Doppelbrau, secretary of an excellent firm of bathroom-fixture jobbers. His was a comfortable house with no architectural manners whatever; a large wooden box with a squat tower, a broad porch, and glossy paint yellow as a yolk. Babbitt disapproved of Mr. and Mrs. Doppelbrau as "Bohemian." From their house came midnight music and obscene laughter; there were neighborhood rumors of bootlegged whisky and fast motor rides. They furnished Babbitt with many happy evenings of discussion, during which he announced firmly, "I'm not strait-laced, and I don't mind seeing a fellow throw in a drink once in a while, but when it comes to deliberately trying to get away with a lot of hell-raising all the while like the Doppelbraus do, it's too rich for my blood!"

On the other side of Babbitt lived Howard Littlefield,

23

Ph. D., in a strictly modern house whereof the lower part
was dark red tapestry brick, with a leaded oriel, the upper
part of pale stucco like spattered clay, and the roof red-tiled.
Littlefield was the Great Scholar of the neighborhood; the authority on everything in the world except babies, cooking, and
motors. He was a Bachelor of Arts of Blodgett College, and a
Doctor of Philosophy in economics of Yale. He was the em-
ployment-manager and publicity-counsel of the Zenith Street
Traction Company. He could, on ten hours' notice, appear before the board of aldermen or the state legislature and prove,
absolutely, with figures all in rows and with precedents from
Poland and New Zealand, that the street-car company loved
the Public and yearned over its employees; that all its stock
was owned by Widows and Orphans; and that whatever it
desired to do would benefit property-owners by increasing
rental values, and help the poor by lowering rents. All his
acquaintances turned to Littlefield when they desired to
know the date of the battle of Saragossa, the definition of the
word "sabotage," the future of the German mark, the trans-
lation of *"hinc illæ lachrimæ,"* or the number of products
of coal tar. He awed Babbitt by confessing that he often sat up
till midnight reading the figures and footnotes in Government
reports, or skimming (with amusement at the author's mis-
takes) the latest volumes of chemistry, archeology, and ich-
thyology.

But Littlefield's great value was as a spiritual example.
Despite his strange learnings he was as strict a Presbyterian
and as firm a Republican as George F. Babbitt. He con-
firmed the business men in the faith. Where they knew only
by passionate instinct that their system of industry and manners was perfect, Dr. Howard Littlefield proved it to them,
out of history, economics, and the confessions of reformed
radicals.

Babbitt had a good deal of honest pride in being the neighbor of such a savant, and in Ted's intimacy with Eunice Littlefield. At sixteen Eunice was interested in no statistics save
those regarding the ages and salaries of motion-picture
stars, but—as Babbitt definitively put it—"she was her father's
daughter."

The difference between a light man like Sam Doppelbrau
and a really fine character like Littlefield was revealed in their
appearances. Doppelbrau was disturbingly young for a man
of forty-eight. He wore his derby on the back of his head,
and his red face was wrinkled with meaningless laughter. But

Littlefield was old for a man of forty-two. He was tall, broad, thick; his gold-rimmed spectacles were engulfed in the folds of his long face; his hair was a tossed mass of greasy blackness; he puffed and rumbled as he talked; his Phi Beta Kappa key shone against a spotty black vest; he smelled of old pipes; he was altogether funereal and archidiaconal; and to real-estate brokerage and the jobbing of bathroom-fixtures he added an aroma of sanctity.

This morning he was in front of his house, inspecting the grass parking between the curb and the broad cement sidewalk. Babbitt stopped his car and leaned out to shout "Mornin'!" Littlefield lumbered over and stood with one foot up on the running-board.

"Fine morning," said Babbitt, lighting—illegally early—his second cigar of the day.

"Yes, it's a might fine morning," said Littlefield.

"Spring coming along fast now."

"Yes, it's real spring now, all right," said Littlefield.

"Still cold nights, though. Had to have a couple blankets, on the sleeping-porch last night."

"Yes, it wasn't any too warm last night," said Littlefield.

"But I don't anticipate we'll have any more real cold weather now."

"No, but still, there was snow at Tiflis, Montana, yesterday," said the Scholar, "and you remember the blizzard they had out West three days ago—thirty inches of snow at Greeley, Colorado—and two years ago we had a snow-squall right here in Zenith on the twenty-fifth of April."

"Is that a fact! Say, old man, what do you think about the Republican candidate? Who'll they nominate for president? Don't you think it's about time we had a real business administration?"

"In my opinion, what the country needs, first and foremost, is a good, sound, business-like conduct of its affairs. What we need is—a business administration!" said Littlefield.

"I'm glad to hear you say that! I certainly am glad to hear you say that! I didn't know how you'd feel about it, with all your associations with colleges and so on, and I'm glad you feel that way. What the country needs—just at this present juncture—is neither a college president nor a lot of monkeying with foreign affairs, but a good—sound—economical—business—administration, that will give us a chance to have something like a decent turnover."

"Yes. It isn't generally realized that even in China the

schoolmen are giving way to more practical men, and of course you can see what that implies."

"Is that a fact! Well, well!" breathed Babbitt, feeling much calmer, and much happier about the way things were going in the world. "Well, it's been nice to stop and parleyvoo a second. Guess I'll have to get down to the office now and sting a few clients. Well, so long, old man. See you to-night. So long."

II

They had labored, these solid citizens. Twenty years before, the hill on which Floral Heights was spread, with its bright roofs and immaculate turf and amazing comfort, had been a wilderness of rank second-growth elms and oaks and maples. Along the precise streets were still a few wooded vacant lots, and the fragment of an old orchard. It was brilliant to-day; the apple boughs were lit with fresh leaves like torches of green fire. The first white of cherry blossoms flickered down a gully, and robins clamored.

Babbitt sniffed the earth, chuckled at the hysteric robins as he would have chuckled at kittens or at a comic movie. He was, to the eye, the perfect office-going executive—a well-fed man in a correct brown soft hat and frameless spectacles, smoking a large cigar, driving a good motor along a semi-suburban parkway. But in him was some genius of authentic love for his neighborhood, his city, his clan. The winter was over; the time was come for the building, the visible growth, which to him was glory. He lost his dawn depression; he was ruddily cheerful when he stopped on Smith Street to leave the brown trousers, and to have the gasoline-tank filled.

The familiarity of the rite fortified him: the sight of the tall red iron gasoline-pump, the hollow-tile and terra-cotta garage, the window full of the most agreeable accessories—shiny casings, spark-plugs with immaculate porcelain jackets, tire-chains of gold and silver. He was flattered by the friendliness with which Sylvester Moon, dirtiest and most skilled of motor mechanics, came out to serve him. "Mornin', Mr. Babbitt!" said Moon, and Babbitt felt himself a person of importance, one whose name even busy garagemen remembered—not one of these cheap-sports flying around in flivvers. He admired the ingenuity of the automatic dial, clicking off gallon by gallon; admired the smartness of the sign: "A fill in time saves getting stuck—gas to-day 31 cents"; admired the rhythmic gurgle of the gasoline as it flowed into the tank, and the mechanical regularity with which Moon turned the handle.

"How much we takin' to-day?" asked Moon, in a manner which combined the independence of the great specialist, the friendliness of a familiar gossip, and respect for a man of weight in the community, like George F. Babbitt.

"Fill 'er up."

"Who you rootin' for for Republican candidate, Mr. Babbitt?"

"It's too early to make any predictions yet. After all, there's still a good month and two weeks—no, three weeks—must be almost three weeks—well, there's more than six weeks in all before the Republican convention, and I feel a fellow ought to keep an open mind and give all the candidates a show—look 'em all over and size 'em up, and then decide carefully."

"That's a fact, Mr. Babbitt."

"But I'll tell you—and my stand on this is just the same as it was four years ago, and eight years ago, and it'll be my stand four years from now—yes, and eight years from now! What I tell everybody, and it can't be too generally understood, is that what we need first, last, and all the time is a good, sound business administration!"

"By golly, that's right!"

"How do those front tires look to you?"

"Fine! Fine! Wouldn't be much work for garages if everybody looked after their car the way you do."

"Well, I do try and have some sense about it." Babbitt paid his bill, said adequately, "Oh, keep the change," and drove off in an ecstasy of honest self-appreciation. It was with the manner of a Good Samaritan that he shouted at a respectable-looking man who was waiting for a trolley car, "Have a lift?" As the man climbed in Babbitt condescended, "Going clear down-town? Whenever I see a fellow waiting for a trolley, I always make it a practice to give him a lift —unless, of course, he looks like a bum."

"Wish there were more folks that were so generous with their machines," dutifully said the victim of benevolence.

"Oh, no, 'tain't a question of generosity, hardly. Fact, I always feel—I was saying to my son just the other night— it's a fellow's duty to share the good things of this world with his neighbors, and it gets my goat when a fellow gets stuck on himself and goes around tooting his horn merely because he's charitable."

The victim seemed unable to find the right answer. Babbitt boomed on:

"Pretty punk service the Company giving us on these carlines. Nonsense to only run the Portland Road cars once even seven minutes. Fellow gets mighty cold on a winter morning, waiting on a street corner with the wind nipping at his ankles."

"That's right. The Street Car Company don't care a damn what kind of a deal they give us. Something ought to happen to 'em."

Babbitt was alarmed. "But still, of course it won't do to just keep knocking the Traction Company and not realize the difficulties they're operating under, like these cranks that want municipal ownership. The way these workmen hold up the Company for high wages is simply a crime, and of course the burden falls on you and me that have to pay a seven-cent fare! Fact, there's remarkable service on all their lines —considering."

"Well—" uneasily.

"Darn fine morning," Babbitt explained. "Spring coming along fast."

"Yes, it's real spring now."

The victim had no originality, no wit, and Babbitt fell into a great silence and devoted himself to the game of beating trolley cars to the corner: a spurt, a tail-chase, nervous speeding between the huge yellow side of the trolley and the jagged row of parked motors, shooting past just as the trolley stopped—a rare game and valiant.

And all the while he was conscious of the loveliness of Zenith. For weeks together he noticed nothing but clients and the vexing To Rent signs of rival brokers. To-day, in mysterious malaise, he raged or rejoiced with equal nervous swiftness, and to-day the light of spring was so winsome that he lifted his head and saw.

He admired each district along his familiar route to the office: The bungalows and shrubs and winding irregular driveways of Floral Heights. The one-story shops on Smith Street, a glare of plate-glass and new yellow brick; groceries and laundries and drug-stores to supply the more immediate needs of East Side housewives. The market gardens in Dutch Hollow, their shanties patched with corrugated iron and stolen doors. Billboards with crimson goddesses nine feet tall advertising cinema films, pipe tobacco, and talcum power. The old "mansions" along Ninth Street, S. E., like aged dandies in filthy linen; wooden castles turned into boarding-houses, with muddy walks and rusty hedges, jostled by fast-intruding garages, cheap apartment-houses, and fruit-stands conducted by bland, sleek Athenians. Across the belt of railroad-tracks, factories with high-perched water-tanks and tall stacks—factories producing condensed milk, paper boxes, lighting-fixtures, motor cars. Then the business center, the thickening darting traffic, the crammed trolleys unloading, and high doorways of marble and polished granite.

It was big—and Babbitt respected bigness in anything; in mountains, jewels, muscles, wealth, or words. He was, for a spring-enchanted moment, the lyric and almost unselfish lover of Zenith. He thought of the outlying factory suburbs; of the Chaloosa River with its strangely eroded banks; of the orchard-dappled Tonawanda Hills to the North, and all the fat dairy land and big barns and comfortable herds. As he dropped his passenger he cried, "Gosh, I feel pretty good this morning!"

III

Epochal as starting the car was the drama of parking it before he entered his office. As he turned from Oberlin Avenue round the corner into Third Street, N.E., he peered ahead for a space in the line of parked cars. He angrily just missed a space as a rival driver slid into it. Ahead, another car was leaving the curb, and Babbitt slowed up, holding out his hand to the cars pressing on him from behind, agitatedly motioning an old woman to go ahead, avoiding a truck which bore down on him from one side. With front wheels nicking the wrought-steel bumper of the car in front, he stopped, feverishly cramped his steering-wheel, slid back into the vacant space and, with eighteen inches of room, manœuvered to bring the car level with the curb. It was a virile adventure masterfully executed. With satisfaction he locked a thief-proof steel wedge on the front wheel, and crossed the street to his real-estate office on the ground floor of the Reeves Building.

The Reeves Building was as fireproof as a rock and as efficient as a typewriter; fourteen stories of yellow pressed brick, with clean, upright, unornamented lines. It was filled with the offices of lawyers, doctors, agents for machinery, for emery wheels, for wire fencing, for mining-stock. Their gold signs shone on the windows. The entrance was too modern to be flamboyant with pillars; it was quiet, shrewd, neat.

Along the Third Street side were a Western Union Telegraph
Office, the Blue Delft Candy Shop, Shotwell's Stationery
Shop, and the Babbitt-Thompson Realty Company.

Babbitt could have entered his office from the street, as
customers did, but it made him feel an insider to go through
the corridor of the building and enter by the back door.
Thus he was greeted by the villagers.

The little unknown people who inhabited the Reeves Building corridors—elevator-runners, starter, engineers, superintendent, and the doubtful-looking lame man who conducted the
news and cigar stand—were in no way city-dwellers. They
were rustics, living in a constricted valley, interested only
in one another and in The Building. Their Main Street was
the entrance hall, with its stone floor, severe marble ceiling,
and the inner windows of the shops. The liveliest place on
the street was the Reeves Building Barber Shop, but this was
also Babbitt's one embarrassment. Himself, he patronized the
glittering Pompeian Barber Shop in the Hotel Thornleigh,
and every time he passed the Reeves shop—ten times a day,
a hundred times—he felt untrue to his own village.

Now, as one of the squirearchy, greeted with honorable
salutations by the villagers, he marched into his office, and
peace and dignity were upon him, and the morning's dis-
sonances all unheard.

They were heard again, immediately.

Stanley Graff, the outside salesman, was talking on the
telephone with tragic lack of that firm manner which disci-
plines clients: "Say, uh, I think I got just the house that
would suit you—the Percival House, in Linton. . . . Oh, you've
seen it. Well, how'd it strike you? . . . Huh? . . . Oh," irreso-
lutely, "oh, I see."

As Babbitt marched into his private room, a coop with semi-
partition of oak and frosted glass, at the back of the office,
he reflected how hard it was to find employees who had his
own faith that he was going to make sales.

There were nine members of the staff, besides Babbitt and
his partner and father-in-law, Henry Thompson, who rarely
came to the office. The nine were Stanley Graff, the outside
salesman—a youngish man given to cigarettes and the playing
of pool; old Mat Penniman, general utility man, collector
of rents and salesman of insurance—broken, silent, gray;
a mystery, reputed to have been a "crack" real-estate man
with a firm of his own in haughty Brooklyn; Chester Kirby
Laylock, resident salesman out at the Glen Oriole acreage

development—an enthusiastic person with a silky mustache
and much family; Miss Theresa McGoun, the swift and rather
pretty stenographer; Miss Wilberta Bannigan, the thick, slow,
laborious accountant and file-clerk; and four freelance part-
time commission salesmen.

As he looked from his own cage into the main room Babbitt
mourned, "McGoun's a good stenog., smart's a whip, but
Stan Graff and all those bums—" The zest of the spring
morning was smothered in the stale office air.

Normally he admired the office, with a pleased surprise
that he should have created this sure lovely thing; normally
he was stimulated by the clean newness of it and the air of
bustle; but to-day it seemed flat—the tiled floor, like a bathroom, the ocher-colored metal ceiling, the faded maps on the
hard plaster walls, the chairs of varnished pale oak, the
desks and filing-cabinets of steel painted in olive drab. It
was a vault, a steel chapel where loafing and laughter were
raw sin.

He hadn't even any satisfaction in the new water-cooler!
And it was the very best of water-coolers, up-to-date, scientific, and right-thinking. It had cost a great deal of money
(in itself a virtue). It possessed a non-conducting fiber ice-
container, a porcelain water-jar (guaranteed hygienic), a drip-
less non-clogging sanitary faucet, and machine-painted decorations in two tones of gold. He looked down the relentless
stretch of tiled floor at the water-cooler, and assured himself
that no tenant of the Reeves Building had a more expensive
one, but he could not recapture the feeling of social superiority
it had given him. He astoundingly grunted, "I'd like to
beat it off to the woods right now. And loaf all day. And
go to Gunch's again to-night, and play poker, and cuss as
much as I feel like, and drink a hundred and nine-thousand
bottles of beer."

He sighed; he read through his mail; he shouted "Msgoun,"
which meant "Miss McGoun"; and began to dictate.

This was his own version of his first letter:

"Omar Gribble, send it to his office, Miss McGoun, yours
of twentieth to hand and in reply would say look here, Gribble,
I'm awfully afraid if we go on shilly-shallying like this we'll
just naturally lose the Allen sale, I had Allen up on carpet
day before yesterday and got right down to cases and think
I can assure you—uh, uh, no, change that: all my experience
indicates he is all right, means to do business, looked into his
financial record which is fine—that sentence seems to be a

little balled up, Miss McGoun; make a couple sentences out of it if you have to, period, new paragraph.

"He is perfectly willing to pro rate the special assessment and strikes me, am dead sure there will be no difficulty in getting him to pay for title insurance, so now for heaven's sake let's get busy—no, make that: so now let's go to it and get down—no, that's enough—you can tie those sentences up a little better when you type 'em, Miss McGoun—your sincerely, etcetera."

This is the version of his letter which he received, typed, from Miss McGoun that afternoon:

> BABBITT-THOMPSON REALTY CO.
> Homes for Folks
> Reeves Bldg., Oberlin Avenue & 3d St., N.E.
> Zenith

Omar Gribble, Esq.,
576 North American Building,
Zenith.

Dear Mr. Gribble:

Your letter of the twentieth to hand. I must say I'm awfully afraid that if we go on shilly-shallying like this we'll just naturally lose the Allen sale. I had Allen up on the carpet day before yesterday, and got right down to cases. All my experience indicates that he means to do business. I have also looked into his financial record, which is fine.

He is perfectly willing to pro rate the special assessment and there will be no difficulty in getting him to pay for title insurance.

So let's go!

Yours sincerely,

As he read and signed it, in his correct flowing business-college hand, Babbitt reflected, "Now that's a good, strong letter, and clear's a bell. Now what the— I never told McGoun to make a third paragraph there! Wish she'd quit trying to improve on my dictation! But what I can't understand is: why can't Stan Graff or Chet Laylock write a letter like that? With punch! With a kick!"

The most important thing he dictated that morning was the fortnightly form-letter, to be mimeographed and sent out to a thousand "prospects." It was diligently imitative of the best literary models of the day; of heart-to-heart-talk advertisements, "sales-pulling" letters, discourses on the "development of Will-power," and hand-shaking house-organs, as richly poured forth by the new school of Poets of Business. He had painfully written out a first draft, and he intoned it now like a poet delicate and distrait:

SAY, OLD MAN!

I just want to know can I do you a whaleuva favor? Honest! No kidding! I know you're interested in getting a house, not merely a place where you hang up the old bonnet but a love-nest for the wife and kiddies—and maybe for the flivver out beyant (be sure and spell that b-e-y-a-n-t, Miss McGoun) the spud garden. Say, did you ever stop to think that we're here to save you trouble? That's how we make a living—folks don't pay us for our lovely beauty! Now take a look:

Sit right down at the handsome carved mahogany escritoire and shoot us in a line telling us just what you want, and if we can find it we'll come hopping down your lane with the good tidings, and if we can't, we won't bother you. To save your time, just fill out the blank enclosed. On request will also send blank regarding store properties in Floral Heights, Silver Grove, Linton, Bellevue, and all East Side residential districts.

Yours for service,

P.S.—Just a hint of some plums we can pick for you— some genuine bargains that came in to-day:

SILVER GROVE.—Cute four-room California bungalow, a.m.i., garage, dandy shade tree, swell neighborhood, handy car line. $3700, $780 down and balance liberal, Babbitt-Thompson terms, cheaper than rent.

DORCHESTER.—A corker! Artistic two-family house, all oak trim, parquet floors, lovely gas log, big porches, colonial, HEATED ALL-WEATHER GARAGE, a bargain at $11,250.

Dictation over, with its need of sitting and thinking instead of bustling around and making a noise and really doing something, Babbitt sat creakily back in his revolving desk-chair and beamed on Miss McGoun. He was conscious of her as a girl, of black bobbed hair against demure cheeks. A longing which was indistinguishable from loneliness enfeebled him. While she waited, tapping a long, precise pencil-point on the desk-tablet, he half identified her with the fairy girl of his dreams. He imagined their eyes meeting with terrifying recognition; imagined touching her lips with frightened reverence and— She was chirping, "Any more, Mist' Babbitt?" He grunted, "That winds it up, I guess," and turned heavily away.

For all his wandering thoughts, they had never been more intimate than this. He often reflected, "Nev' forget how old

Jake Offutt said a wise bird never goes love-making in his
own office or his own home. Start trouble. Sure. But—"

In twenty-three years of married life he had peered uneasily at every graceful ankle, every soft shoulder; in thought he
had treasured them; but not once had he hazarded respectability by adventuring. Now, as he calculated the cost of re-
papering the Styles house, he was restless again, discontented
about nothing and everything, ashamed of his discontent-
ment, and lonely for the fairy girl.

chapter 4

I T was a morning of artistic creation. Fifteen minutes after
the purple prose of Babbitt's form-letter, Chester Kirby
Laylock, the resident salesman at Glen Oriole, came in to
report a sale and submit an advertisement. Babbitt disapproved of Laylock, who sang in choirs and was merry at
home over games of Hearts and Old Maid. He had a tenor
voice, wavy chestnut hair, and a mustache like a camel's-
hair brush. Babbitt considered it excusable in a family-
man to growl, "Seen this new picture of the kid—husky
little devil, eh?" but Laylock's domestic confidences were as
bubbling as a girl's.

"Say, I think I got a peach of an ad for the Glen, Mr.
Babbitt. Why don't we try something in poetry? Honest,
it'd have wonderful pulling-power. Listen:

> 'Mid pleasures and palaces,
>   Wherever you may roam,
> You just provide the little bride
>   And we'll provide the home.

Do you get it? See—like 'Home Sweet Home.' Don't you—"

"Yes, yes, yes, hell yes, of course I get it. But— Oh, I
think we'd better use something more dignified and forceful,
like 'We lead, others follow,' or 'Eventually, why not now?'
Course I believe in using poetry and humor and all that junk

when it turns the trick, but with a high-class restricted development like the Glen we better stick to the more dignified approach, see how I mean? Well, I guess that's all, this morning, Chet."

II

By a tragedy familiar to the world of art, the April enthusiasm of Chet Laylock served only to stimulate the talent of the older craftsman, George F. Babbitt. He grumbled to Stanley Graff, "That tan-colored voice of Chet's gets on my nerves," yet he was aroused and in one swoop he wrote:

DO YOU RESPECT YOUR LOVED ONES?

When the last sad rites of bereavement are over, do you know for certain that you have done your best for the Departed? You haven't unless they lie in the Cemetery Beautiful

LINDEN LANE

the only strictly up-to-date burial place in or near Zenith, where exquisitely gardened plots look from daisy-dotted hill-slopes across the smiling fields of Dorchester.

Sole agents
BABBITT-THOMPSON REALTY COMPANY
Reeves Building

He rejoiced, "I guess that'll show Chan Mott and his weedy old Wildwood Cemetery something about modern merchandizing!"

III

He sent Mat Penniman to the recorder's office to dig out the names of the owners of houses which were displaying For Rent signs of other brokers; he talked to a man who desired to lease a store-building for a pool-room; he ran over the list of home-leases which were about to expire; he sent Thomas Bywaters, a street-car conductor who played at real estate in spare time, to call on side-street "prospects" who were unworthy the strategies of Stanley Graff. But he had spent his credulous excitement of creation, and these routine details annoyed him. One moment of heroism he had, in discovering a new way of stopping smoking.

He stopped smoking at least once a month. He went through with it like the solid citizen he was: admitted the evils of tobacco, courageously made resolves, laid out plans to check the vice, tapered off his allowance of cigars, and expounded the pleasures of virtuousness to every one he met. He did everything, in fact, except stop smoking.

Two months before, by ruling out a schedule, noting down the hour and minute of each smoke, and ecstatically increasing the intervals between smokes, he had brought himself down to three cigars a day. Then he had lost the schedule.

A week ago he had invented a system of leaving his cigar-case and cigarette-box in an unused drawer at the bottom of the correspondence-file, in the outer office. "I'll just naturally be ashamed to go poking in there all day long, making a fool of myself before my own employees!" he reasoned. By the end of three days he was trained to leave his desk, walk to the file, take out and light a cigar, without knowing that he was doing it.

This morning it was revealed to him that it had been too easy to open the file. Lock it, that was the thing! Inspired, he rushed out and locked up his cigars, his cigarettes, and even his box of safety matches; and the key to the file drawer he hid in his desk. But the crusading passion of it made him so tobacco-hungry that he immediately recovered the key, walked with forbidding dignity to the file, took out a cigar and a match—"but only one match; if ole cigar goes out, it'll by golly have to stay out!" Later, when the cigar did go out, he took one more match from the file, and when a buyer and a seller came in for a conference at eleven-thirty, naturally he had to offer them cigars. His conscience protested, "Why, ing you're smoking with them!" but he bullied it, "Oh, shut up! I'm busy now. Of course by-and-by——" There was no by-and-by, yet his belief that he had crushed the unclean habit made him feel noble and very happy. When he called up Paul Riesling he was, in his moral splendor, unusually eager.

He was fonder of Paul Riesling than of any one on earth except himself and his daughter Tinka. They had been classmates, roommates, in the State University, but always he thought of Paul Riesling, with his dark slimness, his precisely parted hair, his nose-glasses, his hesitant speech, his moodiness, his love of music, as a younger brother, to be petted and protected. Paul had gone into his father's business, after graduation; he was now a wholesaler and small manufacturer of prepared-paper roofing. But Babbitt strenuously believed and lengthily announced to the world of Good Fellows that Paul could have been a great violinist or painter or writer. "Why say, the letters that boy sent me on his trip to the Canadian Rockies, they just absolutely make you see the place as if you were standing there. Believe me, he could have given any of these bloomin' authors a whale of a run for their money!"

Yet on the telephone they said only:

"South 343. No, no, no! I said *South*—South 343. Say, operator, what the dickens is the trouble? Can't you get me South 343? Why certainly they'll answer. Oh, hello, 343? Wanta speak Mist' Riesling, Mist' Babbitt talking. . . . 'Lo, Paul?"

"Yuh."

" 'S George speaking."

"Yuh."

"How's old socks?"

"Fair to middlin'. How're you?"

"Fine, Paulibus. Well, what do you know?"

"Oh, nothing much."

"Where you been keepin' yourself?"

"Oh, just stickin' round. What's up, Georgie?"

"How 'bout lil lunch 's noon?"

"Be all right with me, I guess. Club?"

"Yuh. Meet you there twelve-thirty."

"A' right. Twelve-thirty. S' long, Georgie."

IV

His morning was not sharply marked into divisions. Interwoven with correspondence and advertisement-writing were a thousand nervous details: calls from clerks who were incessantly and hopefully seeking five furnished rooms and bath at sixty dollars a month; advice to Mat Penniman on getting money out of tenants who had no money.

Babbitt's virtues as a real-estate broker—as the servant of society in the department of finding homes for families and shops for distributors of food—were steadiness and diligence. He was conventionally honest, he kept his records of buyers and sellers complete, he had experience with leases and titles and an excellent memory for prices. His shoulders were broad enough, his voice deep enough, his relish of hearty humor strong enough, to establish him as one of the ruling caste of Good Fellows. Yet his eventual importance to mankind was perhaps lessened by his large and complacent ignorance of all architecture save the types of houses turned out by speculative builders; all landscape gardening save the use of curving roads, grass, and six ordinary shrubs; and all the commonest axioms of economics. He serenely believed that the one purpose of the real-estate business was to make money for George F. Babbitt. True, it was a good advertisement at Boosters' Club lunches, and all the varieties of Annual Banquets to which Good Fellows were invited, to speak sonorously of Unselfish Public Service, the Broker's Obligation to Keep Inviolate the Trust of His Clients, and a thing called Ethics, whose nature was confusing but if you had it you were a High-class Realtor and if you hadn't you were a shyster, a piker, and a fly-by-night. These virtues awakened Confidence, and enabled you to handle Bigger Propositions. But they didn't imply that you were to be impractical and refuse to take twice the value of a house if a buyer was such an idiot that he didn't jew you down on the asking-price.

Babbitt spoke well—and often—at these orgies of commercial righteousness about the "realtor's function as a seer of the future development of the community, and as a prophetic engineer clearing the pathway for inevitable changes" —which meant that a real-estate broker could make money by guessing which way the town would grow. This guessing he called Vision.

In an address at the Boosters' Club he had admitted, "It is at once the duty and the privilege of the realtor to know everything about his own city and its environs. Where a surgeon is a specialist on every vein and mysterious cell of the human body, and the engineer upon electricity in all its phases, or every bolt of some great bridge majestically arching o'er a mighty flood, the realtor must know his city, inch by inch, and all its faults and virtues."

Though he did know the market-price, inch by inch, of certain districts of Zenith, he did not know whether the police force was too large or too small, or whether it was in alliance with gambling and prostitution. He knew the means of fire-proofing buildings and the relation of insurance-rates to fire-proofing, but he did not know how many firemen there were in the city, how they were trained and paid, or how complete their apparatus. He sang eloquently the advantages of proximity of school-buildings to rentable homes, but he did not know—he did not know that it was worth while to know—whether the city schoolrooms were properly heated, lighted, ventilated, furnished; he did not know how the teachers were chosen; and though he chanted "One of the boasts of Zenith is that we pay our teachers adequately," that was because he had read the statement in the *Advocate-Times*.

Himself, he could not have given the average salary of teachers in Zenith or anywhere else.

He had heard it said that "conditions" in the County Jail and the Zenith City Prison were not very "scientific;" he had, with indignation at the criticism of Zenith, skimmed through a report in which the notorious pessimist Seneca Doane, the radical lawyer, asserted that to throw boys and young girls into a bull-pen crammed with men suffering from syphilis, delirium tremens, and insanity was not the perfect way of educating them. He had controverted the report by growling, "Folks that think a jail ought to be a bloomin' Hotel Thornleigh make me sick. If people don't like a jail, let 'em behave 'emselves and keep out of it. Besides, these reform cranks always exaggerate." That was the beginning and quite completely the end of his investigations into Zenith's charities and corrections; and as to the "vice districts" he brightly expressed it, "Those are things that no decent man monkeys with. Besides, smatter fact, I'll tell you confidentially: it's a protection to our daughters and to decent women to have a district where tough nuts can raise cain. Keeps 'em away from our own homes."

As to industrial conditions, however, Babbitt had thought a great deal, and his opinions may be coördinated as follows:

"A good labor union is of value because it keeps out radical unions, which would destroy property. No one ought to be forced to belong to a union, however. All labor agitators who try to force men to join a union should be hanged. In fact, just between ourselves, there oughtn't to be any unions allowed at all; and as it's the best way of fighting the unions, every business man ought to belong to an employers'-association and to the Chamber of Commerce. In union there is strength. So any selfish hog who doesn't join the Chamber of Commerce ought to be forced to."

In nothing—as the expert on whose advice families moved to new neighborhoods to live there for a generation—was Babbitt more splendidly innocent than in the science of sanitation. He did not know a malaria-bearing mosquito from a bat; he knew nothing about tests of drinking water; and in the matters of plumbing and sewage he was as unlearned as he was voluble. He often referred to the excellence of the bathrooms in the houses he sold. He was fond of explaining why it was that no European ever bathed. Some one had told him, when he was twenty-two, that all cesspools were unhealthy, and he still denounced them. If a client impertinently wanted him to sell a house which had a cesspool, Babbitt always spoke about it—before accepting the house and selling it.

When he laid out the Glen Oriole acreage development, when he ironed woodland and dipping meadow into a glenless, orioleless, sunburnt flat prickly with small boards displaying the names of imaginary streets, he righteously put in a complete sewage-system. It made him feel superior; it enabled him to sneer privily at the Martin Lumsen development, Avonlea, which had a cesspool; and it provided a chorus for the full-page advertisements in which he announced the beauty, convenience, cheapness, and supererogatory healthfulness of Glen Oriole. The only flaw was that the Glen Oriole sewers had insufficient outlet, so that waste remained in them, not very agreeably, while the Avonlea cesspool was a Waring septic tank.

The whole of the Glen Oriole project was a suggestion that Babbitt, though he really did hate men recognized as swindlers, was not too unreasonably honest. Operators and buyers prefer that brokers should not be in competition with them as operators and buyers themselves, but attend to their clients' interests only. It was supposed that the Babbitt-Thompson Company were merely agents for Glen Oriole, serving the real owner, Jake Offutt, but the fact was that Babbitt and Thompson owned sixty-two per cent. of the Glen, the president and purchasing agent of the Zenith Street Traction Company owned twenty-eight per cent., and Jake Offutt (a gang-politician, a small manufacturer, a tobacco-chewing old farceur who enjoyed dirty politics, business diplomacy, and cheating at poker) had only ten per cent., which Babbitt and the Traction officials had given to him for "fixing" health inspectors and fire inspectors and a member of the State Transportation Commission.

But Babbitt was virtuous. He advocated, though he did not practise, the prohibition of alcohol; he praised, though he did not obey, the laws against motor-speeding; he paid his debts; he contributed to the church, the Red Cross, and the Y. M. C. A.; he followed the custom of his clan and cheated only as it was sanctified by precedent; and he never descended to trickery—though, as he explained to Paul Riesling:

"Course I don't mean to say that every ad I write is literally true or that I always believe everything I say when I give some buyer a good strong selling-spiel. You see—you see it's like this: In the first place, maybe the owner of the property exaggerated when he put it into my hands, and it certainly isn't my place to go proving my principal a liar! And then most folks are so darn crooked themselves that they expect a fellow to do a little lying, so if I was fool enough to never whoop the ante I'd get the credit for lying anyway! In self-defense I got to toot my own horn, like a lawyer defending a client—his bounden duty, ain't it, to bring out the poor dub's good points? Why, the Judge himself would bawl out a lawyer that didn't, even if they both knew the guy was guilty! But even so, I don't pad out the truth like Cecil Rountree or Thayer or the rest of these realtors. Fact, I think a fellow that's willing to deliberately up and profit by lying ought to be shot!"

Babbitt's value to his clients was rarely better shown than this morning, in the conference at eleven-thirty between himself, Conrad Lyte, and Archibald Purdy.

V

Conrad Lyte was a real-estate speculator. He was a nervous speculator. Before he gambled he consulted bankers, lawyers, architects, contracting builders, and all of their clerks and stenographers who were willing to be cornered and give him advice. He was a bold entrepreneur, and he desired nothing more than complete safety in his investments, freedom from attention to details, and the thirty or forty per cent. profit which, according to all authorities, a pioneer deserves for his risks and foresight. He was a stubby man with a cap-like mass of short gray curls and clothes which, no matter how well cut, seemed shaggy. Below his eyes were semicircular hollows, as though silver dollars had been pressed against them and had left an imprint.

Particularly and always Lyte consulted Babbitt, and trusted in his slow cautiousness.

Six months ago Babbitt had learned that one Archibald Purdy, a grocer in the indecisive residential district known as Linton, was talking of opening a butcher shop beside his grocery. Looking up the ownership of adjoining parcels of land, Babbitt found that Purdy owned his present shop but did not own the one available lot adjoining. He advised Conrad Lyte to purchase this lot, for eleven thousand dollars, though an appraisal on a basis of rents did not indicate its value as above nine thousand. The rents, declared Babbitt, were too low; and by waiting they could make Purdy come to their price. (This was Vision.) He had to bully Lyte into buying. His first act as agent for Lyte was to increase the rent of the battered store-building on the lot. The tenant said a number of rude things, but he paid.

Now, Purdy seemed ready to buy, and his delay was going to cost him ten thousand extra dollars—the reward paid by the community to Mr. Conrad Lyte for the virtue of employing a broker who had Vision and who understood Talking Points, Strategic Values, Key Situations, Underappraisals, and the Psychology of Salesmanship.

Lyte came to the conference exultantly. He was fond of Babbitt, this morning, and called him "old hoss." Purdy, the grocer, a long-nosed man and solemn, seemed to care less for Babbitt and for Vision, but Babbitt met him at the street door to the office and guided him toward the private room with affectionate little cries of "This way, Brother Purdy!" He took from the correspondence-file the entire box of cigars and forced them on his guests. He pushed their chairs two inches forward and three inches back, which gave an hospitable note, then leaned back in his desk-chair and looked plump and jolly. But he spoke to the weakling grocer with firmness.

"Well, Brother Purdy, we been having some pretty tempting offers from butchers and a slew of other folks for that lot next to your store, but I persuaded Brother Lyte that we ought to give you a shot at the property first. I said to Lyte, 'It'd be a rotten shame,' I said, 'if somebody went and opened a combination grocery and meat market right next door and ruined Purdy's nice little business.' Especially—" Babbitt leaned forward, and his voice was harsh, "—it would be hard luck if one of these cash-and-carry chain-stores got in there and started cutting prices below cost till they got rid of competition and forced you to the wall!"

Purdy snatched his thin hands from his pockets, pulled up his trousers, thrust his hands back into his pockets, tilted in the heavy oak chair, and tried to look amused, as he struggled:

"Yes, they're bad competition. But I guess you don't realize the Pulling Power that Personality has in a neighborhood business."

The great Babbitt smiled. "That's so. Just as you feel, old man. We thought we'd give you first chance. All right then—"

"Now look here!" Purdy wailed. "I know f'r a fact that a piece of property 'bout same size, right near, sold for less 'n eighty-five hundred, 'twa'n't two years ago, and here you fellows are asking me twenty-four thousand dollars! Why, I'd have to mortgage— I wouldn't mind so much paying twelve thousand but— Why good God, Mr. Babbitt, you're asking more 'n twice its value! And threatening to ruin me if I don't take it!"

"Purdy, I don't like your way of talking! I don't like it one little bit! Supposing Lyte and I were stinking enough to want to ruin any fellow human, don't you suppose we know it's to our own selfish interest to have everybody in Zenith prosperous? But all this is beside the point. Tell you what we'll do: We'll come down to twenty-three thousand—five thousand down and the rest on mortgage—and if you want to wreck the old shack and rebuild, I guess I can get Lyte here to loosen up for a building-mortgage on good liberal terms. Heavens, man, we'd be glad to oblige you! We don't like these foreign grocery trusts any better 'n you do! But it isn't reasonable to expect us to sacrifice eleven thousand or more just for neighborliness, is it! How about it, Lyte? You willing to come down?"

By warmly taking Purdy's part, Babbitt persuaded the benevolent Mr. Lyte to reduce his price to twenty-one thousand dollars. At the right moment Babbitt snatched from a drawer the agreement he had had Miss McGoun type out a week ago and thrust it into Purdy's hands. He genially shook his fountain pen to make certain that it was flowing, handed it to Purdy, and approvingly watched him sign.

The work of the world was being done. Lyte had made something over nine thousand dollars, Babbitt had made a four-hundred-and-fifty dollar commission, Purdy had, by the sensitive mechanism of modern finance, been provided with a business-building, and soon the happy inhabitants of Linton would have meat lavished upon them at prices only a little higher than those down-town.

It had been a manly battle, but after it Babbitt drooped. This was the only really amusing contest he had been planning. There was nothing ahead save details of leases, appraisals, mortgages.

He muttered, "Makes me sick to think of Lyte carrying off most of the profit when I did all the work, the old skinflint! And— What else have I got to do to-day? . . . Like to take a good long vacation. Motor trip. Something."

He sprang up, rekindled by the thought of lunching with Paul Riesling.

chapter 5

B ABBITT'S preparations for leaving the office to its feeble self during the hour and a half of his lunch-period were somewhat less elaborate than the plans for a general European war.

He fretted to Miss McGoun, "What time you going to lunch? Well, make sure Miss Bannigan is in then. Explain to her that if Wiedenfeldt calls up, she's to tell him I'm already having the title traced. And oh, b' the way, remind me to-morrow to have Penniman trace it. Now if anybody comes in looking for a cheap house, remember we got to shove that Bangor Road place off onto somebody. If you need me, I'll be at the Athletic Club. And—uh— And—uh— I'll be back by two."

He dusted the cigar-ashes off his vest. He placed a difficult unanswered letter on the pile of unfinished work, that he might not fail to attend to it that afternoon. (For three noons, now, he had placed the same letter on the unfinished pile.) He scrawled on a sheet of yellow backing-paper the memorandum: "See abt apt h drs," which gave him an agreeable feeling of having already seen about the apartment-house doors.

He discovered that he was smoking another cigar. He threw it away, protesting, "Darn it, I thought you'd quit this darn smoking!" He courageously returned the cigar-box to the correspondence-file, locked it up, hid the key in a more difficult place, and raged, "Ought to take care of myself. And need more exercise—walk to the club, every single noon—just what I'll do—every noon—cut out this motoring all the time."

The resolution made him feel exemplary. Immediately after it he decided that this noon it was too late to walk.

It took but little more time to start his car and edge it into the traffic than it would have taken to walk the three and a half blocks to the club.

II

As he drove he glanced with the fondness of familiarity at the buildings.

A stranger suddenly dropped into the business-center of Zenith could not have told whether he was in a city of Oregon or Georgia, Ohio or Maine, Oklahoma or Manitoba. But to Babbitt every inch was individual and stirring. As always he noted that the California Building across the way was three stories lower, therefore three stories less beautiful, than his own Reeves Building. As always when he passed the Parthenon Shoe Shine Parlor, a one-story hut which beside the granite and red-brick ponderousness of the old California Building resembled a bath-house under a cliff, he commented, "Gosh, ought to get my shoes shined this afternoon. Keep forgetting it." At the Simplex Office Furniture Shop, the National Cash Register Agency, he yearned for a dictaphone, for a typewriter which would add and multiply, as a poet yearns for quartos or a physician for radium.

At the Nobby Men's Wear Shop he took his left hand off the steering-wheel to touch his scarf, and thought well of himself as one who bought expensive ties "and could pay cash for 'em, too, by golly;" and at the United Cigar Store, with its crimson and gold alertness, he reflected, "Wonder if I need some cigars—idiot—plumb forgot—going t' cut down my fool smoking." He looked at his bank, the Miners' and Drovers' National, and considered how clever and solid he was to bank with so marbled an establishment. His high moment came in the clash of traffic when he was halted at the corner beneath the lofty Second National Tower. His car was banked with four others in a line of steel restless as cavalry, while the cross-town traffic, limousines and enormous moving-vans and insistent motor-cycles, poured by; on the farther corner, pneumatic riveters rang on the sun-plated skeleton of a new building; and out of this tornado flashed the inspiration of a familiar face, and a fellow Booster shouted, "H' are you, George!" Babbitt waved in neighborly affection, and slid on with the traffic as the policeman lifted his hand. He noted how quickly his car picked up. He felt superior and powerful, like a shuttle of polished steel darting in a vast machine.

As always he ignored the next two blocks, decayed blocks not yet reclaimed from the grime and shabbiness of the Zenith of 1885. While he was passing the five-and-ten-cent store, the Dakota Lodging House, Concordia Hall with its lodge-rooms and the offices of fortune-tellers and chiropractors, he thought of how much money he made, and he boasted a little and worried a little and did old familiar sums:

"Four hundred fifty plunks this morning from the Lyte deal. But taxes due. Let's see: I ought to pull out eight thousand net this year, and save fifteen hundred of that—no, not if I put up garage and— Let's see: six hundred and forty clear last month, and twelve times six-forty makes—makes—let see: six times twelve is seventy-two hundred and— Oh rats, anyway, I'll make eight thousand—gee now, that's not so bad; mighty few fellows pulling down eight thousand dollars a year—eight thousand good hard iron dollars—bet there isn't more than five per cent. of the people in the whole United States that make more than Uncle George does, by golly! Right up at the top of the heap! But— Way expenses are— Family wasting gasoline, and always dressed like millionaires, and sending that eighty a month to Mother— And all these stenographers and salesmen gouging me for every cent they can get—"

The effect of his scientific budget-planning was that he felt at once triumphantly wealthy and perilously poor, and in the midst of these dissertations he stopped his car, rushed into a small news-and-miscellany shop, and bought the electric cigar-lighter which he had coveted for a week. He dodged his conscience by being jerky and noisy, and by shouting at the clerk, "Guess this will prett' near pay for itself in matches, eh?"

It was a pretty thing, a nickeled cylinder with an almost silvery socket, to be attached to the dashboard of his car. It was not only, as the placard on the counter observed, "a dandy little refinement, lending the last touch of class to a gentleman's auto," but a priceless time-saver. By freeing him from halting the car to light a match, it would in a month or two easily save ten minutes.

As he drove on he glanced at it. "Pretty nice. Always wanted one," he said wistfully. "The one thing a smoker needs, too."

Then he remembered that he had given up smoking.

"Darn it!" he mourned. "Oh well, I suppose I'll hit a cigar once in a while. And— Be a great convenience for other folks. Might make just the difference in getting chummy with some fellow that would put over a sale. And— Certainly looks nice there. Certainly is a mighty clever little jigger. Gives the last touch of refinement and class. I— By golly,

I guess I can afford it if I want to! Not going to be the only member of this family that never has a single doggone luxury!"

Thus, laden with treasure, after three and a half blocks of romantic adventure, he drove up to the club.

III

The Zenith Athletic Club is not athletic and it isn't exactly a club, but it is Zenith in perfection. It has an active and smoke-misted billiard room, it is represented by baseball and football teams, and in the pool and the gymnasium a tenth of the members sporadically try to reduce. But most of its three thousand members use it as a café in which to lunch, play cards, tell stories, meet customers, and entertain out-of-town uncles at dinner. It is the largest club in the city, and its chief hatred is the conservative Union Club, which all sound members of the Athletic call "a rotten, snobbish, dull, expensive old hole—not one Good Mixer in the place—you couldn't hire me to join." Statistics show that no member of the Athletic has ever refused election to the Union, and of those who are elected, sixty-seven per cent. resign from the Athletic and are thereafter heard to say, in the drowsy sanctity of the Union lounge, "The Athletic would be a pretty good hotel, if it were more exclusive."

The Athletic Club building is nine stories high, yellow brick with glassy roof-garden above and portico of huge lime-stone columns below. The lobby, with its thick pillars of porous Caen stone, its pointed vaulting, and a brown glazed-tile floor like well-baked bread-crust, is a combination of cathedral-crypt and rathskeller. The members rush into the lobby as though they were shopping and hadn't much time for it. Thus did Babbitt enter, and to the group standing by the cigar-counter he whooped, "How's the boys? How's the boys? Well, well, fine day!"

Jovially they whooped back—Vergil Gunch, the coal-dealer, Sidney Finkelstein, the ladies'-ready-to-wear buyer for Parcher & Stein's department-store, and Professor Joseph K. Pumphrey, owner of the Riteway Business College and instructor in Public Speaking, Business English, Scenario Writing, and Commercial Law. Though Babbitt admired this savant, and appreciated Sidney Finkelstein as "a mighty smart buyer and a good liberal spender," it was to Vergil Gunch that he turned with enthusiasm. Mr. Gunch was president of the Boosters' Club, a weekly lunch-club, local chapter of a national organization which promoted sound business and friendliness among Regular Fellows. He was also no less an official than Esteemed Leading Knight in the Benevolent and Protective Order of Elks, and it was rumored that at the next election he would be a candidate for Exalted Ruler. He was a jolly man, given to oratory and to chumminess with the arts. He called on the famous actors and vaudeville artists when they came to town, gave them cigars, addressed them by their first names, and—sometimes —succeeded in bringing them to the Boosters' lunches to give The Boys a Free Entertainment. He was a large man with hair *en brosse,* and he knew the latest jokes, but he played poker close to the chest. It was at his party that Babbitt had sucked in the virus of to-day's restlessness.

Gunch shouted, "How's the old Bolsheviki? How do you feel, the morning after the night before?"

"Oh, boy! Some head! That was a regular party you threw, Verg! Hope you haven't forgotten I took that last cute little jack-pot!" Babbitt bellowed. (He was three feet from Gunch.)

"That's all right now! What I'll hand you next time, Georgie! Say, juh notice in the paper the way the New York Assembly stood up to the reds?"

"You bet I did. That was fine, eh? Nice day to-day."

"Yes, it's one mighty fine spring day, but nights still cold."

"Yeh, you're right they are! Had to have coupla blankets last night, out on the sleeping-porch. Say, Sid," Babbitt turned to Finkelstein, the buyer, "got something wanta ask you about. I went out and bought me an electric cigar-lighter for the car, this noon, and—"

"Good hunch!" said Finkelstein, while even the learned Professor Pumphrey, a bulbous man with a pepper-and-salt cutaway and a pipe-organ voice, commented, "That makes a dandy accessory. Cigar-lighter gives tone to the dashboard."

"Yep, finally decided I'd buy me one. Got the best on the market, the clerk said it was. Paid five bucks for it. Just wondering if I got stuck. What do they charge for 'em at the store, Sid?"

Finkelstein asserted that five dollars was not too great a sum, not for a really high-class lighter which was suitably nickeled and provided with connections of the very best quality. "I always say—and believe me, I base it on a pretty fairly extensive mercantile experience—the best is the cheapest in the long run. Of course if a fellow wants to be a Jew about it, he can get cheap junk, but in the long *run*, the cheapest thing is—the best you can get! Now you take here just th' other day: I got a new top for my old boat and some upholstery, and I paid out a hundred and twenty-six fifty, and of course a lot of fellows would say that was too much —Lord, if the Old Folks—they live in one of these hick towns up-state and they simply can't get onto the way a city fellow's mind works, and then, of course, they're Jews, and they'd lie right down and die if they knew Sid had anted up a hundred and twenty-six bones. But I don't figure I was stuck, George, not a bit. Machine looks brand new now—not that it's so darned old, of course; had it less 'n three years, but I give it hard service; never drive less 'n a hundred miles on Sunday and, uh— Oh, I don't really think you got stuck, George. In the *long* run, the best is, you might say, it's un-questionably the cheapest."

"That's right," said Vergil Gunch. "That's the way I look at it. If a fellow is keyed up to what you might call intensive living, the way you get it here in Zenith—all the hustle and mental activity that's going on with a bunch of live-wires like the Boosters and here in the Z.A.C., why, he's got to save his nerves by having the best."

Babbitt nodded his head at every fifth word in the roaring rhythm; and by the conclusion, in Gunch's renowned humor-ous vein, he was enchanted:

"Still, at that, George, don't know's you can afford it. I've heard your business has been kind of under the eye of the gov'ment since you stole the tail of Eathorne Park and sold it!"

"Oh, you're a great little josher, Verg. But when it comes to kidding, how about this report that you stole the black marble steps off the post-office and sold 'em for high-grade coal!" In delight Babbitt patted Gunch's back, stroked his arm.

"That's all right, but what I want to know is: who's the real-estate shark that bought that coal for his apartment-houses?"

"I guess that'll hold you for a while, George!" said Finkel-stein. "I'll tell you, though, boys, what I did hear: George's missus went into the gents' wear department at Parcher's to buy him some collars, and before she could give his neck-size the clerk slips her some thirteens. 'How juh know the size?' says Mrs. Babbitt, and the clerk says, 'Men that let their wives buy collars for 'em always wear thirteen, madam.'

How's that! That's pretty good, eh? How's that, eh? I guess
that'll about fix you, George!"

"I—I—" Babbitt sought for amiable insults in answer. He
stopped, stared at the door. Paul Riesling was coming in.
Babbitt cried, "See you later, boys," and hastened across the
lobby. He was, just then, neither the sulky child of the sleeping-porch, the domestic tyrant of the breakfast table, the
crafty money-changer of the Lyte-Purdy conference, nor the
blaring Good Fellow, the Josher and Regular Guy, of the
Athletic Club. He was an older brother to Paul Riesling, swift
to defend him, admiring him with a proud and credulous
love passing the love of women. Paul and he shook hands
solemnly; they smiled as shyly as though they had been parted three years, not three days—and they said:

"How's the old horse-thief?"

"All right, I guess. How're you, you poor shrimp?"

"I'm first-rate, you second-hand hunk o' cheese."

Reassured thus of their high fondness, Babbitt grunted,
"You're a fine guy, you are! Ten minutes late!" Riesling
snapped, "Well, you're lucky to have a chance to lunch with
a gentleman!" They grinned and went into the Neronian washroom, where a line of men bent over the bowls inset along a
prodigious slab of marble as in religious prostration before
their own images in the massy mirror. Voices thick, satisfied,
authoritative, hurtled along the marble walls, bounded from
the ceiling of lavender-bordered milky tiles, while the lords
of the city, the barons of insurance and law and fertilizers
and motor tires, laid down the law for Zenith; announced
that the day was warm—indeed, indisputably of spring; that
wages were too high and the interest on mortgages too low;
that Babe Ruth, the eminent player of baseball, was a noble
man; and that "those two nuts at the Climax Vaudeville Theater this week certainly are a slick pair of actors." Babbitt,
though ordinarily his voice was the surest and most episcopal of all, was silent. In the presence of the slight dark reticence of Paul Riesling, he was awkward, he desired to be
quiet and firm and deft.

The entrance lobby of the Athletic Club was Gothic, the
washroom Roman Imperial, the lounge Spanish Mission, and
the reading-room in Chinese Chippendale, but the gem of the
club was the dining-room, the masterpiece of Ferdinand Reit-
man, Zenith's busiest architect. It was lofty and half-tim-
bered, with Tudor leaded casements, an oriel, a somewhat
musicianless musicians'-gallery, and tapestries believed to

illustrate the granting of Magna Charta. The opens beams had been hand-adzed at Jake Offutt's car-body works, the hinges were of hand-wrought iron, the wainscot studded with handmade wooden pegs, and at one end of the room was a heraldic and hooded stone fireplace which the club's advertising-pamphlet asserted to be not only larger than any of the fireplaces in European castles but of a draught incomparably more scientific. It was also much cleaner, as no fire had ever been built in it.

Half of the tables were mammoth slabs which seated twenty or thirty men. Babbitt usually sat at the one near the door, with a group including Gunch, Finkelstein, Professor Pumphrey, Howard Littlefield, his neighbor, T. Cholmondeley Frink, the poet and advertising-agent, and Orville Jones, whose laundry was in many ways the best in Zenith. They composed a club within the club, and merrily called themselves "The Roughnecks." To-day as he passed their table the Roughnecks greeted him, "Come on, sit in! You 'n' Paul too proud to feed with poor folks? Afraid somebody might stick you for a bottle of Bevo, George? Strikes me you swells are getting awful darn exclusive!"

He thundered, "You bet! We can't afford to have our reps ruined by being seen with you tightwads!" and guided Paul to one of the small tables beneath the musicians'-gallery. He felt guilty. At the Zenith Athletic Club, privacy was very bad form. But he wanted Paul to himself.

That morning he had advocated lighter lunches and now he ordered nothing but English mutton chop, radishes, peas, deep-dish apple pie, a bit of cheese, and a pot of coffee with cream, adding, as he did invariably, "And uh— Oh, and you might give me an order of French fried potatoes." When the chop came he vigorously peppered it and salted it. He always peppered and salted his meat, and vigorously, before tasting it.

Paul and he took up the spring-like quality of the spring, the virtues of the electric cigar-lighter, and the action of the New York State Assembly. It was not till Babbitt was thick and disconsolate with mutton grease that he flung out:

"I wound up a nice little deal with Conrad Lyte this morning that put five hundred good round plunks in my pocket. Petty nice—pretty nice! And yet— I don't know what's the matter with me to-day. Maybe it's an attack of spring fever, or staying up too late at Verg Gunch's, or maybe it's just the winter's work piling up, but I've felt kind of down in the mouth all day long. Course I wouldn't beef about it to the fellows at the Roughnecks' Table there, but you— Ever feel that way, Paul? Kind of comes over me: here I've pretty much done all the things I ought to; supported my family, and got a good house and a six-cylinder car, and built up a nice little business, and I haven't any vices 'specially, except smoking—and I'm practically cutting that out, by the way. And I belong to the church, and play enough golf to keep in trim, and I only associate with good decent fellows. And yet, even so, I don't know that I'm entirely satisfied!"

It was drawled out, broken by shouts from the neighboring tables, by mechanical love-making to the waitress, by stertorous grunts as the coffee filled him with dizziness and indigestion. He was apologetic and doubtful, and it was Paul, with his thin voice, who pierced the fog:

"Good Lord, George, you don't suppose it's any novelty to me to find that we hustlers, that think we're so all-fired successful, aren't getting much out of it? You look as if you expected me to report you as seditious! You know what my own life's been."

"I know, old man."

"I ought to have been a fiddler, and I'm a pedler of tar-roofing! And Zilla— Oh, I don't want to squeal, but you know as well as I do about how inspiring a wife she is. . . . Typical instance last evening: We went to the movies. There was a big crowd waiting in the lobby, us at the tail-end. She began to push right through it with her 'Sir, how dare you?' manner— Honestly, sometimes when I look at her and see how she's always so made up and stinking of perfume and looking for trouble and kind of always yelping, 'I tell yuh I'm a lady, damn yuh!'—why, I want to kill her! Well, she keeps elbowing through the crowd, me after her, feeling good and ashamed, till she's almost up to the velvet rope and ready to be the next let in. But there was a little squirt of a man there—probably been waiting half an hour—I kind of admired the little cuss—and he turns on Zilla and says, perfectly polite, 'Madam, why are you trying to push past me?' And she simply—God, I was so ashamed!—she rips out at him, 'You're no gentleman,' and she drags me into it and hollers, 'Paul, this person insulted me!' and the poor skate he got ready to fight.

"I made out I hadn't heard them—sure! same as you wouldn't hear a boiler-factory!—and I tried to look away— I can tell you exactly how every tile looks in the ceiling of that lobby; there's one with brown spots on it like the face of the devil—and all the time the people there—they were packed in like sardines—they kept making remarks about us, and Zilla went right on talking about the little chap, and screeching that 'folks like him oughtn't to be admitted in a place that's *supposed* to be for ladies and gentlemen,' and 'Paul, will you kindly call the manager, so I can report this dirty rat?' and— Oof! Maybe I wasn't glad when I could sneak inside and hide in the dark!

"After twenty-four years of that kind of thing, you don't expect me to fall down and foam at the mouth when you hint that this sweet, clean, respectable, moral life isn't all it's cracked up to be, do you? I can't even talk about it, except to you, because anybody else would think I was yellow. Maybe I am. Don't care any longer. . . . Gosh, you've had to stand a lot of whining from me, first and last, Georgie!"

"Rats, now, Paul, you've never really what you could call whined. Sometimes— I'm always blowing to Myra and the kids about what a whale of a realtor I am, and yet sometimes I get a sneaking idea I'm not such a Pierpont Morgan as I let on to be. But if I ever do help by jollying you along, old Paulski, I guess maybe Saint Pete may let me in after all!"

"Yuh, you're an old blow-hard, Georgie, you cheerful cut-throat, but you've certainly kept me going."

"Why don't you divorce Zilla?"

"Why don't I! If I only could! If she'd just give me the chance! You couldn't hire her to divorce me, no, nor desert me. She's too fond of her three squares and a few pounds of nut-center chocolates in between. If she'd only be what they call unfaithful to me! George, I don't want to be too much of a stinker; back in college I'd 've thought a man who could say that ought to be shot at sunrise. But honestly, I'd be tickled to death if she'd really go making love with somebody. Fat chance! Of course she'll flirt with anything—you know how she holds hands and laughs—that laugh—that horrible brassy laugh—the way she yaps, 'You naughty man, you better be careful or my big husband will be after you!'— and the guy looking me over and thinking, 'Why, you cute little thing, you run away now or I'll spank you!' And she'll let him go just far enough so she gets some excitement out of it and then she'll begin to do the injured innocent and have a beautiful time wailing, 'I didn't think you were that kind of a person.' They talk about these *demi-vierges* in stories—"

"These *whats?*"

"—but the wise, hard, corseted, old married women like Zilla are worse than any bobbed-haired girl that ever went boldly out into this-here storm of life—and kept her umbrella slid up her sleeve! But rats, you know what Zilla is. How she nags—nags—nags. How she wants everything I can buy her, and a lot that I can't, and how absolutely unreasonable she is, and when I get sore and try to have it out with her she plays the Perfect Lady so well that even I get fooled and get all tangled up in a lot of 'Why did you say's' and 'I didn't mean's.' I'll tell you, Georgie: You know my tastes are pretty fairly simple—in the matter of food, at least. Course, as you're always complaining, I do like decent cigars—not those Flor de Cabagos you're smoking—"

"That's all right now! That's a good two-for. By the way, Paul, did I tell you I decided to practically cut out smok—"

"Yes you— At the same time, if I can't get what I like, why, I can do without it. I don't mind sitting down to burnt steak, with canned peaches and store cake for a thrilling little dessert afterwards, but I do draw the line at having to sympathize with Zilla because she's so rotten bad-tempered that the cook has quit, and she's been so busy sitting in a dirty lace negligée all afternoon, reading about some brave manly Western hero, that she hasn't had time to do any cooking. You're always talking about 'morals'—meaning monogamy, I suppose. You've been the rock of ages to me, all right, but you're essentially a simp. You—"

"Where d' you get that 'simp,' little man? Let me tell you—"

"—love to look earnest and inform the world that it's the 'duty of responsible business men to be strictly moral, as an example to the community.' In fact you're so earnest about morality, old Georgie, that I hate to think how essentially immoral you must be underneath. All right, you can—"

"Wait, wait now! What's—"

"—talk about morals all you want to, old thing, but believe me, if it hadn't been for you and an occasional evening playing the violin to Terrill O'Farrell's 'cello, and three or four darling girls that let me forget this beastly joke they call 'respectable life,' I'd 've killed myself years ago.

"And business! The roofing business! Roofs for cowsheds! Oh, I don't mean I haven't had a lot of fun out of the Game;

out of putting it over on the labor unions, and seeing a big
check coming in, and the business increasing. But what's
the use of it? You know, my business isn't distributing roofing
—it's principally keeping my competitors from distributing
roofing. Same with you. All we do is cut each other's throats
and make the public pay for it!"

"Look here now, Paul! You're pretty darn near talking
socialism!"

"Oh yes, of course I don't really exactly mean that—I
s'pose. Course—competition—brings out the best—survival
of the fittest—but— But I mean: Take all these fellows we
know, the kind right here in the club now, that seem to be
perfectly content with their home-life and their businesses,
and that boost Zenith and the Chamber of Commerce and
holler for a million population. I bet if you could cut into
their heads you'd find that one-third of 'em are sure-enough
satisfied with their wives and kids and friends and their
offices; and one-third feel kind of restless but won't admit it;
and one-third are miserable and know it. They hate the whole
peppy, boosting, go-ahead game, and they're bored by their
wives and think their families are fools—at least when they
come to forty or forty-five they're bored—and they hate business, and they'd go— Why do you suppose there's so many
'mysterious' suicides? Why do you suppose so many Substantial Citizens jumped right into the war? Think it was
all patriotism?"

Babbitt snorted, "What do you expect? Think we were
sent into the world to have a soft time and—what is it?—
'float on flowery beds of ease'? Think Man was just made to
be happy?"

"Why not? Though I've never discovered anybody that
knew what the deuce Man really was made for!"

"Well we know—not just in the Bible alone, but it stands
to reason—a man who doesn't buckle down and do his duty,
even if it does bore him sometimes, is nothing but a—well,
he's simply a weakling. Mollycoddle, in fact! And what do
you advocate? Come down to cases! If a man is bored by his
wife, do you seriously mean he has a right to chuck her and
take a sneak, or even kill himself?"

"Good Lord, I don't know what 'rights' a man has! And
I don't know the solution of boredom. If I did, I'd be the
one philosopher that had the cure for living. But I do know
that about ten times as many people find their lives dull, and
unnecessarily dull, as ever admit it; and I do believe that if

we busted out and admitted it sometimes, instead of being nice and patient and loyal for sixty years, and then nice and patient and dead for the rest of eternity, why, maybe, possibly, we might make life more fun."

They drifted into a maze of speculation. Babbitt was elephantishly uneasy. Paul was bold, but not quire sure about what he was being bold. Now and then Babbitt suddenly agreed with Paul in an admission which contradicted all his defense of duty and Christian patience, and at each admission he had a curious reckless joy. He said at last:

"Look here, old Paul, you do a lot of talking about kicking things in the face, but you never kick. Why don't you?"

"Nobody does. Habit too strong. But— Georgie, I've been thinking of one mild bat—oh, don't worry, old pillar of monogamy; it's highly proper. It seems to be settled now, isn't it—though of course Zilla keeps rooting for a nice expensive vacation in New York and Atlantic City, with the bright lights and the bootlegged cocktails and a bunch of lounge-lizards to dance with—but the Babbitts and the Rieslings are sure-enough going to Lake Sunasquam, aren't we? Why couldn't you and I make some excuse—say business in New York—and get up to Maine four or five days before they do, and just loaf by ourselves and smoke and cuss and be natural?"

"Great! Great idea!" Babbitt admired.

Not for fourteen years had he taken a holiday without his wife, and neither of them quite believed they could commit this audacity. Many members of the Athletic Club did go camping without their wives, but they were officially dedicated to fishing and hunting, whereas the sacred and unchangeable sports of Babbitt and Paul Riesling were golfing, motoring, and bridge. For either the fishermen or the golfers to have changed their habits would have been an infraction of their self-imposed discipline which would have shocked all right-thinking and regularized citizens.

Babbitt blustered, "Why don't we just put our foot down and say, 'We're going on ahead of you, and that's all there is to it!' Nothing criminal in it. Simply say to Zilla—"

"You don't say anything to Zilla simply. Why, Georgie, she's almost as much of a moralist as you are, and if I told her the truth she'd believe we were going to meet some dames in New York. And even Myra—she never nags you, the way Zilla does, but she'd worry. She'd say, 'Don't you *want* me to go to Maine with you? I shouldn't dream of going unless you wanted me;' and you'd give in to save her feelings. Oh, the devil! Let's have a shot at duck-pins."

During the game of duck-pins, a juvenile form of bowling, Paul was silent. As they came down the steps of the club, not more than half an hour after the time at which Babbitt had sternly told Miss McGoun he would be back, Paul sighed, "Look here, old man, oughtn't to talk about Zilla way I did."

"Rats, old man, it lets off steam."

"Oh, I know! After spending all noon sneering at the conventional stuff, I'm conventional enough to be ashamed of saving my life by busting out with my fool troubles!"

"Old Paul, your nerves are kind of on the bum. I'm going to take you away. I'm going to rig this thing. I'm going to have an important deal in New York and—and sure, of course!—I'll need you to advise me on the roof of the building! And the ole deal will fall through, and there'll be nothing for us but to go on ahead to Maine. I—Paul, when it comes right down to it, I don't care whether you bust loose or not. I do like having a rep for being one of the Bunch, but if you ever needed me I'd chuck it and come out for you every time! Not of course but what you're—course I don't mean you'd ever do anything that would put—that would put a decent position on the fritz but— See how I mean? I'm kind of a clumsy old codger, and I need your fine Eyetalian hand. We— Oh, hell, I can't stand here gassing all day! On the job! S' long! Don't take any wooden money, Paulibus! See you soon! S' long!"

chapter 6

HE forgot Paul Riesling in an afternoon of not unagreeable details. After a return to his office, which seemed to have staggered on without him, he drove a "prospect" out to view a four-flat tenement in the Linton district. He was inspired by the customer's admiration of the new cigar-lighter. Thrice its novelty made him use it, and thrice he hurled half-smoked cigarettes from the car, protesting, "I *got* to quit smoking so blame much!"

Their ample discussion of every detail of the cigar-lighter led them to speak of electric flat-irons and bed-warmers. Babbitt apologized for being so shabbily old-fashioned as still to use a hot-water bottle, and he announced that he would have the sleeping-porch wired at once. He had enormous and poetic admiration, though very little understanding, of all mechanical devices. They were his symbols of truth and beauty. Regarding each new intricate mechanism—metal lathe, two-jet carburetor, machine gun, oxyacetylene welder—he learned one good realistic-sounding phrase, and used it over and over, with a delightful feeling of being technical and initiated.

The customer joined him in the worship of machinery, and they came buoyantly up to the tenement and began that examination of plastic slate roof, kalamein doors, and seven-eighths-inch blind-nailed flooring, began those diplomacies of hurt surprise and readiness to be persuaded to do something they had already decided to do, which would some day result in a sale.

One the way back Babbitt picked up his partner and father-in-law, Henry T. Thompson, at his kitchen-cabinet works, and they drove through South Zenith, a high-colored, banging, exciting region: new factories of hollow tile with gigantic wire-glass windows, surly old red-brick factories stained with tar, high-perched water-tanks, big red trucks like locomotives, and, on a score of hectic side-tracks, far-wandering freight-cars from the New York Central and apple orchards, the Great Northern and wheat-plateaus, the Southern Pacific and orange groves.

They talked to the secretary of the Zenith Foundry Company about an interesting artistic project—a cast-iron fence for Linden Lane Cemetery. They drove on to the Zeeco Motor Company and interviewed the sales-manager, Noël Ryland, about a discount on a Zeeco car for Thompson. Babbitt and Ryland were fellow-members of the Boosters' Club, and no Booster felt right if he bought anything from another Booster without receiving a discount. But Henry Thompson growled, "Oh, t' hell with 'em! I'm not going to crawl around mooching discounts, not from nobody." It was one of the differences between Thompson, the old-fashioned, lean Yankee, rugged, traditional, stage type of American business man, and Babbitt, the plump, smooth, efficient, up-to-the-minute and otherwise perfected modern. Whenever Thompson twanged, "Put your John Hancock on that line," Babbitt was as much amused by the antiquated provincialism as any proper Englishman by any American. He knew himself to be of a breeding altogether more esthetic and sensitive than Thompson's. He was a college graduate, he played golf, he often smoked cigarettes instead of cigars, and when he went to Chicago he took a room with a private bath. "The whole thing is," he explained to Paul Riesling, "these old codgers lack the subtlety that you got to have to-day."

This advance in civilization could be carried too far, Babbitt perceived. Noël Ryland, sales-manager of the Zeeco, was a frivolous graduate of Princeton, while Babbitt was a sound and standard ware from that great department-store, the State University. Ryland wore spats, he wrote long letters about City Planning and Community Singing, and, though he was a Booster, he was known to carry in his pocket small volumes of poetry in a foreign language. All this was going too far. Henry Thompson was the extreme of insularity, and Noël Ryland the extreme of frothiness, while between them, supporting the state, defending the evangelical churches and domestic brightness and sound business, were Babbitt and his friends.

With this just estimate of himself—and with the promise of a discount on Thompson's car—he returned to his office in triumph.

But as he went through the corridor of the Reeves Building he sighed, "Poor old Paul! I got to— Oh, damn Noël Ryland! Damn Charley McKelvey! Just because they make more money than I do, they think they're so superior. I wouldn't be found dead in their stuffy old Union Club! I— Somehow, to-day, I don't feel like going back to work. Oh well—"

II

He answered telephone calls, he read the four o'clock mail, he signed his morning's letters, he talked to a tenant about repairs, he fought with Stanley Graff.

Young Graff, the outside salesman, was always hinting that

he deserved an increase of commission, and to-day he complained, "I think I ought to get a bonus if I put through the Heiler sale. I'm chasing around and working on it every single evening, almost."

Babbitt frequently remarked to his wife that it was better to "con your office-help along and keep 'em happy 'stead of jumping on 'em and poking 'em up—get more work out of 'em that way," but this unexampled lack of appreciation hurt him, and he turned on Graff:

"Look here, Stan; let's get this clear. You've got an idea somehow that it's you that do all the selling. Where d' you get that stuff? Where d' you think you'd be if it wasn't for our capital behind you, and our lists of properties, and all the prospects we find for you? All you got to do is follow up our tips and close the deal. The hall-porter could sell Babbitt-Thompson listings! You say you're engaged to a girl, but have to put in your evenings chasing after buyers. Well, why the devil shouldn't you? What do you want to do? Sit around holding her hand? Let me tell you, Stan, if your girl is worth her salt, she'll be glad to know you're out hustling, making some money to furnish the home-nest, instead of doing the lovey-dovey. The kind of fellow that kicks about working overtime, that wants to spend his evenings reading trashy novels or spooning and exchanging a lot of nonsense and foolishness with some girl, he ain't the kind of upstanding, energetic young man, with a future—and with Vision!—that we want here. How about it? What's your Ideal, anyway? Do you want to make money and be a responsible member of the community, or do you want to be a loafer, with no Inspiration or Pep?"

Graff was not so amenable to Vision and Ideals as usual. "You bet I want to make money! That's why I want that bonus! Honest, Mr. Babbitt, I don't want to get fresh, but this Heiler house is a terror. Nobody'll fall for it. The flooring is rotten and the walls are full of cracks."

"That's exactly what I mean! To a salesman with a love for his profession, it's hard problems like that that inspire him to do his best. Besides, Stan— Matter o' fact, Thompson and I are against bonuses, as a matter of principle. We like you, and we want to help you so you can get married, but we can't be unfair to the others on the staff. If we start giving you bonuses, don't you see we're going to hurt the feeling and be unjust to Penniman and Laylock? Right's right, and discrimination is unfair, and there ain't going to be any of it in this office! Don't get the idea, Stan, that because during the war salesmen were hard to hire, now, when there's a lot of men out of work, there aren't a slew of bright young fellows that would be glad to step in and enjoy your opportunities, and not act as if Thompson and I were his enemies and not do any work except for bonuses. How about it, heh? How about it?"

"Oh—well—gee—of course—" sighed Graff, as he went out, crabwise.

Babbitt did not often squabble with his employees. He liked to like the people about him; he was dismayed when they did not like him. It was only when they attacked the sacred purse that he was frightened into fury, but then, being a man given to oratory and high principles, he enjoyed the sound of his own vocabulary and the warmth of his own virtue. Today he had so passionately indulged in self-approval that he wondered whether he had been entirely just:

"After all, Stan isn't a boy any more. Oughtn't to call him so hard. But rats, got to haul folks over the coals now and then for their own good. Unpleasant duty, but— I wonder if Stan is sore? What's he saying to McGoun out there?"

So chill a wind of hatred blew from the outer office that the normal comfort of his evening home-going was ruined. He was distressed by losing that approval of his employees to which an executive is always slave. Ordinarily he left the office with a thousand enjoyable fussy directions to the effect that there would undoubtedly be important tasks to-morrow, and Miss McGoun and Miss Bannigan would do well to be there early, and for heaven's sake remind him to call up Conrad Lyte soon 's he came in. To-night he departed with feigned and apologetic liveliness. He was as afraid of his still-faced clerks—of the eyes focused on him, Miss McGoun staring with head lifted from her typing, Miss Bannigan looking over her ledger, Mat Penniman craning around at his desk in the dark alcove, Stanley Graff sullenly expressionless—as a parvenu before the bleak propriety of his butler. He hated to expose his back to their laughter, and in his effort to be casually merry he stammered and was raucously friendly and oozed wretchedly out of the door.

But he forgot his misery when he saw from Smith Street the charms of Floral Heights; the roofs of red tile and green slate, the shining new sun-parlors, and the stainless walls.

III

He stopped to inform Howard Littlefield, his scholarly neighbor, that though the day had been springlike the evening might be cold. He went in to shout "Where are you?" at his wife, with no very definite desire to know where she was. He examined the lawn to see whether the furnace-man had raked it properly. With some satisfaction and a good deal of discussion of the matter with Mrs. Babbitt, Ted, and Howard Littlefield, he concluded that the furnace-man had not raked it properly. He cut two tufts of wild grass with his wife's largest dressmaking-scissors; he informed Ted that it was all nonsense having a furnace-man—"big husky fellow like you ought to do all the work around the house;" and privately he meditated that it was agreeable to have it known throughout the neighborhood that he was so prosperous that his son never worked around the house.

He stood on the sleeping-porch and did his day's exercises: arms out sidewise for two minutes, up for two minutes, while he muttered, "Ought take more exercise; keep in shape;" then went in to see whether his collar needed changing before dinner. As usual it apparently did not.

The Lettish-Croat maid, a powerful woman, beat the dinner-gong.

The roast of beef, roasted potatoes, and string beans were excellent this evening and, after an adequate sketch of the day's progressive weather-states, his four-hundred-and-fifty-dollar fee, his lunch with Paul Riesling, and the proven merits of the new cigar-lighter, he was moved to a benign, "Sort o' thinking about buying a new car. Don't believe we'll get one till next year, but still, we might."

Verona, the older daughter, cried, "Oh, Dad, if you do, why don't you get a sedan? That would be perfectly slick! A closed car is so much more comfy than an open one."

"Well now, I don't know about that. I kind of like an open car. You get more fresh air that way."

"Oh, shoot, that's just because you never tried a sedan. Let's get one. It's got a lot more class," said Ted.

"A closed car does keep the clothes nicer," from Mrs. Babbitt; "You don't get your hair blown all to pieces," from Verona; "It's a lot sportier," from Ted; and from Tinka, the youngest, "Oh, let's have a sedan! Mary Ellen's father has got one." Ted wound up, "Oh, everybody's got a closed car now, except us!"

Babbitt faced them: "I guess you got nothing very terrible to complain about! Anyway, I don't keep a car just to enable you children to look like millionaires! And I like an open car, so you can put the top down on summer evenings and go out for a drive and get some good fresh air. Besides—A closed car costs more money."

"Aw, gee whiz, if the Doppelbraus can afford a closed car, I guess we can!" prodded Ted.

"Humph! I make eight thousand a year to his seven! But I don't blow it all in and waste it and throw it around, the way he does! Don't believe in this business of going and spending a whole lot of money to show off and——"

They went, with ardor and some thoroughness, into the matters of streamline bodies, hill-climbing power, wire wheels, chrome steel, ignition systems, and body colors. It was much more than a study of transportation. It was an aspiration for knightly rank. In the city of Zenith, in the barbarous twentieth century, a family's motor indicated its social rank as precisely as the grades of the peerage determined the rank of an English family—indeed, more precisely, considering the opinion of old county families upon newly created brewery barons and woolen-mill viscounts. The details of precedence we never officially determined. There was no court to decide whether the second son of a Pierce Arrow limousine should go in to dinner before the first son of a Buick roadster, but of their respective social importance there was no doubt; and where Babbitt as a boy had aspired to the presidency, his son Ted aspired to a Packard twin-six and an established position in the motored gentry.

The favor which Babbitt had won from his family by speaking of a new car evaporated as they realized that he didn't intend to buy one this year. Ted lamented, "Oh, punk! The old boat looks as if it'd had fleas and been scratching its varnish off." Mrs. Babbitt said abstractedly, "Snoway talkcher father." Babbitt raged, "If you're too much of a high-class gentleman, and you belong to the *bon ton* and so on, why, you needn't take the car out this evening." Ted explained, "I didn't mean——" and dinner dragged on with normal domestic delight to the inevitable point at which Babbitt protested, "Come, come now, we can't sit here all evening. Give the girl a chance to clear away the table."

He was fretting, "What a family! I don't know how we all get to scrapping this way. Like to go off some place and be able to hear myself think. . . . Paul . . . Maine . . . Wear old pants, and loaf, and cuss." He said cautiously to his wife, "I've been in correspondence with a man in New York—wants me to see him about a real-estate trade—may not come off till summer. Hope it doesn't break just when we and the Rieslings get ready to go to Maine. Be a shame if we couldn't make the trip there together. Well, no use worrying now."

Verona escaped, immediately after dinner, with no discussion save an automatic "Why don't you ever stay home?" from Babbitt.

In the living-room, in a corner of the davenport, Ted settled down to his Home Study; plain geometry, Cicero, and the agonizing metaphors of Comus.

"I don't see why they give us this old-fashioned junk by Milton and Shakespeare and Wordsworth and all these has-beens," he protested. "Oh, I guess I could stand it to see a show by Shakespeare, if they had swell scenery and put on a lot of dog, but to sit down in cold blood and *read* 'em— These teachers—how do they get that way?"

Mrs. Babbitt, darning socks, speculated, "Yes, I wonder why. Of course I don't want to fly in the face of the professors and everybody, but I do think there's things in Shakespeare—not that I read him much, but when I was young the girls used to show me passages that weren't, really, they weren't at all nice."

Babbitt looked up irritably from the comic strips in the *Evening Advocate*. They composed his favorite literature and art, these illustrated chronicles in which Mr. Mutt hit Mr. Jeff with a rotten egg, and Mother corrected Father's vulgarisms by means of a rolling-pin. With the solemn face of a devotee, breathing heavily through his open mouth, he plodded nightly through every picture, and during the rite he detested interruptions. Furthermore, he felt that on the subject of Shakespeare he wasn't really an authority. Neither the *Advocate-Times*, the *Evening Advocate*, nor the *Bulletin of the Zenith Chamber of Commerce* had ever had an editorial on the matter, and until one of them had spoken he found it hard to form an original opinion. But even at risk of floundering in strange bogs, he could not keep out of an open controversy.

"I'll tell you why you have to study Shakespeare and those.

It's because they're required for college entrance, and that's all there is to it! Personally, I don't see myself why they stuck 'em into an up-to-date high-school system like we have in this state. Be a good deal better if you took Business English, and learned how to write an ad, or letters that would pull. But there it is, and there's no talk, argument, or discussion about it! Trouble with you, Ted, is you always want to do something different! If you're going to law-school—and you are!—I never had a chance to, but I'll see that you do—why, you'll want to lay in all the English and Latin you can get."

"Oh punk. I don't see what's the use of law-school—or even finishing high school. I don't want to go to college 'specially. Honest, there's lot of fellows that have graduated from colleges that don't begin to make as much money as fellows that went to work early. Old Shimmy Peters, that teaches Latin in the High, he's a what-is-it from Columbia and he sits up all night reading a lot of greasy books and he's always spieling about the 'value of languages,' and the poor soak doesn't make but eighteen hundred a year, and no traveling salesman would think of working for that. I know what I'd like to do. I'd like to be an aviator, or own a corking big garage, or else—a fellow was telling me about it yesterday—I'd like to be one of these fellows that the Standard Oil Company sends out to China, and you live in a compound and don't have to do any work, and you get to see the world and pagodas and the ocean and everything! And then I could take up correspondence-courses. That's the real stuff! You don't have to recite to some frosty-faced old dame that's trying to show off to the principal, and you can study any subject you want to. Just listen to these! I clipped out the ads of some swell courses."

He snatched from the back of his geometry half a hundred advertisements of those home-study courses which the energy and foresight of American commerce have contributed to the science of education. The first displayed the portrait of a young man with a pure brow, an iron jaw, silk socks, and hair like patent leather. Standing with one hand in his trousers-pocket and the other extended with chiding forefinger, he was bewitching an audience of men with gray beards, paunches, bald heads, and every other sign of wisdom and prosperity. Above the picture was an inspiring educational symbol—no antiquated lamp or torch or owl of Minerva, but a row of dollar signs. The text ran:

$ $ $ $ $ $ $ $ $

POWER AND PROSPERITY IN PUBLIC SPEAKING

A Yarn Told at the Club

Who do you think I ran into the other evening at the De Luxe Restaurant? Why, old Freddy Durkee, that used to be a dead-or-alive shipping clerk in my old place—Mr. Mouse-Man we used to laughingly call the dear fellow. One time he was so timid he was plumb scared of the Super, and never got credit for the dandy work he did. Him at the De Luxe! And if he wasn't ordering a tony feed with all the "fixings" from celery to nuts! And instead of being embarrassed by the waiters, like he used to be at the little dump where we lunched in Old Lang Syne, he was bossing them around like he was a million-aire!

I cautiously asked him what he was doing. Freddy laughed and said, "Say, old chum, I guess you're wondering what's come over me. You'll be glad to know I'm now Assistant Super at the old shop, and right on the High Road to Prosperity and Domination, and I look forward with confidence to a twelve-cylinder car, and the wife is making things hum in the best society and the kiddies getting a first-class education.

WHAT WE TEACH YOU!

How to address your lodge.

How to give toasts.

How to tell dialect stories.

How to propose to a lady.

How to entertain banquets.

How to make convincing selling-talks.

How to build big vocabulary.

How to create a strong personality.

How to become a rational, powerful and original thinker.

How to be a MASTER MAN!

"Here's how it happened. I ran across an ad of a course that claimed to teach people how to talk easily and on their feet, how to answer complaints, how to lay a proposition before the Boss, how to hit a bank for a loan, how to hold a big audience spellbound with wit, humor, anecdote, inspiration, etc. It was compiled by the Master Orator, Prof. Waldo F. Peet. I was skeptical, too, but I wrote (just *on a postcard,* with name and address) to the publisher for the lessons—sent On Trial, money back if you are not absolutely satisfied. There were eight simple lessons in plain language anybody could understand, and I studied them just a few hours a night, then started practising on the wife. Soon found I could talk right up to the Super and get due credit for all the good work I did. They began to appreciate me and advance me fast, and say, old doggo, what do you think they're paying me now? $6,500 per year! And say, I find I can keep a big audience fascinated, speaking on any topic. As a friend, old boy, I advise you to send for circular (no obligation) and valuable free Art Picture to:—

Babbitt was again without a canon which would enable him to speak with authority. Nothing in motoring or real estate had indicated what a Solid Citizen and Regular Fellow ought to think about culture by mail. He began with hesitation:

"Well—sounds as if it covered the ground. It certainly is a fine thing to be able to orate. I've sometimes thought I had a little talent that way myself, and I know darn well that one reason why a fourflushing old back-number like Chan Mott can get away with it in real estate is just because he can make a good talk, even when he hasn't got a doggone thing to say! And it certainly is pretty cute the way they get out all these courses on various topics and subjects nowadays. I'll tell you, though: No need to blow in a lot of good money on this stuff when you can get a first-rate course in eloquence and English and all that right in your own school—and one of the biggest school buildings in the entire country!"

"That's so," said Mrs. Babbitt comfortably, while Ted complained:

"Yuh, but Dad, they just teach a lot of old junk that isn't any practical use—except the manual training and type-writing and basketball and dancing—and in these correspondence-courses, gee, you can get all kinds of stuff that would come in handy. Say, listen to this one:

CAN YOU PLAY A MAN'S PART?

If you are walking with your mother, sister or best girl and some one passes a slighting remark or uses improper language, won't you be ashamed if you can't take her part? Well, can you?

We teach boxing and self-defense by mail. Many pupils have written saying that after a few lessons they've out-boxed bigger and heavier opponents. The lessons start with simple movements practised before your mirror—holding out your hand for a coin, the breast-stroke in swimming, etc. Before you realize it you are striking scientifically, ducking, guarding and feinting, just as if you had a real opponent before you.

"Oh, baby, maybe I wouldn't like that!" Ted chanted. "I'll tell the world! Gosh, I'd like to take one fellow I know in school that's always shooting off his mouth, and catch him alone—"

"Nonsense! The idea! Most useless thing I ever heard of!" Babbitt fulminated.

"Well, just suppose I was walking with Mama or Rone, and somebody passed a slighting remark or used improper language. What would I do?"

"Why, you'd probably bust the record for the hundred-yard dash!"

"I *would* not! I'd stand right up to any mucker that passed a slighting remark on *my* sister and I'd show him—"

"Look here, young Dempsey! If I ever catch you fighting I'll whale the everlasting daylights out of you—and I'll do it without practising holding out my hand for a coin before the mirror, too!"

"Why, Ted dear," Mrs. Babbitt said placidly, "it's not at all nice, your talking of fighting this way!"

"Well, gosh almighty, that's a fine way to appreciate— And then suppose I was walking with *you*, Ma, and somebody passed a slighting remark—"

"Nobody's going to pass no slighting remarks on nobody," Babbitt observed, "not if they stay home and study their geometry and mind their own affairs instead of hanging around a lot of poolrooms and soda-fountains and places where nobody's got any business to be!"

"But gooooooosh, Dad, if they DID!"

Mrs. Babbitt chirped, "Well, if they did, I wouldn't do them the honor of paying any attention to them! Besides, they never do. You always hear about these women that get followed and insulted and all, but I don't believe a word of it, or it's their own fault, the way some women look at a person. I certainly never 've been insulted by—"

"Aw shoot. Mother, just suppose you *were* sometime! Just *suppose!* Can't you suppose something? Can't you imagine things?"

"Certainly I can imagine things! The idea!"

"Certainly your mother can imagine things—and suppose things! Think you're the only member of this household that's got an imagination?" Babbitt demanded. "But what's the use of a lot of supposing? Supposing never gets you anywhere. No sense supposing when there's a lot of real facts to take into considera—"

"Look here, Dad. Suppose—I mean, just—just suppose you were in your office and some rival real-estate man—"

"Realtor!"

"—some realtor that you hated came in—"

"I don't hate any realtor."

"But suppose you *did!*"

"I don't intend to suppose anything of the kind! There's plenty of fellows in my profession that stoop and hate their competitors, but if you were a little older and understood business, instead of always going to the movies and running around with a lot of fool girls with their dresses up to their knees and powdered and painted and rouged and God knows what all as if they were chorus-girls, then you'd know— and you'd suppose—that if there's any one thing that I stand for in the real-estate circles of Zenith, it is that we ought to always speak of each other only in the friendliest terms and institute a spirit of brotherhood and coöperation, and so I certainly can't suppose and I can't imagine my hating any realtor, not even that dirty, fourflushing society sneak, Cecil Rountree!"

"But—"

"And theres no If, And or But about it! But if I *were* going to lambaste somebody, I wouldn't require any fancy ducks or swimming-strokes before a mirror, or any of these doodads and flipflops! Suppose you were out some place and a fellow called you vile names. Think you'd want to box and jump around like a dancing-master? You'd just lay him out cold (at least I certainly hope any son of mine would!) and then you'd dust off your hands and go on about your business, and that's all there is to it, and you aren't going to have any boxing-lessons by mail, either!"

"Well but— Yes— I just wanted to show how many different kinds of correspondence-courses there are, instead of all the camembert they teach us in the High."

"But I thought they taught boxing in the school gymnasium."

"That's different. They stick you up there and some big stiff amuses himself pounding the stuffin's out of you before you have a chance to learn. Hunka! Not any! But anyway— Listen to some of these others."

The advertisements were truly philanthropic. One of them bore the rousing headline: "Money! Money!! Money!!!" The second announced that "Mr. P. R., formerly making only eighteen a week in a barber shop, writes to us that since taking our course he is now pulling down $5,000 as an Osteo-vitalic Physician;" and the third that "Miss J. L., recently a wrapper in a store, is now getting Ten Real Dollars a day teaching our Hindu System of Vibratory Breathing and Mental Control."

Ted had collected fifty or sixty announcements, from annual reference-books, from Sunday School periodicals, fiction-magazines, and journals of discussion. One benefactor implored, "Don't be a Wallflower—Be More Popular and Make More Money—*You* Can Ukulele or Sing Yourself into Society! By the secret principles of a Newly Discovered System of Music Teaching, any one—man, lady or child—can, without tiresome exercises, special training or long drawn out study, and without waste of time, money or energy, learn to play by note, piano, banjo, cornet, clarinet, saxophone, violin or drum, and learn sight-singing."

The next, under the wistful appeal "Finger Print Detectives Wanted—Big Incomes!" confided: "YOU red-blooded men and women—this is the PROFESSION you have been looking for. There's MONEY in it, BIG money, and that rapid change of scene, that entrancing and compelling interest and fascination, which your active mind and adventurous spirit crave. Think of being the chief figure and directing factor in solving strange mysteries and baffling crimes. This wonderful profession brings you into contact with influential men on the basis of equality, and often calls upon you to travel everywhere, maybe to distant lands—all expenses paid. NO SPECIAL EDUCATION REQUIRED."

"Oh, boy! I guess that wins the fire-brick necklace! Wouldn't it be swell to travel everywhere and nab some famous crook!" whooped Ted.

"Well, I don't think much of that. Doggone likely to get hurt. Still, that music-study stunt might be pretty fair, though. There's no reason why, if efficiency-experts put their minds to it the way they have to routing products in a factory, they couldn't figure out some scheme so a person wouldn't have to monkey with all this practising and exercises that you get in music." Babbitt was impressed, and he had a delightful parental feeling that they two, the men of the family, understood each other.

He listened to the notices of mail-box universities which taught Short-story Writing and Improving the Memory, Motion-picture-acting and Developing the Soul-power, Banking and Spanish, Chiropody and Photography, Electrical Engineering and Window-trimming, Poultry-raising and Chemistry.

"Well—well—" Babbitt sought for adequate expression of his admiration. "I'm a son of a gun! I knew this correspondence-school business had become a mighty profitable game— makes suburban real-estate look like two cents!—but I didn't realize it'd got to be such a reg'lar key-industry! Must rank right up with groceries and movies. Always figured some-body'd come along with the brains to not leave education to a lot of bookworms and impractical theorists but make a big thing out of it. Yes, I can see how a lot of these courses might interest you. I must ask the fellows at the Athletic if they ever realized— But same time, Ted, you know how advertisers, I means some advertisers, exaggerate. I don't know as they'd be able to jam you through these courses as fast as they claim they can."

"Oh sure, Dad; of course." Ted had the immense and joy-ful maturity of a boy who is respectfully listened to by his elders. Babbitt concentrated on him with grateful affection:

"I can see what an influence these courses might have on the whole educational works. Course I'd never admit it pub-licly—fellow like myself, a State U. graduate, it's only decent and patriotic for him to blow his horn and boost the Alma Mater—but smatter of fact, there's a whole lot of valuable time lost even at the U., studying poetry and French and subjects that never brought in anybody a cent. I don't know but what maybe these correspondence-courses might prove to be one of the most important American inventions.

"Trouble with a lot of folks is: they're so blame material; they don't see the spiritual and mental side of American supremacy; they think that inventions like the telephone and the areoplane and wireless—no, that was a Wop invention, but anyway: they think these mechanical improvements are all that we stand for; whereas to a real thinker, he sees that spiritual and, uh, dominating movements like Efficiency, and Rotarianism, and Prohibition, and Democracy are what compose our deepest and truest wealth. And maybe this new principle in education-at-home may be another—may be another factor. I tell you, Ted, we've got to have Vision—"

"I think those correspondence-courses are terrible!"

The philosophers gasped. It was Mrs. Babbitt who had made this discord in their spiritual harmony, and one of Mrs. Babbitt's virtues was that, except during dinner-parties, when she was transformed into a raging hostess, she took care of the house and didn't bother the males by thinking. She went on firmly:

"It sounds awful to me, the way they coax those poor young folks to think they're learning something, and nobody 'round to help them and— You two learn so quick, but me, I always was slow. But just the same—"

Babbitt attended to her: "Nonsense! Get just as much,

studying at home. You don't think a fellow learns any more because he blows in his father's hard-earned money and sits around in Morris chairs in a swell Harvard dormitory with pictures and shields and table-covers and those doodads, do you? I tell you, I'm a college man—I *know!* There is one objection you might make though. I certainly do protest against any effort to get a lot of fellows out of barber shops and factories into the professions. They're too crowded already, and what'll we do for workmen if all those fellows go and get educated?"

Ted was leaning back, smoking a cigarette without reproof. He was, for the moment, sharing the high thin air of Babbitt's speculation as though he were Paul Riesling or even Dr. Howard Littlefield. He hinted:

"Well, what do you think then, Dad? Wouldn't it be a good idea if I could go off to China or some peppy place, and study engineering or something by mail?"

"No, and I'll tell you why, son. I've found out it's a mighty nice thing to be able to say you're a B.A. Some client that doesn't know what you are and thinks you're just a plug business man, he gets to shooting off his mouth about economics or literature or foreign trade conditions, and you just ease in something like, 'When I was in college—course I got my B.A. in sociology and all that junk—' Oh, it puts an awful crimp in their style! But there wouldn't be any class to saying 'I got the degree of Stamp-licker from the Bezuzus Mail-order University!' You see— My dad was a pretty good old coot, but he never had much style to him, and I had to work darn hard to earn my way through college. Well, it's been worth it, to be able to associate with the finest gentlemen in Zenith, at the clubs and so on, and I wouldn't want you to drop out of the gentlemen class—the class that are just as red-blooded as the Common People but still have power and personality. It would kind of hurt me if you did that, old man!"

"I know, Dad! Sure! All right. I'll stick to it. Say! Gosh! Gee whiz! I forgot all about those kids I was going to take to the chorus rehearsal. I'll have to duck!"

"But you haven't done all your home-work."

"Do it first thing in the morning."

"Well—"

Six times in the past sixty days Babbitt had stormed, "You will not 'do it first thing in the morning'! You'll do it right now!" but to-night he said, "Well, better hustle," and his smile was the rare shy radiance he kept for Paul Riesling.

IV

"Ted's a good boy," he said to Mrs. Babbitt.

"Oh, he is!"

"Who's these girls he's going to pick up? Are they nice decent girls?"

"I don't know. Oh dear, Ted never tells me anything any more. I don't understand what's come over the children of this generation. I used to have to tell Papa and Mama everything, but seems like the children to-day have just slipped away from all control."

"I hope they're decent girls. Course Ted's no longer a kid, and I wouldn't want him to, uh, get mixed up and everything."

"George: I wonder if you oughtn't to take him aside and tell him about—Things!" She blushed and lowered her eyes.

"Well, I don't know. Way I figure it, Myra, no sense suggesting a lot of Things to a boy's mind. Think up enough devilment by himself. But I wonder— It's kind of a hard question. Wonder what Littlefield thinks about it?"

"Course Papa agrees with you. He says all this—Instruction—is— He says 'tisn't decent."

"Oh, he does, does he! Well, let me tell you that whatever Henry T. Thompson thinks—about morals, I mean, though course you can't beat the old duffer—"

"Why, what a way to talk of Papa!"

"—simply can't beat him at getting in on the ground floor of a deal, but let me tell you whenever he springs any ideas about higher things and education, then I know I think just the opposite. You may not regard me as any great brainshark, but believe me, I'm a regular college president, compared with Henry T.! Yes sir, by golly, I'm going to take Ted aside and tell him why I lead a strictly moral life."

"Oh, will you? When?"

"When? When? What's the use of trying to pin me down to When and Why and Where and How and When? That's the trouble with women, that's why they don't make high-class executives; they haven't any sense of diplomacy. When the proper opportunity and occasion arises so it just comes in natural, why then I'll have a friendly little talk with him and —and— Was that Tinka hollering up-stairs? She ought to been asleep, long ago."

He prowled through the living-room, and stood in the sun-parlor, that glass-walled room of wicker chairs and swinging couch in which they loafed on Sunday afternoons. Outside, only the lights of Doppelbrau's house and the dim presence of Babbitt's favorite elm broke the softness of April night.

"Good visit with the boy. Getting over feeling cranky, way I did this morning. And restless. Though, by golly, I will have a few days alone with Paul in Maine! . . . That devil Zilla! . . . But . . . Ted's all right. Whole family all right. And good business. Not many fellows make four hundred and fifty bucks, practically half of a thousand dollars, easy as I did to-day! Maybe when we all get to rowing it's just as much my fault as it is theirs. Oughtn't to get grouchy like I do. But— Wish I'd been a pioneer, same as my grand-dad. But then, wouldn't have a house like this. I— Oh, gosh, *I don't know!*"

He thought moodily of Paul Riesling, of their youth together, of the girls they had known.

When Babbitt had graduated from the State University, twenty-four years ago, he had intended to be a lawyer. He had been a ponderous debater in college; he felt that he was an orator; he saw himself becoming governor of the state. While he read law he worked as a real-estate salesman. He saved money, lived in a boarding-house, supped on poached egg on hash. The lively Paul Riesling (who was certainly going off to Europe to study violin, next month or next year) was his refuge till Paul was bespelled by Zilla Colbeck, who laughed and danced and drew men after her plump and gaily wagging finger.

Babbitt's evenings were barren then, and he found comfort only in Paul's second cousin, Myra Thompson, a sleek and gentle girl who showed her capacity by agreeing with the ardent young Babbitt that of course he was going to be governor some day. Where Zilla mocked him as a country boy, Myra said indignantly that he was ever so much solider than the young dandies who had been born in the great city of Zenith—an ancient settlement in 1897, one hundred and five years old, with two hundred thousand population, the queen and wonder of all the state and, to the Catawba boy, George Babbitt, so vast and thunderous and luxurious that he was flattered to know a girl ennobled by birth in Zenith.

Of love there was no talk between them. He knew that if he was to study law he could not marry for years; and Myra was distinctly a Nice Girl—one didn't kiss her, one didn't "think about her that way at all" unless one was going to marry her. But she was a dependable companion. She was always ready to go skating, walking; always content to hear his discourses on the great things he was going to do, the distressed poor whom he would defend against the Unjust Rich, the speeches he would make at Banquets, the inexactitudes of popular thought which he would correct.

One evening when he was weary and soft-minded, he saw that she had been weeping. She had been left out of a party given by Zilla. Somehow her head was on his shoulder and he was kissing away the tears—and she raised her head to say trustingly, "Now that we're engaged, shall we be married soon or shall we wait?"

Engaged? It was his first hint of it. His affection for this brown tender woman thing went cold and fearful, but he could not hurt her, could not abuse her trust. He mumbled something about waiting, and escaped. He walked for an hour, trying to find a way of telling her that it was a mistake. Often, in the month after, he got near to telling her, but it was pleasant to have a girl in his arms, and less and less could he insult her by blurting that he didn't love her. He himself had no doubt. The evening before his marriage was an agony, and the morning wild with the desire to flee.

She made him what is known as a Good Wife. She was loyal, industrious, and at rare times merry. She passed from a feeble disgust at their closer relations into what promised to be ardent affection, but it drooped into bored routine. Yet she existed only for him and for the children, and she was as sorry, as worried as himself, when he gave up the law and trudged on in a rut of listing real estate.

"Poor kid, she hasn't had much better time than I have," Babbitt reflected, standing in the dark sun-parlor. "But— I wish I could 've had a whirl at law and politics. Seen what I could do. Well— Maybe I've made more money as it is."

He returned to the living-room but before he settled down he smoothed his wife's hair, and she glanced up, happy and somewhat surprised.

HE solemnly finished the last copy of the *American Magazine*, while his wife sighed, laid away her darning, and looked enviously at the lingerie designs in a women's magazine. The room was very still.

It was a room which observed the best Floral Heights standards. The gray walls were divided into artificial paneling by strips of white-enameled pine. From the Babbitts' former house had come two much-carved rocking-chairs, but the other chairs were new, very deep and restful, upholstered in blue and gold-striped velvet. A blue velvet davenport faced the fireplace, and behind it was a cherrywood table and a tall piano-lamp with a shade of golden silk. (Two out of every three houses in Floral Heights had before the fireplace a davenport, a mahogany table real or imitation, and a piano-lamp or a reading-lamp with a shade of yellow or rose silk.)

On the table was a runner of gold-threaded Chinese fabric, four magazines, a silver box containing cigarette-crumbs, and three "gift-books"—large, expensive editions of fairy-tales illustrated by English artists and as yet unread by any Babbitt save Tinka.

In a corner by the front windows was a large cabinet Victrola. (Eight out of every nine Floral Heights houses had a cabinet phonograph.)

Among the pictures, hung in the exact center of each gray panel, were a red and black imitation English hunting-print, an anemic imitation boudoir-print with a French caption of whose morality Babbitt had always been rather suspicious, and a "hand-colored" photograph of a Colonial room—rag rug, maiden spinning, cat demure before a white fireplace. (Nineteen out of every twenty houses in Floral Heights had either a hunting-print, a *Madame Fait la Toilette* print,

77

a colored photograph of a New England house, a photograph
of a Rocky Mountain, or all four.)

It was a room as superior in comfort to the "parlor" of
Babbitt's boyhood as his motor was superior to his father's
buggy. Though there was nothing in the room that was interesting, there was nothing that was offensive. It was as neat,
and as negative, as a block of artificial ice. The fireplace was
unsoftened by downy ashes or by sooty brick; the brass fire-
irons were of immaculate polish; and the grenadier andirons
were like samples in a shop, desolate, unwanted, lifeless things
of commerce.

Against the wall was a piano, with another piano-lamp, but
no one used it save Tinka. The hard briskness of the phonograph contented them; their store of jazz records made them
feel wealthy and cultured; and all they knew of creating music
was the nice adjustment of a bamboo needle. The books on
the table was unspotted and laid in rigid parallels; not one
corner of the carpet-rug was curled; and nowhere was there
a hockey-stick, a torn picture-book, an old cap, or a gre-
garious and disorganizing dog.

II

At home, Babbitt never read with absorption. He was concentrated enough at the office but here he crossed his legs and
fidgeted. When his story was interesting he read the best,
that is the funniest, paragraphs to his wife; when it did not
hold him he coughed, scratched his ankles and his right ear,
thrust his left thumb into his vest pocket, jingled his silver,
whirled the cigar-cutter and the keys on one end of his
watch-chain, yawned, rubbed his nose, and found errands to
do. He went upstairs to put on his slippers—his elegant
slippers of seal-brown, shaped like medieval shoes. He brought
up an apple from the barrel which stood by the trunk-closet
in the basement.

"An apple a day keeps the doctor away," he enlightened
Mrs. Babbitt, for quite the first time in fourteen hours.

"That's so."

"An apple is Nature's best regulator."

"Yes, it——"

"Trouble with women is, they never have sense enough to
form regular habits."

"Well, I—"

"Always nibbling and eating between meals."

"George!" She looked up from her reading. "Did you have a light lunch to-day, like you were going to? I did!"

This malicious and unprovoked attack astounded him. "Well, maybe it wasn't as light as— Went to lunch with Paul and didn't have much chance to diet. Oh, you needn't to grin like a chessy cat! If it wasn't for me watching out and keeping an eye on our diet— I'm the only member of this family that appreciates the value of oatmeal for breakfast. I—"

She stooped over her story while he piously sliced and gulped down the apple, discoursing:

"One thing I've done: cut down my smoking.

"Had kind of a run-in with Graff in the office. He's getting too darn fresh. I'll stand for a good deal, but once in a while I got to assert my authority, and I jumped him. 'Stan,' I said— Well, I told him just exactly where he got off.

"Funny kind of a day. Makes you feel restless.

"Wellllllllll, uh—" That sleepiest sound in the world, the terminal yawn. Mrs. Babbitt yawned with it, and looked grateful as he droned, "How about going to bed, eh? Don't suppose Rone and Ted will be in till all hours. Yep, funny kind of a day; not terribly warm but yet— Gosh, I'd like— Some day I'm going to take a long motor trip."

"Yes, we'd enjoy that," she yawned.

He looked away from her as he realized that he did not wish to have her go with him. As he locked doors and tried windows and set the heat regulator so that the furnace-drafts would open automatically in the morning, he sighed a little, heavy with a lonely feeling which perplexed and frightened him. So absent-minded was he that he could not remember which window-catches he had inspected, and through the darkness, fumbling at unseen perilous chairs, he crept back to try them all over again. His feet were loud on the steps as he clumped upstairs at the end of this great and treacherous day of veiled rebellions.

III

Before breakfast he always reverted to up-state village boy-hood, and shrank from the complex urban demands of shaving, bathing, deciding whether the current shirt was clean enough for another day. Whenever he stayed home in the evening he went to bed early, and thriftily got ahead in those dismal duties. It was his luxurious custom to shave while sitting snugly in a tubful of hot water. He may be viewed to-night as a plump, smooth, pink, baldish, podgy goodman, robbed of the importance of spectacles, squatting in breast-high water, scraping his lather-smeared cheeks with a safety-razor like a tiny lawn-mower, and with melancholy dignity clawing through the water to recover a slippery and active piece of soap.

He was lulled to dreaming by the caressing warmth. The light fell on the inner surface of the tub in a pattern of deli-cate wrinkled lines which slipped with a green sparkle over the curving porcelain as the clear water trembled. Babbitt lazily watched it; noted that along the silhouette of his legs against the radiance on the bottom of the tub, the shadows of the air-bubbles clinging to the hairs were reproduced as strange jungle mosses. He patted the water, and the reflected light capsized and leaped and volleyed. He was content and childish. He played. He shaved a swath down the calf of one plump leg.

The drain-pipe was dripping, a dulcet and lively song: drip-pety drip drip dribble, drippety drip drip drip. He was en-chanted by it. He looked at the solid tub, the beautiful nickel taps, the tiled walls of the room, and felt virtuous in the possession of this splendor.

He roused himself and spoke gruffly to his bath-things. "Come here! You've done enough fooling!" he reproved the treacherous soap, and defied the scratchy nail-brush with "Oh, you would, would you!" He soaped himself, and rinsed him-self, and austerely rubbed himself; he noted a hole in the Turkish towel, and meditatively thrust a finger through it, and marched back to the bedroom, a grave and unbending citizen.

There was a moment of gorgeous abandon, a flash of melo-drama such as he found in traffic-driving, when he laid out a clean collar, discovered that it was frayed in front, and tore it up with a magnificent yeeeeeing sound.

Most important of all was the preparation of his bed and the sleeping-porch.

It is not known whether he enjoyed his sleeping-porch be-cause of the fresh air or because it was the standard thing to have a sleeping-porch.

Just as he was an Elk, a Booster, and a member of the Chamber of Commerce, just as the priests of the Presbyte-rian Church determined his every religious belief and the senators who controlled the Republican Party decided in little smoky rooms in Washington what he should think about disarmament, tariff, and Germany, so did the large national advertisers fix the surface of his life, fix what he believed to be his individuality. These standard advertised wares—toothpastes, socks, tires, cameras, instantaneous hot-water heaters—were his symbols and proofs of excellence; at first the signs, then the substitutes, for joy and passion and wisdom.

But none of these advertised tokens of financial and social success was more significant than a sleeping-porch with a sun-parlor below.

The rites of preparing for bed were elaborate and unchanging. The blankets had to be tucked in at the foot of his cot. (Also, the reason why the maid hadn't tucked in the blankets had to be discussed with Mrs. Babbitt.) The rag rug was adjusted so that his bare feet would strike it when he arose in the morning. The alarm clock was wound. The hot-water bottle was filled and placed precisely two feet from the bottom of the cot.

These tremendous undertakings yielded to his determination; one by one they were announced to Mrs. Babbitt and smashed through to accomplishment. At last his brow cleared, and in his "Gnight!" rang virile power. But there was yet need of courage. As he sank into sleep, just at the first exquisite relaxation, the Doppelbrau car came home. He bounced into wakefulness, lamenting, "Why the devil can't some people never get to bed at a reasonable hour?" So familiar was he with the process of putting up his own car that he awaited each step like an able executioner condemned to his own rack.

The car insultingly cheerful on the driveway. The car door opened and banged shut, then the garage door slid open, grating on the sill, and the car door again. The motor raced for the climb up into the garage and raced once more, explosively, before it was shut off. A final opening and slamming of the car door. Silence then, a horrible silence filled with waiting, till the leisurely Mr. Doppelbrau had examined the state of his tires and had at last shut the garage door. Instantly, for Babbitt, a blessed state of oblivion.

IV

At that moment in the city of Zenith, Horace Updike was making love to Lucile McKelvey in her mauve drawing-room on Royal Ridge, after their return from a lecture by an eminent English novelist. Updike was Zenith's professional bachelor; a slim-waisted man of forty-six with an effeminate voice and taste in flowers, cretonnes, and flappers. Mrs. McKelvey was red-haired, creamy, discontented, exquisite, rude, and honest. Updike tried his invariable first maneuver— touching her nervous wrist.

"Don't be an idiot!" she said.

"Do you mind awfully?"

"No! That's what I mind!"

He changed to conversation. He was famous at conversation. He spoke reasonably of psychoanalysis, Long Island polo, and the Ming platter he had found in Vancouver. She promised to meet him in Deauville, the coming summer, "though," she sighed, "it's becoming too dreadfully banal; nothing but Americans and frowsy English baronesses."

And at that moment in Zenith, a cocaine-runner and a prostitute were drinking cocktails in Healey Hanson's saloon on Front Street. Since national prohibition was now in force, and since Zenith was notoriously law-abiding, they were compelled to keep the cocktails innocent by drinking them out of tea-cups. The lady threw her cup at the cocaine-runner's head. He worked his revolver out of the pocket in his sleeve, and casually murdered her.

At that moment in Zenith, two men sat in a laboratory. For thirty-seven hours now they had been working on a report of their investigations of synthetic rubber.

At that moment in Zenith, there was a conference of four union officials as to whether the twelve thousand coal-miners within a hundred miles of the city should strike. Of these men one resembled a testy and prosperous grocer, one a Yankee carpenter, one a soda-clerk, and one a Russian Jewish actor. The Russian Jew quoted Kautsky, Gene Debs, and Abraham Lincoln.

At that moment a G. A. R. veteran was dying. He had come from the Civil War straight to a farm which, though it was officially within the city-limits of Zenith, was primitive as the backwoods. He had never ridden in a motor car, never seen a bath-tub, never read any book save the Bible, Mc-Guffey's readers, and religious tracts; and he believed that the earth is flat, that the English are the Lost Ten Tribes of Israel, and that the United States is a democracy.

At that moment the steel and cement town which composed the factory of the Pullmore Tractor Company of Zenith was running on night shift to fill an order of tractors for the Polish army. It hummed like a million bees, glared through its wide windows like a volcano. Along the high wire fences, searchlights played on cinder-lined yards, switch-tracks, and armed guards on patrol.

At that moment Mike Monday was finishing a meeting. Mr. Monday, the distinguished evangelist, the best-known Protestant pontiff in America, had once been a prize-fighter. Satan had not dealt justly with him. As a prize-fighter he gained nothing but his crooked nose, his celebrated vocabulary, and his stage-presence. The service of the Lord had been more profitable. He was about to retire with a fortune. It had been well earned, for, to quote his last report, "Rev. Mr. Monday, the Prophet with a Punch, has shown that he is the world's greatest salesman of salvation, and that by efficient organization the overhead of spiritual regeneration may be kept down to an unprecedented rock-bottom basis. He has converted over two hundred thousand lost and price-less souls at an average cost of less than ten dollars a head."

Of the larger cities of the land, only Zenith had hesitated to submit its vices to Mike Monday and his expert recla-mation corps. The more enterprising organizations of the city had voted to invite him—Mr. George F. Babbitt had once praised him in a speech at the Boosters' Club. But there was opposition from certain Episcopalian and Congregational-ist ministers, those renegades whom Mr. Monday so finely called "a bunch of gospel-pushers with dish-water instead of blood, a gang of squealers that need more dust on the knees of their pants and more hair on their skinny old chests." This opposition had been crushed when the secretary of the Chamber of Commerce had reported to a committee of man-ufacturers that in every city where he had appeared, Mr. Monday had turned the minds of workmen from wages and hours to higher things, and thus averted strikes. He was im-mediately invited.

An expense fund of forty thousand dollars had been un-derwritten; out on the County Fair Grounds a Mike Monday Tabernacle had been erected, to seat fifteen thousand people. In it the prophet was at this moment concluding his message:

"There's a lot of smart college professors and tea-guzzling slobs in this burg that say I'm a roughneck and a never-wuz-zer and my knowledge of history is not-yet. Oh, there's a gang of woolly-whiskered book-lice that think they know more than Almighty God, and prefer a lot of Hun science and smutty German criticism to the straight and simple

Word of God. Oh, there's a swell bunch of Lizzie boys and lemon-suckers and pie-faces and infidels and beer-bloated scribblers that love to fire off their filthy mouths and yip that Mike Monday is vulgar and full of mush. Those pups are saying now that I hog the gospel-show, that I'm in it for the coin. Well, now listen, folks! I'm going to give those birds a chance! They can stand right up here and tell me to my face that I'm a galoot and a liar and a hick! Only if they do—if they do!—don't faint with surprise if some of those rum-dumm liars get one good swift poke from Mike, with all the kick of God's Flaming Righteousness behind the wallop! Well, come on, folks! Who says it? Who says Mike Monday is a four-flush and a yahoo? Huh? Don't I see anybody standing up? Well, there you are! Now I guess the folks in this man's town will quit listening to all this kyoodling from behind the fence; I guess you'll quit listening to the guys that pan and roast and kick and beef, and vomit out filthy atheism; and all of you 'll come in, with every grain of pep and reverence you got, and boost all together for Jesus Christ and his everlasting mercy and tenderness!"

v

At that moment Seneca Doane, the radical lawyer, and Dr. Kurt Yavitch, the histologist (whose report on the destruction of epithelial cells under radium had made the name of Zenith known in Munich, Prague, and Rome), were talking in Doane's library.

"Zenith's a city with gigantic power—gigantic buildings, gigantic machines, gigantic transportation," meditated Doane.

"I hate your city. It has standardized all the beauty out of life. It is one big railroad station—with all the people taking tickets for the best cemeteries," Dr. Yavitch said placidly.

Doane roused. "I'm hanged if it is! You make me sick, Kurt, with your perpetual whine about 'standardization.' Don't you suppose any other nation is 'standardized?' Is anything more standardized than England, with every house that can afford it having the same muffins at the same tea-hour, and every retired general going to exactly the same evensong at the same gray stone church with a square tower, and every golfing prig in Harris tweeds saying 'Right you are!' to every other prosperous ass? Yet I love England. And for standardization—just look at the sidewalk cafés in France and the love-making in Italy!

"Standardization is excellent, *per se*. When I buy an Ingersoll watch or a Ford, I get a better tool for less money, and I know precisely what I'm getting, and that leaves me more time and energy to be individual in. And— I remember once in London I saw a picture of an American suburb, in a toothpaste ad on the back of the *Saturday Evening Post*— an elm-lined snowy street of these new houses, Georgian some of 'em, or with low raking roofs and— The kind of street you'd find here in Zenith, say in Floral Heights. Open. Trees. Grass. And I was homesick! There's no other country in the world that has such pleasant houses. And I don't care if they *are* standardized. It's a corking standard!

"No, what I fight in Zenith is standardization of thought, and, of course, the traditions of competition. The real villains of the piece are the clean, kind, industrious Family Men who use every known brand of trickery and cruelty to insure the prosperity of their cubs. The worst thing about these fellows is that they're so good and, in their work at least, so intelligent. You can't hate them properly, and yet their standardized minds are the enemy.

"Then this boosting— Sneakingly I have a notion that Zenith is a better place to live in than Manchester or Glasgow or Lyons or Berlin or Turin—"

"It is not, and I have lift in most of them," murmured Dr. Yavitch.

"Well, matter of taste. Personally, I prefer a city with a future so unknown that it excites my imagination. But what I particularly want—"

"You," said Dr. Yavitch, "are a middle-road liberal, and you haven't the slightest idea what you want. I, being a revolutionist, know exactly what I want—and what I want now is a drink."

VI

At that moment in Zenith, Jake Offutt, the politician, and Henry T. Thompson were in conference. Offutt suggested, "The thing to do is to get your fool son-in-law, Babbitt, to put it over. He's one of these patriotic guys. When he grabs a piece of property for the gang, he makes it look like we were dyin' of love for the dear peepul, and I do love to buy respectability—reasonable. Wonder how long we can keep it up, Hank? We're safe as long as the good little boys like George Babbitt and all the nice respectable labor-leaders think you and me are rugged patriots. There's swell pick-

ings for an honest politician here, Hank: a whole city working
to provide cigars and fried chicken and dry martinis for us,
and rallying to our banner with indignation, oh, fierce indignation, whenever some squealer like this fellow Seneca Doane
comes along! Honest, Hank, a smart codger like me ought
to be ashamed of himself if he didn't milk cattle like them,
when they come around mooing for it! But the Traction gang
can't get away with grand larceny like it used to. I wonder
when— Hank, I wish we could fix some way to run this fellow Seneca Doane out of town. It's him or us!"

At that moment in Zenith, three hundred and forty or
fifty thousand Ordinary People were asleep, a vast unpene-
trated shadow. In the slum beyond the railroad tracks, a
young man who for six months had sought work turned on
the gas and killed himself and his wife.

At that moment Lloyd Mallam, the poet, owner of the Hafiz
Book Shop, was finishing a rondeau to show how diverting
was life amid the feuds of medieval Florence, but how dull
it was in so obvious a place as Zenith.

And at that moment George F. Babbitt turned ponderously in bed—the last turn, signifying that he'd had enough of
this worried business of falling asleep and was about it in
earnest.

Instantly he was in the magic dream. He was somewhere
among unknown people who laughed at him. He slipped away,
ran down the paths of a midnight garden, and at the gate the
fairy child was waiting. Her dear and tranquil hand caressed
his cheek. He was gallant and wise and well-beloved; warm
ivory were her arms; and beyond perilous moors the brave
sea glittered.

chapter 8

THE great events of Babbitt's spring were the secret buying of real-estate options in Linton for certain street-
traction officials, before the public announcement that the
Linton Avenue Car Line would be extended, and a dinner

which was, as he rejoiced to his wife, not only "a regular society spread but a real sure-enough highbrow affair, with some of the keenest intellects and the brightest bunch of little women in town." It was so absorbing an occasion that he almost forgot his desire to run off to Maine with Paul Riesling.

Though he had been born in the village of Catawba, Babbitt had risen to that metropolitan social plane on which hosts have as many as four people at dinner without planning it for more than an evening or two. But a dinner of twelve, with flowers from the florist's and all the cut-glass out, staggered even the Babbitts.

For two weeks they studied, debated, and arbitrated the list of guests.

Babbitt marveled, "Of course we're up-to-date ourselves, but still, think of us entertaining a famous poet like Chum Frink, a fellow that on nothing but a poem or so every day and just writing a few advertisements pulls down fifteen thousand berries a year!"

"Yes, and Howard Littlefield. Do you know, the other evening Eunice told me her papa speaks three languages!" said Mrs. Babbitt.

"Huh! That's nothing! So do I—American, baseball, and poker!"

"I don't think it's nice to be funny about a matter like that. Think how wonderful it must be to speak three languages, and so useful and— And with people like that, I don't see why we invite the Orville Joneses."

"Well now, Orville is a mighty up-and-coming fellow!"

"Yes, I know, but— A laundry!"

"I'll admit a laundry hasn't got the class of poetry or real estate, but just the same, Orvy is mighty deep. Ever start him spieling about gardening? Say, that fellow can tell you the name of every kind of tree, and some of their Greek and Latin names too! Besides, we owe the Joneses a dinner. Besides, gosh, we got to have some boob for audience, when a bunch of hot-air artists like Frink and Littlefield get going."

"Well, dear—I meant to speak of this—I do think that as host you ought to sit back and listen, and let your guests have a chance to talk once in a while!"

"Oh, you do, do you! Sure! I talk all the time! And I'm just a business man—oh sure!—I'm no Ph.D. like Littlefield, and no poet, and I haven't anything to spring! Well, let me tell you, just the other day your darn Chum Frink comes up to me at the club begging to know what I thought about the Springfield school-bond issue. And who told him? I did! You bet your life I told him! Little me! I certainly did! He came up and asked me, and I told him all about it! You bet! And he was darn glad to listen to me and— Duty as a host! I guess I know my duty as a host and let me tell you—"

In fact, the Orville Joneses were invited.

II

On the morning of the dinner, Mrs. Babbitt was restive.

"Now, George, I want you to be sure and be home early to-night. Remember, you have to dress."

"Uh-huh. I see by the *Advocate* that the Presbyterian General Assembly has voted to quit the Interchurch World Movement. That—"

"George! Did you hear what I said? You must be home in time to dress to-night."

"Dress! Hell! I'm dressed now! Think I'm going down to the office in my B.V.D.'s?"

"I will not have you talking indecently before the children! And you do have to put on your dinner-jacket!"

"I guess you mean my Tux. I tell you, of all the doggone nonsensical nuisances that was ever invented—"

Three minutes later, after Babbitt had wailed, "Well, I don't know whether I'm going to dress or *not*" in a manner which showed that he was going to dress, the discussion moved on.

"Now, George, you mustn't forget to call in at Vecchia's on the way home and get the ice cream. Their delivery-wagon is broken down, and I don't want to trust them to send it by—"

"All right! You told me that before breakfast!"

"Well, I don't want you to forget. I'll be working my head off all day long, training the girl that's to help with the dinner—"

"All nonsense, anyway, hiring an extra girl for the feed. Matilda could perfectly well—"

"—and I have to go out and buy the flowers, and fix them, and set the table, and order the salted almonds, and look at the chickens, and arrange for the children to have their supper upstairs and— And I simply must depend on you to go to Vecchia's for the ice cream."

"All riiiiight! Gosh, I'm going to get it!"

"All you have to do is to go in and say you want the ice cream that Mrs. Babbitt ordered yesterday by 'phone, and it will be all ready for you."

At ten-thirty she telephoned to him not to forget the ice cream from Vecchia's.

He was surprised and blasted then by a thought. He wondered whether Floral Heights dinners were worth the hideous toil involved. But he repented the sacrilege in the excitement of buying the materials for cocktails.

Now this was the manner of obtaining alcohol under the reign of righteousness and prohibition:

He drove from the severe rectangular streets of the modern business center into the tangled byways of Old Town—jagged blocks filled with sooty warehouses and lofts; on into The Arbor, once a pleasant orchard but now a morass of lodging-houses, tenements, and brothels. Exquisite shivers chilled his spine and stomach, and he looked at every policeman with intense innocence, as one who loved the law, and admired the Force, and longed to stop and play with them. He parked his car a block from Healey Hanson's saloon, worrying, "Well, rats, if anybody did see me, they'd think I was here on business."

He entered a place curiously like the saloons of ante-prohibition days, with a long greasy bar with sawdust in front and streaky mirror behind, a pine table at which a dirty old man dreamed over a glass of something which resembled whisky, and with two men at the bar, drinking something which resembled beer, and giving that impression of forming a large crowd which two men always give in a saloon. The bartender, a tall pale Swede with a diamond in his lilac scarf, stared at Babbitt as he stalked plumply up to the bar and whispered, "I'd, uh— Friend of Hanson's sent me here. Like to get some gin."

The bartender gazed down on him in the manner of an outraged bishop. "I guess you got the wrong place, my friend. We sell nothing but soft drinks here." He cleaned the bar with a rag which would itself have done with a little cleaning, and glared across his mechanically moving elbow.

The old dreamer at the table petitioned the bartender, "Say, Oscar, listen."

Oscar did not listen.

"Aw, say, Oscar, listen, will yuh? Say, lis-sen!"

The decayed and drowsy voice of the loafer, the agreeable stink of beer-dregs, threw a spell of inanition over Babbitt.

The bartender moved grimly toward the crowd of two men. Babbitt followed him as delicately as a cat, and wheedled, "Say, Oscar, I want to speak to Mr. Hanson."

"Whajuh wanta see him for?"

"I just want to talk to him. Here's my card."

It was a beautiful card, an engraved card, a card in the blackest black and the sharpest red, announcing that Mr. George F. Babbitt was Estates, Insurance, Rents. The bartender held it as though it weighed ten pounds, and read it as though it were a hundred words long. He did not bend from his episcopal dignity, but he growled, "I'll see if he's around."

From the back room he brought an immensely old young man, a quiet sharp-eyed man, in tan silk shirt, checked vest hanging open, and burning brown trousers—Mr. Healey Hanson. Mr. Hanson said only "Yuh?" but his implacable and contemptuous eyes queried Babbitt's soul, and he seemed not at all impressed by the new dark-gray suit for which (as he had admitted to every acquaintance at the Athletic Club) Babbitt had paid a hundred and twenty-five dollars.

"Glad meet you, Mr. Hanson. Say, uh— I'm George Babbitt of the Babbitt-Thompson Realty Company. I'm a great friend of Jake Offutt's."

"Well, what of it?"

"Say, uh, I'm going to have a party, and Jake told me you'd be able to fix me up with a little gin." In alarm, in obsequiousness, as Hanson's eyes grew more bored, "You telephone to Jake about me, if you want to."

Hanson answered by jerking his head to indicate the entrance to the back room, and strolled away. Babbitt melodramatically crept into an apartment containing four round tables, eleven chairs, a brewery calendar, and a smell. He waited. Thrice he saw Healey Hanson saunter through, humming, hands in pockets, ignoring him.

By this time Babbitt had modified his valiant morning vow, "I won't pay one cent over seven dollars a quart" to "I might pay ten." On Hansons next weary entrance he besought, "Could you fix that up?" Hanson scowled, and grated, "Just a minute—Pete's sake—just a min-ute!" In growing meekness Babbitt went on waiting till Hanson casually reappeared with a quart of gin—what is euphemistically known as a quart—in his disdainful long white hands.

"Twelve bucks," he snapped.

"Say, uh, but say, cap'n, Jake thought you'd be able to fix me up for eight or nine a bottle."

"Nup. Twelve. This is the real stuff, smuggled from Canada. This is none o' your neutral spirits with a drop of juniper extract," the honest merchant said virtuously. "Twelve bones—if you want it. Course y' understand I'm just doing this anyway as a friend of Jake's."

"Sure! Sure! I understand!" Babbitt gratefully held out twelve dollars. He felt honored by contact with greatness as Hanson yawned, stuffed the bills, uncounted, into his radiant vest, and swaggered away.

He had a number of titillations out of concealing the gin-bottle under his coat and out of hiding it in his desk. All afternoon he snorted and chuckled and gurgled over his ability to "give the Boys a real shot in the arm to-night." He was, in fact, so exhilarated that he was within a block of his house before he remembered that there was a certain matter, mentioned by his wife, of fetching ice cream from Vecchia's. He explained, "Well, darn it—" and drove back.

Vecchia was not a caterer, he was The Caterer of Zenith. Most coming-out parties were held in the white and gold ballroom of the Maison Vecchia; at all nice teas the guests recognized the five kinds of Vecchia sandwiches and the seven kinds of Vecchia cakes; and all really smart dinners ended, as on a resolving chord, in Vecchia Neapolitan ice cream in one of the three reliable molds—the melon mold, the round mold like a layer cake, and the long brick.

Vecchia's shop had pale blue woodwork, tracery of plaster roses, attendants in frilled aprons, and glass shelves of "kisses" with all the refinement that inheres in whites of eggs. Babbitt felt heavy and thick amid this professional daintiness, and as he waited for the ice cream he decided, with hot prickles at the back of his neck, that a girl customer was giggling at him. He went home in a touchy temper. The first thing he heard was his wife's agitated:

"George! *Did* you remember to go to Vecchia's and get the ice cream?"

"Say! Look here! Do I ever forget to do things?"

"Yes! Often!"

"Well now, it's darn seldom I do, and it certainly makes me tired, after going into a pink-tea joint like Vecchia's and having to stand around looking at a lot of half-naked young girls, all rouged up like they were sixty and eating a lot of stuff that simply ruins their stomachs—"

"Oh, it's too bad about you! I've noticed how you hate to look at pretty girls!"

With a jar Babbitt realized that his wife was too busy to be impressed by that moral indignation with which males rule the world, and he went humbly up-stairs to dress. He had an impression of a glorified dining-room, of cut-glass, candles, polished wood, lace, silver, roses. With the awed swelling of the heart suitable to so grave a business as giving a dinner, he slew the temptation to wear his plaited dress-shirt for a fourth time, took out an entirely fresh one, tightened his black bow, and rubbed his patent-leather pumps with a handkerchief. He glanced with pleasure at his garnet and silver studs. He smoothed and patted his ankles, transformed by silk socks from the sturdy shanks of George Babbitt to the elegant limbs of what is called a Clubman. He stood before the pier-glass, viewing his trim dinner-coat, his beautiful triple-braided trousers; and murmured in lyric beatitude, "By golly, I don't look so bad. I certainly don't look like Catawba. If the hicks back home could see me in this rig, they'd have a fit!"

He moved majestically down to mix the cocktails. As he chipped ice, as he squeezed oranges, as he collected vast stores of bottles, glasses, and spoons at the sink in the pantry, he felt as authoritative as the bartender at Healey Hanson's saloon. True, Mrs. Babbitt said he was under foot, and Matilda and the maid hired for the evening brushed by him, elbowed him, shrieked "Pleasopn door," as they tottered through with trays, but in this high moment he ignored them.

Besides the new bottle of gin, his cellar consisted of one half-bottle of Bourbon whisky, a quarter of a bottle of Italian vermouth, and approximately one hundred drops of orange bitters. He did not possess a cocktail-shaker. A shaker was proof of dissipation, the symbol of a Drinker, and Babbitt disliked being known as a Drinker even more than he liked a Drink. He mixed by pouring from an ancient gravy-boat into a handleless pitcher; he poured with a noble dignity, holding his alembics high beneath the powerful Mazda globe, his face hot, his shirt-front a glaring white, the copper sink a scoured red-gold.

He tasted the sacred essence. "Now, by golly, if that isn't pretty near one fine old cocktail! Kind of a Bronx, and yet like a Manhattan. Ummmmmm! Hey, Myra, want a little nip before the folks come?"

Bustling into the dining-room, moving each glass a quarter of an inch, rushing back with resolution implacable on her face, her gray and silver-lace party frock protected by a denim towel, Mrs. Babbitt glared at him, and rebuked him, "Certainly not!"

"Well," in a loose, jocose manner, "I think the old man will!"

The cocktail filled him with a whirling exhilaration behind which he was aware of devastating desires—to rush places in fast motors, to kiss girls, to sing, to be witty. He sought to regain his lost dignity by announcing to Matilda:

"I'm going to stick this pitcher of cocktails in the refrigerator. Be sure you don't upset any of 'em."

"Yeh."

"Well, be sure now. Don't go putting anything on this top shelf."

"Yeh."

"Well, be—" He was dizzy. His voice was thin and distant. "Whee!" With enormous impressiveness he commanded, "Well, be sure now," and minced into the safety of the livingroom. He wondered whether he could persuade "as slow a bunch as Myra and the Littlefields to go some place aft' dinner and raise Cain and maybe dig up smore booze." He perceived that he had gifts of profligacy which had been neglected.

By the time the guests had come, including the inevitable late couple for whom the others waited with painful amiability, a great gray emptiness had replaced the purple swirling in Babbitt's head, and he had to force the tumultuous greetings suitable to a host on Floral Heights.

The guests were Howard Littlefield, the doctor of philosophy who furnished publicity and comforting economics to the Street Traction Company; Vergil Gunch, the coal-dealer, equally powerful in the Elks and in the Boosters' Club; Eddie Swanson, the agent for the Javelin Motor Car, who lived across the street; and Orville Jones, owner of the Lily White Laundry, which justly announced itself "the biggest, busiest, bulliest cleanerie shoppe in Zenith." But, naturally, the most distinguished of all was T. Cholmondeley Frink, who was not only the author of "Poemulations," which, syndicated daily in sixty-seven leading newspapers, gave him one of the largest audiences of any poet in the world, but also an optimistic lecturer and the creator of "Ads that Add." Despite the searching philosophy and high morality of his verses, they were humorous and easily understood by any child of twelve; and it added a neat air of pleasantry to them that they were set not as verse but as prose. Mr. Frink was known from Coast to Coast as "Chum."

With them were six wives, more or less—it was hard to tell, so early in the evening, as at first glance they all looked alike, and as they all said, "Oh, *isn't* this nice!" in the same tone of determined liveliness. To the eye, the men were less similar: Littlefield, a hedge-scholar, tall and horse-faced; Chum Frink, a trifle of a man with soft and mouse-like hair, advertising his profession as poet by a silk cord on his eye-glasses; Vergil Gunch, broad, with coarse black hair *en brosse;* Eddie Swanson, a bald and bouncing young man who showed his taste for elegance by an evening waistcoat of figured black silk with glass buttons; Orville Jones, a steady-looking, stubby, not very memorable person, with a hemp-colored toothbrush mustache. Yet they were all so well fed and clean, they all shouted " 'Evenin', Georgie!" with such robustness, that they seemed to be cousins, and the strange thing is that the longer one knew the women, the less alike they seemed; while the longer one knew the men, the more alike their bold patterns appeared.

The drinking of the cocktails was as canonical a rite as the mixing. The company waited, uneasily, hopefully, agreeing in a strained manner that the weather had been rather warm and slightly cold, but still Babbitt said nothing about drinks. They became despondent. But when the late couple (the Swansons) had arrived, Babbitt hinted, "Well, folks, do you think you could stand breaking the law a little?"

They looked at Chum Frink, the recognized lord of language. Frink pulled at his eye-glass cord as at a bell-rope, he cleared his throat and said that which was the custom:

"I'll tell you, George; I'm a law-abiding man, but they do say Verg Gunch is a regular yegg, and of course he's bigger 'n I am, and I just can't figure out what I'd do if he tried to force me into anything criminal!"

Gunch was roaring, "Well, I'll take a chance—" when Frink held up his hand and went on, "So if Verg and you insist, Georgie, I'll park my car on the wrong side of the street, because I take it for granted that's the crime you're hinting at!"

There was a great deal of laughter. Mrs. Jones asserted, "Mr. Frink is simply too killing! You'd think he was so innocent!"

Babbitt clamored, "How did you guess it, Chum? Well, you-all just wait a moment while I go out and get the—keys to your cars!" Through a froth of merriment he brought the

shining promise, the mighty tray of glasses with the cloudy
yellow cocktails in the glass pitcher in the center. The men
babbled, "Oh, gosh, have a look!" and "This gets me right
where I live!" and "Let me at it!" But Chum Frink, a traveled
man and not unused to woes, was stricken by the thought
that the potion might be merely fruit-juice with a little neutral
spirits. He looked timorous as Babbitt, a moist and ecstatic
almoner, held out a glass, but as he tasted it he piped, "Oh,
man, let me dream on! It ain't true, but don't waken me! Jus'
lemme slumber!"

Two hours before, Frink had completed a newspaper lyric
beginning:

> I sat alone and groused and thunk, and scratched my head
> and sighed and wunk, and groaned, "There still are boobs,
> alack, who'd like the old-time gin-mill back; that den that
> makes a sage a loon, the vile and smelly old saloon!" I'll
> never miss their poison booze, whilst I the bubbling spring
> can use, that leaves my head at merry morn as clear as any
> babe new-born!

Babbitt drank with the others; his moment's depression was
gone; he perceived that these were the best fellows in the
world; he wanted to give them a thousand cocktails. "Think
you could stand another?" he cried. The wives refused, with
giggles, but the men, speaking in a wide, elaborate, enjoyable
manner, gloated, "Well, sooner than have you get sore at
me, Georgie—"

"You got a little dividend coming," said Babbitt to each of
them, and each intoned, "Squeeze it, Georgie, squeeze it!"

When, beyond hope, the pitcher was empty, they stood and
talked about prohibition. The men leaned back on their heels,
put their hands in their trousers-pockets, and proclaimed
their views with the booming profundity of a prosperous
male repeating a thoroughly hackneyed statement about a
matter of which he knows nothing whatever.

"Now, I'll tell you," said Vergil Gunch; "way I figure it is
this, and I can speak by the book, because I've talked to a
lot of doctors and fellows that ought to know, and the way
I see it is that it's a good thing to get rid of the saloon,
but they ought to let a fellow have beer and light wines."

Howard Littlefield observed, "What isn't generally realized
is that it's a dangerous prop'sition to invade the rights
of personal liberty. Now, take this for instance: The King of
—Bavaria? I think it was Bavaria—yes, Bavaria, it was—in
1862, March, 1862, he issued a proclamation against public

grazing of live-stock. The peasantry had stood for overtaxa-
tion without the slightest complaint, but when this proclamation came out, they rebelled. Or it may have been Saxony.
But it just goes to show the dangers of invading the rights of
personal liberty."

"That's it—no one got a right to invade personal liberty,"
said Orville Jones.

"Just the same, you don't want to forget prohibition is a
mighty good thing for the working-classes. Keeps 'em from
wasting their money and lowering their productiveness,"
said Vergil Gunch.

"Yes, that's so. But the trouble is the manner of enforcement," insisted Howard Littlefield. "Congress didn't understand the right system. Now, if I'd been running the thing, I'd
have arranged it so that the drinker himself was licensed,
and then we could have taken care of the shiftless workman
—kept him from drinking—and yet not 've interfered with
the rights—with the personal liberty—of fellows like ourselves."

They bobbed their heads, looked admiringly at one another, and stated, "That's so, that would be the stunt."

"The thing that worries me is that a lot of these guys will
take to cocaine," sighed Eddie Swanson.

They bobbed more violently, and groaned, "That's so, there
is a danger of that."

Chum Frink chanted, "Oh, say, I got hold of a swell
new receipt for home-made beer the other day. You take—"

Gunch interrupted, "Wait! Let me tell you mine!" Littlefield
snorted, "Beer! Rats! Thing to do is to ferment cider!"
Jones insisted, "I've got the receipt that does the business!"
Swanson begged, "Oh, say, lemme tell you the story—" But
Frink went on resolutely, "You take and save the shells
from peas, and pour six gallons of water on a bushel of
shells and boil the mixture till—"

Mrs. Babbitt turned toward them with yearning sweetness; Frink hastened to finish even his best beer-recipe; and
she said gaily, "Dinner is served."

There was a good deal of friendly argument among the
men as to which should go in last, and while they were
crossing the hall from the living-room to the dining-room
Vergil Gunch made them laugh by thundering, "If I can't sit
next to Myra Babbitt and hold her hand under the table, I
won't play—I'm goin' home." In the dining-room they
stood embarrassed while Mrs. Babbitt fluttered, "Now, let me

see— Oh, I was going to have some nice hand-painted place-cards for you but— Oh, let me see; Mr. Frink, you sit there."

The dinner was in the best style of women's-magazine art, whereby the salad was served in hollowed apples, and everything but the invincible fried chicken resembled something else.

Ordinarily the men found it hard to talk to the women; flirtation was an art unknown on Floral Heights, and the realms of offices and of kitchens had no alliances. But under the inspiration of the cocktails, conversation was violent. Each of the men still had a number of important things to say about prohibition, and now that each had a loyal listener in his dinner-partner he burst out:

"I found a place where I can get all the hootch I want at eight a quart—"

"Did you read about this fellow that went and paid a thousand dollars for ten cases of red-eye that proved to be nothing but water? Seems this fellow was standing on the corner and fellow comes up to him—"

"They say there's a whole raft of stuff being smuggled across at Detroit—"

"What I always say is—what a lot of folks don't realize about prohibition—"

"And then you get all this awful poison stuff—wood alcohol and everything—"

"Course I believe in it on principle, but I don't propose to have anybody telling me what I got to think and do. No American 'll ever stand for that!"

But they all felt that it was rather in bad taste for Orville Jones—and he not recognized as one of the wits of the occasion anyway—to say, "In fact, the whole thing about prohibition is this: it isn't the initial cost, it's the humidity."

Not till the one required topic had been dealt with did the conversation become general.

It was often and admiringly said of Vergil Gunch, "Gee, that fellow can get away with murder! Why, he can pull a Raw One in mixed company and all the ladies 'll laugh their heads off, but me, gosh, if I crack anything that's just the least bit off color I get the razz for fair!" Now Gunch delighted them by crying to Mrs. Eddie Swanson, youngest of the women, "Louetta! I managed to pinch Eddie's doorkey out of his pocket, and what say you and me sneak across the street

when the folks aren't looking? Got something," with a
gorgeous leer, "awful important to tell you!"

The women wriggled, and Babbitt was stirred to like
naughtiness. "Say, folks, I wished I dared show you a book I
borrowed from Doc Patten!"

"Now, George! The idea!" Mrs. Babbitt warned him.

"This book—racy isn't the word! It's some kind of an
anthropological report about—about Customs, in the South
Seas, and what it doesn't *say!* It's a book you can't buy. Verg,
I'll lend it to you."

"Me first!" insisted Eddie Swanson. "Sounds spicy!"

Orville Jones announced, "Say, I heard a Good One the
other day about a coupla Swedes and their wives," and, in
the best Jewish accent, he resolutely carried the Good One
to a slightly disinfected ending. Gunch capped it. But the
cocktails waned, the seekers dropped back into cautious
reality.

Chum Frink had recently been on a lecture-tour among the
small towns, and he chuckled, "Awful good to get back to
civilization! I certainly been seeing some hick towns! I mean—
Course the folks there are the best on earth, but, gee whiz,
those Main Street burgs are slow, and you fellows can't hardly
appreciate what it means to be here with a bunch of live
ones!"

"You bet!" exulted Orville Jones. "They're the best folks on
earth, those small-town folks, but, oh, mama! what conversation! Why, say, they can't talk about anything but the weather
and the ne-oo Ford, by heckalorum!"

"That's right. They all talk about just the same things,"
said Eddie Swanson.

"Don't they, though! They just say the same things over
and over," said Vergil Gunch.

"Yes, it's really remarkable. They seem to lack all power of
looking at things impersonally. They simply go over and over
the same talk about Fords and the weather and so on," said
Howard Littlefield.

"Still, at that, you can't blame 'em. They haven't got any
intellectual stimulus such as you get up here in the city,"
said Chum Frink.

"Gosh, that's right," said Babbitt. "I don't want you highbrows to get stuck on yourselves but I must say it keeps a
fellow right up on his toes to sit in with a poet and with
Howard, the guy that put the con in economics! But these
small-town boobs, with nobody but each other to talk to, no

wonder they get so sloppy and uncultured in their speech, and so balled-up in their thinking!"

Orville Jones commented, "And, then take our other advantages—the movies, frinstance. These Yapville sports think they're all-get-out if they have one change of bill a week, where here in the city you got your choice of a dozen dif-f'rent movies any evening you want to name!"

"Sure, and the inspiration we get from rubbing up against high-class hustlers every day and getting jam full of ginger," said Eddie Swanson.

"Same time," said Babbitt, "no sense excusing these rube burgs too easy. Fellow's own fault if he doesn't show the initiative to up and beat it to the city, like we done—did. And, just speaking in confidence among friends, they're jealous as the devil of a city man. Every time I go up to Catawba I have to go around apologizing to the fellows I was brought up with because I've more or less succeeded and they haven't. And if you talk natural to 'em, way we do here, and show finesse and what you might call a broad point of view, why, they think you're putting on side. There's my own half-brother Martin—runs the little ole general store my Dad used to keep. Say, I'll bet he don't know there is such a thing as a Tux—as a dinner-jacket. If he was to come in here now, he'd think we were a bunch of—of— Why, gosh, I swear, he wouldn't know what to think! Yes, sir, they're jealous!"

Chum Frink agreed, "That's so. But what I mind is their lack of culture and appreciation of the Beautiful—if you'll excuse me for being highbrow. Now, I like to give a high-class lecture, and read some of my best poetry—not the newspaper stuff but the magazine things. But say, when I get out in the tall grass, there's nothing will take but a lot of cheesy old stories and slang and junk that if any of us were to indulge in it here, he'd get the gate so fast it would make his head swim."

Vergil Gunch summed it up: "Fact is, we're mighty lucky to be living among a bunch of city-folks, that recognize artistic things and business-punch equally. We'd feel pretty glum if we got stuck in some Main Street burg and tried to wise up the old codgers to the kind of life we're used to here. But, by golly, there's this you got to say for 'em: Every small American town is trying to get population and modern ideals. And darn if a lot of 'em don't put it across! Somebody starts panning a rube crossroads, telling how he was there in 1900 and it consisted of one muddy street, count 'em, one, and nine hundred human clams. Well, you go back there in 1920, and you find pavements and a swell little hotel and a first-class ladies' ready-to-wear shop—real perfection, in fact! You don't want to just look at what these small towns are, you want to look at what they're aiming to become, and they all got an ambition that in the long run is going to make 'em the finest spots on earth—they all want to be just like Zenith!"

III

However intimate they might be with T. Cholmondeley Frink as a neighbor, as a borrower of lawn-mowers and monkey-wrenches, they knew that he was also a Famous Poet and a distinguished advertising-agent; that behind his easiness were sultry literary mysteries which they could not penetrate. But to-night, in the gin-evolved confidence, he admitted them to the arcanum:

"I've got a literary problem that's worrying me to death. I'm doing a series of ads for the Zeeco Car and I want to make each of 'em a real little gem—reg'lar stylistic stuff. I'm all for this theory that perfection is the stunt, or nothing at all, and these are as tough things as I ever tackled. You might think it'd be harder to do my poems—all these Heart Topics: home and fireside and happiness—but they're cinches. You can't go wrong on 'em; you know what sentiments any decent go-ahead fellow must have if he plays the game, and you stick right to 'em. But the poetry of industrialism, now there's a literary line where you got to open up new territory. Do you know the fellow who's really *the* American genius? The fellow who you don't know his name and I don't either, but his work ought to be preserved so's future generations can judge our American thought and originality to-day? Why, the fellow that writes the Prince Albert Tobacco ads! Just listen to this:

It's P.A. that jams such joy in jimmy pipes. Say—bet you've often bent-an-ear to that spill-of-speech about hopping from five to f-i-f-t-y p-e-r by "stepping on her a bit!" Guess that's going some, all right—BUT—just among ourselves, you better start a rapidwhiz system to keep tabs as to how fast you'll buzz from low smoke spirits to *tip-top-high*—once you line up behind a jimmy pipe that's all aglow with that peach-of-a-pal, Prince Albert.

Prince Albert is john-on-the-job—always joy'usly more-*ish* in flavor; always delightfully cool and fragrant! For a fact, you never hooked such double-decked, copper-riveted, two-fisted smoke enjoyment!

Go to a pipe—speed-o-quick like you light on a good thing! Why—packed with Prince Albert you can play a joy'us jimmy straight across the boards! *And you know what that means!"*

"Now that," caroled the motor agent, Eddie Swanson, "that's what I call he-literature! That Prince Albert fellow—though, gosh, there can't be just one fellow that writes 'em; must be a big board of classy ink-slingers in conference, but anyway: now, him, he doesn't write for long-haired pikers, he writes for Regular Guys, he writes for *me*, and I tip my benny to him! The only thing is: I wonder if it sells the goods? Course, like all these poets, this Prince Albert fellow lets his idea run away with him. It makes elegant reading, but it don't say nothing. I'd never go out and buy Prince Albert Tobacco after reading it, because it doesn't tell me anything about the stuff. It's just a bunch of fluff."

Frink faced him: "Oh, you're crazy! Have I got to sell you the idea of Style? Anyway, that's the kind of stuff I'd like to do for the Zeeco. But I simply can't. So I decided to stick to the straight poetic, and I took a shot at a highbrow ad for the Zeeco. How do you like this:

The long white trail is calling—calling—and it's over the hills and far away for every man or woman that has red blood in his veins and on his lips the ancient song of the buccaneers. It's away with dull drudging, and a fig for care. Speed—glorious Speed—it's more than just a moment's exhilaration—it's Life for you and me! This great new truth the makers of the Zeeco Car have considered as much as price and style. It's fleet as the antelope, smooth as the glide of a swallow, yet powerful as the charge of a bull-elephant. Class breathes in every line. Listen, brother! You'll never know what the high art of hiking is till you TRY LIFE'S ZIPPINGEST ZEST—THE ZEECO!

"Yes," Frink mused, "that's got an elegant color to it, if I do say so, but it ain't got the originality of 'spill-of-speech!' "

The whole company sighed with sympathy and admiration.

chapter 9

BABBITT was fond of his friends, he loved the importance of being host and shouting, "Certainly, you're going to have smore chicken—the idea!" and he appreciated the genius of T. Cholmondeley Frink, but the vigor of the cocktails was gone, and the more he ate the less joyful he felt. Then the amity of the dinner was destroyed by the nagging of the Swansons.

In Floral Heights and the other prosperous sections of Zenith, especially in the "young married set," there were many women who had nothing to do. Though they had few servants, yet with gas stoves, electric ranges and dish-washers and vacuum cleaners, and tiled kitchen walls, their houses were so convenient that they had little housework, and much of their food came from bakeries and delicatessens. They had but two, one, or no children; and despite the myth that the Great War had made work respectable, their husbands objected to their "wasting time and getting a lot of crank ideas" in unpaid social work, and still more to their causing a rumor, by earning money, that they were not adequately supported. They worked perhaps two hours a day, and the rest of the time they ate chocolates, went to the motion-pictures, went window-shopping, went in gossiping twos and threes to card-parties, read magazines, thought timorously of the lovers who never appeared, and accumulated a splendid restlessness which they got rid of by nagging their husbands. The husbands nagged back.

Of these naggers the Swansons were perfect specimens.

Throughout the dinner Eddie Swanson had been complaining, publicly, about his wife's new frock. It was, he submitted, too short, too low, too immodestly thin, and much too expensive. He appealed to Babbitt:

"Honest, George, what do you think of that rag Louetta went and bought? Don't you think it's the limit?"

"What's eating you, Eddie? I call it a swell little dress."

"Oh, it is, Mr. Swanson. It's a sweet frock," Mrs. Babbitt protested.

"There now, do you see, smarty! You're such an authority on clothes!" Louetta raged, while the guests ruminated and peeped at her shoulders.

"That's all right now," said Swanson. "I'm authority enough so I know it was a waste of money, and it makes me tired to see you not wearing out a whole closetful of clothes you got already. I've expressed my idea about this before, and you know good and well you didn't pay the least bit of attention. I have to camp on your trail to get you to do anything—"

There was much more of it, and they all assisted, all but Babbitt. Everything about him was dim except his stomach, and that was a bright scarlet disturbance. "Had too much grub; oughtn't to eat this stuff," he groaned—while he went on eating, while he gulped down a chill and glutinous slice of the ice-cream brick, and cocoanut cake as oozy as shaving-cream. He felt as though he had been stuffed with clay; his body was bursting, his throat was bursting, his brain was hot mud; and only with agony did he continue to smile and shout as became a host on Floral Heights.

He would, except for his guests, have fled outdoors and walked off the intoxication of food, but in the haze which filled the room they sat forever, talking, talking, while he agonized, "Darn fool to be eating all this—not 'nother mouthful," and discovered that he was again tasting the sickly welter of melted ice cream on his plate. There was no magic in his friends; he was not uplifted when Howard Littlefield produced from his treasure-house of scholarship the information that the chemical symbol for raw rubber is $C_{10}H_{16}$, which turns into isoprene, $2C_5H_8$. Suddenly, without precedent, Babbitt was not merely bored but admitting that he was bored. It was ecstasy to escape from the table, from the torture of a straight chair, and loll on the davenport in the living-room.

The others, from their fitful unconvincing talk, their expressions of being slowly and painfully smothered, seemed to be suffering from the toil of social life and the horror of good food as much as himself. All of them accepted with relief the suggestion of bridge.

Babbitt recovered from the feeling of being bored. He won at bridge. He was again able to endure Vergil Gunch's inexorable heartiness. But he pictured loafing with Paul Riesling beside a lake in Maine. It was as overpowering and imaginative as homesickness. He had never seen Maine, yet he beheld the shrouded mountains, the tranquil lake of evening. "That boy Paul's worth all these ballyhooing highbrows put together," he muttered; and, "I'd like to get away from—everything."

Even Louetta Swanson did not rouse him.

Mrs. Swanson was pretty and pliant. Babbitt was not an analyst of women, except as to their tastes in Furnished Houses to Rent. He divided them into Real Ladies, Working Women, Old Cranks, and Fly Chickens. He mooned over their charms but he was of opinion that all of them (save the women of his own family) were "different" and "mysterious." Yet he had known by instinct that Louetta Swanson could be approached. Her eyes and lips were moist. Her face tapered from a broad forehead to a pointed chin, her mouth was thin but strong and avid, and between her brows were two outcurving and passionate wrinkles. She was thirty, perhaps, or younger. Gossip had never touched her, but every man naturally and instantly rose to flirtatiousness when he spoke to her, and every woman watched her with stilled blankness.

Between games, sitting on the davenport, Babbitt spoke to her with the requisite gallantry, that sonorous Floral Heights gallantry which is not flirtation but a terrified flight from it:

"You're looking like a new soda-fountain to-night, Louetta."

"Am I?"

"Ole Eddie kind of on the rampage."

"Yes. I get so sick of it."

"Well, when you get tired of hubby, you can run off with Uncle George."

"If I ran away— Oh, well—"

"Anybody ever tell you your hands are awful pretty?"

She looked down at them, she pulled the lace of her sleeves over them, but otherwise she did not heed him. She was lost in unexpressed imaginings.

Babbitt was too languid this evening to pursue his duty of being a captivating (though strictly moral) male. He ambled back to the bridge-tables. He was not much thrilled when Mrs. Frink, a small twittering woman, proposed that they "try and do some spiritualism and table-tipping—you know Chum can make the spirits come—honest, he just scares me!"

The ladies of the party had not emerged all evening, but now, as the sex given to things of the spirit while the men warred against base things material, they took command and cried, "Oh, let's!" In the dimness the men were rather solemn and foolish, but the goodwives quivered and adored as they sat about the table. They laughed, "Now, you be good or I'll tell!" when the men took their hands in the circle.

Babbitt tingled with a slight return of interest in life as Louetta Swanson's hand closed on his with quiet firmness.

All of them hunched over, intent. They startled as some one drew a strained breath. In the dusty light from the hall they looked unreal, they felt disembodied. Mrs. Gunch squeaked, and they jumped with unnatural jocularity, but at Frink's hiss they sank into subdued awe. Suddenly, incredibly, they heard a knocking. They stared at Frink's half-revealed hands and found them lying still. They wriggled, and pretended not to be impressed.

Frink spoke with gravity: "Is some one there?" A thud. "Is one knock to be the sign for 'yes'?" A thud. "And two for 'no'?" A thud.

"Now, ladies and gentlemen, shall we ask the guide to put us into communication with the spirit of some great one passed over?" Frink mumbled.

Mrs. Orville Jones begged, "Oh, let's talk to Dante! We studied him at the Reading Circle. You know who he was, Orvy."

"Certainly I know who he was! The Wop poet. Where do you think I was raised?" from her insulted husband.

"Sure—the fellow that took the Cook's Tour to Hell. I've never waded through his po'try, but we learned about him in the U.," said Babbitt.

"Page Mr. Dannnnnty!" intoned Eddie Swanson.

"You ought to get him easy, Mr. Frink, you and he being fellow-poets," said Louetta Swanson.

"Fellow-poets, rats! Where d' you get that stuff?" protested Vergil Gunch. "I suppose Dante showed a lot of speed for an old-timer—not that I've actually read him, of course—but to come right down to hard facts, he wouldn't stand one-two-three if he had to buckle down to practical literature and turn out a poem for the newspaper-syndicate every day, like Chum does!"

"That's so," from Eddie Swanson. "Those old birds could

take their time. Judas Priest, I could write poetry myself if I had a whole year for it, and just wrote about that old-fashioned junk like Dante wrote about."

Frink demanded, "Hush, now! I'll call him. . . . O, Laughing Eyes, emerge forth into the, uh, the ultimates and bring hither the spirit of Dante, that we mortals may list to his words of wisdom."

"You forgot to give um the address: 1658 Brimstone Avenue. Fiery Heights, Hell," Gunch chuckled, but the others felt that this was irreligious. And besides—"probably it was just Chum making the knocks, but still, if there did happen to be something to all this, be exciting to talk to an old fellow belonging to—way back in early times—"

A thud. The spirit of Dante had come to the parlor of George F. Babbitt.

He was, it seemed, quite ready to answer their questions. He was "glad to be with them, this evening."

Frink spelled out the messages by running through the alphabet till the spirit intepreter knocked at the right letter.

Littlefield asked, in a learned tone, "Do you like it in the Paradiso, Messire?"

"We are very happy on the higher plane, Signor. We are glad that you are studying this great truth of spiritualism," Dante replied.

The circle moved with an awed creaking of stays and shirt-fronts. "Suppose—suppose there were something to this?"

Babbitt had a different worry. "Suppose Chum Frink was really one of these spiritualists! Chum had, for a literary fellow, always seemed to be a Regular Guy; he belonged to the Chatham Road Presbyterian Church and went to the Boosters' lunches and liked cigars and motors and racy stories. But suppose that secretly— After all, you never could tell about these darn highbrows; and to be an out-and-out spiritualist would be almost like being a socialist!"

No one could long be serious in the presence of Vergil Gunch. "Ask Dant' how Jack Shakespeare and old Verg'— the guy they named after me—are gettin' along, and don't they wish they could get into the movie game!" he blared, and instantly all was mirth. Mrs. Jones shrieked, and Eddie Swanson desired to know whether Dante didn't catch cold with nothing on but his wreath.

The pleased Dante made humble answer.

But Babbitt—the curst discontent was torturing him again, and heavily, in the impersonal darkness, he pondered, "I

don't— We're all so flip and think we're so smart. There'd
be— A fellow like Dante— I wish I'd read some of his
pieces. I don't suppose I ever will, now."

He had, without explanation, the impression of a slaggy
cliff and on it, in silhouette against menacing clouds, a lone
and austere figure. He was dismayed by a sudden contempt for
his surest friends. He grasped Louetta Swanson's hand, and
found the comfort of human warmth. Habit came, a veteran
warrior; and he shook himself. "What the deuce is the matter with me, this evening?"

He patted Louetta's hand, to indicate that he hadn't meant
anything improper by squeezing it, and demanded of Frink,
"Say, see if you can get old Dant' to spiel us some of his
poetry. Talk up to him. Tell him, *'Buena giorna, señor,
com sa va, wie geht's? Keskersaykersa* a little pome, *señor?'* "

II

The lights were switched on; the women sat on the fronts of
their chairs in that determined suspense whereby a wife
indicates that as soon as the present speaker has finished,
she is going to remark brightly to her husband, "Well, dear, I
think per-*haps* it's about time for us to be saying good-
night." For once Babbitt did not break out in blustering efforts
to keep the party going. He had—there was something he
wished to think out— But the psychical research had started
them off again. ("Why didn't they go home! Why didn't they
go home!") Though he was impressed by the profundity of
the statement, he was only half-enthusiastic when Howard
Littlefield lectured, "The United States is the only nation in
which the government is a Moral Ideal and not just a social
arrangement." ("True—true—weren't they *ever* going home?")
He was usually delighted to have an "inside view" of the mo-
mentous world of motors but to-night he scarcely listened to
Eddie Swanson's revelation: "If you want to go above the
Javelin class, the Zeeco is a mighty good buy. Couple weeks
ago, and mind you, this was a fair, square test, they took
a Zeeco stock touring-car and they slid up the Tonawanda
hill on high, and fellow told me—" ("Zeeco—good boat but
— Were they planning to stay all night?")

They really were going, with a flutter of "We did have the
best time!"

Most aggressively friendly of all was Babbitt, yet as he bur-
bled he was reflecting, "I got through it, but for a while

there I didn't hardly think I'd last out." He prepared to taste that most delicate pleasure of the host: making fun of his guests in the relaxation of midnight. As the door closed he yawned voluptuously, chest out, shoulders wriggling, and turned cynically to his wife.

She was beaming. "Oh, it was nice, wasn't it! I know they enjoyed every minute of it. Don't you think so?"

He couldn't do it. He couldn't mock. It would have been like sneering at a happy child. He lied ponderously: "You bet! Best party this year, by a long shot."

"Wasn't the dinner good! And honestly I thought the fried chicken was delicious!"

"You bet! Fried to the Queen's taste. Best fried chicken I've tasted for a coon's age."

"Didn't Matilda fry it beautifully! And don't you think the soup was simply delicious?"

"It certainly was! It was corking! Best soup I've tasted since Heck was a pup!" But his voice was seeping away. They stood in the hall, under the electric light in its square box-like shade of red glass bound with nickel. She stared at him.

"Why, George, you don't sound—you sound as if you hadn't really enjoyed it."

"Sure I did! Course I did!"

"George! What is it?"

"Oh, I'm kind of tired, I guess. Been pounding pretty hard at the office. Need to get away and rest up a little."

"Well, we're going to Maine in just a few weeks now, dear."

"Yuh—" Then he was pouring it out nakedly, robbed of reticence. "Myra: I think it'd be a good thing for me to get up there early."

"But you have this man you have to meet in New York about business."

"What man? Oh, sure. Him. Oh, that's all off. But I want to hit Maine early—get in a little fishing, catch me a big trout, by golly!" A nervous, artificial laugh.

"Well, why don't we do it? Verona and Matilda can run the house between them, and you and I can go any time, if you think we can afford it."

"But that's— I've been feeling so jumpy lately, I thought maybe it might be a good thing if I kind of got off by myself and sweat it out of me."

"George! Don't you *want* me to go along?" She was too wretchedly in earnest to be tragic, or gloriously insulted, or anything save dumpy and defenseless and flushed to the red steaminess of a boiled beet.

"Of course I do! I just meant—" Remembering that Paul Riesling had predicted this, he was as desperate as she. "I mean, sometimes it's a good thing for an old grouch like me to go off and get it out of his system." He tried to sound paternal. "Then when you and the kids arrive—I figured maybe I might skip up to Maine just a few days ahead of you —I'd be ready for a real bat, see how I mean?" He coaxed her with large booming sounds, with affable smiles, like a popular preacher blessing an Easter congregation, like a humorous lecturer completing his stint of eloquence, like all perpetrators of masculine wiles.

She stared at him, the joy of festival drained from her face. "Do I bother you when we go on vacations? Don't I add anything to your fun?"

He broke. Suddenly, dreadfully, he was hysterical, he was a yelping baby. "Yes, yes, yes! Hell, yes! But can't you understand I'm shot to pieces? I'm all in! I got to take care of myself! I tell you, I got to— I'm sick of everything and everybody! I got to—"

It was she who was mature and protective now. "Why, of course! You shall run off by yourself! Why don't you get Paul to go along, and you boys just fish and have a good time?" She patted his shoulder—reaching up to it—while he shook with palsied helplessness, and in that moment was not merely by habit fond of her but clung to her strength.

She cried cheerily, "Now up-stairs you go, and pop into bed. We'll fix it all up. I'll see to the doors. Now skip!"

For many minutes, for many hours, for a bleak eternity, he lay awake, shivering, reduced to primitive terror, comprehending that he had won freedom, and wondering what he could do with anything so unknown and so embarrassing as freedom.

chapter 10

NO apartment-house in Zenith had more resolutely experimented in condensation than the Revelstoke Arms, in which Paul and Zilla Riesling had a flat. By sliding the beds into low closets the bedrooms were converted into living-rooms. The kitchens were cupboards each containing an electric range, a copper sink, a glass refrigerator, and, very intermittently, a Balkan maid. Everything about the Arms was excessively modern, and everything was compressed—except the garages.

The Babbitts were calling on the Rieslings at the Arms. It was a speculative venture to call on the Rieslings; interesting and sometimes disconcerting. Zilla was an active, strident, full-blown, high-bosomed blonde. When she condescended to be good-humored she was nervously amusing. Her comments on people were saltily satiric and penetrative of accepted hypocrisies. "That's so!" you said, and looked sheepish. She danced wildly, and called on the world to be merry, but in the midst of it she would turn indignant. She was always becoming indignant. Life was a plot against her, and she exposed it furiously.

She was affable to-night. She merely hinted that Orville Jones wore a toupé, that Mrs. T. Cholmondeley Frink's singing resembled a Ford going into high, and that the Hon. Otis Deeble, mayor of Zenith and candidate for Congress, was a flatulent fool (which was quite true). The Babbitts and Rieslings sat doubtfully on stone-hard brocade chairs in the small living-room of the flat, with its mantel unprovided with a fireplace, and its strip of heavy gilt fabric upon a glaring new player-piano, till Mrs. Riesling shrieked, "Come on! Let's put some pep in it! Get out your fiddle, Paul, and I'll try to make Georgie dance decently."

The Babbitts were in earnest. They were plotting for the

escape to Maine. But when Mrs. Babbitt hinted with plump smilingness, "Does Paul get as tired after the winter's work as Georgie does?" then Zilla remembered an injury; and when Zilla Riesling remembered an injury the world stopped till something had been done about it.

"Does he get tired? No, he doesn't get tired, he just goes crazy, that's all! You think Paul is so reasonable, oh, yes, and he loves to make out he's a little lamb, but he's stubborn as a mule. Oh, if you had to live with him—! You'd find out how sweet he is! He just pretends to be meek so he can have his own way. And me, I get the credit for being a terrible old crank, but if I didn't blow up once in a while and get something started, we'd die of dry-rot. He never wants to go any place and— Why, last evening, just because the car was out of order—and that was his fault, too, because he ought to have taken it to the service-station and had the battery looked at—and he didn't want to go down to the movies on the trolley. But we went, and then there was one of those impudent conductors, and Paul wouldn't do a thing.

"I was standing on the platform waiting for the people to let me into the car, and this beast, this conductor, hollered at me, 'Come on, you, move up!' Why, I've never had anybody speak to me that way in all my life! I was so astonished I just turned to him and said—I thought there must be some mistake, and so I said to him, perfectly pleasant, 'Were you speaking to me?' and he went on and bellowed at me, 'Yes, I was! You're keeping the whole car from starting!' he said, and then I saw he was one of these dirty ill-bred hogs that kindness is wasted on, and so I stopped and looked right at him, and I said, 'I—beg—your—pardon, I am not doing anything of the kind,' I said, 'it's the people ahead of me, who won't move up,' I said, 'and furthermore, let me tell you, young man, that you're a low-down, foul-mouthed, impertinent skunk,' I said, 'and you're no gentleman! I certainly intend to report you, and we'll see,' I said, 'whether a lady is to be insulted by any drunken bum that chooses to put on a ragged uniform, and I'd thank you,' I said, 'to keep your filthy abuse to yourself.' And then I waited for Paul to show he was half a man and come to my defense, and he just stood there and pretended he hadn't heard a word, and so I said to him, 'Well,' I said—"

"Oh, cut it, cut it, Zill!" Paul groaned. "We all know I'm a mollycoddle, and you're a tender bud, and let's let it go at that."

"Let it go?" Zilla's face was wrinkled like the Medusa, her voice was a dagger of corroded brass. She was full of the joy of righteousness and bad temper. She was a crusader and, like every crusader, she exulted in the opportunity to be vicious in the name of virtue. "Let it go? If people knew how many things I've let go—"

"Oh, quit being such a bully."

"Yes, a fine figure you'd cut if I didn't bully you! You'd lie abed till noon and play your idiotic fiddle till midnight! You're born lazy, and you're born shiftless, and you're born cowardly, Paul Riesling—"

"Oh, now, don't say that, Zilla; you don't mean a word of it!" protested Mrs. Babbitt.

"I will say that, and I mean every single last word of it!"

"Oh, now, Zilla, the idea!" Mrs. Babbitt was maternal and fussy. She was no older than Zilla, but she seemed so —at first. She was placid and puffy and mature, where Zilla, at forty-five, was so bleached and tight-corseted that you knew only that she was older than she looked. "The idea of talking to poor Paul like that!"

"Poor Paul is right! We'd both be poor, we'd be in the poorhouse, if I didn't jazz him up!"

"Why, now, Zilla, Georgie and I were just saying how hard Paul's been working all year, and we were thinking it would be lovely if the Boys could run off by themselves. I've been coaxing George to go up to Maine ahead of the rest of us, and get the tired out of his system before we come, and I think it would be lovely if Paul could manage to get away and join him."

At this exposure of his plot to escape, Paul was startled out of impassivity. He rubbed his fingers. His hands twitched.

Zilla bayed, "Yes! You're lucky! You can let George go, and not have to watch him. Fat old Georgie! Never peeps at another woman! Hasn't got the spunk!"

"The hell I haven't!" Babbitt was fervently defending his priceless immorality when Paul interrupted him—and Paul looked dangerous. He rose quickly; he said gently to Zilla:

"I suppose you imply I have a lot of sweethearts."

"Yes, I do!"

"Well, then, my dear, since you ask for it— There hasn't been a time in the last ten years when I haven't found some nice little girl to comfort me, and as long as you continue your amiability I shall probably continue to deceive you. It isn't hard. You're so stupid."

Zilla gibbered; she howled; words could not be distinguished in her slaver of abuse.

Then the bland George F. Babbitt was transformed. If Paul was dangerous, if Zilla was a snake-locked fury, if the neat emotions suitable to the Revelstoke Arms had been slashed into raw hatreds, it was Babbitt who was the most formidable. He leaped up. He seemed very large. He seized Zilla's shoulder. The cautions of the broker were wiped from his face, and his voice was cruel:

"I've had enough of all this damn nonsense! I've known you for twenty-five years, Zil, and I never knew you to miss a chance to take your disappointments out on Paul. You're not wicked. You're worse. You're a fool. And let me tell you that Paul is the finest boy God ever made. Every decent person is sick and tired of your taking advantage of being a woman and springing every mean innuendo you can think of. Who the hell are you that a person like Paul should have to ask your *permission* to go with me? You act like you were a combination of Queen Victoria and Cleopatra. You fool, can't you see how people snicker at you, and sneer at you?"

Zilla was sobbing, "I've never—I've never—nobody ever talked to me like this in all my life!"

"No, but that's the way they talk behind your back! Always! They say you're a scolding old woman. Old, by God!"

That cowardly attack broke her. Her eyes were blank. She wept. But Babbitt glared stolidly. He felt that he was the all-powerful official in charge; that Paul and Mrs. Babbitt looked on him with awe; that he alone could handle this case.

Zilla writhed. She begged, "Oh, they don't!"

"They certainly do!"

"I've been a bad woman! I'm terribly sorry! I'll kill myself! I'll do anything. Oh, I'll— What do you want?"

She abased herself completely. Also, she enjoyed it. To the connoisseur of scenes, nothing is more enjoyable than a thorough, melodramatic, egoistic humility.

"I want you to let Paul beat it off to Maine with me," Babbitt demanded.

"How can I help his going? You've just said I was an idiot and nobody paid any attention to me."

"Oh, you can help it, all right, all right! What you got to do is to cut out hinting that the minute he gets out of your sight, he'll go chasing after some petticoat. Matter fact, that's the way you start the boy off wrong. You ought to have more sense—"

"Oh, I will, honestly, I will, George. I know I was bad. Oh, forgive me, all of you, forgive me—"

She enjoyed it.

So did Babbitt. He condemned magnificently and forgave piously, and as he went parading out with his wife he was grandly explanatory to her:

"Kind of a shame to bully Zilla, but course it was the only way to handle her. Gosh, I certainly did have her crawling!"

She said calmly, "Yes. You were horrid. You were showing off. You were having a lovely time thinking what a great fine person you were!"

"Well, by golly! Can you beat it! Of course I might of expected you to not stand by me! I might of expected you'd stick up for your own sex!"

"Yes. Poor Zilla, she's so unhappy. She takes it out on Paul. She hasn't a single thing to do, in that little flat. And she broods too much. And she used to be so pretty and gay, and she resents losing it. And you were just as nasty and mean as you could be. I'm not a bit proud of you—or of Paul, boasting about his horrid love-affairs!"

He was sulkily silent; he maintained his bad temper at a high level of outraged nobility all the four blocks home. At the door he left her, in self-approving haughtiness, and tramped the lawn.

With a shock it was revealed to him: "Gosh, I wonder if she was right—if she was partly right?" Overwork must have flayed him to abnormal sensitiveness; it was one of the few times in his life when he had queried his eternal excellence; and he perceived the summer night, smelled the wet grass. Then: "I don't care! I've pulled it off. We're going to have our spree. And for Paul, I'd do anything."

II

They were buying their Maine tackle at Ijams Brothers', the Sporting Goods Mart, with the help of Willis Ijams, fellow member of the Boosters' Club. Babbitt was completely mad. He trumpeted and danced. He muttered to Paul, "Say, this is pretty good, eh? To be buying the stuff, eh? And good old Willis Ijams himself coming down on the floor to wait on us! Say, if those fellows that are getting their kit for the North Lakes knew we were going clear up to Maine, they'd have a fit, eh? . . . Well, come on, Brother Ijams—Willis, I mean. Here's your chance! We're a couple of easy marks! Whee! Let me at it! I'm going to buy out the store!"

He gloated on fly-rods and gorgeous rubber hip-boots, on tents with celluloid windows and folding chairs and ice-boxes. He simple-heartedly wanted to buy all of them. It was the Paul whom he was always vaguely protecting who kept him from his drunken desires.

But even Paul lightened when Willis Ijams, a salesman with poetry and diplomacy, discussed flies. "Now, of course, you boys know," he said, "the great scrap is between dry flies and wet flies. Personally, I'm for dry flies. More sporting."

"That's so. Lots more sporting," fulminated Babbitt, who knew very little about flies either wet or dry.

"Now if you'll take my advice, Georgie, you'll stock up well on these pale evening dims, and silver sedges, and red ants. Oh, boy, there's a fly, that red ant!"

"You bet! That's what it is—a fly!" rejoiced Babbitt.

"Yes, sir, that red ant," said Ijams, "is a real honest-to-God *fly!*"

"Oh, I guess ole Mr. Trout won't come a-hustling when I drop one of those red ants on the water!" asserted Babbitt, and his thick wrists made a rapturous motion of casting.

"Yes, and the landlocked salmon will take it, too," said Ijams, who had never seen a landlocked salmon.

"Salmon! Trout! Say, Paul, can you see Uncle George with his khaki pants on haulin' 'em in, some morning 'bout seven? Whee!"

III

They were on the New York express, incredibly bound for Maine, incredibly without their families. They were free, in a man's world, in the smoking-compartment of the Pullman.

Outside the car window was a glaze of darkness stippled with the gold of infrequent mysterious lights. Babbitt was immensely conscious, in the sway and authoritative clatter of the train, of going, of going on. Leaning toward Paul he grunted, "Gosh, pretty nice to be hiking, eh?"

The small room, with its walls of ocher-colored steel, was filled mostly with the sort of men he classified as the Best Fellows You'll Ever Meet—Real Good Mixers. There were four of them on the long seat; a fat man with a shrewd fat face, a knife-edged man in a green velour hat, a very young young man with an imitation amber cigarette-holder, and Babbitt. Facing them, on two movable leather chairs, were Paul and a lanky, old-fashioned man, very cunning, with wrinkles bracketing his mouth. They all read newspapers or trade journals, boot-and-shoe journals, crockery journals, and waited for the joys of conversation. It was the very young man, now making his first journey by Pullman, who began it.

"Say, gee, I had a wild old time in Zenith!" he gloried. "Say, if a fellow knows the ropes there he can have as wild a time as he can in New York!"

"Yuh, I bet you simply raised the old Ned. I figured you were a bad man when I saw you get on the train!" chuckled the fat one.

The others delightedly laid down their papers.

"Well, that's all right now! I guess I seen some things in the Arbor you never seen!" complained the boy.

"Oh, I'll bet you did! I bet you lapped up the malted milk like a reg'lar little devil!"

Then, the boy having served as introduction, they ignored him and charged into real talk. Only Paul, sitting by himself, reading at a serial story in a newspaper, failed to join them, and all but Babbitt regarded him as a snob, an eccentric, a person of no spirit.

Which of them said which has never been determined, and does not matter, since they all had the same ideas and expressed them always with the same ponderous and brassy assurance. If it was not Babbitt who was delivering any given verdict, at least he was beaming on the chancellor who did deliver it.

"At that, though," announced the first, "they're selling quite some booze in Zenith. Guess they are everywhere. I don't know how you fellows feel about prohibition, but the way it strikes me is that it's a mighty beneficial thing for the poor zob that hasn't got any will-power but for fellows like us, it's an infringement of personal liberty."

"That's a fact. Congress had got no right to interfere with a fellow's personal liberty," contended the second.

A man came in from the car, but as all the seats were full he stood up while he smoked his cigarette. He was an Outsider; he was not one of the Old Families of the smoking-compartment. They looked upon him bleakly and, after trying to appear at ease by examining his chin in the mirror, he gave it up and went out in silence.

"Just been making a trip through the South. Business conditions not very good down there," said one of the council.

"Is that a fact! Not very good, eh?"

"No, didn't strike me they were up to normal."

"Not up to normal. eh?"

"No, I wouldn't hardly say they were."

The whole council nodded sagely and decided, "Yump, not hardly up to snuff."

"Well, business conditions ain't what they ought to be out West, neither, not by a long shot."

"That's a fact. And I guess the hotel business feels it. That's one good thing, though: These hotels that've been charging five bucks a day—yes, and maybe six-seven!—for a rotten room are going to be darn glad to get four, and maybe give you a little service."

"That's a fact. Say, uh, speaknubout hotels, I hit the St. Francis at San Francisco for the first time, the other day, and, say, it certainly is a first-class place."

"You're right, brother! The St. Francis is a swell place— absolutely A1."

"That's a fact. I'm right with you. It's a first-class place."

"Yuh, but say, any of you fellows ever stay at the Rippleton, in Chicago? I don't want to knock—I believe in boosting wherever you can—but say, of all the rotten dumps that pass 'emselves off as first-class hotels, that's the worst. I'm going to *get* those guys, one of these days, and I told 'em so. You know how I am—well, maybe you don't know, but I'm accustomed to first-class accommodations, and I'm perfectly willing to pay a reasonable price. I got into Chicago late the other night, and the Rippleton's near the station—I'd never been there before, but I says to the taxi-driver—I always believe in taking a taxi when you get in late; may cost a little more money, but, gosh, it's worth it when you got to be up early next morning and out selling a lot of crabs—and I said to him, 'Oh, just drive me over to the Rippleton.'

"Well, we got there, and I breezed up to the desk and said to the clerk, 'Well, brother, got a nice room with bath for Cousin Bill?' Saaaay! You'd 'a' thought I'd sold him a second, or asked him to work on Yom Kippur! He hands me the cold-boiled stare and yaps, 'I dunno, friend, I'll see,' and he ducks behind the rigamajig they keep track of the rooms on. Well, I guess he called up the Credit Association and the American Security League to see if I was all right—he certainly took long enough—or maybe he just went to sleep; but finally he comes out and looks at me like it hurts him, and croaks, 'I think I can let you have a room with bath.' 'Well, that's awful nice of you—sorry to trouble you—how much 'll it set me back?' I says, real sweet. 'It'll cost you seven bucks a day, friend,' he says.

"Well, it was late, and anyway, it went down on my expense-account—gosh, if I'd been paying it instead of the firm, I'd 'a' tramped the streets all night before I'd 'a' let any hick tavern stick me seven great big round dollars, believe me! So I lets it go at that. Well, the clerk wakes a nice young bell-hop—fine lad—not a day over seventy-nine years old—fought at the Battle of Gettysburg and doesn't know it's over yet—thought I was one of the Confederates, I guess, from the way he looked at me—and Rip van Winkle took me up to something—I found out afterwards they called it a room, but first I thought there'd been some mistake—I thought they were putting me in the Salvation Army collection-box! At seven *per* each and every *diem!* Gosh!"

"Yuh, I've heard the Rippleton was pretty cheesy. Now, when I go to Chicago I always stay at the Blackstone or the La Salle—first-class places."

"Say, any of you fellows ever stay at the Birchdale at Terre Haute? How is it?"

"Oh, the Birchdale is a first-class hotel."

(Twelve minutes of conference on the state of hotels in South Bend, Flint, Dayton, Tulsa, Wichita, Fort Worth, Winona, Erie, Fargo, and Moose Jaw.)

"Speaknubout prices," the man in the velour hat observed, fingering the elk-tooth on his heavy watch-chain, "I'd like to know where they get this stuff about clothes coming down. Now, you take this suit I got on." He pinched his trousers-leg. "Four years ago I paid forty-two fifty for it, and it was real sure-'nough value. Well, here the other day I went into a store back home and asked to see a suit, and the fellow yanks out some hand-me-downs that, honest, I wouldn't put on a hired man. Just out of curiosity I asks him, 'What you charging for that junk?' 'Junk,' he says, 'what d' you mean junk? That's a swell piece of goods, all wool—' Like hell! It was nice vegetable wool, right off the Ole Plantation! 'It's all wool,' he says, 'and we get sixty-seven ninety for it.' 'Oh, you do, do you!' I says. 'Not from me you don't,' I says, and I walks right out on him. You bet! I says to the wife,

'Well,' I said, 'as long as your strength holds out and you can go on putting a few more patches on papa's pants, we'll just pass up buying clothes.' "

"That's right, brother. And just look at collars, frinstance—"

"Hey! Wait!" the fat man protested. "What's the matter with collars! I'm selling collars! D' you realize the cost of labor on collars is still two hundred and seven per cent. above—"

They voted that if their old friend the fat man sold collars, then the price of collars was exactly what it should be; but all other clothing was tragically too expensive. They admired and loved one another now. They went profoundly into the science of business, and indicated that the purpose of manufacturing a plow or a brick was so that it might be sold. To them, the Romantic Hero was no longer the knight, the wandering poet, the cowpuncher, the aviator, nor the brave young district attorney, but the great sales-manager, who had an Analysis of Merchandizing Problems on his glass-topped desk, whose title of nobility was "Go-getter," and who devoted himself and all his young samurai to the cosmic purpose of Selling—not of selling anything in particular, for or to anybody in particular, but pure Selling.

The shop-talk roused Paul Riesling. Though he was a player of violins and an interestingly unhappy husband, he was also a very able salesman of tar-roofing. He listened to the fat man's remarks on "the value of house-organs and bulletins as a method of jazzing-up the Boys out on the road;" and he himself offered one or two excellent thoughts on the use of two-cent stamps on circulars. Then he committed an offense against the holy law of the Clan of Good Fellows. He became highbrow.

They were entering a city. On the outskirts they passed a steel-mill which flared in scarlet and orange flame that licked at the cadaverous stacks, at the iron-sheathed walls and sullen converters.

"My Lord, look at that—beautiful!" said Paul.

"You bet it's beautiful, friend. That's the Shelling-Horton Steel Plant, and they tell me old John Shelling made a good three million bones out of munitions during the war!" the man with the velour hat said reverently.

"I didn't mean—I mean it's lovely the way the light pulls that picturesque yard, all littered with junk, right out of the darkness," said Paul.

They stared at him, while Babbitt crowed, "Paul there has certainly got one great little eye for picturesque places and quaint sights and all that stuff. 'D of been an author or something if he hadn't gone into the roofing line."

Paul looked annoyed. (Babbitt sometimes wondered if Paul appreciated his loyal boosting.) The man in the velour hat grunted, "Well, personally, I think Shelling-Horton keep their works awful dirty. Bum routing. But I don't suppose there's any law against calling 'em 'picturesque' if it gets you that way!"

Paul sulkily returned to his newspaper and the conversation logically moved on to trains.

"What time do we get into Pittsburg?" asked Babbitt.

"Pittsburg? I think we get in at—no, that was last year's schedule—wait a minute—let's see—got a time-table right here."

"I wonder if we're on time?"

"Yuh, sure, we must be just about on time."

"No, we aren't—we were seven minutes late, last station."

"Were we? Straight? Why, gosh, I thought we were right on time."

"No, we're about seven minutes late."

"Yuh, that's right; seven minutes late."

The porter entered—a negro in white jacket with brass buttons.

"How late are we, George?" growled the fat man.

" 'Deed, I don't know, sir. I think we're about on time," said the porter, folding towels and deftly tossing them up on the rack above the washbowls. The council stared at him gloomily and when he was gone they wailed:

"I don't know what's come over these niggers, nowadays. They never give you a civil answer."

"That's a fact. They're getting so they don't have a single bit of respect for you. The old-fashioned coon was a fine old cuss—he knew his place—but these young dinges don't want to be porters or cotton-pickers. Oh, no! They got to be lawyers and professors and Lord knows what all! I tell you, it's becoming a pretty serious problem. We ought to get together and show the black man, yes, and the yellow man, his place. Now, I haven't got one particle of race-prejudice. I'm the first to be glad when a nigger succeeds—so long as he stays where he belongs and doesn't try to usurp the rightful authority and business ability of the white man."

"That's the i.! And another thing we got to do," said the

man with the velour hat (whose name was Koplinsky), "is to keep these damn foreigners out of the country. Thank the Lord, we're putting a limit on immigration. These Dagoes and Hunkies have got to learn that this is a white man's country, and they ain't wanted here. When we've assimilated the foreigners we got here now and learned 'em the principles of Americanism and turned 'em into regular folks, why then maybe we'll let in a few more."

"You bet. That's a fact," they observed, and passed on to lighter topics. They rapidly reviewed motor-car prices, tire-mileage, oil-stocks, fishing, and the prospects for the wheat-crop in Dakota.

But the fat man was impatient at this waste of time. He was a veteran traveler and free of illusions. Already he had asserted that he was "an old he-one." He leaned forward, gathered in their attention by his expression of sly humor, and grumbled, "Oh, hell, boys, let's cut out the formality and get down to the stories!"

They became very lively and intimate.

Paul and the boy vanished. The others slid forward on the long seat, unbuttoned their vests, thrust their feet up on the chairs, pulled the stately brass cuspidors nearer, and ran the green window-shade down on its little trolley, to shut them in from the uncomfortable strangeness of night. After each bark of laughter they cried, "Say, jever hear the one about—" Babbitt was expansive and virile. When the train stopped at an important station, the four men walked up and down the cement platform, under the vast smoky train-shed roof, like a stormy sky, under the elevated footways, beside crates of ducks and sides of beef, in the mystery of an unknown city. They strolled abreast, old friends and well content. At the long-drawn "Alllll aboarrrrrd"—like a mountain call at dusk —they hastened back into the smoking-compartment, and till two of the morning continued the droll tales, their eyes damp with cigar-smoke and laughter. When they parted they shook hands, and chuckled, "Well, sir, it's been a great session. Sorry to bust it up. Mighty glad to met you."

Babbitt lay awake in the close hot tomb of his Pullman berth, shaking with remembrance of the fat man's limerick about the lady who wished to be wild. He raised the shade; he lay with a puffy arm tucked between his head and the skimpy pillow, looking out on the sliding silhouettes of trees, and village lamps like exclamation-points. He was very happy.

chapter 11

THEY had four hours in New York between trains. The one thing Babbitt wished to see was the Pennsylvania Hotel, which had been built since his last visit. He stared up at it, muttering, "Twenty-two hundred rooms and twenty-two hundred baths! That's got everything in the world beat. Lord, their turnover must be—well, suppose price of rooms is four to eight dollars a day, and I suppose maybe some ten and—four times twenty-two hundred—say six times twenty-two hundred—well, anyway; with restaurants and everything, say summers between eight and fifteen thousand a day. Every day! I never thought I'd see a thing like that! Some town! Of course the average fellow in Zenith has got more Individual Initiative than the fourflushers here, but I got to hand it to New York. Yes, sir, town, you're all right—some ways. Well, old Paulski, I guess we've seen everything that's worth while. How'll we kill the rest of the time? Movie?"

But Paul desired to see a liner. "Always wanted to go to Europe—and, by thunder, I will, too, some day before I pass out," he sighed.

From a rough wharf on the North River they stared at the stern of the *Aquitania* and her stacks and wireless antennæ lifted above the dock-house which shut her in.

"By golly," Babbitt droned, "wouldn't be so bad to go over to the Old Country and take a squint at all these ruins, and the place where Shakespeare was born. And think of being able to order a drink whenever you wanted one! Just range up to a bar and holler out loud, 'Gimme a cocktail, and darn the police!' Not bad at all. What juh like to see, over there, Paulibus?"

Paul did not answer. Babbitt turned. Paul was standing with clenched fists, head drooping, staring at the liner as in terror. His thin body, seen against the summer-glaring planks of the wharf, was childishly meager.

Again, "What would you hit for on the other side, Paul?"

Scowling at the steamer, his breast heaving, Paul whispered, "Oh, my God!" While Babbitt watched him anxiously he snapped, "Come on, let's get out of this," and hastened down the wharf, not looking back.

"That's funny," considered Babbitt. "The boy didn't care for seeing the ocean boats after all. I thought he'd be interested in 'em."

II

Though he exulted, and made sage speculations about locomotive horse-power, as their train climbed the Maine mountain-ridge and from the summit he looked down the shining way among the pines; though he remarked, "Well, by golly!" when he discovered that the station at Katadumcook, the end of the line, was an aged freight-car; Babbitt's moment of impassioned release came when they sat on a tiny wharf on Lake Sunasquam, awaiting the launch from the hotel. A raft had floated down the lake; between the logs and the shore, the water was transparent, thin-looking, flashing with minnows. A guide in black felt hat with trout-flies in the band, and flannel shirt of a peculiarly daring blue, sat on a log and whittled and was silent. A dog, a good country dog, black and woolly gray, a dog rich in leisure and in meditation, scratched and grunted and slept. The thick sunlight was lavish on the bright water, on the rim of gold-green balsam boughs, the silver birches and tropic ferns, and across the lake it burned on the sturdy shoulders of the mountains. Over everything was a holy peace.

Silent, they loafed on the edge of the wharf, swinging their legs above the water. The immense tenderness of the place sank into Babbitt, and he murmured, "I'd just like to sit here—the rest of my life—and whittle—and sit. And never hear a typewriter. Or Stan Graff fussing in the 'phone. Or Rone and Ted scrapping. Just sit. Gosh!"

He patted Paul's shoulder. "How does it strike you, old snoozer?"

"Oh, it's darn good, Georgie. There's something sort of eternal about it."

For once, Babbit understood him.

III

Their launch rounded the bend; at the head of the lake, under a mountain slope, they saw the little central dining-shack of their hotel and the crescent of squat log cottages which served as bedrooms. They landed, and endured the critical examination of the habitués who had been at the hotel for a whole week. In their cottage, with its high stone fireplace, they hastened, as Babbitt expressed it, to "get into some regular he-togs." They came out; Paul in an old gray suit and soft white shirt; Babbitt in khaki shirt and vast and flapping khaki trousers. It was excessively new khaki; his rimless spectacles belonged to a city office; and his face was not tanned but a city pink. He made a discordant noise in the place. But with infinite satisfaction he slapped his legs and crowed, "Say, this is getting back home, eh?"

They stood on the wharf before the hotel. He winked at Paul and drew from his back pocket a plug of chewing-tobacco, a vulgarism forbidden in the Babbitt home. He took a chew, beaming and wagging his head as he tugged at it. "Um! Um! Maybe I haven't been hungry for a wad of eating-tobacco! Have some?"

They looked at each other in a grin of understanding. Paul took the plug, gnawed at it. They stood quiet, their jaws working. They solemnly spat, one after the other, into the placid water. They stretched voluptuously, with lifted arms and arched backs. From beyond the mountains came the shuffling sound of a far-off train. A trout leaped, and fell back in a silver circle. They sighed together.

IV

They had a week before their families came. Each evening they planned to get up early and fish before breakfast. Each morning they lay abed till the breakfast-bell, pleasantly conscious that there were no efficient wives to rouse them. The mornings were cold; the fire was kindly as they dressed.

Paul was distressingly clean, but Babbitt reveled in a good sound dirtiness, in not having to shave till his spirit was moved to it. He treasured every grease spot and fish-scale on his new khaki trousers.

All morning they fished unenergetically, or tramped the dim and aqueous-lighted trails among rank ferns and moss sprinkled with crimson bells. They slept all afternoon, and till midnight played stud-poker with the guides. Poker was a serious business to the guides. They did not gossip; they shuffled the thick greasy cards with a deft ferocity menacing to the "sports;" and Joe Paradise, king of guides, was sarcastic to loiterers who halted the game even to scratch.

At midnight, as Paul and he blundered to their cottage over the pungent wet grass, and pine-roots confusing in the darkness, Babbitt rejoiced that he did not have to explain to his wife where he had been all evening.

They did not talk much. The nervous loquacity and opinionation of the Zenith Athletic Club dropped from them. But when they did talk they slipped into the naïve intimacy of college days. Once they drew their canoe up to the bank of Sunasquam Water, a stream walled in by the dense green of the hardhack. The sun roared on the green jungle but in the shade was sleepy peace, and the water was golden and rippling. Babbitt drew his hand through the cool flood, and mused:

"We never thought we'd come to Maine together!"

"No. We've never done anything the way we thought we would. I expected to live in Germany with my granddad's people, and study the fiddle."

"That's so. And remember how I wanted to be a lawyer and go into politics? I still think I might have made a go of it, I've kind of got the gift of the gab—anyway, I can think on my feet, and make some kind of a spiel on most anything, and of course that's the thing you need in politics. By golly, Ted's going to law-school, even if I didn't! Well— I guess it's worked out all right. Myra's been a fine wife. And Zilla means well, Paulibus."

"Yes. Up here, I figure out all sorts of plans to keep her amused. I kind of feel life is going to be different, now that we're getting a good rest and can go back and start over again."

"I hope so, old boy." Shyly: "Say, gosh, it's been awful nice to sit around and loaf and gamble and act regular, with you along, you old horse-thief!"

"Well, you know what it means to me, Georgie. Saved my life."

The shame of emotion overpowered them; they cursed a little, to prove they were good rough fellows; and in a mellow silence, Babbitt whistling while Paul hummed, they paddled back to the hotel.

V

Though it was Paul who had seemed overwrought, Babbitt who had been the protecting big brother, Paul became clear-eyed and merry, while Babbitt sank into irritability. He uncovered layer on layer of hidden weariness. At first he had played nimble jester to Paul and for him sought amusements; by the end of the week Paul was nurse, and Babbitt accepted favors with the condescension one always shows a patient nurse.

The day before their families arrived, the women guests at the hotel bubbled, "Oh, isn't it nice! You must be so excited;" and the proprieties compelled Babbitt and Paul to look excited. But they went to bed early and grumpy.

When Myra appeared she said at once, "Now, we want you boys to go on playing around just as if we weren't here."

The first evening, he stayed out for poker with the guides, and she said in placid merriment, "My! You're a regular bad one!" The second evening, she groaned sleepily, "Good heavens, are you going to be out every single night?" The third evening, he didn't play poker.

He was tired now in every cell. "Funny! Vacation doesn't seem to have done me a bit of good," he lamented. "Paul's frisky as a colt, but I swear, I'm crankier and nervouser than when I came up here."

He had three weeks of Maine. At the end of the second week he began to feel calm, and interested in life. He planned an expedition to climb Sachem Mountain, and wanted to camp overnight at Box Car Pond. He was curiously weak, yet cheerful, as though he had cleansed his veins of poisonous energy and was filling them with wholesome blood.

He ceased to be irritated by Ted's infatuation with a waitress (his seventh tragic affair this year); he played catch with Ted, and with pride taught him to cast a fly in the pine-shadowed silence of Skowtuit Pond.

At the end he sighed, "Hang it, I'm just beginning to enjoy my vacation. But, well, I feel a lot better. And it's going to be one great year! Maybe the Real Estate Board will elect me president, instead of some fuzzy old-fashioned faker like Chan Mott."

On the way home, whenever he went into the smoking-compartment he felt guilty at deserting his wife and angry at being expected to feel guilty, but each time he triumphed, "Oh, this is going to be a great year, a great old year!"

chapter 12

ALL the way home from Maine, Babbitt was certain that he was a changed man. He was converted to serenity. He was going to cease worrying about business. He was going to have more "interests"—theaters, public affairs, reading. And suddenly, as he finished an especially heavy cigar, he was going to stop smoking.

He invented a new and perfect method. He would buy no tobacco; he would depend on borrowing it; and, of course, he would be ashamed to borrow often. In a spasm of righteousness he flung his cigar-case out of the smoking-compartment window. He went back and was kind to his wife about nothing in particular; he admired his own purity, and decided, "Absolutely simple. Just a matter of will-power." He started a magazine serial about a scientific detective. Ten miles on, he was conscious that he desired to smoke. He ducked his head, like a turtle going into its shell; he appeared uneasy; he skipped two pages in his story and didn't know it. Five miles later, he leaped up and sought the porter. "Say, uh, George, have you got a—" The porter looked patient. "Have you got a time-table?" Babbitt finished. At the next stop he went out and bought a cigar. Since it was to be his last before he reached Zenith, he finished it down to an inch stub.

Four days later he again remembered that he had stopped smoking, but he was too busy catching up with his office-work to keep it remembered.

II

Baseball, he determined, would be an excellent hobby. "No sense a man's working his fool head off. I'm going out to the

127

Game three times a week. Besides, fellow ought to support the home team."

He did go and support the team, and enhance the glory of Zenith, by yelling "Attaboy!" and "Rotten!" He performed the rite scrupulously. He wore a cotton handkerchief about his collar; he became sweaty; he opened his mouth in a wide loose grin; and drank lemon soda out of a bottle. He went to the Game three times a week, for one week. Then he compromised on watching the *Advocate-Times* bulletin-board. He stood in the thickest and steamiest of the crowd, and as the boy up on the lofty platform recorded the achievements of Big Bill Bostwick, the pitcher, Babbitt remarked to complete strangers, "Pretty nice! Good work!" and hastened back to the office.

He honestly believed that he loved baseball. It is true that he hadn't, in twenty-five years, himself played any baseball except back-lot catch with Ted—very gentle, and strictly limited to ten minutes. But the game was a custom of his clan, and it gave outlet for the homicidal and side-taking instincts which Babbitt called "patriotism" and "love of sport."

As he approached the office he walked faster and faster, muttering, "Guess better hustle." All about him the city was hustling, for hustling's sake. Men in motors were hustling to pass one another in the hustling traffic. Men were hustling to catch trolleys, with another trolley a minute behind, and to leap from the trolleys, to gallop across the sidewalk, to hurl themselves into buildings, into hustling express elevators. Men in dairy lunches were hustling to gulp down the food which cooks had hustled to fry. Men in barber shops were snapping, "Jus' shave me once over. Gotta hustle." Men were feverishly getting rid of visitors in offices adorned with the signs, "This Is My Busy Day" and "The Lord Created the World in Six Days—You Can Spiel All You Got to Say in Six Minutes." Men who had made five thousand, year before last, and ten thousand last year, were urging on nerve-yelping bodies and parched brains so that they might make twenty thousand this year; and the men who had broken down immediately after making their twenty thousand dollars were hustling to catch trains, to hustle through the vacations which the hustling doctors had ordered.

Among them Babbitt hustled back to his office, to sit down with nothing much to do except see that the staff looked as though they were hustling.

III

Every Saturday afternoon he hustled out to his country club and hustled through nine holes of golf as a rest after the week's hustle.

In Zenith it was as necessary for a Successful Man to belong to a country club as it was to wear a linen collar. Babbitt's was the Outing Golf and Country Club, a pleasant gray-shingled building with a broad porch, on a daisy-starred cliff above Lake Kennepoose. There was another, the Tonawanda Country Club, to which belonged Charles McKelvey, Horace Updike, and the other rich men who lunched not at the Athletic but at the Union Club. Babbitt explained with frequency, "You couldn't hire me to join the Tonawanda, even if I did have a hundred and eighty bucks to throw away on the initiation fee. At the Outing we've got a bunch of real human fellows, and the finest lot of little women in town—just as good at joshing as the men—but at the Tonawanda there's nothing but these would-be's in New York getups, drinking tea! Too much dog altogether. Why, I wouldn't join the Tonawanda even if they— I wouldn't join it on a bet!"

When he had played four or five holes, he relaxed a bit, his tobacco-fluttering heart beat more normally, and his voice slowed to the drawling of his hundred generations of peasant ancestors.

IV

At least once a week Mr. and Mrs. Babbitt and Tinka went to the movies. Their favorite motion-picture theater was the Château, which held three thousand spectators and had an orchestra of fifty pieces which played Arrangements from the Operas and suites portraying a Day on the Farm, or a Four-alarm Fire. In the stone rotunda, decorated with crown-embroidered velvet chairs and almost medieval tapestries, parrakeets sat on gilded lotos columns.

With exclamations of "Well, by golly!" and "You got to go some to beat this dump!" Babbitt admired the Château. As he stared across the thousands of heads, a gray plain in the dimness, as he smelled good clothes and mild perfume and chewing-gum, he felt as when he had first seen a moun-

tain and realized how very, very much earth and rock there
was in it.

He liked three kinds of films: pretty bathing girls with
bare legs; policemen or cowboys and an industrious shooting of revolvers; and funny fat men who ate spaghetti. He
chuckled with immense, moist-eyed sentimentality at inter-
ludes portraying puppies, kittens, and chubby babies; and
he wept at deathbeds and old mothers being patient in
mortgaged cottages. Mrs. Babbitt preferred the pictures in
which handsome young women in elaborate frocks moved
through sets ticketed as the drawing-rooms of New York
millionaires. As for Tinka, she preferred, or was believed
to prefer, whatever her parents told her to.

All his relaxations—baseball, golf, movies, bridge, motoring, long talks with Paul at the Athletic Club, or at the Good
Red Beef and Old English Chop House—were necessary to
Babbitt, for he was entering a year of such activity as he
had never known.

chapter 13

IT was by accident that Babbitt had his opportunity to
address the S. A. R. E. B.

The S. A. R. E. B., as its members called it, with the universal passion for mysterious and important-sounding initials,
was the State Association of Real Estate Boards; the organization of brokers and operators. It was to hold its annual
convention at Monarch, Zenith's chief rival among the cities
of the state. Babbitt was an official delegate; another was
Cecil Rountree, whom Babbitt admired for his picaresque
speculative building, and hated for his social position, for
being present at the smartest dances on Royal Ridge. Rountree was chairman of the convention program-committee.

Babbitt had growled to him, "Makes me tired the way

these doctors and profs and preachers put on lugs about being 'professional men.' A good realtor has to have more knowledge and finesse than any of 'em."

"Right you are! I say: Why don't you put that into a paper, and give it at the S. A. R. E. B.?" suggested Rountree.

"Well, if it would help you in making up the program— Tell you: the way I look at it is this: First place, we ought to insist that folks call us 'realtors' and not 'real-estate men.' Sounds more like a reg'lar profession. Second place— What is it distinguishes a profession from a mere trade, business, or occupation? What is it? Why, it's the public service and the skill, the trained skill, and the knowledge and, uh, all that, whereas a fellow that merely goes out for the jack, he never considers the—public service and trained skill and so on. Now as a professional—"

"Rather! That's perfectly bully! Perfectly corking! Now you write it in a paper," said Rountree, as he rapidly and firmly moved away.

II

However accustomed to the literary labors of advertisements and correspondence, Babbitt was dismayed on the evening when he sat down to prepare a paper which would take a whole ten minutes to read.

He laid out a new fifteen-cent school exercise-book on his wife's collapsible sewing-table, set up for the event in the living-room. The household had been bullied into silence; Verona and Ted requested to disappear, and Tinka threatened with "If I hear one sound out of you—if you holler for a glass of water one single solitary time— You better not, that's all!" Mrs. Babbitt sat over by the piano, making a nightgown and gazing with respect while Babbitt wrote in the exercise-book, to the rhythmical wiggling and squeaking of the sewing-table.

When he rose, damp and jumpy, and his throat dusty from cigarettes, she marveled, "I don't see how you can just sit down and make up things right out of your own head!"

"Oh, it's the training in constructive imagination that a fellow gets in modern business life."

He had written seven pages, whereof the first page set forth:

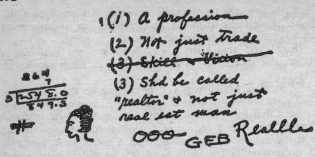

The other six pages were rather like the first.

For a week he went about looking important. Every morning, as he dressed, he thought aloud: "Jever stop to consider, Myra, that before a town can have buildings or prosperity or any of those things, some realtor has got to sell 'em the land? All civilization starts with him. Jever realize that?" At the Athletic Club he led unwilling men aside to inquire, "Say, if you had to read a paper before a big convention, would you start in with the funny stories or just kind of scatter 'em all through?" He asked Howard Littlefield for a "set of statistics about real-estate sales; something good and impressive," and Littlefield provided something exceedingly good and impressive.

But it was to T. Cholmondeley Frink that Babbitt most often turned. He caught Frink at the club every noon, and demanded, while Frink looked hunted and evasive, "Say, Chum—you're a shark on this writing stuff—how would you put this sentence, see here in my manuscript—manuscript—now where the deuce is that?—oh, yes, here. Would you say 'We ought not also to alone think?' or 'We ought also not to think alone?' or—"

One evening when his wife was away and he had no one to impress, Babbitt forgot about Style, Order, and the other mysteries, and scrawled off what he really thought about the real-estate business and about himself, and he found the paper written. When he read it to his wife she yearned, "Why, dear, it's splendid; beautifully written, and so clear and interesting, and such splendid ideas! Why, it's just—it's just splendid!"

Next day he cornered Chum Frink and crowed, "Well, old son, I finished it last evening! Just lammed it out! I used to think you writing-guys must have a hard job making up pieces, but Lord, it's a cinch. Pretty soft for you fellows; you certainly earn your money easy! Some day when I get ready to retire, guess I'll take to writing and show you boys how to do it. I always used to think I could write better stuff, and more punch and originality, than all this stuff you see printed, and now I'm doggone sure of it!"

He had four copies of the paper typed in black with a gorgeous red title, had them bound in pale blue manilla, and affably presented one to old Ira Runyon, the managing editor of the *Advocate-Times*, who said yes, indeed yes, he was very glad to have it, and he certainly would read it all through—as soon as he could find time.

Mrs. Babbitt could not go to Monarch. She had a women's-club meeting. Babbitt said that he was very sorry.

III

Besides the five official delegates to the convention—Babbitt, Rountree, W. A. Rogers, Alvin Thayer, and Elbert Wing—there were fifty unofficial delegates, most of them with their wives.

They met at the Union Station for the midnight train to Monarch. All of them, save Cecil Rountree, who was such a snob that he never wore badges, displayed celluloid buttons the size of dollars and lettered "We zoom for Zenith." The official delegates were magnificent with silver and magenta ribbons. Martin Lumsen's little boy Willy carried a tasseled banner inscribed "Zenith the Zip City—Zeal, Zest and Zowie —1,000,000 in 1935." As the delegates arrived, not in taxicabs but in the family automobile driven by the oldest son or by Cousin Fred, they formed impromptu processions through the station waiting-room.

It was a new and enormous waiting-room, with marble pilasters, and frescoes depicting the exploration of the Chaloosa River Valley by Père Emile Fauthoux in 1740. The benches were shelves of ponderous mahogany; the newsstand a marble kiosk with a brass grill. Down the echoing spaces of the hall the delegates paraded after Willy Lumsen's banner, the men waving their cigars, the women conscious of their new frocks and strings of beads, all singing to the tune of Auld Lang Syne the official City Song, written by Chum Frink:

> Good old Zenith,
> Our kin and kith,

> Wherever we may be,
> Hats in the ring,
> We blithely sing
> Of thy Prosperity.

Warren Whitby, the broker, who had a gift of verse for banquets and birthdays, had added to Frink's City Song a special verse for the realtors' convention:

> Oh, here we come,
> The fellows from
> Zenith, the Zip Citee.
> We wish to state
> In real estate
> There's none so live as we.

Babbitt was stirred to hysteric patriotism. He leaped on a bench, shouting to the crowd:

"What's the matter with Zenith?"

"She's all right!"

"What's best ole town in the U. S. A.?"

"Zeeeeeen-ith!"

The patient poor people waiting for the midnight train stared in unenvious wonder—Italian women with shawls, old weary men with broken shoes, roving road-wise boys in suits which had been flashy when they were new but which were faded now and wrinkled.

Babbitt perceived that as an official delegate he must be more dignified. With Wing and Rogers he tramped up and down the cement platform beside the waiting Pullmans. Motor-driven baggage-trucks and red-capped porters carrying bags sped down the platform with an agreeable effect of activity. Arc-lights glared and stammered overhead. The glossy yellow sleeping-cars shone impressively. Babbitt made his voice to be measured and lordly; he thrust out his abdomen and rumbled, "We got to see to it that the convention lets the Legislature understand just where they get off in this matter of taxing realty transfers." Wing uttered approving grunts and Babbitt swelled—gloated—

The blind of a Pullman compartment was raised, and Babbitt looked into an unfamiliar world. The occupant of the compartment was Lucile McKelvey, the pretty wife of the millionaire contractor. Possibly, Babbitt thrilled, she was going to Europe! On the seat beside her was a bunch of orchids and violets, and a yellow paper-bound book which seemed foreign. While he stared, she picked up the book, then glanced out of the window as though she was bored.

She must have looked straight at him, and he had met her, but she gave no sign. She languidly pulled down the blind, and he stood still, a cold feeling of insignificance in his heart.

But on the train his pride was restored by meeting delegates from Sparta, Pioneer, and other smaller cities of the state, who listened respectfully when, as a magnifico from the metropolis of Zenith, he explained politics and the value of a Good Sound Business Administration. They fell joyfully into shop-talk, the purest and most rapturous form of conversation:

"How'd this fellow Rountree make out with this big apartment-hotel he was going to put up? Whadde do? Get out bonds to finance it?" asked a Sparta broker.

"Well, I'll tell you," said Babbitt. "Now if I'd been handling it—"

"So," Elbert Wing was droning, "I hired this shop-window for a week, and put up a big sign, 'Toy Town for Tiny Tots,' and stuck in a lot of doll houses and some dinky little trees, and then down at the bottom, 'Baby Likes This Dollydale, but Papa and Mama Will Prefer Our Beautiful Bungalows,' and you know, that certainly got folks talking, and first week we sold—"

The trucks sang "lickety-lick, lickety-lick" as the train ran through the factory district. Furnaces spurted flame, and power-hammers were clanging. Red lights, green lights, furious white lights rushed past, and Babbitt was important again, and eager.

IV

He did a voluptuous thing: he had his clothes pressed on the train. In the morning, half an hour before they reached Monarch, the porter came to his berth and whispered, "There's a drawing-room vacant, sir. I put your suit in there." In tan autumn overcoat over his pajamas, Babbitt slipped down the green-curtain-lined aisle to the glory of his first private compartment. The porter indicated that he knew Babbitt was used to a man-servant; he held the ends of Babbitt's trousers, that the beautifully sponged garment might not be soiled, filled the bowl in the private washroom, and waited with a towel.

To have a private washroom was luxurious. However enlivening a Pullman smoking-compartment was by night, even to Babbitt it was depressing in the morning, when it was jammed with fat men in woolen undershirts, every hook filled with wrinkled cottony shirts, the leather seat piled with dingy toilet-kits, and the air nauseating with the smell of soap and toothpaste. Babbitt did not ordinarily think much of privacy, but now he reveled in it, reveled in his valet, and purred with pleasure as he gave the man a tip of a dollar and a half.

He rather hoped that he was being noticed as, in his newly pressed clothes, with the adoring porter carrying his suitcase, he disembarked at Monarch.

He was to share a room at the Hotel Sedgwick with W. A. Rogers, that shrewd, rustic-looking Zenith dealer in farmlands. Together they had a noble breakfast, with waffles, and coffee not in exiguous cups but in large pots. Babbitt grew expansive, and told Rogers about the art of writing; he gave a bell-boy a quarter to fetch a morning newspaper from the lobby, and sent to Tinka a post-card: "Papa wishes you were here to bat round with him."

V

The meetings of the convention were held in the ballroom of the Allen House. In an anteroom was the office of the chairman of the executive committee. He was the busiest man in the convention; he was so busy that he got nothing done whatever. He sat at a marquetry table, in a room littered with crumpled paper and, all day long, town-boosters and lobbyists and orators who wished to lead debates came and whispered to him, whereupon he looked vague, and said rapidly, "Yes, yes, that's a fine idea; we'll do that," and instantly forgot all about it, lighted a cigar and forgot that too, while the telephone rang mercilessly and about him men kept beseeching, "Say, Mr. Chairman—say, Mr. Chairman!" without penetrating his exhausted hearing.

In the exhibit-room were plans of the new suburbs of Sparta, pictures of the new state capitol, at Galop de Vache, and large ears of corn with the label, "Nature's Gold, from Shelby County, the Garden Spot of God's Own Country."

The real convention consisted of men muttering in hotel bedrooms or in groups amid the badge-spotted crowd in the hotel-lobby, but there was a show of public meetings.

The first of them opened with a welcome by the mayor of Monarch. The pastor of the First Christian Church of Monarch, a large man with a long damp frontal lock, informed God that the real-estate men were here now.

The venerable Minnemagantic realtor, Major Carlton Tuke, read a paper in which he denounced coöperative stores. William A. Larkin of Eureka gave a comforting prognosis of "The Prospects for Increased Construction," and reminded them that plate-glass prices were two points lower.

The convention was on.

The delegates were entertained, incessantly and firmly. The Monarch Chamber of Commerce gave them a banquet, and the Manufacturers' Association an afternoon reception, at which a chrysanthemum was presented to each of the ladies, and to each of the men a leather bill-fold inscribed "From Monarch the Mighty Motor Mart."

Mrs. Crosby Knowlton, wife of the manufacturer of Fleetwing Automobiles, opened her celebrated Italian garden and served tea. Six hundred real-estate men and wives ambled down the autumnal paths. Perhaps three hundred of them were quietly inconspicuous; perhaps three hundred vigorously exclaimed, "This is pretty slick, eh?", surreptitiously picked the late asters and concealed them in their pockets, and tried to get near enough to Mrs. Knowlton to shake her lovely hand. Without request, the Zenith delegates (except Rountree) gathered round a marble dancing nymph and sang "Here we come, the fellows from Zenith, the Zip Citee."

It chanced that all the delegates from Pioneer belonged to the Brotherly and Protective Order of Elks, and they produced an enormous banner lettered: "B. P. O. E.—Best People on Earth—Boost Pioneer, Oh Eddie." Nor was Galop de Vache, the state capital, to be slighted. The leader of the Galop de Vache delegation was a large, reddish, roundish man, but active. He took off his coat, hurled his broad black felt hat on the ground, rolled up his sleeves, climbed upon the sun-dial, spat, and bellowed:

"We'll tell the world, and the good lady who's giving the show this afternoon, that the bonniest burg in this man's state is Galop de Vache. You boys can talk about your zip, but jus' lemme murmur that old Galop has the largest proportion of home-owning citizens in the state; and when folks own their homes, they ain't starting labor-troubles, and they're raising kids instead of raising hell! Galop de Vache! The town for homey folks! The town that eats 'em alive oh, Bosco! We'll —tell—the—world!"

The guests drove off; the garden shivered into quiet. But

Mrs. Crosby Knowlton sighed as she looked at a marble seat warm from five hundred summers of Amalfi. On the face of a winged sphinx which supported it some one had drawn a mustache in lead-pencil. Crumpled paper napkins were dumped among the Michaelmas daisies. On the walk, like shredded lovely flesh, were the petals of the last gallant rose. Cigarette stubs floated in the goldfish pool, trailing an evil stain as they swelled and disintegrated, and beneath the marble seat, the fragments carefully put together, was a smashed teacup.

VI

As he rode back to the hotel Babbitt reflected, "Myra would have enjoyed all this social agony." For himself he cared less for the garden party than for the motor tours which the Monarch Chamber of Commerce had arranged. Indefatigably he viewed water-reservoirs, suburban trolley-stations, and tanneries. He devoured the statistics which were given to him, and marveled to his roommate, W. A. Rogers, "Of course this town isn't a patch on Zenith; it hasn't got our outlook and natural resources; but did you know—I nev' did till to-day—that they manufactured seven hundred and sixty-three million feet of lumber last year? What d' you think of that!"

He was nervous as the time for reading his paper approached. When he stood on the low platform before the convention, he trembled and saw only a purple haze. But he was in earnest, and when he had finished the formal paper he talked to them, his hands in his pockets, his spectacled face a flashing disk, like a plate set up on edge in the lamplight. They shouted "That's the stuff!" and in the discussion afterward they referred with impressiveness to "our friend and brother, Mr. George F. Babbitt." He had in fifteen minutes changed from a minor delegate to a personage almost as well known as that diplomat of business, Cecil Rountree. After the meeting, delegates from all over the state said, "Hower you, Brother Babbitt?" Sixteen complete strangers called him "George," and three men took him into corners to confide, "Mighty glad you had the courage to stand up and give the Profession a real boost. Now I've always maintained—"

Next morning, with tremendous casualness, Babbitt asked the girl at the hotel news-stand for the newspapers from

Zenith. There was nothing in the *Press*, but in the *Advocate-Times*, on the third page— He gasped. They had printed his picture and a half-column account. The heading was "Sensation at Annual Land-men's Convention. G. F. Babbitt, Prominent Ziptown Realtor, Keynoter in Fine Address."

He murmured reverently, "I guess some of the folks on Floral Heights will sit up and take notice now, and pay a little attention to old Georgie!"

VII

It was the last meeting. The delegations were presenting the claims of their several cities to the next year's convention. Orators were announcing that "Galop de Vache, the Capital City, the site of Kremer College and the Upholtz Knitting Works, is the recognized center of culture and high-class enterprise;" and that "Hamburg, the Big Little City with the Logical Location, where every man is open-handed and every woman a heaven-born hostess, throws wide to you her hospitable gates."

In the midst of these more diffident invitations, the golden doors of the ballroom opened with a blatting of trumpets, and a circus parade rolled in. It was composed of the Zenith brokers, dressed as cowpunchers, bareback riders, Japanese jugglers. At the head was big Warren Whitby, in the bear-skin and gold-and-crimson coat of a drum-major. Behind him, as a clown, beating a bass drum, extraordinarily happy and noisy, was Babbitt.

Warren Whitby leaped on the platform, made merry play with his baton, and observed, "Boyses and girlses, the time has came to get down to cases. A dyed-in-the-wool Zenithite sure loves his neighbors, but we've made up our minds to grab this convention off our neighbor burgs like we've grabbed the condensed-milk business and the paper-box business and—"

J. Harry Barmhill, the convention chairman, hinted, "We're grateful to you, Mr. Uh, but you must give the other boys a chance to hand in their bids now."

A fog-horn voice blared, "In Eureka we'll promise free motor rides through the prettiest country—"

Running down the aisle, clapping his hands, a lean bald young man cried, "I'm from Sparta! Our Chamber of Commerce has wired me they've set aside eight thousand dollars, in real money, for the entertainment of the convention!"

A clerical-looking man rose to clamor, "Money talks! Move we accept the bid from Sparta!"

It was accepted.

VIII

The Committee on Resolutions was reporting. They said that Whereas Almighty God in his beneficent mercy had seen fit to remove to a sphere of higher usefulness some thirty-six realtors of the state the past year, Therefore it was the sentiment of this convention assembled that they were sorry God had done it, and the secretary should be, and hereby was, instructed to spread these resolutions on the minutes, and to console the bereaved families by sending them each a copy.

A second resolution authorized the president of the S.A.R.E.B. to spend fifteen thousand dollars in lobbying for sane tax measures in the State Legislature. This resolution had a good deal to say about Menaces to Sound Business and clearing the Wheels of Progress from ill-advised and short-sighted obstacles.

The Committee on Committees reported, and with startled awe Babbitt learned that he had been appointed a member of the Committee on Torrens Titles.

He rejoiced, "I said it was going to be a great year! Georgie, old son, you got big things ahead of you! You're a natural-born orator and a good mixer and— Zowie!"

IX

There was no formal entertainment provided for the last evening. Babbitt had planned to go home, but that afternoon the Jered Sassburgers of Pioneer suggested that Babbitt and W. A. Rogers have tea with them at the Catalpa Inn.

Teas were not unknown to Babbitt—his wife and he earnestly attended them at least twice a year—but they were sufficiently exotic to make him feel important. He sat at a glass-covered table in the Art Room of the Inn, with its painted rabbits, mottoes lettered on birch bark, and waitresses being artistic in Dutch caps; he ate insufficient lettuce sandwiches, and was lively and naughty with Mrs. Sassburger, who was as smooth and large-eyed as a cloak-model. Sassburger and he had met two days before, so they were calling each other "Georgie" and "Sassy."

Sassburger said prayerfully, "Say, boys, before you go, seeing this is the last chance, I've *got it,* up in my room, and

Miriam here is the best little mixologist in the Stati Unidos, like us Italians say."

With wide flowing gestures, Babbitt and Rogers followed the Sassburgers to their room. Mrs. Sassburger shrieked, "Oh, how terrible!" when she saw that she had left a chemise of sheer lavender crêpe on the bed. She tucked it into a bag, while Babbitt giggled, "Don't mind us; we're a couple o' little divvils!"

Sassburger telephoned for ice, and the bell-boy who brought it said, prosaically and unprompted, "Highball glasses or cocktail?" Miriam Sassburger mixed the cocktails in one of those dismal, nakedly white water-pitchers which exist only in hotels. When they had finished the first round she proved by intoning "Think you boys could stand another —you got a dividend coming" that, though she was but a woman, she knew the complete and perfect rite of cocktail-drinking.

Outside, Babbitt hinted to Rogers, "Say, W. A., old rooster, it comes over me that I could stand it if we didn't go back to the lovin' wives, this handsome *Abend,* but just kind of stayed in Monarch and threw a party, heh?"

"George, you speak with the tongue of wisdom and sagash-iteriferousness. El Wing's wife has gone on to Pittsburg. Let's see if we can't gather him in."

At half-past seven they sat in their room, with Elbert Wing and two up-state delegates. Their coats were off, their vests open, their faces red, their voices emphatic. They were finishing a bottle of corrosive bootlegged whisky and imploring the bell-boy, "Say, son, can you get us some more of this embalming fluid?" They were smoking large cigars and dropping ashes and stubs on the carpet. With windy guffaws they were telling stories. They were, in fact, males in a happy state of nature.

Babbitt sighed, "I don't know how it strikes you hellions, but personally I like this busting loose for a change, and kicking over a couple of mountains and climbing up on the North Pole and waving the aurora borealis around."

The man from Sparta, a grave, intense youngster, babbled, "Say! I guess I'm as good a husband as the run of the mill, but God, I do get so tired of going home every evening, and nothing to see but the movies. That's why I go out and drill with the National Guard. I guess I got the nicest little wife in my burg, but— Say! Know what I wanted to do as a kid? Know what I wanted to do? Wanted to be a big chemist.

Tha's what I wanted to do. But Dad chased me out on the road selling kitchenware, and here I'm settled down—settled for *life*—not a chance! Oh, who the devil started this funeral talk? How 'bout 'nother lil drink? 'And a-noth-er drink wouldn' do 's 'ny harmmmmmmm.' "

"Yea. Cut the sob-stuff," said W. A. Rogers genially. "You boys know I'm the village songster? Come on now—sing up:

> Said the old Obadiah to the young Obadiah,
> 'I am dry, Obadiah, I am dry.'
> Said the young Obadiah to the old Obadiah,
> 'So am I, Obadiah, so am I.' "

x

They had dinner in the Moorish Grillroom of the Hotel Sedgwick. Somewhere, somehow, they seemed to have gathered in two other comrades: a manufacturer of fly-paper and a dentist. They all drank whisky from tea-cups, and they were humorous, and never listened to one another, except when W. A. Rogers "kidded" the Italian waiter.

"Say, Gooseppy," he said innocently, "I want a couple o' fried elephants' ears."

"Sorry, sir, we haven't any."

"Huh? No elephants' ears? What do you know about that!" Rogers turned to Babbitt. "Pedro says the elephants' ears are all out!"

"Well, I'll be switched!" said the man from Sparta, with difficulty hiding his laughter.

"Well, in that case, Carlo, just bring me a hunk o' steak and a couple o' bushels o' French fried potatoes and some peas," Rogers went on. "I suppose back in dear old sunny It' the Eyetalians get their fresh garden peas out of the can."

"No, sir, we have very nice peas in Italy."

"Is that a fact! Georgie, do you hear that? They get their fresh garden peas out of the garden, in Italy! By golly, you live and learn, don't you, Antonio, you certainly do live and learn, if you live long enough and keep your strength. All right, Garibaldi, just shoot me in that steak, with about two printers'-reams of French fried spuds on the promenade deck, *comprehenez-vous*, Michelovitch Angeloni?"

Afterward Elbert Wing admired, "Gee, you certainly did have that poor Dago going, W. A. He couldn't make you out at all!"

In the *Monarch Herald,* Babbitt found an advertisement which he read aloud, to applause and laughter:

Old Colony Theatre

Shake the Old Dogs to the
WROLLICKING WRENS
The bonniest bevy of beauteous
bathing babes in burlesque.
Pete Menutti and his
Oh, Gee, Kids.

This is the straight steer, Benny, the painless chicklets of the Wrollicking Wrens are the cuddlingest bunch that ever hit town. Steer the feet, get the card board, and twist the pupils to the PDQest show ever. You will get 111% on your kale in this fun-fest. The Calroza Sisters are sure some lookers and will give you a run for your gelt. Jock Silbersteen is one of the pepper lads and slips you a dose of real laughter. Shoot the up and down to Jackson and West for graceful tappers. They run 1-2 under the wire. Provin and Adams will blow the blues in their laugh skit "Hootch Mon!" Something doing, boys. Listen to what the Hep Bird twitters.

"Sounds like a juicy show to me. Let's all take it in," said Babbitt.

But they put off departure as long as they could. They were safe while they sat here, legs firmly crossed under the table, but they felt unsteady; they were afraid of navigating the long and slippery floor of the grillroom under the eyes of the other guests and the too-attentive waiters.

When they did venture, tables got in their way, and they sought to cover embarrassment by heavy jocularity at the coatroom. As the girl handed out their hats, they smiled at her, and hoped that she, a cool and expert judge, would feel that they were gentlemen. They croaked at one another, "Who owns the bum lid?" and "You take a good one, George; I'll take what's left," and to the check-girl they stammered, "Better come along, sister! High, wide, and fancy evening ahead!" All of them tried to tip her, urging one another, "No! Wait! Here! I got it right here!" Among them, they gave her three dollars.

XI

Flamboyantly smoking cigars they sat in a box at the burlesque show, their feet up on the rail, while a chorus of twenty daubed, worried, and inextinguishably respectable gran-

dams swung their legs in the more elementary chorus-evolu-
tions, and a Jewish comedian made vicious fun of Jews.
In the entr'actes they met other lone delegates. A dozen of
them went in taxicabs out to Bright Blossom Inn, where the
blossoms were made of dusty paper festooned along a room
low and stinking, like a cow-stable no longer wisely used.

Here, whisky was served openly, in glasses. Two or three
clerks, who on pay-day longed to be taken for millionaires,
sheepishly danced with telephone-girls and manicure-girls
in the narrow space between the tables. Fantastically whirled
the professionals, a young man in sleek evening-clothes and
a slim mad girl in emerald silk, with amber hair flung up as
jaggedly as flames. Babbitt tried to dance with her. He
shuffled along the floor, too bulky to be guided, his steps un-
related to the rhythm of the jungle music, and in his stag-
gering he would have fallen, had she not held him with supple
kindly strength. He was blind and deaf from prohibition-
era alcohol; he could not see the tables, the faces. But he was
overwhelmed by the girl and her young pliant warmth.

When she had firmly returned him to his group, he remembered, by a connection quite untraceable, that his mother's
mother had been Scotch, and with head thrown back, eyes
closed, wide mouth indicating ecstasy, he sang, very slowly
and richly, "Loch Lomond."

But that was the last of his mellowness and jolly companionship. The man from Sparta said he was a "bum singer,"
and for ten minutes Babbitt quarreled with him, in a loud, unsteady, heroic indignation. They called for drinks till the
manager insisted that the place was closed. All the while
Babbitt felt a hot raw desire for more brutal amusements.
When W. A. Rogers drawled, "What say we go down the line
and look over the girls?" he agreed savagely. Before they
went, three of them secretly made appointments with the
professional dancing girl, who agreed "Yes, yes, sure, darling"
to everything they said, and amiably forgot them.

As they drove back through the outskirts of Monarch, down
streets of small brown wooden cottages of workmen,
characterless as cells, as they rattled across warehouse-districts
which by drunken night seemed vast and perilous, as they
were borne toward the red lights and violent automatic pianos
and the stocky women who simpered, Babbitt was frightened.
He wanted to leap from the taxicab, but all his body was
a murky fire, and he groaned, "Too late to quit now," and
knew that he did not want to quit.

There was, they felt, one very humorous incident on the way. A broker from Minnemagantic said, "Monarch is a lot sportier than Zenith. You Zenith tightwads haven't got any joints like these here." Babbitt raged, "That's a dirty lie! Snothin' you can't find in Zenith. Believe me, we got more houses and hootch-parlors an' all kinds o' dives than any burg in the state."

He realized they were laughing at him; he desired to fight; and forgot it in such musty unsatisfying experiments as he had not known since college.

In the morning, when he returned to Zenith, his desire for rebellion was partly satisfied. He had retrograded to a shame-faced contentment. He was irritable. He did not smile when W. A. Rogers complained, "Ow, what a head! I certainly do feel like the wrath of God this morning. Say! I know what was the trouble! Somebody went and put alcohol in my booze last night."

Babbitt's excursion was never known to his family, nor to any one in Zenith save Rogers and Wing. It was not officially recognized even by himself. If it had any consequences, they have not been discovered.

chapter 14

THIS autumn a Mr. W. G. Harding, of Marion, Ohio, was appointed President of the United States, but Zenith was less interested in the national campaign than in the local election. Seneca Doane, though he was a lawyer and a graduate of the State University, was candidate for mayor of Zenith on an alarming labor ticket. To oppose him the Democrats and Republicans united on Lucas Prout, a mattress-manufacturer with a perfect record for sanity. Mr. Prout was supported by the banks, the Chamber of Commerce, all the decent newspapers, and George F. Babbitt.

Babbitt was precinct-leader on Floral Heights, but his district was safe and he longed for stouter battling. His convention paper had given him the beginning of a reputation for oratory, so the Republican-Democratic Central Committee sent him to the Seventh Ward and South Zenith, to address small audiences of workmen and clerks, and wives uneasy with their new votes. He acquired a fame enduring for weeks. Now and then a reporter was present at one of his meetings, and the headlines (though they were not very large) indicated that George F. Babbitt had addressed Cheering Throng, and Distinguished Man of Affairs had pointed out the Fallacies of Doane. Once, in the rotogravure section of the Sunday *Advocate-Times*, there was a photograph of Babbitt and a dozen other business men, with the caption "Leaders of Zenith Finance and Commerce Who Back Prout."

He deserved his glory. He was an excellent campaigner. He had faith; he was certain that if Lincoln were alive, he would be electioneering for Mr. W. G. Harding—unless he came to Zenith and electioneered for Lucas Prout. He did not confuse audiences by silly subtleties; Prout represented honest industry, Seneca Doane represented whining laziness, and you could take your choice. With his broad shoulders and vigorous voice, he was obviously a Good Fellow; and, rarest of all, he really liked people. He almost liked common workmen. He wanted them to be well paid, and able to afford high rents—though, naturally, they must not interfere with the reasonable profits of stockholders. Thus nobly endowed, and keyed high by the discovery that he was a natural orator, he was popular with audiences, and he raged through the campaign, renowned not only in the Seventh and Eighth Wards but even in parts of the Sixteenth.

II

Crowded in his car, they came driving up to Turnverein Hall, South Zenith—Babbitt, his wife, Verona, Ted, and Paul and Zilla Riesling. The hall was over a delicatessen shop, in a street banging with trolleys and smelling of onions and gasoline and fried fish. A new appreciation of Babbitt filled all of them, including Babbitt.

"Don't know how you keep it up, talking to three bunches in one evening. Wish I had your strength," said Paul; and Ted exclaimed to Verona, "The old man certainly does know how to kid these roughnecks along!"

Men in black sateen shirts, their faces new-washed but with a hint of grime under their eyes, were loitering on the broad stairs up to the hall. Babbitt's party politely edged through them and into the whitewashed room, at the front of which was a dais with a red-lush throne and a pine altar painted watery blue, as used nightly by the Grand Masters and Supreme Potentates of innumerable lodges. The hall was full. As Babbitt pushed through the fringe standing at the back, he heard the precious tribute, "That's him!" The chairman bustled down the center aisle with an impressive, "The speaker? All ready, sir! Uh—let's see—what was the name, sir?"

Then Babbitt slid into a sea of eloquence:

"Ladies and gentlemen of the Sixteenth Ward, there is one who cannot be with us here to-night, a man than whom there is no more stalwart Trojan in all the political arena —I refer to our leader, the Honorable Lucas Prout, standard-bearer of the city and county of Zenith. Since he is not here, I trust that you will bear with me if, as a friend and neighbor, as one who is proud to share with you the common blessing of being a resident of the great city of Zenith, I tell you in all candor, honesty, and sincerity how the issues of this critical campaign appear to one plain man of business—to one who, brought up to the blessings of poverty and of manual labor, has, even when Fate condemned him to sit at a desk, yet never forgotten how it feels, by heck, to be up at five-thirty and at the factory with the ole dinner-pail in his hardened mitt when the whistle blew at seven, unless the owner sneaked in ten minutes on us and blew it early! (Laughter.) To come down to the basic and fundamental issues of this campaign, the greater error, insincerely promulgated by Seneca Doane—"

There were workmen who jeered—young cynical workmen, for the most part foreigners, Jews, Swedes, Irishmen, Italians —but the older men, the patient, bleached, stooped carpenters and mechanics, cheered him; and when he worked up to his anecdote of Lincoln their eyes were wet.

Modestly, busily, he hurried out of the hall on delicious applause, and sped off to his third audience of the evening. "Ted, you better drive," he said. "Kind of all in after that spiel. Well, Paul, how'd it go? Did I get 'em?"

"Bully! Corking! You had a lot of pep."

Mrs. Babbitt worshiped, "Oh, it was fine! So clear and interesting, and such nice ideas. When I hear you orating I realize I don't appreciate how profoundly you think and what a splendid brain and vocabulary you have. Just—splendid."

But Verona was irritating. "Dad," she worried, "how do you know that public ownership of utilities and so on and so forth will always be a failure?"

Mrs. Babbitt reproved, "Rone, I should think you could see and realize that when your father's all worn out with orating, it's no time to expect him to explain these complicated subjects. I'm sure when he's rested he'll be glad to explain it to you. Now let's all be quiet and give Papa a chance to get ready for his next speech. Just think! Right now they're gathering in Maccabee Temple, and *waiting* for us!"

III

Mr. Lucas Prout and Sound Business defeated Mr. Seneca Doane and Class Rule, and Zenith was again saved. Babbitt was offered several minor appointments to distribute among poor relations, but he preferred advance information about the extension of paved highways, and this a grateful administration gave to him. Also, he was one of only nineteen speakers at the dinner with which the Chamber of Commerce celebrated the victory of righteousness.

His reputation for oratory established, at the dinner of the Zenith Real Estate Board he made the Annual Address. The *Advocate-Times* reported this speech with unusual fullness:

"One of the livest banquets that has recently been pulled off occurred last night in the annual Get-Together Fest of the Zenith Real Estate Board, held in the Venetian Ball Room of the O'Hearn House. Mine host Gil O'Hearn had as usual done himself proud and those assembled feasted on such an assemblage of plates as could be rivaled nowhere west of New York, if there, and washed down the plenteous feed with the cup which inspired but did not inebriate in the shape of cider from the farm of Chandler Mott, president of the board and who acted as witty and efficient chairman.

"As Mr. Mott was suffering from slight infection and sore throat, G. F. Babbitt made the principal talk. Besides outlining the progress of Torrensing real estate titles, Mr. Babbitt spoke in part as follows:

"'In rising to address you, with my impromptu speech carefully tucked into my vest pocket, I am reminded of the story of the two Irishmen, Mike and Pat, who were riding on the Pullman. Both of them, I forgot to say, were sailors in the Navy. It seems Mike had the lower berth and by and by he heard a terrible racket from the upper, and when he yelled up to find out what the trouble was, Pat answered, "Shure an' bedad an' how can I ever get a night's sleep at all, at all? I been trying to get into this darned little hammock ever since eight bells!"

" 'Now, gentlemen, standing up here before you, I feel a good deal like Pat, and maybe after I've spieled along for a while, I may feel so darn small that I'll be able to crawl into a Pullman hammock with no trouble at all, at all!

" 'Gentlemen, it strikes me that each year at this annual occasion when friend and foe get together and lay down the battle-ax and let the waves of good-fellowship waft them up the flowery slopes of amity, it behooves us, standing together eye to eye and shoulder to shoulder as fellow-citizens of the best city in the world, to consider where we are both as regards ourselves and the common weal.

" 'It is true that even with our 361,000 or practically 362,000 population, there are, by the last census, almost a score of larger cities in the United States. But, gentlemen, if by the next census we do not stand at least tenth, then I'll be the first to request any knocker to remove my shirt and to eat the same, with the compliments of G. F. Babbitt, Esquire! It may be true that New York, Chicago, and Philadelphia will continue to keep ahead of us in size. But aside from these three cities, which are notoriously so overgrown that no decent white man nobody who loves his wife and kiddies and God's good out-o'-doors and likes to shake the hand of his neighbor in greeting, would want to live in them—and let me tell you right here and now, I wouldn't trade a high-class Zenith acreage development for the whole length and breadth of Broadway or State Street!—aside from these three, it's evident to any one with a head for facts that Zenith is the finest example of American life and prosperity to be found anywhere.

" 'I don't mean to say we're perfect. We've got a lot to do in the way of extending the paving of motor boulevards, for, believe me, it's the fellow with four to ten thousand a year, say, and an automobile and a nice little family in a bungalow on the edge of town, that makes the wheels of progress go round!

" 'That's the type of fellow that's ruling America to-day; in fact, it's the ideal type to which the entire world must tend, if there's to be a decent, well-balanced, Christian, go-

ahead future for this little old planet! Once in a while I just
naturally sit back and size up this Solid American Citizen,
with a whale of a lot of satisfaction.

" 'Our Ideal Citizen—I picture him first and foremost as
being busier than a bird-dog, not wasting a lot of good time
in day-dreaming or going to sassiety teas or kicking about
things that are none of his business, but putting the zip into
some store or profession or art. At night he lights up a good
cigar, and climbs into the little old 'bus, and maybe cusses the
carburetor, and shoots out home. He mows the lawn, or
sneaks in some practice putting, and then he's ready for
dinner. After dinner he tells the kiddies a story, or takes the
family to the movies, or plays a few fists of bridge, or reads
the evening paper, and a chapter or two of some good lively
Western novel if he has a taste for literature, and maybe
the folks next-door drop in and they sit and visit about their
friends and the topics of the day. Then he goes happily to
bed, his conscience clear, having contributed his mite to the
prosperity of the city and to his own bank-account.

" 'In politics and religion this Sane Citizen is the canniest
man on earth; and in the arts he invariably has a natural
taste which makes him pick out the best, every time. In no
country in the world will you find so many reproductions of
the Old Masters and of well-known paintings on parlor walls
as in these United States. No country has anything like our
number of phonographs, with not only dance records and
comic but also the best operas, such as Verdi, rendered by the
world's highest-paid singers.

" 'In other countries, art and literature are left to a lot of
shabby bums living in attics and feeding on booze and
spaghetti, but in America the successful writer or picture-
painter is indistinguishable from any other decent business
man; and I, for one, am only too glad that the man who has
the rare skill to season his message with interesting reading
matter and who shows both purpose and pep in handling his
literary wares has a chance to drag down his fifty thousand
bucks a year, to mingle with the biggest executives on terms
of perfect equality, and to show as big a house and as swell
a car as any Captain of Industry! But, mind you, it's the
appreciation of the Regular Guy who I have been depicting
which has made this possible, and you got to hand as much
credit to him as to the authors themselves.

"Finally, but most important, our Standardized Citizen,
even if he is a bachelor, is a lover of the Little Ones, a

supporter of the hearthstone which is the basic foundation of our civilization, first, last, and all the time, and the thing that most distinguishes us from the decayed nations of Europe.

" 'I have never yet toured Europe—and as a matter of fact, I don't know that I care to such an awful lot, as long as there's our own mighty cities and mountains to be seen—but, the way I figure it out, there must be a good many of our own sort of folks abroad. Indeed, one of the most enthusiastic Rotarians I ever met boosted the tenets of one-hundred-per-cent pep in a burr that smacked o' bonny Scutlond and all ye bonny braes o' Bobby Burns. But same time, one thing that distinguishes us from our good brothers, the hustlers over there, is that they're willing to take a lot off the snobs and journalists and politicians, while the modern American business man knows how to talk right up for himself, knows how to make it good and plenty clear that he intends to run the works. He doesn't have to call in some highbrow hired-man when it's necessary for him to answer the crooked critics of the sane and efficient life. He's not dumb, like the old-fashioned merchant. He's got a vocabulary and a punch.

" 'With all modesty, I want to stand up here as a representative business man and gently whisper, "Here's our kind of folks! Here's the specifications of the Standardized American Citizen! Here's the new generation of Americans: fellows with hair on their chests and smiles in their eyes and adding-machines in their offices. We're not doing any boasting, but we like ourselves first-rate, and if you don't like us, look out—better get under cover before the cyclone hits town!"

" 'So! In my clumsy way I have tried to sketch the Real He-man, the fellow with Zip and Bang. And it's because Zenith has so large a proportion of such men that it's the most stable, the greatest of our cities. New York also has its thousands of Real Folks, but New York is cursed with un-numbered foreigners. So are Chicago and San Francisco. Oh, we have a golden roster of cities—Detroit and Cleveland with their renowned factories, Cincinnati with its great machine-tool and soap products, Pittsburg and Birmingham with their steel, Kansas City and Minneapolis and Omaha that open their bountiful gates on the bosom of the ocean-like wheat-lands, and countless other magnificent sister-cities, for, by the last census, there were no less than sixty-eight glorious American burgs with a population of over one hundred thousand! And all these cities stand together for power and purity, and against foreign ideas and communism—Atlanta with Hartford, Rochester with Denver, Milwaukee with Indianapolis, Los Angeles with Scranton, Portland, Maine, with Portland, Oregon. A good live wire from Baltimore or Seattle or Duluth is the twin-brother of every like fellow booster from Buffalo or Akron, Fort Worth or Oskaloosa!

" 'But it's here in Zenith, the home for manly men and womanly women and bright kids, that you find the largest proportion of these Regular Guys, and that's what sets it in a class by itself; that's why Zenith will be remembered in history as having set the pace for a civilization that shall endure when the old time-killing ways are gone forever and the day of earnest efficient endeavor shall have dawned all round the world!

" 'Some time I hope folks will quit handing all the credit to a lot of moth-eaten, mildewed, out-of-date, old, European dumps, and give proper credit to the famous Zenith spirit, that clean fighting determination to win Success that has made the little old Zip City celebrated in every land and clime, wherever condensed milk and pasteboard cartons are known! Believe me, the world has fallen too long for these worn-out countries that aren't producing anything but bootblacks and scenery and booze, that haven't got one bathroom per hundred people, and that don't know a loose-leaf ledger from a slip-cover; and it's just about time for some Zenithite to get his back up and holler for a show-down!

" 'I tell you, Zenith and her sister-cities are producing a new type of civilization. There are many resemblances between Zenith and these other burgs, and I'm darn glad of it! The extraordinary, growing, and sane standardization of stores, offices, streets, hotels, clothes, and newspapers throughout the United States shows how strong and enduring a type is ours.

" 'I always like to remember a piece that Chum Frink wrote for the newspapers about his lecture-tours. It is doubtless familiar to many of you, but if you will permit me, I'll take a chance and read it. It's one of the classic poems, like "If" by Kipling, or Ella Wheeler Wilcox's "The Man Worth While"; and I always carry this clipping of it in my note-book:

> When I am out upon the road, a poet with a pedler's load,
> I mostly sing a hearty song, and take a chew and hike along,
> a-handing out my samples fine of Cheero Brand of sweet
> sunshine, and peddling optimistic pokes and stable lines of

*japes and jokes to Lyceums and other folks, to Rotarys,
Kiwanis' Clubs, and feel I ain't like other dubs. And then old
Major Silas Satan, a brainy cuss who's always waitin', he
gives his tail a lively quirk, and gets in quick his dirty work.
He fills me up with mullygrubs; my hair the backward
way he rubs; he makes me lonelier than a hound, on Sunday
when the folks ain't round. And then b' gosh, I would
prefer to never be a lecturer, a-ridin' round in classy cars and
smoking fifty-cent cigars, and never more I want to roam;
I simply want to be back home, a-eatin' flap-jacks, hash,
and ham, with folks who savvy whom I am!*

*But when I get that lonely spell, I simply seek the best
hotel, no matter in what town I be—St. Paul, Toledo, or
K.C., in Washington, Schenectady, in Louisville or Albany.
And at that inn it hits my dome that I again am right at
home. If I should stand a lengthy spell in front of that first-
class hotel, that to the drummers loves to cater, across from
some big film theayter; if I should look around and buzz,
and wonder in what town I was, I swear that I could never
tell! For all the crowd would be so swell, in just the same
fine sort of jeans they wear at home, and all the queens with
spiffy bonnets on their beans, and all the fellows standing
round a-talkin' always, I'll be bound, the same good jolly
kind of guff, 'bout autos, politics and stuff and baseball
players of renown that Nice Guys talk in my home town!*

*Then when I entered that hotel, I'd look around and say,
"Well, well!" For there would be the same news-stand, same
magazines and candies grand, same smokes of famous
standard brand, I'd find at home, I'll tell! And when I saw
the jolly bunch come waltzing in for eats at lunch, and
squaring up in natty duds to platters large of French Fried
spuds, why then I'd stand right up and bawl, "I've never left
my home at all!" And all replete I'd sit me down beside some
guy in derby brown upon a lobby chair of plush, and murmur to him in a rush, "Hello, Bill, tell me, good old scout,
how is your stock a-holdin' out?" Then we'd be off, two
solid pals, a-chatterin' like giddy gals of flivvers, weather,
home, and wives, lodge-brothers then for all our lives! So
when Sam Satan makes you blue, good friend, that's what
I'd up and do, for in these States where'er you roam, you
never leave your home sweet home.*

" 'Yes, sir, these other burgs are our true partners in the
great game of vital living. But let's not have any mistake
about this. I claim that Zenith is the best partner and the
fastest-growing partner of the whole caboodle. I trust I may
be pardoned if I give a few statistics to back up my claims.
If they are old stuff to any of you, yet the tidings of prosperity, like the good news of the Bible, never become tedious
to the ears of a real hustler, no matter how oft the sweet

story is told! Every intelligent person knows that Zenith manufactures more condensed milk and evaporated cream, more paper boxes, and more lighting-fixtures, than any other city in the United States, if not in the world. But it is not so universally known that we also stand second in the manufacture of package-butter, sixth in the giant realm of motors and automobiles, and somewhere about third in cheese, leather findings, tar roofing, breakfast food, and overalls!

" 'Our greatness, however, lies not alone in punchful prosperity but equally in that public spirit, that forward-looking idealism and brotherhood, which has marked Zenith ever since its foundation by the Fathers. We have a right, indeed we have a duty toward our fair city, to announce broadcast the facts about our high schools, characterized by their complete plants and the finest school-ventilating systems in the country, bar none; our magnificent new hotels and banks and the paintings and carved marble in their lobbies; and the Second National Tower, the second highest business building in any inland city in the entire country. When I add that we have an unparalleled number of miles of paved streets, bathrooms, vacuum cleaners, and all the other signs of civilization; that our library and art museum are well supported and housed in convenient and roomy buildings; that our park-system is more than up to par, with its handsome driveways adorned with grass, shrubs, and statuary, then I give but a hint of the all-round unlimited greatness of Zenith!

" 'I believe, however, in keeping the best to the last. When I remind you that we have one motor car for every five and seven-eights persons in the city, then I give a rock-ribbed practical indication of the kind of progress and braininess which is synonymous with the name Zenith!

" 'But the way of the righteous is not all roses. Before I close I must call your attention to a problem we have to face, this coming year. The worst menace to sound government is not the avowed socialists but a lot of cowards who work under cover—the long-haired gentry who call themselves "liberals" and "radicals" and "non-partisan" and "intelligentsia" and God only knows how many other trick names! Irresponsible teachers and professors constitute the worst of this whole gang, and I am ashamed to say that several of them are on the faculty of our great State University! The U. is my own Alma Mater, and I am proud to be known as an alumni, but there are certain instructors there who seem to think we ought to turn the conduct of the nation over to hoboes and roustabouts.

" 'Those profs are the snakes to be scotched—they and all their milk-and-water ilk! The American business man is generous to a fault, but one thing he does demand of all teachers and lecturers and journalists: if we're going to pay them our good money, they've got to help us by selling efficiency and whooping it up for rational prosperity! And when it comes to these blab-mouth, fault-finding, pessimistic, cynical University teachers, let me tell you that during this golden coming year it's just as much our duty to bring influence to have those cusses fired as it is to sell all the real estate and gather in all the good shekels we can.

" 'Not till that is done will our sons and daughters see that the ideal of American manhood and culture isn't a lot of cranks sitting around chewing the rag about their Rights and their Wrongs, but a God-fearing, hustling, successful, two-fisted Regular Guy, who belongs to some church with pep and piety to it, who belongs to the Boosters or the Rotarians or the Kiwanis, to the Elks or Moose or Red Men or Knights of Columbus or any one of a score of organizations of good, jolly, kidding, laughing, sweating, upstanding, lend-a-handing Royal Good Fellows, who plays hard and works hard, and whose answer to his critics is a square-toed boot that'll teach the grouches and smart alecks to respect the He-man and get out and root for Uncle Samuel, U.S.A.!' "

IV

Babbitt promised to become a recognized orator. He entertained a Smoker of the Men's Club of the Chatham Road Presbyterian Church with Irish, Jewish, and Chinese dialect stories.

But in nothing was he more clearly revealed as the Prominent Citizen than in his lecture on "Brass Tacks Facts on Real Estate," as delivered before the class in Sales Methods at the Zenith Y.M.C.A.

The *Advocate-Times* reported the lecture so fully that Vergil Gunch said to Babbitt, "You're getting to be one of the classiest spellbinders in town. Seems 's if I couldn't pick up a paper without reading about your well-known eloquence. All this guff ought to bring a lot of business into your office. Good work! Keep it up!"

"Go on, quit your kidding," said Babbitt feebly, but at this tribute from Gunch, himself a man of no mean oratorical fame, he expanded with delight and wondered how, before his vacation, he could have questioned the joys of being a solid citizen.

chapter 15

HIS march to greatness was not without disastrous stumbling.

Fame did not bring the social advancement which the Babbitts deserved. They were not asked to join the Tonawanda Country Club nor invited to the dances at the Union. Himself, Babbitt fretted, he didn't "care a fat hoot for all these highrollers, but the wife would kind of like to be Among Those Present." He nervously awaited his university class-dinner and an evening of furious intimacy with such social leaders as Charles McKelvey the millionaire contractor, Max Kruger the banker, Irving Tate the tool-manufacturer, and Adelbert Dobson the fashionable interior decorator. Theoretically he was their friend, as he had been in college, and when he encountered them they still called him "Georgie," but he didn't seem to encounter them often, and they never invited him to dinner (with champagne and a butler) at their houses on Royal Ridge.

All the week before the class-dinner he thought of them. "No reason why we shouldn't become real chummy now!"

II

Like all true American diversions and spiritual outpourings, the dinner of the men of the Class of 1896 was thoroughly organized. The dinner-committee hammered like a sales-corporation. Once a week they sent out reminders:

TICKLER NO. 3

Old man, are you going to be with us at the livest Friendship Feed the alumni of the good old U have ever known? The alumnæ of '08 turned out 60% strong. Are we boys going to be beaten by a bunch of skirts? Come on, fellows, let's work up some real genuine enthusiasm and all boost together for the snappiest dinner yet! Elegant eats, short ginger-talks, and memories shared together of the brightest, gladdest days of life.

The dinner was held in a private room at the Union Club. The club was a dingy building, three pretentious old dwellings knocked together, and the entrance-hall resembled a potato cellar, yet the Babbitt who was free of the magnificence of the Athletic Club entered with embarrassment. He nodded to the doorman, an ancient proud negro with brass buttons and a blue tail-coat, and paraded through the hall, trying to look like a member.

Sixty men had come to the dinner. They made islands and eddies in the hall; they packed the elevator and the corners of the private dining-room. They tried to be intimate and enthusiastic. They appeared to one another exactly as they had in college—as raw youngsters whose present mustaches, baldnesses, paunches, and wrinkles were but jovial disguises put on for the evening. "You haven't changed a particle!" they marveled. The men whom they could not recall they addressed, "Well, well, great to see you again, old man. What are you— Still doing the same thing?"

Some one was always starting a cheer or a college song, and it was always thinning into silence. Despite their resolution to be democratic they divided into two sets: the men with dress-clothes and the men without. Babbitt (extremely in dress-clothes) went from one group to the other. Though he was, almost frankly, out for social conquest, he sought Paul Riesling first. He found him alone, neat and silent.

Paul sighed, "I'm no good at this handshaking and 'well, look who's here' bunk."

"Rats now, Paulibus, loosen up and be a mixer! Finest bunch of boys on earth! Say, you seem kind of glum. What's matter?"

"Oh, the usual. Run-in with Zilla."

"Come on! Let's wade in and forget our troubles."

He kept Paul beside him, but worked toward the spot where Charles McKelvey stood warming his admirers like a furnace.

McKelvey had been the hero of the Class of '96; not only football captain and hammer-thrower but debater, and passable in what the State University considered scholarship. He had gone on, had captured the construction-company once owned by the Dodsworths, best-known pioneer family of Zenith. He built state capitols, skyscrapers, railway terminals. He was a heavy-shouldered, big-chested man, but not sluggish. There was a quiet humor in his eyes, a syrup-smooth quickness in his speech, which intimidated politicians and warned reporters; and in his presence the most intelligent scientist or the most sensitive artist felt thin-blooded, unworldly, and a little shabby. He was, particularly when he was influencing legislatures or hiring labor-spies, very easy and lovable and gorgeous. He was baronial; he was a peer in the rapidly crystallizing American aristocracy, inferior only to the haughty Old Families. (In Zenith, an Old Family is one which came to town before 1840.) His power was the greater because he was not hindered by scruples, by either the vice or the virtue of the older Puritan tradition.

McKelvey was being placidly merry now with the great, the manufacturers and bankers, the land-owners and lawyers and surgeons who had chauffeurs and went to Europe. Babbitt squeezed among them. He liked McKelvey's smile as much as the social advancement to be had from his favor. If in Paul's company he felt ponderous and protective, with McKelvey he felt slight and adoring.

He heard McKelvey say to Max Kruger, the banker, "Yes, we'll put up Sir Gerald Doak." Babbitt's democratic love for titles became a rich relish. "You know, he's one of the biggest iron-men in England, Max. Horribly well-off. . . . Why, hello, old Georgie! Say, Max, George Babbitt is getting fatter than I am!"

The chairman shouted, "Take your seats, fellows!"

"Shall we make a move, Charley?" Babbitt said casually to McKelvey.

"Right. Hello, Paul! How's the old fiddler? Planning to sit anywhere special, George? Come on, let's grab some seats. Come on, Max. Georgie, I read about your speeches in the campaign. Bully work!"

After that, Babbitt would have followed him through fire. He was enormously busy during the dinner, now bumblingly cheering Paul, now approaching McKelvey with "Hear, you're going to build some piers in Brooklyn," now noting how enviously the failures of the class, sitting by themselves in a weedy group, looked up to him in his association with the nobility, now warming himself in the Society Talk of McKelvey and Max Kruger. They spoke of a "jungle dance" for which Mona Dodsworth had decorated her house with thousands of orchids. They spoke, with an excellent imitation of casualness, of a dinner in Washington at which McKelvey had met a Senator, a Balkan princess, and an English major-general. McKelvey called the princess "Jenny," and let it be known that he had danced with her.

Babbitt was thrilled, but not so weighted with awe as to be silent. If he was not invited by them to dinner, he was yet accustomed to talking with bank-presidents, congressmen, and clubwomen who entertained poets. He was bright and referential with McKelvey:

"Say, Charley, juh remember in Junior year how we chartered a sea-going hack and chased down to Riverdale, to the big show Madame Brown used to put on? Remember how you beat up that hick constabule that tried to run us in, and we pinched the pants-pressing sign and took and hung it on Prof. Morrison's door? Oh, gosh, those were the days!"

Those, McKelvey agreed, were the days.

Babbitt had reached "It isn't the books you study in college but the friendships you make that counts" when the men at head of the table broke into song. He attacked McKelvey:

"It's a shame, uh, shame to drift apart because our, uh, business activities lie in different fields. I've enjoyed talking over the good old days. You and Mrs. McKelvey must come to dinner some night."

Vaguely, "Yes, indeed—"

"Like to talk to you about the growth of real estate out beyond your Grantsville warehouse. I might be able to tip you off to a thing or two, possibly."

"Splendid! We must have dinner together, Georgie. Just let me know. And it will be a great pleasure to have your wife and you at the house," said McKelvey, much less vaguely.

Then the chairman's voice, the prodigious voice which once had roused them to cheer defiance at rooters from Ohio or Michigan or Indiana, whooped, "Come on, you wombats! All together in the long yell!" Babbitt felt that life would never be sweeter than now, when he joined with Paul Riesling and the newly recovered hero, McKelvey, in:

Baaaaaattle-ax
Get an ax,
Bal-ax,
Get-nax,
Who, who? The U.!
Hooroo!

III

The Babbitts invited the McKelveys to dinner, in early December, and the McKelveys not only accepted but, after changing the date once or twice, actually came.

The Babbitts somewhat thoroughly discussed the details of the dinner, from the purchase of a bottle of champagne to the number of salted almonds to be placed before each person. Especially did they mention the matter of the other guests. To the last Babbitt held out for giving Paul Riesling the benefit of being with the McKelveys. "Good old Charley would like Paul and Verg Gunch better than some highfalutin' Willy boy," he insisted, but Mrs. Babbitt interrupted his observations with, "Yes—perhaps— I think I'll try to get some Lynnhaven oysters," and when she was quite ready she invited Dr. J. T. Angus, the oculist, and a dismally respectable lawyer named Maxwell, with their glittering wives.

Neither Angus nor Maxwell belonged to the Elks or to the Athletic Club; neither of them had ever called Babbitt "brother" or asked his opinions on carburetors. The only "human people" whom she invited, Babbitt raged, were the Littlefields; and Howard Littlefield at times became so statistical that Babbitt longed for the refreshment of Gunch's, "Well, old lemon-pie-face, what's the good word?"

Immediately after lunch Mrs. Babbitt began to set the table for the seven-thirty dinner to the McKelveys, and Babbitt was, by order, home at four. But they didn't find anything for him to do, and three times Mrs. Babbitt scolded, "Do please try to keep out of the way!" He stood in the door of the garage, his lips drooping, and wished that Littlefield or Sam Doppelbrau or somebody would come along and talk to him. He saw Ted sneaking about the corner of the house.

"What's the matter, old man?" said Babbitt.

"Is that you, thin, owld one? Gee, Ma Certainly is on the warpath! I told her Rone and I would jus' soon not be let in on the fiesta to-night, and she bit me. She says I got to take a bath, too. But, say, the Babbitt men will be some lookers to-night! Little Theodore in a dress-suit!"

"The Babbitt men!" Babbitt liked the sound of it. He put his
arm about the boy's shoulder. He wished that Paul Riesling
had a daughter, so that Ted might marry her. "Yes, your
mother is kind of rouncing round, all right," he said, and they
laughed together, and sighed together, and dutifully went in
to dress.

The McKelveys were less than fifteen minutes late.

Babbitt hoped that the Doppelbraus would see the Mc-
Kelveys' limousine, and their uniformed chauffeur, waiting in
front.

The dinner was well cooked and incredibly plentiful, and
Mrs. Babbitt had brought out her grandmother's silver candle-
sticks. Babbitt worked hard. He was good. He told none of the
jokes he wanted to tell. He listened to the others. He started
Maxwell off with a resounding, "Let's hear about your trip to
the Yellowstone." He was laudatory, extremely laudatory.
He found opportunities to remark that Dr. Angus was a
benefactor to humantiy, Maxwell and Howard Littlefield profound scholars, Charles McKelvey an inspiration to ambitious youth, and Mrs. McKelvey an adornment to the social
circles of Zenith, Washington, New York, Paris, and numbers
of other places.

But he could not stir them. It was a dinner without a soul.
For no reason that was clear to Babbitt, heaviness was over
them and they spoke laboriously and unwillingly.

He concentrated on Lucile McKelvey, carefully not looking at her blanched lovely shoulder and the tawny silken band
which supported her frock.

"I suppose you'll be going to Europe pretty soon again,
won't you?" he invited.

"I'd like awfully to run over to Rome for a few weeks."

"I suppose you see a lot of pictures and music and curios
and everything there."

"No, what I really go for is: there's a little *trattoria* on the
Via della Scrofa where you get the best *fettuccine* in the
world."

"Oh, I— Yes. That must be nice to try that. Yes."

At a quarter to ten McKelvey discovered with profound
regret that his wife had a headache. He said blithely, as
Babbitt helped him with his coat, "We must lunch together
some time, and talk over the old days."

When the others had labored out, at half-past ten, Babbitt
turned to his wife, pleading, "Charley said he had a corking

time and we must lunch—said they wanted to have us up to the house for dinner before long."

She achieved, "Oh, it's just been one of those quiet evenings that are often so much more enjoyable than noisy parties where everybody talks at once and doesn't really settle down to—nice quiet enjoyment."

But from his cot on the sleeping-porch he heard her weeping, slowly, without hope.

IV

For a month they watched the social columns, and waited for a return dinner-invitation.

As the hosts of Sir Gerald Doak, the McKelveys were headlined all the week after the Babbitts' dinner. Zenith ardently received Sir Gerald (who had come to America to buy coal). The newspapers interviewed him on prohibition, Ireland, unemployment, naval aviation, the rate of exchange, tea-drinking *versus* whisky-drinking, the psychology of American women, and daily life as lived by English county families. Sir Gerald seemed to have heard of all those topics. The McKelveys gave him a Singhalese dinner, and Miss Elnora Pearl Bates, society editor of the *Advocate-Times*, rose to her highest lark note. Babbitt read aloud at breakfast-table:

'Twixt the original and Oriental decorations, the strange and delicious food, and the personalities both of the distinguished guests, the charming hostess and the noted host, never has Zenith seen a more recherche affair than the Ceylon dinner-dance given last evening by Mr. and Mrs. Charles McKelvey to Sir Gerald Doak. Methought as we —fortunate one!—were privileged to view that fairy and foreign scene, nothing at Monte Carlo or the choicest ambassadorial sets of foreign capitals could be more lovely. It is not for nothing that Zenith is in matters social rapidly becoming known as the choosiest inland city in the country.

Though he is too modest to admit it, Lord Doak gives a cachet to our smart quartier such as it has not received since the ever-memorable visit of the Earl of Sittingbourne. Not only is he of the British peerage, but he is also, on dit, a leader of the British metal industries. As he comes from Nottingham, a favorite haunt of Robin Hood, though now, we are informed by Lord Doak, a live modern city of 275,573 inhabitants, and important lace as well as other industries, we like to think that perhaps through his veins runs some of the blood, both virile red and bonny blue, of that earlier lord o' the good greenwood, the roguish Robin. The lovely Mrs. McKelvey never was more fascinating than last evening in her black net gown relieved by dainty bands of silver and at her exquisite waist a glowing cluster of Aaron Ward roses.

Babbitt said bravely, "I hope they don't invite us to meet this Lord Doak guy. Darn sight rather just have a nice quite little dinner with Charley and the Missus."

At the Zenith Athletic Club they discussed it amply. "I s'pose we'll have to call McKelvey 'Lord Chaz' from now on," said Sidney Finkelstein.

"It beats all get-out," meditated that man of data, Howard Littlefield, "how hard it is for some people to get things straight. Here they call this fellow 'Lord Doak' when it ought to be 'Sir Gerald.' "

Babbitt marvelled, "Is that a fact! Well, well! 'Sir Gerald,' eh? That's what you call um, eh? Well, sir, I'm glad to know that."

Later he informed his salesmen, "It's funnier 'n a goat the way some folks that, just because they happen to lay up a big wad, go entertaining famous foreigners, don't have any more idea 'n a rabbit how to address 'em so's to make 'em feel at home!"

That evening, as he was driving home, he passed Mc-Kelvey's limousine and saw Sir Gerald, a large, ruddy, pop-eyed, Teutonic Englishman whose dribble of yellow mustache gave him an aspect sad and doubtful. Babbitt drove on slowly, oppressed by futility. He had a sudden, unexplained, and horrible conviction that the McKelveys were laughing at him.

He betrayed his depression by the violence with which he informed his wife, "Folks that really tend to business haven't got the time to waste on a bunch like the McKelveys. This society stuff is like any other hobby; if you devote your-self to it, you get on. But I like to have a chance to visit with you and the children instead of all this idiotic chasing round."

They did not speak of the McKelveys again.

V

It was a shame, at this worried time, to have to think about the Overbrooks.

Ed Overbrook was a classmate of Babbitt who had been a failure. He had a large family and a feeble insurance business out in the suburb of Dorchester. He was gray and thin and unimportant. He had always been gray and thin and unimportant. He was the person whom, in any group, you forgot to introduce, then introduced with extra enthusiasm. He had admired Babbitt's good-fellowship in college, had admired ever since his power in real estate, his beautiful house and wonderful clothes. It pleased Babbitt, though it bothered him with a sense of responsibility. At the class-dinner he had seen poor Overbrook, in a shiny blue serge business-suit, being diffident in a corner with three other failures. He had gone over and been cordial: "Why, hello, young Ed! I hear you're writing all the insurance in Dorchester now. Bully work!"

They recalled the good old days when Overbrook used to write poetry. Overbrook embarrassed him by blurting, "Say, Georgie, I hate to think of how we been drifting apart. I wish you and Mrs. Babbitt would come to dinner some night."

Babbitt boomed, "Fine! Sure! Just let me know. And the wife and I want to have you at the house." He forgot it, but unfortunately Ed Overbrook did not. Repeatedly he telephoned to Babbitt, inviting him to dinner. "Might as well go and get it over," Babbitt groaned to his wife. "But don't it simply amaze you the way the poor fish doesn't know the first thing about social etiquette? Think of him 'phoning me, instead of his wife sitting down and writing us a regular bid! Well, I guess we're stuck for it. That's the trouble with all this class-brother hooptedoodle."

He accepted Overbrook's next plaintive invitation, for an evening two weeks off. A dinner two weeks off, even a family dinner, never seems so appalling, till the two weeks have astoundingly disappeared and one comes dismayed to the ambushed hour. They had to change the date, because of their own dinner to the McKelveys, but at last they gloomily drove out to the Overbrooks' house in Dorchester.

It was miserable from the beginning. The Overbrooks had dinner at six-thirty, while the Babbitts never dined before seven. Babbitt permitted himself to be ten minutes late. "Let's make it as short as possible. I think we'll duck out quick. I'll say I have to be at the office extra early to-morrow," he planned.

The Overbrook house was depressing. It was the second story of a wooden two-family dwelling; a place of baby-carriages, old hats hung in the hall, cabbage-smell, and a Family Bible on the parlor table. Ed Overbrook and his wife were as awkward and threadbare as usual, and the other guests were two dreadful families whose names Babbitt never caught and never desired to catch. But he was touched, and disconcerted, by the tactless way in which Overbrook praised him: "We're mighty proud to have old George here to-night! Of course you've all read about his speeches and oratory in the papers—and the boy's good-looking, too, eh?—but what I always think of is back in college, and what a great old mixer he was, and one of the best swimmers in the class."

Babbitt tried to be jovial; he worked at it; but he could find nothing to interest him in Overbrook's timorousness, the blankness of the other guests, or the drained stupidity of Mrs. Overbrook, with her spectacles, drab skin, and tight-drawn hair. He told his best Irish story, but it sank like soggy cake. Most bleary moment of all was when Mrs. Overbrook, peering out of her fog of nursing eight children and cooking and scrubbing, tried to be conversational.

"I suppose you go to Chicago and New York right along, Mr. Babbitt," she prodded.

"Well, I get to Chicago fairly often."

"It must be awfully interesting. I suppose you take in all the theaters."

"Well, to tell the truth, Mrs. Overbrook, thing that hits me best is a great big beefsteak at a Dutch restaurant in the Loop!"

They had nothing more to say. Babbitt was sorry, but there was no hope; the dinner was a failure. At ten, rousing out of the stupor of meaningless talk, he said as cheerily as he could, " 'Fraid we got to be starting, Ed. I've got a fellow coming to see me early to-morrow." As Overbrook helped him with his coat, Babbitt said, "Nice to rub up on the old days! We must have lunch together, P.D.Q."

Mrs. Babbitt sighed, on their drive home, "It was pretty terrible. But how Mr. Overbrook does admire you!"

"Yep. Poor cuss! Seems to think I'm a little tin archangel, and the best-looking man in Zenith."

"Well, you're certainly not that but— Oh, Georgie, you don't suppose we have to invite them to dinner at our house now, do we?"

"Ouch! Gaw, I hope not!"

"See here, now, George! You didn't say anything about it to Mr. Overbrook, did you?"

"No! Gee! No! Honest, I didn't! Just made a bluff about having him to lunch some time."

"Well. . . . Oh, dear. . . . I don't want to hurt their feelings. But I don't see how I could stand another evening like this one. And suppose somebody like Dr. and Mrs. Angus came in when we had the Overbrooks there, and thought they were friends of ours!"

For a week they worried, "We really ought to invite Ed and his wife, poor devils!" But as they never saw the Overbrooks, they forgot them, and after a month or two they said, "That really was the best way, just to let it slide. It wouldn't be kind to *them* to have them here. They'd feel so out of place and hard-up in our home."

They did not speak of the Overbrooks again.

chapter 16

THE certainty that he was not going to be accepted by the McKelveys made Babbitt feel guilty and a little absurd. But he went more regularly to the Elks; at a Chamber of Commerce luncheon he was oratorical regarding the wickedness of strikes; and again he saw himself as a Prominent Citizen.

His clubs and associations were food comfortable to his spirit.

Of a decent man in Zenith it was required that he should belong to one, preferably two or three, of the innumerous "lodges" and prosperity-boosting lunch-clubs; to the Rotarians, the Kiwanis, or the Boosters; to the Oddfellows, Moose, Masons, Red Men, Woodmen, Owls, Eagles, Maccabees, Knights of Pythias, Knights of Columbus, and other secret orders characterized by a high degree of heartiness, sound morals, and reverence for the Constitution. There were four reasons for joining these orders: It was the thing to do. It was good for business, since lodge-brothers frequently became customers. It gave to Americans unable to become Geheimräte or Commendatori such unctuous honorifics as High Worthy Recording Scribe and Grand Hoogow to add to the commonplace distinctions of Colonel, Judge, and Professor. And it permitted the swaddled American husband to stay away from home for one evening a week. The lodge was his piazza, his pavement café. He could shoot pool and talk man-talk and be obscene and valiant.

Babbitt was what he called a "joiner" for all these reasons.

Behind the gold and scarlet banner of his public achievements was the dun background of office-routine: leases, sales-contracts, lists of properties to rent. The evenings of oratory and committees and lodges stimulated him like brandy, but every morning he was sandy-tongued. Week by week he accumulated nervousness. He was in open disagreement with his outside salesman, Stanley Graff; and once, though her charms had always kept him nickeringly polite to her, he snarled at Miss McGoun for changing his letters.

But in the presence of Paul Riesling he relaxed. At least once a week they fled from maturity. On Saturday they played golf, jeering, "As a golfer, you're a fine tennis-player," or they motored all Sunday afternoon, stopping at village lunchrooms to sit on high stools at a counter and drink coffee from thick cups. Sometimes Paul came over in the evening with his violin, and even Zilla was silent as the lonely man who had lost his way and forever crept down unfamiliar roads spun out his dark soul in music.

II

Nothing gave Babbitt more purification and publicity than his labors for the Sunday School.

His church, the Chatham Road Presbyterian, was one of the largest and richest, one of the most oaken and velvety, in Zenith. The pastor was the Reverend John Jennison Drew, M.A., D.D., LL.D. (The M.A. and the D.D. were from Elbert University, Nebraska, the LL.D. from Waterbury College, Oklahoma.) He was eloquent, efficient, and versatile. He presided at meetings for the denunciation of unions or the elevation of domestic service, and confided to the audiences that as a poor boy he had carried newspapers. For the Saturday edition of the *Evening Advocate* he wrote editorials on "The Manly Man's Religion" and "The Dollars and Sense Value of Christianity," which were printed in bold type surrounded by a wiggly border. He often said that he was "proud to be known as primarily a business man" and that he certainly was not going to "permit the old Satan to monopolize all the pep and punch." He was a thin, rustic-faced young man with gold spectacles and a bang of dull brown hair, but when he hurled himself into oratory he glowed with power. He admitted that he was too much the scholar and poet to imitate the evangelist, Mike Monday, yet he had once awakened his fold to new life, and to larger collections, by the challenge, "My brethren, the real cheap skate is the man who won't lend to the Lord!"

He had made his church a true community center. It contained everything but a bar. It had a nursery, a Thursday evening supper with a short bright missionary lecture afterward, a gymnasium, a fortnightly motion-picture show, a library of technical books for young workmen—though, unfortunately, no younger workman ever entered the church except to wash the windows or repair the furnace—and a sewing-circle which made short little pants for the children of the poor while Mrs. Drew read aloud from earnest novels.

Though Dr. Drew's theology was Presbyterian, his church-building was gracefully Episcopalian. As he said, it had the "most perdurable features of those noble ecclesiastical monuments of grand Old England which stand as symbols of the eternity of faith, religious and civil." It was built of cheery iron-spot brick in an improved Gothic style, and the main auditorium had indirect lighting from electric globes in lavish alabaster bowls.

On a December morning when the Babbitts went to church, Dr. John Jennison Drew was unusually eloquent. The crowd was immense. Ten brisk young ushers, in morning coats with white roses, were bringing folding chairs up from the basement. There was an impressive musical program, conducted by Sheldon Smeeth, educational director of the Y.M.C.A., who also sang the offertory. Babbitt cared less for this, because some misguided person had taught young Mr. Smeeth to smile, smile, smile while he was singing, but with all the appreciation of a fellow-orator he admired Dr. Drew's sermon. It had the intellectual quality which distinguished the Chatham Road congregation from the grubby chapels on Smith Street.

"At this abundant harvest-time of all the year," Dr. Drew chanted, "when, though stormy the sky and laborious the path to the drudging wayfarer, yet the hovering and bodiless spirit swoops back o'er all the labors and desires of the past twelve months, oh, then it seems to me there sounds behind all our apparent failures the golden chorus of greeting

from those passed happily on; and lo! on the dim horizon
we see behind dolorous clouds the mighty mass of mountains
—mountains of melody, mountains of mirth, mountains of
might!"

"I certainly do like a sermon with culture and thought
in it," meditated Babbitt.

At the end of the service he was delighted when the pastor, actively shaking hands at the door, twittered, "Oh,
Brother Babbitt, can you wait a jiffy? Want your advice."

"Sure, doctor! You bet!"

"Drop into my office. I think you'll like the cigars there."

Babbitt did like the cigars. He also liked the office, which
was distinguished from other offices only by the spirited
change of the familiar wall-placard to "This is the Lord's
Busy Day." Chum Frink came in, then William W. Eathorne.

Mr. Eathorne was the seventy-year-old president of the
First State Bank of Zenith. He still wore the delicate patches
of side-whiskers which had been the uniform of bankers in
1870. If Babbitt was envious of the Smart Set of the Mc-
Kelveys, before William Washington Eathorne he was rev-
erent. Mr. Eathorne had nothing to do with the Smart Set.
He was above it. He was the great-grandson of one of the
five men who founded Zenith, in 1792, and he was of the
third generation of bankers. He could examine credits, make
loans, promote or injure a man's business. In his presence
Babbitt breathed quickly and felt young.

The Reverend Dr. Drew bounced into the room and flow-
ered into speech:

"I've asked you gentlemen to stay so I can put a proposition before you. The Sunday School needs bucking up. It's
the fourth largest in Zenith, but there's no reason why we
should take anybody's dust. We ought to be first. I want to
request you, if you will, to form a committee of advice and
publicity for the Sunday School; look it over and make any
suggestions for its betterment, and then, perhaps, see that
the press gives us some attention—give the public some really
helpful and constructive news instead of all these murders
and divorces."

"Excellent," said the banker.

Babbitt and Frink were enchanted to join him.

III

If you had asked Babbitt what his religion was, he would
have answered in sonorous Boosters'-Club rhetoric, "My re-

ligion is to serve my fellow men, to honor my brother as
myself, and to do my bit to make life happier for one and
all." If you had pressed him for more detail, he would
have announced, "I'm a member of the Presbyterian Church,
and naturally, I accept its doctrines." If you had been so
brutal as to go on, he would have protested, "There's no use
discussing and arguing about religion; it just stirs up bad
feeling."

Actually, the content of his theology was that there was a
supreme being who had tried to make us perfect, but pre-
sumably had failed; that if one was a Good Man he would
go to a place called Heaven (Babbitt unconsciously pictured
it as rather like an excellent hotel with a pivate garden), but
if one was a Bad Man, that is, if he murdered or committed
burglary or used cocaine or had mistresses or sold non-exist-
ent real estate, he would be punished. Babbitt was uncertain,
however, about what he called "this business of Hell." He
explained to Ted, "Of course I'm pretty liberal; I don't exactly believe in a fire-and-brimstone Hell. Stands to reason,
though, that a fellow can't get away with all sorts of Vice
and not get nicked for it, see how I mean?"

Upon this theology he rarely pondered. The kernel of his
practical religion was that it was respectable, and beneficial
to one's business, to be seen going to services; that the church
kept the Worst Elements from being still worse; and that the
pastor's sermons, however dull they might seem at the time
of taking, yet had a voodooistic power which "did a fellow
good—kept him in touch with Higher Things."

His first investigations for the Sunday School Advisory
Committee did not inspire him.

He liked the Busy Folks' Bible Class, composed of mature
men and women and addressed by the old-school physician,
Dr. T. Atkins Jordan, in a sparkling style comparable to that
of the more refined humorous after-dinner speakers, but
when he went down to the junior classes he was disconcerted. He heard Sheldon Smeeth, educational director of
the Y.M.C.A. and leader of the church-choir, a pale but
strenuous young man with curly hair and a smile, teaching a
class of sixteen-year-old boys. Smeeth lovingly admonished
them, "Now, fellows, I'm going to have a Heart to Heart
Talk Evening at my house next Thursday. We'll get off by
ourselves and be frank about our Secret Worries. You can
just tell old Sheldy anything, like all the fellows do at the
Y. I'm going to explain frankly about the horrible practises

a kiddy falls into unless he's guided by a Big Brother, and about the perils and glory of Sex." Old Sheldy beamed damply; the boys looked ashamed; and Babbitt didn't know which way to turn his embarrassed eyes.

Less annoying but also much duller were the minor classes which were being instructed in philosophy and Oriental ethnology by earnest spinsters. Most of them met in the highly varnished Sunday School room, but there was an overflow to the basement, which was decorated with varicose water-pipes and lighted by small windows high up in the oozing wall. What Babbitt saw, however, was the First Congregational Church of Catawba. He was back in the Sunday School of his boyhood. He smelled again that polite stuffiness to be found only in church parlors; he recalled the case of drab Sunday School books: "Hetty, a Humble Heroine" and "Josephus, a Lad of Palestine;" he thumbed once more the high-colored text-cards which no boy wanted but no boy liked to throw away, because they were somehow sacred; he was tortured by the stumbling rote of thirty-five years ago, as in the vast Zenith church he listened to:

"Now, Edgar, you read the next verse. What does it mean when it says it's easier for a camel to go through a needle's eye? What does this teach us? Clarence! Please don't wiggle so! If you had studied your lesson you wouldn't be so fidgety. Now, Earl, what is the lesson Jesus was trying to teach his disciples? The one thing I want you to especially remember, boys, is the words, 'With God all things are possible.' Just think of that always—Clarence, *please* pay attention— just say 'With God all things are possible' whenever you feel discouraged, and, Alec, will you read the next verse; if you'd pay attention you wouldn't lose your place!"

Drone—drone—drone—gigantic bees that boomed in a cavern of drowsiness—

Babbitt started from his open-eyed nap, thanked the teacher for "the privilege of listening to her splendid teaching," and staggered on to the next circle.

After two weeks of this he had no suggestions whatever for the Reverend Dr. Drew.

Then he discovered a world of Sunday School journals, an enormous and busy domain of weeklies and monthlies which were as technical, as practical and forward-looking, as the real-estate columns or the shoe-trade magazines. He bought half a dozen of them at a religious book-shop and till after midnight he read them and admired.

He found many lucrative tips on "Focusing Appeals," "Scouting for New Members," and "Getting Prospects to Sign up with the Sunday School." He particularly liked the word "prospects," and he was moved by the rubric:

"The moral springs of the community's life lie deep in its Sunday Schools—its schools of religious instruction and inspiration. Neglect now means loss of spiritual vigor and moral power in years to come. . . . Facts like the above, followed by a straight-arm appeal, will reach folks who can never be laughed or jollied into doing their part."

Babbitt admitted, "That's so. I used to skin out of the ole Sunday School at Catawba every chance I got, but same time, I wouldn't be where I am to-day, maybe, if it hadn't been for its training in—in moral power. And all about the Bible. Great literature. Have to read some of it again, one of these days."

How scientifically the Sunday School could be organized he learned from an article in the *Westminster Adult Bible Class*:

"The second vice-president looks after the fellowship of the class. She chooses a group to help her. These become ushers. Every one who comes gets a glad hand. No one goes away a stranger. One member of the group stands on the doorstep and invites passers-by to come in."

Perhaps most of all Babbitt appreciated the remarks by William H. Ridgway in the *Sunday School Times:*

"If you have a Sunday School class without any pep and get-up-and-go in it, that is, without interest, that is uncertain in attendance, that acts like a fellow with the spring fever, let old Dr. Ridgway write you a prescription. Rx. Invite the Bunch for Supper."

The Sunday School journals were as well rounded as they were practical. They neglected none of the arts. As to music the *Sunday School Times* advertised that C. Harold Lowden, "known to thousands through his sacred compositions," had written a new masterpiece, "entitled 'Yearning for You.' The poem, by Harry D. Kerr, is one of the daintiest you could imagine and the music is indescribably beautiful. Critics are agreed that it will sweep the country. May be made into a charming sacred song by substituting the hymn words, 'I Heard the Voice of Jesus Say.' "

Even manual training was adequately considered. Babbitt noted an ingenious way of illustrating the resurrection of Jesus Christ:

"Model for Pupils to Make. Tomb with Rolling Door. —Use a square covered box turned upside down. Pull the cover forward a little to form a groove at the bottom. Cut a square door, also cut a circle of cardboard to more than cover the door. Cover the circular door and the tomb thickly with stiff mixture of sand, flour and water and let it dry. It was the heavy circular stone over the door the women found 'rolled away' on Easter morning. This is the story we are to 'Go—tell.' "

In their advertisements the Sunday School journals were thoroughly efficient. Babbitt was interested in a preparation which "takes the place of exercise for sedentary men by building up depleted nerve tissue, nourishing the brain and the digestive system." He was edified to learn that the selling of Bibles was a hustling and strictly competitive industry, and as an expert on hygiene he was pleased by the Sanitary Communion Outfit Company's announcement of "an improved and satisfactory outfit throughout, including highly polished beautiful mahogany tray. This tray eliminates all noise, is lighter and more easily handled than others and is more in keeping with the furniture of the church than a tray of any other material."

IV

He dropped the pile of Sunday School journals.

He pondered, "Now, there's a real he-world. Corking!

"Ashamed I haven't sat in more. Fellow that's an influence in the community—shame if he doesn't take part in a real virile hustling religion. Sort of Christianity Incorporated, you might say.

"But with all reverence.

"Some folks might claim these Sunday School fans are undignified and unspiritual and so on. Sure! Always some skunk to spring things like that! Knocking and sneering and tearing-down—so much easier than building up. But me, I certainly hand it to these magazines. They've brought ole George F. Babbitt into camp, and that's the answer to the critics!

"The more manly and practical a fellow is, the more he ought to lead the enterprising Christian life. Me for it! Cut out this carelessness and boozing and— Rone! Where the devil you been? This is a fine time o' night to be coming in!"

THERE are but three or four old houses in Floral Heights, and in Floral Heights an old house is one which was built before 1880. The largest of these is the residence of William Washington Eathorne, president of the First State Bank.

The Eathorne Mansion preserves the memory of the "nice parts" of Zenith as they appeared from 1860 to 1900. It is a red brick immensity with gray sandstone lintels and a roof of slate in courses of red, green, and dyspeptic yellow. There are two anemic towers, one roofed with copper, the other crowned with castiron ferns. The porch is like an open tomb; it is supported by squat granite pillars above which hang frozen cascades of brick. At one side of the house is a huge stained-glass window in the shape of a keyhole.

But the house has an effect not at all humorous. It embodies the heavy dignity of those Victorian financiers who ruled the generation between the pioneers and the brisk "sales-engineers" and created a somber oligarchy by gaining control of banks, mills, land, railroads, mines. Out of the dozen contradictory Zeniths which together make up the true and complete Zenith, none is so powerful and enduring yet none so unfamiliar to the citizens as the small, still, dry, polite, cruel Zenith of the William Eathornes; and for that tiny hierarchy the other Zeniths unwittingly labor and insignificantly die.

Most of the castles of the testy Victorian tetrarchs are gone now or decayed into boarding-houses, but the Eathorne Mansion remains virtuous and aloof, reminiscent of London, Back Bay, Rittenhouse Square. Its marble steps are scrubbed daily, the brass plate is reverently polished, and the lace curtains are as prim and superior as William Washington Eathorne himself.

With a certain awe Babbitt and Chum Frink called on Eathorne for a meeting of the Sunday School Advisory Committee; with uneasy stillness they followed a uniformed maid through catacombs of reception-rooms to the library. It was as unmistakably the library of a solid old banker as Eathorne's side-whiskers were the side-whiskers of a solid old banker. The books were most of them Standard Sets, with the correct and traditional touch of dim blue, dim gold, and glossy calf-skin. The fire was exactly correct and traditional; a small, quiet, steady fire, reflected by polished fire-irons. The oak desk was dark and old and altogether perfect; the chairs were gently supercilious.

Eathorne's inquiries as to the healths of Mrs. Babbitt, Miss Babbitt, and the Other Children were softly paternal, but Babbitt had nothing with which to answer him. It was indecent to think of using the "How's tricks, ole socks?" which gratified Virgil Gunch and Frink and Howard Littlefield—men who till now had seemed successful and urbane. Babbitt and Frink sat politely, and politely did Eathorne observe, opening his thin lips just wide enough to dismiss the words, "Gentlemen, before we begin our conference—you may have felt the cold in coming here—so good of you to save an old man the journey—shall we perhaps have a whisky toddy?"

So well trained was Babbitt in all the conversation that befits a Good Fellow that he almost disgraced himself with "Rather than make trouble, and always providin' there ain't any enforcement officers hiding in the waste-basket—" The words died choking in his throat. He bowed in flustered obedience. So did Chum Frink.

Eathorne rang for the maid.

The modern and luxurious Babbitt had never seen any one ring for a servant in a private house, except during meals. Himself, in hotels, had rung for bell-boys, but in the house you didn't hurt Matilda's feelings; you went out in the hall and shouted for her. Nor had he, since prohibition, known any one to be casual about drinking. It was extraordinary merely to sip his toddy and not cry, "Oh, maaaaan, this hits me right where I live!" And always, with the ecstasy of youth meeting greatness, he marveled, "That little fuzzy-face there, why, he could make me or break me! If he told my banker to call my loans—! Gosh! That quarter-sized

squirt! And looking like he hadn't got a single bit of hustle
to him! I wonder— Do we Boosters throw too many fits
about pep?"

From this thought he shuddered away, and listened de-
voutly to Eathorne's ideas on the advancement of the Sunday School, which were very clear and very bad.

Diffidently Babbitt outlined his own suggestions:

"I think if you analyze the needs of the school, in fact,
going right at it as if it was a merchandizing problem, of
course the one basic and fundamental need is growth. I pre-
sume we're all agreed we won't be satisfied till we build
up the biggest darn Sunday School in the whole state, so the
Chatham Road Presbyterian won't have to take anything off
anybody. Now about jazzing up the campaign for prospects:
they've already used contesting teams, and given prizes to the
kids that bring in the most members. And they made a mistake there: the prizes were a lot of folderols and doodads
like poetry books and illustrated Testaments, instead of something a real live kid would want to work for, like real cash or
a speedometer for his motor cycle. Course I suppose it's all
fine and dandy to illustrate the lessons with these decorated
book-marks and blackboard drawings and so on, but when it
comes down to real he-hustling, getting out and drumming up
customers—or members, I mean, why, you got to make it
worth a fellow's while.

"Now, I want to propose two stunts: First, divide the
Sunday School into four armies, depending on age. Everybody gets a military rank in his own army according to how
many members he brings in, and the duffers that lie down on
us and don't bring in any, they remain privates. The pastor
and superintendent rank as generals. And everybody has got
to give salutes and all the rest of that junk, just like a regular
army, to make 'em feel it's worth while to get rank.

"Then, second: Course the school has its advertising committee, but, Lord, nobody ever really works good—nobody
works well just for the love of it. The thing to do is to be
practical and up-to-date, and hire a real paid press-
agent for the Sunday School—some newspaper fellow who
can give part of his time."

"Sure, you bet!" said Chum Frink.

"Think of the nice juicy bits he could get in!" Babbitt
crowed. "Not only the big, salient, vital facts, about how
fast the Sunday School—and the collection—is growing, but
a lot of humorous gossip and kidding: about how some blow-

hard fell down on his pledge to get new members, or the good time the Sacred Trinity class of girls had at their wienie-wurst party. And on the side, if he had time, the press-agent might even boost the lessons themselves—do a little advertising for all the Sunday Schools in town, in fact. No use being hoggish toward the rest of 'em, providing we can keep the bulge on 'em in membership. Frinstance, he might get the papers to— Course I haven't got a literary training like Frink here, and I'm just guessing how the pieces ought to be written, but take frinstance, suppose the week's lesson is about Jacob; well, the press-agent might get in something that would have a fine moral, and yet with a trick headline that'd get folks to read it—say like: *Jake Fools the Old Man; Makes Getaway with Girl and Bankroll.* See how I mean? That'd get their interest! Now, course, Mr. Eathorne, you're con-servative, and maybe you feel these stunts would be undigni-fied, but honestly, I believe they'd bring home the bacon."

Eathorne folded his hands on his comfortable little belly and purred like an aged pussy:

"May I say, first, that I have been very much pleased by your analysis of the situation, Mr. Babbitt. As you surmise, it's necessary in My Position to be conservative, and per-haps endeavor to maintain a certain standard of dignity. Yet I think you'll find me somewhat progressive. In our bank, for example, I hope I may say that we have as modern a method of publicity and advertising as any in the city. Yes, I fancy you'll find us oldsters quite cognizant of the shifting spiritual values of the age. Yes, oh yes. And so, in fact, it pleases me to be able to say that though personally I might prefer the sterner Presbyterianism of an earlier era—"

Babbitt finally gathered that Eathorne was willing.

Chum Frink suggested as part-time press-agent one Ken-neth Escott, reporter on the *Advocate-Times.*

They parted on a high plane of amity and Christian help-fulness.

Babbitt did not drive home, but toward the center of the city. He wished to be by himself and exult over the beauty of intimacy with William Washington Eathorne.

II

A snow-blanched evening of ringing pavements and eager lights.

Great golden lights of trolley-cars sliding along the packed snow of the roadway. Demure lights of little houses. The belching glare of a distant foundry, wiping out the sharp-edged stars. Lights of neighborhood drug stores where friends gossiped, well pleased, after the day's work.

The green light of a police-station, and greener radiance on the snow; the drama of a patrol-wagon—gong beating like a terrified heart, headlights scorching the crystal-sparkling street, driver not a chauffeur but a policeman proud in uniform, another policeman perilously dangling on the step at the back, and a glimpse of the prisoner. A murderer, a burglar, a coiner cleverly trapped?

An enormous graystone church with a rigid spire; dim light in the Parlors, and cheerful droning of choir-practise. The quivering green mercury-vapor light of a photo-engraver's loft. Then the storming lights of down-town; parked cars with ruby tail-lights; white arched entrances to movie theaters, like frosty mouths of winter caves; electric signs—serpents and little dancing men of fire; pink-shaded globes and scarlet jazz music in a cheap up-stairs dance-hall; lights of Chinese restaurants, lanterns painted with cherry-blossoms and with pagodas, hung against lattices of lustrous gold and black. Small dirty lamps in small stinking lunch-rooms. The smart shopping-district, with rich and quiet light on crystal pendants and furs and suave surfaces of polished wood in velvet-hung reticent windows. High above the street, an unexpected square hanging in the darkness, the window of an office where some one was working late, for a reason unknown and stimulating. A man meshed in bankruptcy, an ambitious boy, an oil-man suddenly become rich?

The air was shrewd, the snow was deep in uncleared alleys, and beyond the city, Babbitt knew, were hillsides of snow-drift among wintry oaks, and the curving ice-enchanted river.

He loved his city with passionate wonder. He lost the accumulated weariness of business-worry and expansive oratory; he felt young and potential. He was ambitious. It was not enough to be a Vergil Gunch, an Orville Jones. No. "They're bully fellows, simply lovely, but they haven't got any finesse." No. He was going to be an Eathorne; delicately rigorous, coldly powerful.

"That's the stuff. The wallop in the velvet mitt. Not let anybody get fresh with you. Been getting careless about my diction. Slang. Colloquial. Cut it out. I was first-rate at rhetoric in college. Themes on— Anyway, not bad. Had

too much of this hooptedoodle and good-fellow stuff. I—
Why couldn't I organize a bank of my own some day? And
Ted succeed me!"

He drove happily home, and to Mrs. Babbitt he was a William Washington Eathorne, but she did not notice it.

III

Young Kenneth Escott, reporter on the *Advocate-Times,*
was appointed press-agent of the Chatham Road Presbyterian
Sunday School. He gave six hours a week to it. At least
he was paid for giving six hours a week. He had friends on
the *Press* and the *Gazette* and he was not (officially) known
as a press-agent. He procured a trickle of insinuating items
about neighborliness and the Bible, about class-suppers, jolly
but educational, and the value of the Prayer-life in attaining
financial success.

The Sunday School adopted Babbitt's system of military
ranks. Quickened by this spiritual refreshment, it had a
boom. It did not become the largest school in Zenith—the
Central Methodist Church kept ahead of it by methods which
Dr. Drew scored as "unfair, undignified, un-American, un-
gentlemanly, and unchristian"—but it climbed from fourth
place to second, and there was rejoicing in heaven, or at least
in that portion of heaven included in the parsonage of Dr.
Drew, while Babbitt had much praise and good repute.

He had received the rank of colonel on the general staff of
the school. He was plumply pleased by salutes on the street
from unknown small boys; his ears were tickled to ruddy
ecstasy by hearing himself called "Colonel;" and if he did not
attend Sunday School merely to be thus exalted, certainly he
thought about it all the way there.

He was particularly pleasant to the press-agent, Kenneth
Escott; he took him to lunch at the Athletic Club and had
him at the house for dinner.

Like many of the cocksure young men who forage about
cities in apparent contentment and who express their cynicism
in supercilious slang, Escott was shy and lonely. His shrewd
starveling face broadened with joy at dinner, and he blurted,
"Gee whillikins, Mrs. Babbitt, if you knew how good it is to
have home eats again!"

Escott and Verona liked each other. All evening they
"talked about ideas." They discovered that they were Radicals. True, they were sensible about it. They agreed that all

communists were criminals; that this *vers libre* was tommy-
rot; and that while there ought to be universal disarmament,
of course Great Britain and the United States must, on
behalf of oppressed small nations, keep a navy equal to the
tonnage of all the rest of the world. But they were so revolu-
tionary that they predicted (to Babbitt's irritation) that there
would some day be a Third Party which would give trouble to
the Republicans and Democrats.

Escott shook hands with Babbitt three times, at parting.
Babbitt mentioned his extreme fondness for Eathorne.

Within a week three newspapers presented accounts of Babbitt's sterling labors for religion, and all of them tactfully
mentioned William Washington Eathorne as his collaborator.

Nothing had brought Babbitt quite so much credit at the
Elks, the Athletic Club, and the Boosters'. His friends had
always congratulated him on his oratory, but in their praise
was doubt, for even in speeches advertising the city there was
something highbrow and degenerate, like writing poetry. But
now Orville Jones shouted across the Athletic dining-room,
"Here's the new director of the First State Bank!" Grover
Butterbaugh, the eminent wholesaler of plumbers' supplies,
chuckled, "Wonder you mix with common folks, after
holding Eathorne's hand!" And Emil Wengert, the jeweler,
was at last willing to discuss buying a house in Dorchester.

IV

When the Sunday School campaign was finished, Babbitt
suggested to Kenneth Escott, "Say, how about doing a little
boosting for Doc Drew personally?"

Escott grinned. "You trust the doc to do a little boosting
for himself, Mr. Babbitt! There's hardly a week goes by
without his ringing up the paper to say if we'll chase a reporter up to his Study, he'll let us in on the story about the swell
sermon he's going to preach on the wickedness of short
skirts, or the authorship of the Pentateuch. Don't you worry
about him. There's just one better publicity-grabber in town,
and that's this Dora Gibson Tucker that runs the Child
Welfare and the Americanization League, and the only reason
she's got Drew beaten is because she has got *some* brains!"

"Well, now Kenneth, I don't think you ought to talk that
way about the doctor. A preacher has to watch his interests,
hasn't he? You remember that in the Bible about—about
being diligent in the Lord's business, or something?"

"All right, I'll get something in if you want me to, Mr. Babbitt, but I'll have to wait till the managing editor is out of town, and then blackjack the city editor."

Thus it came to pass that in the Sunday *Advocate-Times*, under a picture of Dr. Drew at his earnestest, with eyes alert, jaw as granite, and rustic lock flamboyant, appeared an inscription—a wood-pulp tablet conferring twenty-four hours' immortality:

The Rev. Dr. John Jennison Drew, M.A., pastor of the beautiful Chatham Road Presbyterian Church in lovely Floral Heights, is a wizard soul-winner. He holds the local record for conversions. During his shepherdhood an average of almost a hundred sin-weary persons per year have declared their resolve to lead a new life and have found a harbor of refuge and peace.

Everything zips at the Chatham Road Church. The subsidiary organizations are keyed to the top-notch of efficiency. Dr. Drew is especially keen on good congregational singing. Bright cheerful hymns are used at every meeting, and the special Sing Services attract lovers of music and professionals from all parts of the city.

On the popular lecture platform as well as in the pulpit Dr. Drew is a renowned word-painter, and during the course of the year he receives literally scores of invitations to speak at varied functions both here and elsewhere.

v

Babbitt let Dr. Drew know that he was responsible for this tribute. Dr. Drew called him "brother," and shook his hand a great many times.

During the meetings of the Advisory Committee, Babbitt had hinted that he would be charmed to invite Eathorne to dinner, but Eathorne had murmured, "So nice of you—old man, now—almost never go out." Surely Eathorne would not refuse his own pastor. Babbitt said boyishly to Drew:

"Say, doctor, now we've put this thing over, strikes me it's up to the dominie to blow the three of us to a dinner!"

"Bully! You bet! Delighted!" cried Dr. Drew, in his manliest way. (Some one had once told him that he talked like the late President Roosevelt.)

"And, uh, say, doctor, be sure and get Mr. Eathorne to come. Insist on it. It's, uh— I think he sticks around home too much for his own health."

Eathorne came.

It was a friendly dinner. Babbitt spoke gracefully of the stabilizing and educational value of bankers to the community. They were, he said, the pastors of the fold of commerce. For the first time Eathorne departed from the topic of Sunday Schools, and asked Babbitt about the progress of his business. Babbitt answered modestly, almost filially.

A few months later, when he had a chance to take part in the Street Traction Company's terminal deal, Babbitt did not care to go to his own bank for a loan. It was rather a quiet sort of deal and, if it had come out, the Public might not have understood. He went to his friend Mr. Eathorne; he was welcomed, and received the loan as a private venture; and they both profited in their pleasant new association.

After that, Babbitt went to church regularly, except on spring Sunday mornings which were obviously meant for motoring. He announced to Ted, "I tell you, boy, there's no stronger bulwark of sound conservatism than the evangelical church, and no better place to make friends who'll help you to gain your rightful place in the community than in your own church-home!"

chapter 18

THOUGH he saw them twice daily, though he knew and amply discussed every detail of their expenditures, yet for weeks together Babbitt was no more conscious of his children than of the buttons on his coat-sleeves.

The admiration of Kenneth Escott made him aware of Verona.

She had become secretary to Mr. Gruensberg of the Gruensberg Leather Company; she did her work with the thoroughness of a mind which reveres details and never quite understands them; but she was one of the people who give an agitating impression of being on the point of doing something desperate—of leaving a job or a husband—without ever doing it. Babbitt was so hopeful about Escott's hesitant ardors that he became the playful parent. When he returned from the Elks he peered coyly into the living-room and gurgled, "Has our Kenny been here to-night?" He never credited Verona's protest, "Why, Ken and I are just good friends, and we only talk about Ideas. I won't have all this sentimental nonsense, that would spoil everything."

It was Ted who most worried Babbitt.

With conditions in Latin and English but with a triumphant record in manual training, basket-ball, and the organization of dances, Ted was struggling through his Senior year in the East Side High School. At home he was interested only when he was asked to trace some subtle ill in the ignition system of the car. He repeated to his tut-tutting father that he did not wish to go to college or law-school, and Babbitt was equally disturbed by this "shiftlessness" and by Ted's relations with Eunice Littlefield, next door.

Though she was the daughter of Howard Littlefield, that wrought-iron fact-mill, that horse-faced priest of private ownership, Eunice was a midge in the sun. She danced into the house, she flung herself into Babbitt's lap when he was reading, she crumpled his paper, and laughed at him when he adequately explained that he hated a crumpled newspaper as he hated a broken sales-contract. She was seventeen now. Her ambition was to be a cinema actress. She did not merely attend the showing of every "feature film;" she also read the motion-picture magazines, those extraordinary symptoms of the Age of Pep—monthlies and weeklies gorgeously illustrated with portraits of young women who had recently been manicure girls, not very skilful manicure girls, and who, unless their every grimace had been arranged by a director, could not have acted in the Easter cantata of the Central Methodist Church; magazines reporting, quite seriously, in "interviews" plastered with pictures of riding-breeches and California bungalows, the views on sculpture and international politics of blankly beautiful, suspiciously beautiful young men; outlining the plots of films about pure prostitutes and kind-hearted train-robbers; and giving directions for making bootblacks into Celebrated Scenario Authors overnight.

These authorities Eunice studied. She could, she frequently did, tell whether it was in November or December, 1905, that Mack Harker, the renowned screen cowpuncher and badman, began his public career, as chorus man in "Oh,

You Naughty Girlie." On the wall of her room, her father reported, she had pinned up twenty-one photographs of actors. But the signed portrait of the most graceful of the movie heroes she carried in her young bosom.

Babbitt was bewildered by this worship of new gods, and he suspected that Eunice smoked cigarettes. He smelled the cloying reek from up-stairs, and heard her giggling with Ted. He never inquired. The agreeable child dismayed him. Her thin and charming face was sharpened by bobbed hair; her skirts were short, her stockings were rolled, and, as she flew after Ted, above the caressing silk were glimpses of soft knees which made Babbitt uneasy, and wretched that she should consider him old. Sometimes, in the veiled life of his dreams, when the fairy child came running to him she took on the semblance of Eunice Littlefield.

Ted was motor-mad as Eunice was movie-mad.

A thousand sarcastic refusals did not check his teasing for a car of his own. However lax he might be about early rising and the prosody of Vergil, he was tireless in tinkering. With three other boys he bought a rheumatic Ford chassis, built an amazing racer-body out of tin and pine, went skidding round corners in the perilous craft, and sold it at a profit. Babbitt gave him a motor-cycle, and every Saturday afternoon, with seven sandwiches and a bottle of Coca-Cola in his pockets, and Eunice perched eerily on the rumble seat, he went roaring off to distant towns.

Usually Eunice and he were merely neighborhood chums, and quarreled with a wholesome and violent lack of delicacy; but now and then, after the color and scent of a dance, they were silent together and a little furtive, and Babbitt was worried.

Babbitt was an average father. He was affectionate, bullying, opinionated, ignorant, and rather wistful. Like most parents, he enjoyed the game of waiting till the victim was clearly wrong, then virtuously pouncing. He justified himself by croaking, "Well, Ted's mother spoils him. Got to be somebody who tells him what's what, and me, I'm elected the goat. Because I try to bring him up to be a real, decent, human being and not one of these sapheads and lounge-lizards, of course they all call me a grouch!"

Throughout, with the eternal human genius for arriving by the worst possible routes at surprisingly tolerable goals, Babbitt loved his son and warmed to his companionship and would have sacrificed everything for him—if he could have been sure of proper credit.

II

Ted was planning a party for his set in the Senior Class. Babbitt meant to be helpful and jolly about it. From his memory of high-school pleasures back in Catawba he suggested the nicest games: Going to Boston, and charades with stewpans for helmets, and word-games in which you were an Adjective or a Quality. When he was most enthusiastic he discovered that they weren't paying attention; they were only tolerating him. As for the party, it was as fixed and standarized as a Union Club Hop. There was to be dancing in the living-room, a noble collation in the dining-room, and in the hall two tables of bridge for what Ted called "the poor old dumb-bells that you can't get to dance hardly more 'n half the time."

Every breakfast was monopolized by conferences on the affair. No one listened to Babbitt's bulletins about the February weather or to his throat-clearing comments on the head-lines. He said furiously, "If I may be *permitted* to interrupt your engrossing private *conversation*— Juh hear what I *said?*"

"Oh, don't be a spoiled baby! Ted and I have just as much right to talk as you have!" flared Mrs. Babbitt.

On the night of the party he was permitted to look on, when he was not helping Matilda with the Vecchia ice cream and the *petits fours*. He was deeply disquieted. Eight years ago, when Verona had given a high-school party, the children had been featureless gabies. Now they were men and women of the world, very supercilious men and women; the boys condescended to Babbitt, they wore evening-clothes, and with hauteur they accepted cigarettes from silver cases. Babbitt had heard stories of what the Athletic Club called "goings-on" at young parties; of girls "parking" their corsets in the dressing-room, of "cuddling" and "petting," and a presumable increase in what was known as Immorality. To-night he believed the stories. These children seemed bold to him, and cold. The girls wore misty chiffon, coral velvet, or cloth of gold, and around their dipping bobbed hair were shining wreaths. He had it, upon urgent and secret inquiry, that no corsets were known to be parked upstairs; but certainly these eager bodies were not stiff with steel. Their stockings were of lustrous silk, their slippers costly and unnatural, their lips carmined and their eyebrows penciled. They danced cheek to cheek with the boys, and Babbitt sickened with apprehension and unconscious envy.

Worst of them all was Eunice Littlefield, and maddest of all the boys was Ted. Eunice was a flying demon. She slid the length of the room; her tender shoulders swayed; her feet were deft as a weaver's shuttle; she laughed, and enticed Babbitt to dance with her.

Then he discovered the annex to the party.

The boys and girls disappeared occasionally, and he remembered rumors of their drinking together from hip-pocket flasks. He tiptoed round the house, and in each of the dozen cars waiting in the street he saw the points of light from cigarettes, from each of them heard high giggles. He wanted to denounce them but (standing in the snow, peering round the dark corner) he did not dare. He tried to be tactful. When he had returned to the front hall he coaxed the boys, "Say, if any of you fellows are thirsty, there's some dandy ginger ale."

"Oh! Thanks!" they condescended.

He sought his wife, in the pantry, and exploded, "I'd like to go in there and throw some of those young pups out of the house! They talk down to me like I was the butler! I'd like to—"

"I know," she sighed; "only everybody says, all the mothers tell me, unless you stand for them, if you get angry because they go out to their cars to have a drink, they won't come to your house any more, and we wouldn't want Ted left out of things, would we?"

He announced that he would be enchanted to have Ted left out of things, and hurried in to be polite, lest Ted be left out of things.

But, he resolved, if he found that the boys were drinking, he would—well, he'd "hand 'em something that would surprise 'em." While he was trying to be agreeable to large-shouldered young bullies he was earnestly sniffing at them. Twice he caught the reek of prohibition-time whisky, but then, it was only twice—

Dr. Howard Littlefield lumbered in.

He had come, in a mood of solemn parental patronage, to look on. Ted and Eunice were dancing, moving together like one body. Littlefield gasped. He called Eunice. There was a whispered duologue, and Littlefield explained to Babbitt that

Eunice's mother had a headache and needed her. She went off in tears. Babbitt looked after them furiously. "That little devil! Getting Ted into trouble! And Littlefield, the conceited old gas-bag, acting like it was Ted that was the bad influence!"

Later he smelled whisky on Ted's breath.

After the civil farewell to the guests, the row was terrific, a thorough Family Scene, like an avalanche, devastating and without reticences. Babbitt thundered, Mrs. Babbitt wept, Ted was unconvincingly defiant, and Verona in confusion as to whose side she was taking.

For several months there was coolness between the Babbitts and the Littlefields, each family sheltering their lamb from the wolf-cub next door. Babbitt and Littlefield still spoke in pontifical periods about motors and the senate, but they kept bleakly away from mention of their families. Whenever Eunice came to the house she discussed with pleasant intimacy the fact that she had been forbidden to come to the house; and Babbitt tried, with no success whatever, to be fatherly and advisory with her.

III

"Gosh all fishhooks!" Ted wailed to Eunice, as they wolfed hot chocolate, lumps of nougat, and an assortment of glacé nuts, in the mosaic splendor of the Royal Drug Store, "it gets me why Dad doesn't just pass out from being so poky. Every evening he sits there, about half-asleep, and if Rone or I say, 'Oh, come on, let's do something,' he doesn't even take the trouble to think about it. He just yawns and says, 'Naw, this suits me right here.' He doesn't know there's any fun going on anywhere. I suppose he must do some thinking, same as you and I do, but gosh, there's no way of telling it. I don't believe that outside of the office and playing a little bum golf on Saturday he knows there's anything in the world to do except just keep sitting there—sitting there every night—not wanting to go anywhere—not wanting to do anything—thinking us kids are crazy—sitting there—Lord!"

IV

If he was frightened by Ted's slackness, Babbitt was not sufficiently frightened by Verona. She was too safe. She lived too much in the neat little airless room of her mind. Kenneth Escott and she were always under foot. When they were not at home, conducting their cautiously radical courtship over sheets of statistics, they were trudging off to lectures by authors and Hindu philosophers and Swedish lieutenants.

"Gosh," Babbitt wailed to his wife, as they walked home from the Fogartys' bridge-party, "it gets me how Rone and that fellow can be so poky. They sit there night after night, whenever he isn't working, and they don't know there's any fun in the world. All talk and discussion—Lord! Sitting there—sitting there—night after night—not wanting to do anything—thinking I'm crazy because I like to go out and play a fist of cards—sitting there—gosh!"

Then round the swimmer, bored by struggling through the perpetual surf of family life, new combers swelled.

V

Babbitt's father- and mother-in-law, Mr. and Mrs. Henry T. Thompson, rented their old house in the Bellevue district and moved to the Hotel Hatton, that glorified boarding-house filled with widows, red-plush furniture, and the sound of ice-water pitchers. They were lonely there, and every other Sunday evening the Babbitts had to dine with them, on fricasseed chicken, discouraged celery, and cornstarch ice cream, and afterward sit, polite and restrained, in the hotel lounge, while a young woman violinist played songs from the German via Broadway.

Then Babbitt's own mother came down from Catawba to spend three weeks.

She was a kind woman and magnificently uncomprehending. She congratulated the convention-defying Verona on being a "nice, loyal home-body without all these Ideas that so many girls seem to have nowadays;" and when Ted filled the differential with grease, out of pure love of mechanics and filthiness, she rejoiced that he was "so handy around the house and helping his father and all, and not going out with the girls all the time and trying to pretend he was a society fellow."

Babbitt loved his mother, and sometimes he rather liked her, but he was annoyed by her Christian Patience, and he was reduced to pulpiness when she discoursed about a quiet mythical hero called "Your Father":

"You won't remember it, Georgie, you were such a little fellow at the time—my, I remember just how you looked that day, with your goldy brown curls and your lace collar, you always were such a dainty child, and kind of puny and sickly, and you loved pretty things so much and the red tassels on your little bootees and all—and Your Father was taking us to church and a man stopped us and said 'Major'—so many of the neighbors used to call Your Father 'Major;' of course he was only a private in The War but everybody knew that was because of the jealousy of his captain and he ought to have been a high-ranking officer, he had that natural ability to command that so very, very few men have—and this man came out into the road and held up his hand and stopped the buggy and said, 'Major,' he said, 'there's a lot of the folks around here that have decided to support Colonel Scanell for congress, and we want you to join us. Meeting people the way you do in the store, you could help us a lot.'

"Well, Your Father just looked at him and said, 'I certainly shall do nothing of the sort. I don't like his politics,' he said. Well, the man—Captain Smith they used to call him, and heaven only knows why, because he hadn't the shadow or vestige of a right to be called 'Captain' or any other title —this Captain Smith said, 'We'll make it hot for you if you don't stick by your friends, Major.' Well, you know how Your Father was, and this Smith knew it too; he knew what a Real Man he was, and he knew Your Father knew the political situation from A to Z, and he ought to have seen that here was one man he couldn't impose on, but he went on trying to and hinting and trying till Your Father spoke up and said to him, 'Captain Smith,' he said, 'I have a reputation around these parts for being one who is amply qualified to mind his own business and let other folks mind theirs!' and with that he drove on and left the fellow standing there in the road like a bump on a log!"

Babbitt was most exasperated when she revealed his boyhood to the children. He had, it seemed, been fond of barley-sugar; had worn the "loveliest little pink bow in his curls" and corrupted his own name to 'Goo-goo.' He heard (though he did not officially hear) Ted admonishing Tinka, "Come on now, kid; stick the lovely pink bow in your curls and beat it down to breakfast, or Goo-goo will jaw your head off."

Babbitt's half-brother, Martin, with his wife and youngest baby, came down from Catawba for two days. Martin bred cattle and ran the dusty general-store. He was proud of being a freeborn independent American of the good old Yankee stock; he was proud of being honest, blunt, ugly, and disagreeable. His favorite remark was "How much did you pay for that?" He regarded Verona's books, Babbitt's silver pencil, and flowers on the table as citified extravagances, and said so. Babbitt would have quarreled with him but for his gawky wife and the baby, whom Babbitt teased and poked fingers at and addressed:

"I think this baby's a bum, yes, sir, I think this little baby's a bum, he's a bum, yes, sir, he's a bum, that's what he is, he's a bum, this baby's a bum, he's nothing but an old bum, that's what he is—a bum!"

All the while Verona and Kenneth Escott held long inquiries into epistemology; Ted was a disgraced rebel; and Tinka, aged eleven, was demanding that she be allowed to go to the movies thrice a week, "like all the girls."

Babbitt raged, "I'm sick of it! Having to carry three generations. Whole damn bunch lean on me. Pay half of mother's income, listen to Henry T., listen to Myra's worrying, be polite to Mart, and get called an old grouch for trying to help the children. All of 'em depending on me and picking on me and not a damn one of 'em grateful! No relief, and no credit, and no help from anybody. And to keep it up for—good Lord, how long?"

He enjoyed being sick in February; he was delighted by their consternation that he, the rock, should give way.

He had eaten a questionable clam. For two days he was languorous and petted and esteemed. He was allowed to snarl "Oh, let me alone!" without reprisals. He lay on the sleeping-porch and watched the winter sun slide along the taut curtains, turning their ruddy khaki to pale blood red. The shadow of the draw-rope was dense black, in an enticing ripple on the canvas. He found pleasure in the curve of it, sighed as the fading light blurred it. He was conscious of life, and a little sad. With no Vergil Gunches before whom to set his face in resolute optimism, he beheld, and half admitted that he beheld, his way of life as incredibly mechanical. Mechanical business—a brisk selling of badly built houses. Mechanical religion—a dry, hard church, shut off from the real life of the streets, inhumanly respectable as a top-hat. Mechanical golf and dinner-parties and bridge and conversation. Save with Paul Riesling, mechanical friendships—back-slapping and jocular, never daring to essay the test of quietness.

He turned uneasily in bed.

He saw the years, the brilliant winter days and all the

long sweet afternoons which were meant for summery meadows, lost in such brittle pretentiousness. He thought of telephoning about leases, of cajoling men he hated, of making
business calls and waiting in dirty anterooms—hat on knee,
yawning at fly-specked calendars, being polite to office-boys.

"I don't hardly want to go back to work," he prayed. "I'd
like to— I don't know."

But he was back next day, busy and of doubtful temper.

chapter 19

THE Zenith Street Traction Company planned to build
car-repair shops in the suburb of Dorchester, but when
they came to buy the land they found it held, on options,
by the Babbitt-Thompson Realty Company. The purchasing-
agent, the first vice-president, and even the president of the
Traction Company protested against the Babbitt price. They
mentioned their duty toward stockholders, they threatened
an appeal to the courts, though somehow the appeal to the
courts was never carried out and the officials found it wiser
to compromise with Babbitt. Carbon copies of the correspondence are in the company's files, where they may be viewed
by any public commission.

Just after this Babbitt deposited three thousand dollars in
the bank, the purchasing-agent of the Street Traction Company bought a five thousand dollar car, the first vice-president built a home in Devon Woods, and the president was
appointed minister to a foreign country.

To obtain the options, to tie up one man's land without
letting his neighbor know, had been an unusual strain on
Babbitt. It was necessary to introduce rumors about planning garages and stores, to pretend that he wasn't taking any
more options, to wait and look as bored as a poker-player
at a time when the failure to secure a key-lot threatened his

whole plan. To all this was added a nerve-jabbing quarrel with his secret associates in the deal. They did not wish Babbitt and Thompson to have any share in the deal except as brokers. Babbitt rather agreed. "Ethics of the business— broker ought to strictly represent his principles and not get in on the buying," he said to Thompson.

"Ethics, rats! Think I'm going to see that bunch of holy grafters get away with the swag and us not climb in?" snorted old Henry.

"Well, I don't like to do it. Kind of double-crossing."

"It ain't. It's triple-crossing. It's the public that gets double-crossed. Well, now we've been ethical and got it out of our systems, the question is where we can raise a loan to handle some of the property for ourselves, on the Q.T. We can't go to our bank for it. Might come out."

"I could see old Eathorne. He's close as the tomb."

"That's the stuff."

Eathorne was glad, he said, to "invest in character," to make Babbitt the loan and see to it that the loan did not appear on the books of the bank. Thus certain of the options which Babbitt and Thompson obtained were on parcels of real estate which they themselves owned, though the property did not appear in their names.

In the midst of closing this splendid deal, which stimulated business and public confidence by giving an example of increased real-estate activity, Babbitt was overwhelmed to find that he had a dishonest person working for him.

The dishonest one was Stanley Graff, the outside salesman.

For some time Babbitt had been worried about Graff. He did not keep his word to tenants. In order to rent a house he would promise repairs which the owner had not authorized. It was suspected that he juggled inventories of furnished houses so that when the tenant left he had to pay for articles which had never been in the house and the price of which Graff put into his pocket. Babbitt had not been able to prove these suspicions, and though he had rather planned to discharge Graff he had never quite found time for it.

Now into Babbitt's private room charged a red-faced man, panting, "Look here! I've come to raise particular merry hell, and unless you have that fellow pinched, I will!"

"What's— Calm down, o' man. What's trouble?"

"Trouble! Huh! Here's the trouble—"

"Sit down and take it easy! They can hear you all over the building!"

"This fellow Graff you got working for you, he leases me a house. I was in yesterday and signs the lease, all O.K., and he was to get the owner's signature and mail me the lease last night. Well, and he did. This morning I comes down to breakfast and the girl says a fellow had come to the house right after the early delivery and told her he wanted an envelope that had been mailed by mistake, big long envelope with 'Babbitt-Thompson' in the corner of it. Sure enough, there it was, so she lets him have it. And she describes the fellow to me, and it was this Graff. So I 'phones to him and he, the poor fool, he admits it! He says after my lease was all signed he got a better offer from another fellow and he wanted my lease back. Now what you going to do about it?"

"Your name is—?"

"William Varney—W. K. Varney."

"Oh, yes. That was the Garrison house." Babbitt sounded the buzzer. When Miss McGoun came in, he demanded, "Graff gone out?"

"Yes, sir."

"Will you look through his desk and see if there is a lease made out to Mr. Varney on the Garrison house?" To Varney: "Can't tell you how sorry I am this happened. Needless to say, I'll fire Graff the minute he comes in. And of course your lease stands. But there's one other thing I'd like to do. I'll tell the owner not to pay us the commission but apply it to your rent. No! Straight! I want to. To be frank, this thing shakes me up bad. I suppose I've always been a Practical Business Man. Probably I've told one or two fairy stories in my time, when the occasion called for it—you know: sometimes you have to lay things on thick, to impress boneheads. But this is the first time I've ever had to accuse one of my own employees of anything more dishonest than pinching a few stamps. Honest, it would hurt me if we profited by it. So you'll let me hand you the commission? Good!"

II

He walked through the February city, where trucks flung up a spattering of slush and the sky was dark above dark brick cornices. He came back miserable. He, who respected the law, had broken it by concealing the Federal crime of interception of the mails. But he could not see Graff go to jail and his wife suffer. Worse, he had to discharge Graff, and this was a part of office routine which he feared. He

liked people so much, he so much wanted them to like him,
that he could not bear insulting them.

Miss McGoun dashed in to whisper, with the excitement
of an approaching scene, "He's here!"

"Mr. Graff? Ask him to come in."

He tried to make himself heavy and calm in his chair, and
to keep his eyes expressionless. Graff stalked in—a man of
thirty-five, dapper, eye-glassed, with a foppish mustache.

"Want me?" said Graff.

"Yes. Sit down."

Graff continued to stand, grunting, "I suppose that old nut
Varney has been in to see you. Let me explain about him.
He's a regular tightwad, and he sticks out for every cent, and
he practically lied to me about his ability to pay the rent—I
found that out just after we signed up. And then another fellow comes along with a better offer for the house, and I felt
it was my duty to the firm to get rid of Varney, and I was
so worried about it I skun up there and got back the lease.
Honest, Mr. Babbitt, I didn't intend to pull anything crooked.
I just wanted the firm to have all the commis—"

"Wait now, Stan. This may all be true, but I've been having
a lot of complaints about you. Now I don't s'pose you ever
mean to do wrong, and I think if you just get a good lesson
that'll jog you up a little, you'll turn out a first-class realtor
yet. But I don't see how I can keep you on."

Graff leaned against the filing-cabinet, his hands in his
pockets, and laughed. "So I'm fired! Well, old Vision and
Ethics, I'm tickled to death! But I don't want you to think
you can get away with any holier-than-thou stuff. Sure I've
pulled some raw stuff—a little of it—but how could I help
it, in this office?"

"Now, by God, young man—"

"Tut, tut! Keep the naughty temper down, and don't holler,
because everybody in the outside office will hear you. They're
probably listening right now. Babbitt, old dear, you're crooked
in the first place and a damn skinflint in the second. If
you paid me a decent salary I wouldn't have to steal pennies
off a blind man to keep my wife from starving. Us married
just five months, and her the nicest girl living, and you keeping us flat broke all the time, you damned old thief, so you
can put money away for your saphead of a son and your
wishywashy fool of a daughter! Wait, now! You'll by God
take it, or I'll bellow so the whole office will hear it! And
crooked— Say, if I told the prosecuting attorney what I

know about this last Street Traction option steal, both you and me would go to jail, along with some nice, clean, pious, high-up traction guns!"

"Well, Stan, looks like we were coming down to cases. That deal— There was nothing crooked about it. The only way you can get progress is for the broad-gauged men to get things done; and they got to be rewarded—"

"Oh, for Pete's sake, don't get virtuous on me! As I gather it, I'm fired. All right. It's a good thing for me. And if I catch you knocking me to any other firm, I'll squeal all I know about you and Henry T. and the dirty little lickspittle deals that you corporals of industry pull off for the bigger and brainier crooks, and you'll get chased out of town. And me —you're right, Babbitt, I've been going crooked, but now I'm going straight, and the first step will be to get a job in some office where the boss doesn't talk about Ideals. Bad luck, old dear, and you can stick your job up the sewer!"

Babbitt sat for a long time, alternately raging, "I'll have him arrested," and yearning "I wonder— No, I've never done anything that wasn't necessary to keep the Wheels of Progress moving."

Next day he hired in Graff's place Fritz Weilinger, the salesman of his most injurious rival, the East Side Homes and Development Company, and thus at once annoyed his competitor and acquired an excellent man. Young Fritz was a curly-headed, merry, tennis-playing youngster. He made customers welcome to the office. Babbitt thought of him as a son, and in him had much comfort.

III

An abandoned race-track on the outskirts of Chicago, a plot excellent for factory sites, was to be sold, and Jake Offutt asked Babbitt to bid on it for him. The strain of the Street Traction deal and his disappointment in Stanley Graff had so shaken Babbitt that he found it hard to sit at his desk and concentrate. He proposed to his family, "Look here, folks! Do you know who's going to trot up to Chicago for a couple of days—just week-end; won't lose but one day of school—know who's going with that celebrated business-ambassador, George F. Babbitt? Why, Mr. Theodore Roosevelt Babbitt!"

"Hurray!" Ted shouted, and "Oh, maybe the Babbitt men won't paint that lil ole town red!"

And, once away from the familiar implications of home, they were two men together. Ted was young only in his assumption of oldness, and the only realms, apparently, in which Babbitt had a larger and more grown-up knowledge then Ted's were the details of real estate and the phrases of politics. When the other sages of the Pullman smoking-compartment had left them to themselves, Babbitt's voice did not drop into the playful and otherwise offensive tone in which one addresses children but continued its overwhelming and monotonous rumble, and Ted tried to imitate it in his strident tenor:

"Gee, dad, you certainly did show up that poor boot when he got flip about the League of Nations!"

"Well, the trouble with a lot of these fellows is, they simply don't know what they're talking about. They don't get down to facts. . . . What do you think of Ken Escott?"

"I'll tell you, dad: it strikes me Ken is a nice lad; no special faults except he smokes too much; but slow, Lord! Why, if we don't give him a shove the poor dumb-bell never will propose! And Rone just as bad. Slow."

"Yes, I guess you're right. They're slow. They haven't either one of 'em got our pep."

"That's right. They're slow. I swear, dad, I don't know how Rone got into our family! I'll bet, if the truth were known, you were a bad old egg when you were a kid!"

"Well, I wasn't so slow!"

"I'll bet you weren't! I'll bet you didn't miss many tricks!"

"Well, when I was out with the girls I didn't spend all the time telling 'em about the strike in the knitting industry!"

They roared together, and together lighted cigars.

"What are we going to do with 'em?" Babbitt consulted.

"Gosh, I don't know. I swear, sometimes I feel like taking Ken aside and putting him over the jumps and saying to him, 'Young fella me lad, are you going to marry young Rone, or are you going to talk her to death? Here you are getting on toward thirty, and you're only making twenty or twenty-five a week. When you going to develop a sense of responsibility and get a raise? If there's anything that George F. or I can do to help you, call on us, but show a little speed, anyway!' "

"Well, at that, it might not be so bad if you or I talked to him, except he might not understand. He's one of these highbrows. He can't come down to cases and lay his cards

on the table and talk straight out from the shoulder, like
you or I can."

"That's right, he's like all these highbrows."

"That's so, like all of 'em."

"That's a fact."

They sighed, and were silent and thoughtful and happy.

The conductor came in. He had once called at Babbitt's
office, to ask about houses. "H' are you, Mr. Babbitt! We
going to have you with us to Chicago? This your boy?"

"Yes, this is my son Ted."

"Well now, what do you know about that! Here I been
thinking you were a youngster yourself, not a day over forty,
hardly, and you with this great big fellow!"

"Forty? Why, brother, I'll never see forty-five again!"

"Is that a fact! Wouldn't hardly 'a' thought it!"

"Yes, sir, it's a bad give-away for the old man when he
has to travel with a young whale like Ted here!"

"You're right, it is." To Ted: "I suppose you're in college
now."

Proudly, "No, not till next fall. I'm just kind of giving the
diff'rent colleges the once-over now."

As the conductor went on his affable way, huge watch-
chain jingling against his blue chest, Babbitt and Ted gravely considered colleges. They arrived at Chicago late at night;
they lay abed in the morning, rejoicing, "Pretty nice not to
have to get up and get down to breakfast, heh?" They were
staying at the modest Eden Hotel, because Zenith business
men always stayed at the Eden, but they had dinner in the
brocade and crystal Versailles Room of the Regency Hotel.
Babbitt ordered Blue Point oysters with cocktail sauce, a
tremendous steak with a tremendous platter of French fried
potatoes, two pots of coffee, apple pie with ice cream for
both of them and, for Ted, an extra piece of mince pie.

"Hot stuff! Some feed, young fella!" Ted admired.

"Huh! You stick around with me, old man, and I'll show
you a good time!"

They went to a musical comedy and nudged each other at
the matrimonial jokes and the prohibition jokes; they paraded the lobby, arm in arm, between acts, and in the glee
of his first release from the shame which dissevers fathers
and sons Ted chuckled, "Dad, did you ever hear the one
about the three milliners and the judge?"

When Ted had returned to Zenith, Babbitt was lonely. As
he was trying to make alliance between Offutt and certain

Milwaukee interests which wanted the race-track plot, most of his time was taken up in waiting for telephone calls. . . . Sitting on the edge of his bed, holding the portable telephone, asking wearily, "Mr. Sagen not in yet? Didn' he leave any message for me? All right, I'll hold the wire." Staring at a stain on the wall, reflecting that it resembled a shoe, and being bored by this twentieth discovery that it resembled a shoe. Lighting a cigarette; then, bound to the telephone with no ash tray in reach, wondering what to do with this burning menace and anxiously trying to toss it into the tiled bathroom. And last, on the telephone, "No message, eh? All right, I'll call up again."

One afternoon he wandered through snow-rutted streets of which he had never heard, streets of small tenements and two-family houses and marooned cottages. It came to him that he had nothing to do, that there was nothing he wanted to do. He was bleakly lonely in the evening, when he dined by himself at the Regency Hotel. He sat in the lobby afterward, in a plush chair bedecked with the Saxe-Coburg arms, lighting a cigar and looking for some one who would come and play with him and save him from thinking. In the chair next to him (showing the arms of Lithuania) was a half-familiar man, a large red-faced man with pop eyes and a deficient yellow mustache. He seemed kind and insignificant, and as lonely as Babbitt himself. He wore a tweed suit and a reluctant orange tie.

It came to Babbitt with a pyrotechnic crash. The melancholy stranger was Sir Gerald Doak.

Instinctively Babbitt rose, bumbling, "How 're you, Sir Gerald? 'Member we met in Zenith, at Charley McKelvey's? Babbitt's my name—real estate."

"Oh! How d' you do." Sir Gerald shook hands flabbily.

Embarrassed, standing, wondering how he could retreat, Babbitt maundered, "Well, I suppose you been having a great trip since we saw you in Zenith."

"Quite. British Columbia and California and all over the place," he said doubtfully, looking at Babbitt lifelessly.

"How did you find business conditions in British Columbia? Or I suppose maybe you didn't look into 'em. Scenery and sport and so on?"

"Scenery? Oh, capital. But business conditions— You know, Mr. Babbitt, they're having almost as much unemployment as we are." Sir Gerald was speaking warmly now.

"So? Business conditions not so doggone good, eh?"

"No, business conditions weren't at all what I'd hoped to
find them."

"Not good, eh?"

"No, not—not really good."

"That's a darn shame. Well— I suppose you're waiting for
somebody to take you out to some big shindig, Sir
Gerald."

"Shindig? Oh. Shindig. No, to tell you the truth, I was
wondering what the deuce I could do this evening. Don't
know a soul in Tchicahgo. I wonder if you happen to know
whether there's a good theater in this city?"

"Good? Why say, they're running grand opera right now!
I guess maybe you'd like that."

"Eh? Eh? Went to the opera once in London. Covent
Garden sort of thing. Shocking! No, I was wondering if there
was a good cinema—movie."

Babbitt was sitting down, hitching his chair over, shouting,
"Movie? Say, Sir Gerald, I supposed of course you had a raft
of dames waiting to lead you out to some soirée—"

"God forbid!"

"—but if you haven't, what do you say you and me go to
a movie? There's a peach of a film at the Grantham: Bill
Hart in a bandit picture."

"Right-o! Just a moment while I get my coat."

Swollen with greatness, slightly afraid lest the noble
blood of Nottingham change its mind and leave him at any
street corner, Babbitt paraded with Sir Gerald Doak to the
movie palace and in silent bliss sat beside him, trying not to
be too enthusiastic, lest the knight despise his adoration of
six-shooters and broncos. At the end Sir Gerald murmured,
"Jolly good picture, this. So awfully decent of you to take
me. Haven't enjoyed myself so much for weeks. All these
Hostesses—they never let you go to the cinema!"

"The devil you say!" Babbitt's speech had lost the delicate
refinement and all the broad A's with which he had adorned
it, and become hearty and natural. "Well, I'm tickled to
death you liked it, Sir Gerald."

They crawled past the knees of fat women into the aisle;
they stood in the lobby waving their arms in the rite of putting on overcoats. Babbitt hinted, "Say, how about a little
something to eat? I know a place where we could get a swell
rarebit, and we might dig up a little drink—that is, if you
ever touch the stuff."

"Rather! But why don't you come to my room? I've some Scotch—not half bad."

"Oh, I don't want to use up all your hootch. It's darn nice of you, but— You probably want to hit the hay."

Sir Gerald was transformed. He was beefily yearning. "Oh really, now; I haven't had a decent evening for so long! Having to go to all these dances. No chance to discuss business and that sort of thing. Do be a good chap and come along. Won't you?"

"Will I? You bet! I just thought maybe— Say, by golly, it does do a fellow good, don't it, to sit and visit about business conditions, after he's been to these balls and masquerades and banquets and all that society stuff. I often feel that way in Zenith. Sure, you bet I'll come."

"That's awfully nice of you." They beamed along the street. "Look here, old chap, can you tell me, do American cities always keep up this dreadful social pace? All these magnificent parties?"

"Go on now, quit your kidding! Gosh, you with court balls and functions and everything—"

"No, really, old chap! Mother and I—Lady Doak, I should say, we usually play a hand of bezique and go to bed at ten. Bless my soul, I couldn't keep up your beastly pace! And talking! All your American women, they know so much— culture and that sort of thing. This Mrs. McKelvey—your friend—"

"Yuh, old Lucile. Good kid."

"—she asked me which of the galleries I liked best in Florence. Or was it in Firenze? Never been in Italy in my life! And primitives. Did I like primitives. Do you know what the deuce a primitive is?"

"Me? I should say not! But I know what a discount for cash is."

"Rather! So do I, by George! But primitives!"

"Yuh! Primitives!"

They laughed with the sound of a Boosters' luncheon.

Sir Gerald's room was, except for his ponderous and durable English bags, very much like the room of George F. Babbitt; and quite in the manner of Babbitt he disclosed a huge whisky flask, looked proud and hospitable, and chuckled, "Say, when, old chap."

It was after the third drink that Sir Gerald proclaimed, "How do you Yankees get the notion that writing chaps like Bertrand Shaw and this Wells represent us? The real business

England, we think those chaps are traitors. Both our countries have their comic Old Aristocracy—you know, old county families, hunting people and all that sort of thing—and we both have our wretched labor leaders, but we both have a backbone of sound business men who run the whole show."

"You bet. Here's to the real guys!"

"I'm with you! Here's to ourselves!"

It was after the fourth drink that Sir Gerald asked humbly, "What do you think of North Dakota mortgages?" but it was not till after the fifth that Babbitt began to call him "Jerry," and Sir Gerald confided, "I say, do you mind if I pull off my boots?" and ecstatically stretched his knightly feet, his poor, tired, hot, swollen feet out on the bed.

After the sixth, Babbitt irregularly arose. "Well, I better be hiking along. Jerry, you're a regular human being! I wish to thunder we'd been better acquainted in Zenith. Lookit. Can't you come back and stay with me a while?"

"So sorry—must go to New York to-morrow. Most awfully sorry, old boy. I haven't enjoyed an evening so much since I've been in the States. Real talk. Not all this social rot. I'd never have let them give me the beastly title—and I didn't get it for nothing, eh?—if I'd thought I'd have to talk to women about primitives and polo! Goodish thing to have in Nottingham, though; annoyed the mayor most frightfully when I got it; and of course the missus likes it. But nobody calls me 'Jerry' now——" He was almost weeping. "—and nobody in the States has treated me like a friend till to-night! Good-by, old chap, good-by! Thanks awfully!"

"Don't mention it, Jerry. And remember whenever you get to Zenith, the latch-string is always out."

"And don't forget, old boy, if you ever come to Nottingham, Mother and I will be frightfully glad to see you. I shall tell the fellows in Nottingham your ideas about Visions and Real Guys—at our next Rotary Club luncheon."

IV

Babbitt lay abed at his hotel, imagining the Zenith Athletic Club asking him, "What kind of a time d'you have in Chicago?" and his answering, "Oh, fair; ran around with Sir Gerald Doak a lot;" picturing himself meeting Lucile McKelvey and admonishing her, "You're all right, Mrs. Mac, when you aren't trying to pull this highbrow pose. It's just as Gerald Doak says to me in Chicago—oh, yes, Jerry's an old friend of mine—the wife and I are thinking of running over to England to stay with Jerry in his castle, next year—and he said to me, 'Georgie, old bean, I like Lucile first-rate, but you and me, George, we got to make her get over this highty-tighty hooptediddle way she's got.'"

But that evening a thing happened which wrecked his pride.

v

At the Regency Hotel cigar-counter he fell to talking with a salesman of pianos, and they dined together. Babbitt was filled with friendliness and well-being. He enjoyed the gorgeousness of the dining-room: the chandeliers, the looped brocade curtains, the portraits of French kings against panels of gilded oak. He enjoyed the crowd: pretty women, good solid fellows who were "liberal spenders."

He gasped. He stared, and turned away, and stared again. Three tables off, with a doubtful sort of woman, a woman at once coy and withered, was Paul Riesling, and Paul was supposed to be in Akron, selling tar-roofing. The woman was tapping his hand, mooning at him and giggling. Babbitt felt that he had encountered something involved and harmful. Paul was talking with the rapt eagerness of a man who is telling his troubles. He was concentrated on the woman's faded eyes. Once he held her hand and once, blind to the other guests, he puckered his lips as though he was pretending to kiss her. Babbitt had so strong an impulse to go to Paul that he could feel his body uncoiling, his shoulders moving, but he felt, desperately, that he must be diplomatic, and not till he saw Paul paying the check did he bluster to the piano-salesman, "By golly—friend of mine over there—'scuse me second—just say hello to him."

He touched Paul's shoulder, and cried, "Well, when did you hit town?"

Paul glared up at him, face hardening. "Oh, hello, George. Thought you'd gone back to Zenith." He did not introduce his companion. Babbitt peeped at her. She was a flabbily pretty, weakly flirtatious woman of forty-two or three, in an atrocious flowery hat. Her rouging was thorough but unskilful.

"Where you staying, Paulibus?"

The woman turned, yawned, examined her nails. She seemed accustomed to not being introduced.

Paul grumbled, "Campbell Inn, on the South Side."

"Alone?" It sounded insinuating.

"Yes! Unfortunately!" Furiously Paul turned toward the woman, smiling with a fondness sickening to Babbitt. "May! Want to introduce you. Mrs. Arnold, this is my old— acquaintance, George Babbitt."

"Pleasmeech," growled Babbitt, while she gurgled, "Oh, I'm very pleased to meet any friend of Mr. Riesling's, I'm sure."

Babbitt demanded, "Be back there later this evening, Paul? I'll drop down and see you."

"No, better— We better lunch together to-morrow."

"All right, but I'll see you to-night, too, Paul. I'll go down to your hotel, and I'll wait for you!"

chapter 20

HE sat smoking with the piano-salesman, clinging to the warm refuge of gossip, afraid to venture into thoughts of Paul. He was the more affable on the surface as secretly he became more apprehensive, felt more hollow. He was certain that Paul was in Chicago without Zilla's knowledge, and that he was doing things not at all moral and secure. When the salesman yawned that he had to write up his orders, Babbitt left him, left the hotel, in leisurely calm. But savagely he said "Campbell Inn!" to the taxi-driver. He sat agitated on the slippery leather seat, in that chill dimness which smelled of dust and perfume and Turkish cigarettes. He did not heed the snowy lake-front, the dark spaces and sudden bright corners in the unknown land south of the Loop.

The office of the Campbell Inn was hard, bright, new; the night clerk harder and brighter. "Yep?" he said to Babbitt.

"Mr. Paul Riesling registered here?"

"Yep."

"Is he in now?"

"Nope."

"Then if you'll give me his key, I'll wait for him."

"Can't do that, brother. Wait down here if you wanna."

Babbitt had spoken with the deference which all the Clan of Good Fellows give to hotel clerks. Now he said with snarling abruptness:

"I may have to wait some time. I'm Riesling's brother-in-law. I'll go up to his room. D' I look like a sneak-thief?"

His voice was low and not pleasant. With considerable haste the clerk took down the key, protesting, "I never said you looked like a sneak-thief. Just rules of the hotel. But if you want to—"

On his way up in the elevator Babbitt wondered why he was here. Why shouldn't Paul be dining with a respectable married woman? Why had he lied to the clerk about being Paul's brother-in-law? He had acted like a child. He must be careful not to say foolish dramatic things to Paul. As he settled down he tried to look pompous and placid. Then the thought— Suicide. He'd been dreading that, without knowing it. Paul would be just the person to do something like that. He must be out of his head or he wouldn't be confiding in that—that dried-up hag.

Zilla (oh, damn Zilla! how gladly he'd throttle that nagging fiend of a woman!)—she'd probably succeeded at last, and driven Paul crazy.

Suicide. Out there in the lake, way out, beyond the piled ice along the shore. It would be ghastly cold to drop into the water to-night.

Or—throat cut—in the bathroom—

Babbitt flung into Paul's bathroom. It was empty. He smiled, feebly.

He pulled at his choking collar, looked at his watch, opened the window to stare down at the street, looked at his watch, tried to read the evening paper lying on the glass-topped bureau, looked again at his watch. Three minutes had gone by since he had first looked at it.

And he waited for three hours.

He was sitting fixed, chilled, when the doorknob turned. Paul came in glowering.

"Hello," Paul said. "Been waiting?"

"Yuh, little while."

"Well?"

"Well what? Just thought I'd drop in to see how you made out in Akron."

"I did all right. What difference does it make?"

"Why, gosh, Paul, what are you sore about?"

"What are you butting into my affairs for?"

"Why, Paul, that's no way to talk! I'm not butting into nothing. I was so glad to see your ugly old phiz that I just dropped in to say howdy."

"Well, I'm not going to have anybody following me around and trying to boss me. I've had all of that I'm going to stand!"

"Well, gosh, I'm not—"

"I didn't like the way you looked at May Arnold, or the snooty way you talked."

"Well, all right then! If you think I'm a buttinsky, then I'll just butt in! I don't know who your May Arnold is, but I know doggone good and well that you and her weren't talking about tar-roofing, no, nor about playing the violin, neither! If you haven't got any moral consideration for yourself, you ought to have some for your position in the community. The idea of your going around places gawping into a female's eyes like a love-sick pup! I can understand a fellow slipping once, but I don't propose to see a fellow that's been as chummy with me as you have getting started on the downward path and sneaking off from his wife, even as cranky a one as Zilla, to go woman-chasing—"

"Oh, you're a perfectly moral little husband!"

"I am, by God! I've never looked at any woman except Myra since I've been married—practically—and I never will! I tell you there's nothing to immorality. It don't pay. Can't you see, old man, it just makes Zilla still crankier?"

Slight of resolution as he was of body, Paul threw his snow-beaded overcoat on the floor and crouched on a flimsy cane chair. "Oh, you're an old blowhard, and you know less about morality than Tinka, but you're all right, Georgie. But you can't understand that— I'm through. I can't go Zilla's hammering any longer. She's made up her mind that I'm a devil, and— Reg'lar Inquisition. Torture. She enjoys it. It's a game to see how sore she can make me. And me, either it's find a little comfort, any comfort, anywhere, or else do something a lot worse. Now this Mrs. Arnold, she's not so young, but she's a fine woman and she understands a fellow, and she's had her own troubles."

"Yea! I suppose she's one of these hens whose husband 'doesn't understand her'!"

"I don't know. Maybe. He was killed in the war."

Babbitt lumbered up, stood beside Paul patting his shoulder, making soft apologetic noises.

"Honest, George, she's a fine woman, and she's had one hell of a time. We manage to jolly each other up a lot. We tell each other we're the dandiest pair on earth. Maybe we don't believe it, but it helps a lot to have somebody with whom you can be perfectly simple, and not all this discussing—explaining—"

"And that's as far as you go?"

"It is not! Go on! Say it!"

"Well, I don't—I can't say I like it, but—" With a burst which left him feeling large and shining with generosity, "it's none of my darn business! I'll do anything I can for you, if there's anything I can do."

"There might be. I judge from Zilla's letters that 've been forwarded from Akron that she's getting suspicious about my staying away so long. She'd be perfectly capable of having me shadowed, and of coming to Chicago and busting into a hotel dining-room and bawling me out before everybody."

"I'll take care of Zilla. I'll hand her a good fairy-story when I get back to Zenith."

"I don't know—I don't think you better try it. You're a good fellow, but I don't know that diplomacy is your strong point." Babbitt looked hurt, then irritated. "I mean with women! With women, I mean. Course they got to go some to beat you in business diplomacy, but I just mean with women. Zilla may do a lot of rough talking, but she's pretty shrewd. She'd have the story out of you in no time."

"Well, all right, but—" Babbitt was still pathetic at not being allowed to play Secret Agent. Paul soothed:

"Course maybe you might tell her you'd been in Akron and seen me there."

"Why, sure, you bet! Don't I have to go look at that candy-store property in Akron? Don't I? Ain't it a shame I have to stop off there when I'm so anxious to get home? Ain't it a regular shame? I'll say it is! I'll say it's a dog-gone shame!"

"Fine. But for glory hallelujah's sake don't go putting any fancy fixings on the story. When men lie they always try to make it too artistic, and that's why women get suspicious. And— Let's have a drink, Georgie. I've got some gin and a little vermouth."

The Paul who normally refused a second cocktail took a

second now, and a third. He became red-eyed and thick-tongued. He was embarrassingly jocular and salacious.

In the taxicab Babbitt incredulously found tears crowding into his eyes.

II

He had not told Paul of his plan but he did stop at Akron, between trains, for the one purpose of sending to Zilla a post-card with "Had to come here for the day, ran into Paul." In Zenith he called on her. If for public appearances Zilla was over-coiffed, over-painted, and resolutely corseted, for private misery she wore a filthy blue dressing-gown and torn stockings thrust into streaky pink satin mules. Her face was sunken. She seemed to have but half as much hair as Babbitt remembered, and that half was stringy. She sat in a rocker amid a debris of candy-boxes and cheap magazines, and she sounded dolorous when she did not sound derisive. But Babbitt was exceedingly breezy:

"Well, well, Zil, old dear, having a good loaf while hubby's away? That's the idea! I'll bet a hat Myra never got up till ten, while I was in Chicago. Say, could I borrow your thermos—just dropped in to see if I could borrow your thermos bottle. We're going to have a toboggan party—want to take some coffee *mit*. Oh, did you get my card from Akron, saying I'd run into Paul?"

"Yes. What was he doing?"

"How do you mean?" He unbuttoned his overcoat, sat tentatively on the arm of a chair.

"You know how I mean!" She slapped the pages of a magazine with an irritable clatter. "I suppose he was trying to make love to some hotel waitress or manicure girl or somebody."

"Hang it, you're always letting on that Paul goes round chasing skirts. He doesn't, in the first place, and if he did, it would prob'ly be because you keep hinting at him and ding-ing at him so much. I hadn't meant to, Zilla, but since Paul is away, in Akron—"

"He really is in Akron? I know he has some horrible woman that he writes to in Chicago."

"Didn't I tell you I saw him in Akron? What 're you trying to do? Make me out a liar?"

"No, but I just— I get so worried."

"Now, there you are! That's what gets me! Here you love

Paul, and yet you plague him and cuss him out as if you
hated him. I simply can't understand why it is that the more
some folks love people, the harder they try to make 'em miserable."

"You love Ted and Rone—I suppose—and yet you nag
them."

"Oh. Well. That. That's different. Besides, I don't nag 'em.
Not what you'd call nagging. But zize saying: Now, here's
Paul, the nicest, most sensitive critter on God's green earth.
You ought to be ashamed of yourself the way you pan him.
Why, you talk to him like a washerwoman. I'm surprised you
can act so doggone common, Zilla!"

She brooded over her linked fingers. "Oh, I know. I do go
and get mean sometimes, and I'm sorry afterwards. But, oh,
Georgie, Paul is so aggravating! Honestly, I've tried awfully
hard, these last few years, to be nice to him, but just because I
used to be spiteful—or I seemed so; I wasn't, really, but I
used to speak up and say anything that came into my head—
and so he made up his mind that everything was my fault.
Everything can't always be my fault, can it? And now if I get
to fussing, he just turns silent, oh, so dreadfully silent, and
he won't look at me—he just ignores me. He simply isn't
human! And he deliberately keeps it up till I bust out and
say a lot of things I don't mean. So silent— Oh, you righteous men! How wicked you are! How rotten wicked!"

They thrashed things over and over for half an hour. At
the end, weeping drably, Zilla promised to restrain herself.

Paul returned four days later, and the Babbitts and Rieslings went festively to the movies and had chop suey at a
Chinese restaurant. As they walked to the restaurant through
a street of tailor shops and barber shops, the two wives in
front, chattering about cooks, Babbitt murmured to Paul,
"Zil seems a lot nicer now."

"Yes, she has been, except once or twice. But it's too late
now. I just— I'm not going to discuss it, but I'm afraid of
her. There's nothing left. I don't ever want to see her. Some
day I'm going to break away from her. Somehow."

chapter 21

THE International Organization of Boosters' Clubs has become a world-force for optimism, manly pleasantry, and good business. Chapters are to be found now in thirty countries. Nine hundred and twenty of the thousand chapters, however, are in the United States.

None of these is more ardent than the Zenith Boosters' Club.

The second March lunch of the Zenith Boosters was the most important of the year, as it was to be followed by the annual election of officers. There was agitation abroad. The lunch was held in the ballroom of the O'Hearn House. As each of the four hundred Boosters entered he took from a wall-board a huge celluloid button announcing his name, his nickname, and his business. There was a fine of ten cents for calling a Fellow Booster by anything but his nickname at a lunch, and as Babbitt jovially checked his hat the air was radiant with shouts of "Hello, Chet!" and "How're you, Shorty!" and "Top o' the mornin', Mac!"

They sat at friendly tables for eight, choosing places by lot. Babbitt was with Albert Boos the merchant tailor, Hector Seybolt of the Little Sweetheart Condensed Milk Company, Emil Wengert the jeweler, Professor Pumphrey of the Riteway Business College, Dr. Walter Gorbutt, Roy Teegarten the photographer, and Ben Berkey the photo-engraver. One of the merits of the Boosters' Club was that only two persons from each department of business were permitted to join, so that you at once encountered the Ideals of other occupations, and realized the metaphysical oneness of all occupations—plumbing and portrait-painting, medicine and the manufacture of chewing-gum.

Babbitt's table was particularly happy to-day, because Pro-

209

fessor Pumphrey had just had a birthday, and was therefore open to teasing.

"Let's pump Pump about how old he is!" said Emil Wengert.

"No, let's paddle him with a dancing-pump!" said Ben Berkey.

But it was Babbitt who had the applause, with "Don't talk about pumps to that guy! The only pump he knows is a bottle! Honest, they tell me he's starting a class in home-brewing at the ole college!"

At each place was the Boosters' Club booklet, listing the members. Though the object of the club was good-fellowship, yet they never lost sight of the importance of doing a little more business. After each name was the member's occupation. There were scores of advertisements in the booklet, and on one page the admonition: "There's no rule that you have to trade with your Fellow Boosters, but get wise, boy—what's the use of letting all this good money get outside of our happy fambly?" And at each place, to-day, there was a present: a card printed in artistic red and black:

SERVICE AND BOOSTERISM

Service finds its finest opportunity and development only in its broadest and deepest application and the consideration of its perpetual action upon reaction. I believe the highest type of Service, like the most progressive tenets of ethics, senses unceasingly and is motived by active adherence and loyalty to that which is the essential principle of Boosterism—Good Citizenship in all its factors and aspects.

DAD PETERSON

Compliments of Dadbury Peterson Advertising Corp.
"Ads, not Fads, at Dad's"

The Boosters all read Mr. Peterson's aphorism and said they understood it perfectly.

The meeting opened with the regular weekly "stunts." Retiring President Vergil Gunch was in the chair, his stiff hair like a hedge, his voice like a brazen gong of festival. Members who had brought guests introduced them publicly. "This tall red-headed piece of misinformation is the sporting editor of the *Press*," said Willis Ijams; and H. H. Hazen, the druggist, chanted, "Boys, when you're on a long motor tour and finally get to a romantic spot or scene and draw up and remark to the wife, 'This is certainly a romantic place,' it sends a glow right up and down your vertebræ. Well, my guest to-day is from such a place, Harper's Ferry, Virginia, in the beautiful Southland, with memories of good old General Robert E. Lee and of that brave soul, John Brown who, like every good Booster, goes marching on——"

There were two especially distinguished guests: the leading man of the "Bird of Paradise" company, playing this week at the Dodsworth Theater, and the mayor of Zenith, the Hon. Lucas Prout.

Vergil Gunch thundered, "When we manage to grab this celebrated Thespian off his lovely aggregation of beautiful actresses—and I got to admit I butted right into his dressing-room and told him how the Boosters appreciated the high-class artistic performance he's giving us—and don't forget that the treasurer of the Dodsworth is a Booster and will appreciate our patronage—and when on top of that we yank Hizzonor out of his multifarious duties at City Hall, then I feel we've done ourselves proud, and Mr. Prout will now say a few words about the problems and duties——"

By rising vote the Boosters decided which was the handsomest and which the ugliest guest, and to each of them was given a bunch of carnations, donated, President Gunch noted, by Brother Booster H. G. Yeager, the Jennifer Avenue florist.

Each week, in rotation, four Boosters were privileged to obtain the pleasures of generosity and of publicity by donating goods or services to four fellow-members, chosen by lot. There was laughter, this week, when it was announced that one of the contributors was Barnabas Joy, the undertaker. Everybody whispered, "I can think of a coupla good guys to be buried if his donation is a free funeral!"

Through all these diversions the Boosters were lunching on chicken croquettes, peas, fried potatoes, coffee, apple pie, and American cheese. Gunch did not lump the speeches. Presently he called on the visiting secretary of the Zenith Rotary Club, a rival organization. The secretary had the distinction of possessing State Motor Car License Number 5.

The Rotary secretary laughingly admitted that wherever he drove in the state so low a number created a sensation, and though it was pretty nice to have the honor, yet traffic cops remembered it only too darn well, and sometimes he didn't know but what he'd almost as soon have just plain B56,-876 or something like that. Only let any doggone Booster try to get Number 5 away from a live Rotarian next year, and watch the fur fly! And if they'd permit him, he'd wind up by calling for a cheer for the Boosters and Rotarians and the Kiwanis all together!

Babbitt sighed to Professor Pumphrey, "Be pretty nice to have as low a number as that! Everybody 'd say, 'He must be an important guy!' Wonder how he got it? I'll bet he wined and dined the superintendent of the Motor License Bureau to a fare-you-well!"

Then Chum Frink addressed them:

"Some of you may feel that it's out of place here to talk on a strictly highbrow and artistic subject, but I want to come out flatfooted and ask you boys to O.K. the proposition of a Symphony Orchestra for Zenith. Now, where a lot of you make your mistake is in assuming that if you don't like classical music and all that junk, you ought to oppose it. Now, I want to confess that, though I'm a literary guy by profession, I don't care a rap for all this long-haired music. I'd rather listen to a good jazz band any time than to some piece by Beethoven that hasn't any more tune to it than a bunch of fighting cats, and you couldn't whistle it to save your life! But that isn't the point. Culture has become as necessary an adornment and advertisement for a city to-day as pavements or bank-clearances. It's Culture, in theaters and art-galleries and so on, that brings thousands of visitors to New York every year and, to be frank, for all our splendid attainments we haven't yet got the Culture of a New York or Chicago or Boston—or at least we don't get the credit for it. The thing to do then, as a live bunch of go-getters, is to *capitalize Culture;* to go right out and grab it.

"Pictures and books are fine for those that have the time to study 'em, but they don't shoot out on the road and holler 'This is what little old Zenith can put up in the way of Culture.' That's precisely what a Symphony Orchestra does do. Look at the credit Minneapolis and Cincinnati get. An orchestra with first-class musickers and a swell conductor—and I believe we ought to do the thing up brown and get one of the highest-paid conductors on the market, providing he ain't a Hun—it goes right into Beantown and New York and Washington; it plays at the best theaters to the most cultured and moneyed people; it gives such class-advertising as a town can get in no other way; and the guy who is so short-sighted as to crab this orchestra proposition is passing up the chance to impress the glorious name of Zenith on some big New York millionaire that might—that might establish a branch factory here!

"I could also go into the fact that for our daughters who show an interest in highbrow music and may want to teach it, having an A1 local organization is of great benefit, but let's keep this on a practical basis, and I call on you good brothers to whoop it up for Culture and a World-beating Symphony Orchestra!"

They applauded.

To a rustle of excitement President Gunch proclaimed, "Gentleman, we will now proceed to the annual election of officers." For each of the six offices, three candidates had been chosen by a committee. The second name among the candidates for vice-president was Babbitt's.

He was surprised. He looked self-conscious. His heart pounded. He was still more agitated when the ballots were counted and Gunch said, "It's a pleasure to announce that Georgie Babbitt will be the next assistant gavel-wielder. I know of no man who stands more stanchly for common sense and enterprise than good old George. Come on, let's give him our best long yell!"

As they adjourned, a hundred men crushed in to slap his back. He had never known a higher moment. He drove away in a blur of wonder. He lunged into his office, chuckling to Miss McGoun, "Well, I guess you better congratulate your boss! Been elected vice-president of the Boosters!"

He was disappointed. She answered only, "Yes— Oh, Mrs. Babbitt's been trying to get you on the 'phone." But the new salesman, Fritz Weilinger, said, "By golly, chief, say, that's great, that's perfectly great! I'm tickled to death! Congratulations!"

Babbitt called the house, and crowed to his wife, "Heard you were trying to get me, Myra. Say, you got to hand it to little Georgie, this time! Better talk careful! You are now addressing the vice-president of the Boosters' Club!"

"Oh, Georgie—"

"Pretty nice, huh? Willis Ijams is the new president, but when he's away, little old Georgie takes the gavel and whoops 'em up and introduces the speakers—no matter if they're the governor himself—and—"

"George! Listen!"

"—it puts him in solid with big men like Doc Dilling and—"

"George! Paul Riesling—"

"Yes, sure, I'll 'phone Paul and let him know about it right away."

"Georgie! *Listen!* Paul's in jail. He shot his wife, he shot Zilla, this noon. She may not live."

chapter 22

H E drove to the City Prison, not blindly, but with unusual fussy care at corners, the fussiness of an old woman potting plants. It kept him from facing the obscenity of fate.

The attendant said, "Naw, you can't see any of the prisoners till three-thirty—visiting-hour."

It was three. For half an hour Babbitt sat looking at a calendar and a clock on a whitewashed wall. The chair was hard and mean and creaky. People went through the office and, he thought, stared at him. He felt a belligerent defiance which broke into a wincing fear of this machine which was grinding Paul—Paul—

Exactly at half-past three he sent in his name.

The attendant returned with "Riesling says he don't want to see you."

"You're crazy! You didn't give him my name! Tell him it's George wants to see him, George Babbitt."

"Yuh, I told him, all right, all right! He said he didn't want to see you."

"Then take me in anyway."

"Nothing doing. If you ain't his lawyer, if he don't want to see you, that's all there is to it."

"But, my *God*— Say, let me see the warden."

"He's busy. Come on, now, you—" Babbitt reared over him. The attendant hastily changed to a coaxing "You can come back and try to-morrow. Probably the poor guy is off his nut."

Babbitt drove, not at all carefully or fussily, sliding viciously past trucks, ignoring the truckmen's curses, to the City Hall; he stopped with a grind of wheels against the curb, and ran up the marble steps to the office of the Hon. Mr. Lucas Prout, the mayor. He bribed the mayor's doorman with a dollar; he was instantly inside, demanding, "You remember me, Mr. Prout? Babbitt—vice-president of the Boosters—campaigned for you? Say, have you heard about poor Riesling? Well, I want an order on the warden or whatever you call um of the City Prison to take me back and see him. Good. Thanks."

In fifteen minutes he was pounding down the prison corridor to a cage where Paul Riesling sat on a cot, twisted like an old beggar, legs crossed, arms in a knot, biting at his clenched fist.

Paul looked up blankly as the keeper unlocked the cell, admitted Babbitt, and left them together. He spoke slowly: "Go on! Be moral!"

Babbitt plumped on the couch beside him. "I'm not going to be moral! I don't care what happened! I just want to do anything I can. I'm glad Zilla got what was coming to her."

Paul said argumentatively, "Now, don't go jumping on Zilla. I've been thinking; maybe she hasn't had any too easy a time. Just after I shot her— I didn't hardly mean to, but she got to deviling me so I went crazy, just for a second, and pulled out that old revolver you and I used to shoot rabbits with, and took a crack at her. Didn't hardly mean to— After that, when I was trying to stop the blood— It was terrible what it did to her shoulder, and she had beautiful skin— Maybe she won't die. I hope it won't leave her skin all scarred. But just afterward, when I was hunting through the bathroom for some cotton to stop the blood, I ran onto a little fuzzy yellow duck we hung on the tree one Christmas, and I remembered she and I'd been awfully happy then— Hell. I can't hardly believe it's me here." As Babbitt's arm tightened about his shoulder, Paul sighed, "I'm glad you came. But I thought maybe you'd lecture me, and when you've committed a murder, and been brought here and everything —there was a big crowd outside the apartment house, all staring, and the cops took me through it— Oh, I'm not going to talk about it any more."

But he went on, in a monotonous, terrified insane mumble. To divert him Babbitt said, "Why, you got a scar on your cheek."

"Yes. That's where the cop hit me. I suppose cops get a lot of fun out of lecturing murderers, too. He was a big fellow. And they wouldn't let me help carry Zilla down to the ambulance."

"Paul! Quit it! Listen: she won't die, and when it's all over you and I'll go off to Maine again. And maybe we can get that May Arnold to go along. I'll go up to Chicago and ask her. Good woman, by golly. And afterwards I'll see that you get started in business out West somewhere, maybe Seattle —they say that's a lovely city."

Paul was half smiling. It was Babbitt who rambled now. He could not tell whether Paul was heeding, but he droned on till the coming of Paul's lawyer, P. J. Maxwell, a thin, busy, unfriendly man who nodded at Babbitt and hinted, "If Riesling and I could be alone for a moment—"

Babbitt wrung Paul's hands, and waited in the office till Maxwell came pattering out. "Look, old man, what can I do?" he begged.

"Nothing. Not a thing. Not just now," said Maxwell. "Sorry. Got to hurry. And don't try to see him. I've had the doctor give him a shot of morphine, so he'll sleep."

It seemed somehow wicked to return to the office. Babbitt felt as though he had just come from a funeral. He drifted out to the City Hospital to inquire about Zilla. She was not likely to die, he learned. The bullet from Paul's huge old .44 army revolver had smashed her shoulder and torn upward and out.

He wandered home and found his wife radiant with the horrified interest we have in the tragedies of our friends. "Of course Paul isn't altogether to blame, but this is what comes of his chasing after other women instead of bearing his cross in a Christian way," she exulted.

He was too languid to respond as he desired. He said what was to be said about the Christian bearing of crosses, and went out to clean the car. Dully, patiently, he scraped linty grease from the drip-pan, gouged at the mud caked on the wheels. He used up many minutes in washing his hands; scoured them with gritty kitchen soap; rejoiced in hurting his plump knuckles. "Damn soft hands—like a woman's. Aah!"

At dinner, when his wife began the inevitable, he bellowed, "I forbid any of you to say a word about Paul! I'll 'tend to all the talking about this that's necessary, hear me? There's going to be one house in this scandal-mongering town to-night that isn't going to spring the holier-than-thou. And throw those filthy evening papers out of the house!"

But he himself read the papers, after dinner.

Before nine he set out for the house of Lawyer Maxwell.

He was received without cordiality. "Well?" said Maxwell.

"I want to offer my services in the trial. I've got an idea. Why couldn't I go on the stand and swear I was there, and she pulled the gun first and he wrested with her and the gun went off accidentally?"

"And perjure yourself?"

"Huh? Yes, I suppose it would be perjury. Oh— Would it help?"

"But, my dear fellow! Perjury!"

"Oh, don't be a fool! Excuse me, Maxwell; I didn't mean to get your goat. I just mean: I've known and you've known many and many a case of perjury, just to annex some rotten little piece of real estate, and here where it's a case of saving Paul from going to prison, I'd perjure myself black in the face."

"No. Aside from the ethics of the matter, I'm afraid it isn't practicable. The prosecutor would tear your testimony to pieces. It's known that only Riesling and his wife were there at the time."

"Then, look here! Let me go on the stand and swear— and this would be the God's truth—that she pestered him till he kind of went crazy."

"No. Sorry. Riesling absolutely refuses to have any testimony reflecting on his wife. He insists on pleading guilty."

"Then let me get up and testify something—whatever you say. Let me do *something!*"

"I'm sorry, Babbitt, but the best thing you can do—I hate to say it, but you could help us most by keeping strictly out of it."

Babbitt, revolving his hat like a defaulting poor tenant, winced so visibly that Maxwell condescended:

"I don't like to hurt your feelings, but you see we both want to do our best for Riesling, and we mustn't consider any other factor. The trouble with you, Babbitt, is that you're one of these fellows who talk too readily. You like to hear your own voice. If there were anything for which I could put you in the witness-box, you'd get going and give the whole show away. Sorry. Now I must look over some papers— So sorry."

II

He spent most of the next morning nerving himself to face the garrulous world of the Athletic Club. They would talk about Paul; they would be lip-licking and rotten. But at the Roughnecks' Table they did not mention Paul. They spoke with zeal of the coming baseball season. He loved them as he never had before.

III

He had, doubtless from some story-book, pictured Paul's trial as a long struggle, with bitter arguments, a taut crowd, and sudden and overwhelming new testimony. Actually, the trial occupied less than fifteen minutes, largely filled with the evidence of doctors that Zilla would recover and that Paul must have been temporarily insane. Next day Paul was sentenced to three years in the State Penitentiary and taken off— quite undramatically, not handcuffed, merely plodding in a tired way beside a cheerful deputy sheriff—and after saying good-by to him at the station Babbitt returned to his office to realize that he faced a world which, without Paul, was meaningless.

chapter 23

HE was busy, from March to June. He kept himself from the bewilderment of thinking. His wife and the neighbors were generous. Every evening he played bridge or attended the movies, and the days were blank of face and silent.

In June, Mrs. Babbitt and Tinka went East, to stay with relatives, and Babbitt was free to do—he was not quite sure what.

All day long after their departure he thought of the emancipated house in which he could, if he desired, go mad and curse the gods without having to keep up a husbandly front. He considered, "I could have a reg'lar party to-night; stay out till two and not do any explaining afterwards. Cheers!" He telephoned to Vergil Gunch, to Eddie Swanson. Both of them were engaged for the evening, and suddenly he was bored by having to take so much trouble to be riotous.

He was silent at dinner, unusually kindly to Ted and Verona, hesitating but not disapproving when Verona stated her opinion of Kenneth Escott's opinion of Dr. John Jennison Drew's opinion of the opinions of the evolutionists. Ted was working in a garage through the summer vacation, and he related his daily triumphs: how he had found a cracked ball-race, what he had said to the Old Grouch, what he had said to the foreman about the future of wireless telephony.

Ted and Verona went to a dance after dinner. Even the maid was out. Rarely had Babbitt been alone in the house for an entire evening. He was restless. He vaguely wanted something more diverting than the newspaper comic strips to read. He ambled up to Verona's room, sat on her maidenly blue and white bed, humming and grunting in a solid-citizen manner as he examined her books: Conrad's "Rescue," a volume strangely named "Figures of Earth," poetry (quite irregular poetry, Babbitt thought) by Vachel Lindsay, and essays by H. L. Mencken—highly improper essays, making fun of the church and all the decencies. He liked none of the books. In them he felt a spirit of rebellion against niceness and solid-citizenship. These authors—and he supposed they were famous ones, too—did not seem to care about telling a good story which would enable a fellow to forget his troubles. He sighed. He noted a book, "The Three Black Pennies," by Joseph Hergesheimer. Ah, that was something like it! It would be an adventure story, maybe about counterfeiting— detectives sneaking up on the old house at night. He tucked the book under his arm, he clumped down-stairs and solemnly began to read, under the piano-lamp:

"A twilight like blue dust sifted into the shallow fold of the thickly wooded hills. It was early October, but a crisping frost had already stamped the maple trees with gold, the Spanish oaks were hung with patches of wine red, the sumach was brilliant in the darkening underbrush. A pattern of wild geese, flying low and unconcerned above the hills, wavered against the serene ashen evening. Howat Penny, standing in the comparative clearing of a road, decided that the shifting regular flight would not come close enough for a shot. . . . He had no intention of hunting the geese. With the drooping of day his keenness had evaporated; an habitual indifference strengthened, permeating him. . . ."

There it was again: discontent with the good common

ways. Babbitt laid down the book and listened to the stillness. The inner doors of the house were open. He heard from the kitchen the steady drip of the refrigerator, a rhythm demanding and disquieting. He roamed to the window. The summer evening was foggy and, seen through the wire screen, the street-lamps were crosses of pale fire. The whole world was abnormal. While he brooded, Verona and Ted came in and went up to bed. Silence thickened in the sleeping house. He put on his hat, his respectable derby, lighted a cigar, and walked up and down before the house, a portly, worthy, unimaginative figure, humming "Silver Threads among the Gold." He casually considered, "Might call up Paul." Then he remembered. He saw Paul in a jailbird's uniform, but while he agonized he didn't believe the tale. It was part of the unreality of this fog-enchanted evening.

If she were here Myra would be hinting, "Isn't it late, Georgie?" He tramped in forlorn and unwanted freedom. Fog hid the house now. The world was uncreated, a chaos without turmoil or desire.

Through the mist came a man at so feverish a pace that he seemed to dance with fury as he entered the orb of glow from a street-lamp. At each step he brandished his stick and brought it down with a crash. His glasses on their broad pretentious ribbon banged against his stomach. Babbitt incredulously saw that it was Chum Frink.

Frink stopped, focused his vision, and spoke with gravity:

"There's another fool. George Babbitt. Lives for renting howshes—houses. Know who I am? I'm traitor to poetry. I'm drunk. I'm talking too much. I don't care. Know what I could 've been? I could 've been a Gene Field or a James Whitcomb Riley. Maybe a Stevenson. I could 've. Whimsies. 'Magination. Lissen. Lissen to this. Just made it up:

> Glittering summery meadowy noise
> Of beetles and bums and respectable boys.

Hear that? Whimzh—whimsy. I made that up. I don't know what it means! Beginning good verse. Chile's Garden Verses. And whadi write? Tripe! Cheer-up poems. All tripe! Could have written— Too late!"

He darted on with an alarming plunge, seeming always to pitch forward yet never quite falling. Babbitt would have been no more astonished and no less had a ghost skipped out of the fog carrying his head. He accepted Frink with vast apathy; he grunted, "Poor boob!" and straightway forgot him.

He plodded into the house, deliberately went to the refrigerator and rifled it. When Mrs. Babbitt was at home, this was one of the major household crimes. He stood before the covered laundry tubs, eating a chicken leg and half a saucer of raspberry jelly, and grumbling over a clammy cold boiled potato. He was thinking. It was coming to him that perhaps all life as he knew it and vigorously practised it was futile; that heaven as portrayed by the Reverend Dr. John Jennison Drew was neither probable nor very interesting; that he hadn't much pleasure out of making money; that it was of doubtful worth to rear children merely that they might rear children who would rear children. What was it all about? What did he want?

He blundered into the living-room, lay on the davenport, hands behind his head.

What did he want? Wealth? Social position? Travel? Servants? Yes, but only incidentally.

"I give it up," he sighed.

But he did know that he wanted the presence of Paul Riesling; and from that he stumbled into the admission that he wanted the fairy girl—in the flesh. If there had been a woman whom he loved, he would have fled to her, humbled his forehead on her knees.

He thought of his stenographer, Miss McGoun. He thought of the prettiest of the manicure girls at the Hotel Thornleigh barber shop. As he fell asleep on the davenport he felt that he had found something in life, and that he had made a terrifying, thrilling break with everything that was decent and normal.

II

He had forgotten, next morning, that he was a conscious rebel, but he was irritable in the office and at the eleven o'clock drive of telephone calls and visitors he did something he had often desired and never dared: he left the office without excuses to those slave-drivers his employees, and went to the movies. He enjoyed the right to be alone. He came out with a vicious determination to do what he pleased.

As he approached the Roughnecks' Table at the club, everybody laughed.

"Well, here's the millionaire!" said Sidney Finkelstein.

"Yes, I saw him in his Locomobile!" said Professor Pumphrey.

"Gosh, it must be great to be a smart guy like Georgie!" moaned Vergil Gunch. "He's probably stolen all of Dorchester. I'd hate to leave a poor little defenseless piece of property lying around where he could get his hooks on it!"

They had, Babbitt perceived, "something on him." Also, they "had their kidding clothes on." Ordinarily he would have been delighted at the honor implied in being chaffed, but he was suddenly touchy. He grunted, "Yuh, sure; maybe I'll take you guys on as office boys!" He was impatient as the jest elaborately rolled on to its dénouement.

"Of course he may have been meeting a girl," they said, and "No, I think he was waiting for his old roommate, Sir Jerusalem Doak."

He exploded, "Oh, spring it, spring it, you boneheads! What's the great joke?"

"Hurray! George is peeved!" snickered Sidney Finkelstein, while a grin went round the table. Gunch revealed the shocking truth: He had seen Babbitt coming out of a motion-picture theater—at noon!

They kept it up. With a hundred variations, a hundred guffaws, they said that he had gone to the movies during business-hours. He didn't so much mind Gunch, but he was annoyed by Sidney Finkelstein, that brisk, lean, red-headed explainer of jokes. He was bothered, too, by the lump of ice in his glass of water. It was too large; it spun round and burned his nose when he tried to drink. He raged that Finkelstein was like that lump of ice. But he won through; he kept up his banter till they grew tired of the superlative jest and turned to the great problems of the day.

He reflected, "What's the matter with me to-day? Seems like I've got an awful grouch. Only they talk so darn much. But I better steer careful and keep my mouth shut."

As they lighted their cigars he mumbled, "Got to get back," and on a chorus of "If you *will* go spending your mornings with lady ushers at the movies!" he escaped. He heard them giggling. He was embarrassed. While he was most bombastically agreeing with the coat-man that the weather was warm, he was conscious that he was longing to run childishly with his troubles to the comfort of the fairy child.

III

He kept Miss McGoun after he had finished dictating. He searched for a topic which would warm her office impersonality into friendliness.

"Where you going on your vacation?" he purred.

"I think I'll go up-state to a farm do you want me to have the Siddons lease copied this afternoon?"

"Oh, no hurry about it. . . . I suppose you have a great time when you get away from us cranks in the office."

She rose and gathered her pencils. "Oh, nobody's cranky here I think I can get it copied after I do the letters."

She was gone. Babbitt utterly repudiated the view that he had been trying to discover how approachable was Miss Mc-Goun. "Course! knew there was nothing doing!" he said.

IV

Eddie Swanson, the motor-car agent who lived across the street from Babbitt, was giving a Sunday supper. His wife Louetta, young Louetta who loved jazz in music and in clothes and laughter, was at her wildest. She cried, "We'll have a real party!" as she received the guests. Babbitt had un-easily felt that to many men she might be alluring; now he admitted that to himself she was overwhelmingly alluring. Mrs. Babbitt had never quite approved of Louetta; Babbitt was glad that she was not here this evening.

He insisted on helping Louetta in the kitchen: taking the chicken croquettes from the warming-oven, the lettuce sand-wiches from the ice-box. He held her hand, once, and she depressingly didn't notice it. She caroled, "You're a good little mother's-helper, Georgie. Now trot in with the tray and leave it on the side-table."

He wished that Eddie Swanson would give them cocktails; that Louetta would have one. He wanted— Oh, he wanted to be one of these Bohemians you read about. Studio parties. Wild lovely girls who were independent. Not necessarily bad. Certainly not! But not tame, like Floral Heights. How he'd ever stood it all these years—

Eddie did not give them cocktails. True, they supped with mirth, and with several repetitions by Orville Jones of "Any time Louetta wants to come sit on my lap I'll tell this sand-wich to beat it!" but they were respectable, as befitted Sunday evening. Babbitt had discreetly preëmpted a place beside Louetta on the piano bench. While he talked about motors, while he listened with a fixed smile to her account of the film she had seen last Wednesday, while he hoped that she would hurry up and finish her description of the plot, the beauty of the leading man, and the luxury of the setting, he studied her. Slim waist girdled with raw silk, strong brows, ardent eyes, hair parted above a broad forehead— she meant youth to him and a charm which saddened. He thought of how valiant a companion she would be on a long motor tour, exploring mountains, picnicking in a pine grove high above a valley. Her frailness touched him; he was angry at Eddie Swanson for the incessant family bickering. All at once he identified Louetta with the fairy girl. He was startled by the conviction that they had always had a romantic attraction for each other.

"I suppose you're leading a simply terrible life, now you're a widower," she said.

"You bet! I'm a bad little fellow and proud of it. Some evening you slip Eddie some dope in his coffee and sneak across the road and I'll show you how to mix a cocktail," he roared.

"Well, now, I might do it! You never can tell!"

"Well, whenever you're ready, you just hang a towel out of the attic window and I'll jump for the gin!"

Every one giggled at this naughtiness. In a pleased way Eddie Swanson stated that he would have a physician analyze his coffee daily. The others were diverted to a discussion of the more agreeable recent murders, but Babbitt drew Louetta back to personal things:

"That's the prettiest dress I ever saw in my life."

"Do you honestly like it?"

"Like it? Why, say, I'm going to have Kenneth Escott put a piece in the paper saying that the swellest dressed woman in the U. S. is Mrs. E. Louetta Swanson."

"Now, you stop teasing me!" But she beamed. "Let's dance a little. George, you've got to dance with me."

Even as he protested, "Oh, you know what a rotten dancer I am!" he was lumbering to his feet.

"I'll teach you. I can teach anybody."

Her eyes were moist, her voice was jagged with excitement. He was convinced that he had won her. He clasped her, conscious of her smooth warmth, and solemnly he circled in a heavy version of the one-step. He bumped into only one or two people. "Gosh, I'm not doing so bad; hittin' 'em up like a regular stage dancer!" he gloated; and she answered busily, "Yes—yes—I told you I could teach anybody—*don't take such long steps!*"

For a moment he was robbed of confidence; with fearful concentration he sought to keep time to the music. But he was enveloped again by her enchantment. "She's got to like me; I'll make her!" he vowed. He tried to kiss the lock beside her ear. She mechanically moved her head to avoid it, and mechanically she murmured, "Don't!"

For a moment he hated her, but after the moment he was as urgent as ever. He danced with Mrs. Orville Jones, but he watched Louetta swooping down the length of the room with her husband. "Careful! You're getting foolish!" he cautioned himself, the while he hopped and bent his solid knees in dalliance with Mrs. Jones, and to that worthy lady rumbled, "Gee, it's hot!" Without reason, he thought of Paul in that shadowy place where men never dance. "I'm crazy to-night; better go home," he worried, but he left Mrs. Jones and dashed to Louetta's lovely side, demanding, "The next is mine."

"Oh, I'm so hot; I'm not going to dance this one."

"Then," boldly, "come out and sit on the porch and get all nice and cool."

"Well—"

In the tender darkness, with the clamor in the house behind them, he resolutely took her hand. She squeezed his once, then relaxed.

"Louetta! I think you're the nicest thing I know!"

"Well, I think you're very nice."

"Do you? You got to like me! I'm so lonely!"

"Oh, you'll be all right when your wife comes home."

"No, I'm always lonely."

She clasped her hands under her chin, so that he dared not touch her. He sighed:

"When I feel punk and—" He was about to bring in the tragedy of Paul, but that was too sacred even for the diplomacy of love. "—when I get tired out at the office and everything, I like to look across the street and think of you. Do you know I dreamed of you, one time!"

"Was it a nice dream?"

"Lovely!"

"Oh, well, they say dreams go by opposites! Now I must run in."

She was on her feet.

"Oh, don't go in yet! Please, Louetta!"

"Yes, I must. Have to look out for my guests."

"Let 'em look out for 'emselves!"

"I couldn't do that." She carelessly tapped his shoulder and slipped away.

But after two minutes of shamed and childish longing to sneak home he was snorting, "Certainly I wasn't trying to get chummy with her! Knew there was nothing doing, all the time!" and he ambled in to dance with Mrs. Orville Jones, and to avoid Louetta, virtuously and conspicuously.

chapter 24

HIS visit to Paul was as unreal as his night of fog and questioning. Unseeing he went through prison corridors stinking of carbolic acid to a room lined with pale yellow settees pierced in rosettes, like the shoe-store benches he had known as a boy. The guard led in Paul. Above his uniform of linty gray, Paul's face was pale and without expression. He moved timorously in response to the guard's commands; he meekly pushed Babbitt's gifts of tobacco and magazines across the table to the guard for examination. He had nothing to say but "Oh, I'm getting used to it" and "I'm working in the tailor shop; the stuff hurts my fingers."

Babbitt knew that in this place of death Paul was already dead. And as he pondered on the train home something in his own self seemed to have died: a loyal and vigorous faith in the goodness of the world, a fear of public disfavor, a pride in success. He was glad that his wife was away. He admitted it without justifying it. He did not care.

II

Her card read "Mrs. Daniel Judique." Babbitt knew of her as the widow of a wholesale paper-dealer. She must have been forty or forty-two but he thought her younger when he saw her in the office, that afternoon. She had come to inquire about renting an apartment, and he took her away from the unskilled girl accountant. He was nervously attracted by her smartness. She was a slender woman, in a black Swiss frock dotted with white, a cool-looking graceful frock. A broad black hat shaded her face. Her eyes were lustrous, her soft chin of an agreeable plumpness, and her cheeks an even rose. Babbitt wondered afterward if she was made up, but no man living knew less of such arts.

She sat revolving her violet parasol. Her voice was appealing without being coy. "I wonder if you can help me?"

"Be delighted."

"I've looked everywhere and— I want a little flat, just a bedroom, or perhaps two, and sitting-room and kitchenette and bath, but I want one that really has some charm to it, not these dingy places or these new ones with terrible gaudy chandeliers. And I can't pay so dreadfully much. My name's Tanis Judique."

"I think maybe I've got just the thing for you. Would you like to chase around and look at it now?"

"Yes. I have a couple of hours."

In the new Cavendish Apartments, Babbitt had a flat which he had been holding for Sidney Finkelstein, but at the thought of driving beside this agreeable woman he threw over his friend Finkelstein, and with a note of gallantry he proclaimed, "I'll let you see what I can do!"

He dusted the seat of the car for her, and twice he risked death in showing off his driving.

"You do know how to handle a car!" she said.

He liked her voice. There was, he thought, music in it and a hint of culture, not a bouncing giggle like Louetta Swanson's.

He boasted, "You know, there's a lot of these fellows that are so scared and drive so slow that they get in everybody's way. The safest driver is a fellow that knows how to handle his machine and yet isn't scared to speed up when it's necessary, don't you think so?"

"Oh, yes!"

"I bet you drive like a wiz."

"Oh, no—I mean—not really. Of course, we had a car— I mean, before my husband passed on—and I used to make believe drive it, but I don't think any woman ever learns to drive like a man."

"Well, now, there's some mighty good woman drivers."

"Oh, of course, these women that try to imitate men, and play golf and everything, and ruin their complexions and spoil their hands!"

"That's so. I never did like these mannish females."

"I mean—of course, I admire them, dreadfully, and I feel so weak and useless beside them."

"Oh, rats now! I bet you play the piano like a wiz."

"Oh, no—I mean—not really."

"Well, I'll be you do!" He glanced at her smooth hands, her diamond and ruby rings. She caught the glance, snuggled her hands together with a kittenish curving of slim white fingers which delighted him, and yearned:

"I do love to play—I mean—like to drum on the piano, but I haven't had any real training. Mr. Judique used to say I would 've been a good pianist if I'd had any training, but then, I guess he was just flattering me."

"I'll bet he wasn't! I'll bet you've got temperament."

"Oh— Do you like music, Mr. Babbitt?"

"You bet I do! Only I don't know 's I care so much for all this classical stuff."

"Oh, I do! I just love Chopin and all those."

"Do you, honest? Well, of course, I go to lots of these highbrow concerts, but I do like a good jazz orchestra, right up on its toes, with the fellow that plays the bass fiddle spinning it around and beating it up with the bow."

"Oh, I know. I do love good dance music. I love to dance, don't you, Mr. Babbitt?"

"Sure, you bet. Not that I'm very darn good at it, though."

"Oh, I'm sure you are. You ought to let me teach you. I can teach anybody to dance."

"Would you give me a lesson some time?"

"Indeed I would."

Better be careful, or I'll be taking you up on that proposition. I'll be coming up to your flat and making you give me that lesson."

"Ye-es." She was not offended, but she was non-committal. He warned himself, "Have some sense now, you chump! Don't go making a fool of yourself again!" and with loftiness he discoursed:

"I wish I could dance like some of these young fellows, but I'll tell you: I feel it's a man's place to take a full, you might say, a creative share in the world's work and mold conditions and have something to show for his life, don't you think so?"

"Oh, I do!"

"And so I have to sacrifice some of the things I might like to tackle, though I do, by golly, play about as good a game of golf as the next fellow!"

"Oh, I'm sure you do. . . . Are you married?"

"Uh—yes. . . . And, uh, of course official duties—I'm the vice-president of the Boosters' Club, and I'm running one of the committees of the State Association of Real Estate Boards, and that means a lot of work and responsibility—and practically no gratitude for it."

"Oh, I know! Public men never do get proper credit."

They looked at each other with a high degree of mutual respect, and at the Cavendish Apartments he helped her out in a courtly manner, waved his hand at the house as though he were presenting it to her, and ponderously ordered the elevator boy to "hustle and get the keys." She stood close to him in the elevator, and he was stirred but cautious.

It was a pretty flat, of white woodwork and soft blue walls. Mrs. Judique gushed with pleasure as she agreed to take it, and as they walked down the hall to the elevator she touched his sleeve, caroling, "Oh, I'm so glad I went to you! It's such a privilege to meet a man who really Understands. Oh! The flats *some* people have showed me!"

He had a sharp instinctive belief that he could put his arm around her, but he rebuked himself and with excessive politeness he saw her to the car, drove her home. All the way back to his office he raged:

"Glad I had some sense for once. . . . Curse it, I wish I'd tried. She's a darling! A corker! A reg'lar charmer! Lovely eyes and darling lips and that trim waist—never get sloppy, like some women. . . . No, no, no! She's a real cultured lady. One of the brightest little women I've met these many moons. Understands about Public Topics and— But, darn it, why didn't I try? . . . Tanis!"

III

He was harassed and puzzled by it, but he found that he was turning toward youth, as youth. The girl who especially disturbed him—though he had never spoken to her—was the last manicure girl on the right in the Pompeian Barber Shop. She was small, swift, black-haired, smiling. She was nineteen, perhaps, or twenty. She wore thin salmon-colored blouses which exhibited her shoulders and her black-ribboned camisoles.

He went to the Pompeian for his fortnightly hair-trim. As always, he felt disloyal at deserting his neighbor, the Reeves Building Barber Shop. Then, for the first time, he overthrew his sense of guilt. "Doggone it, I don't have to go here if I don't want to! I don't own the Reeves Building! These barbers got nothing on me! I'll doggone well get my hair cut where I doggone well want to! Don't want to hear anything more about it! I'm through standing by people—unless I want to. It doesn't get you anywhere. I'm through!"

The Pompeian Barber Shop was in the basement of the Hotel Thornleigh, largest and most dynamically modern hotel in Zenith. Curving marble steps with a rail of polished brass led from the hotel-lobby down to the barber shop. The interior was of black and white and crimson tiles, with a sensational ceiling of burnished gold, and a fountain in which a massive nymph forever emptied a scarlet cornucopia. Forty barbers and nine manicure girls worked desperately, and at the door six colored porters lurked to greet the customers, to care reverently for their hats and collars, to lead them to a place of waiting where, on a carpet like a tropic isle in the stretch of white stone floor, were a dozen leather chairs and a table heaped with magazines.

Babbitt's porter was an obsequious gray-haired negro who did him an honor highly esteemed in the land of Zenith— greeted him by name. Yet Babbitt was unhappy. His bright particular manicure girl was engaged. She was doing the nails of an overdressed man and giggling with him. Babbitt hated him. He thought of waiting, but to stop the powerful system of the Pompeian was inconceivable, and he was instantly wafted into a chair.

About him was luxury, rich and delicate. One votary was having a violet-ray facial treatment, the next an oil shampoo. Boys wheeled about miraculous electrical massage-machines. The barbers snatched steaming towels from a machine like a a howitzer of polished nickel and disdainfully flung them away after a second's use. On the vast marble shelf facing the chairs were hundreds of tonics, amber and ruby and emerald. It was flattering to Babbitt to have two personal slaves at once—the barber and the bootblack. He would have been completely happy if he could also -have had the manicure girl. The barber snipped at his hair and asked his opinion of the Havre de Grace races, the baseball season, and Mayor Prout. The young negro bootblack hummed "The Camp Meeting Blues" and polished in rhythm to his tune, drawing the shiny shoe-rag so taut at each stroke that it snapped like a banjo string. The barber was an excellent salesman. He made Babbitt feel rich and important by his manner of inquiring, "What is your favorite tonic, sir? Have you time to-day, sir, for a facial massage? Your scalp is a little tight; shall I give you a scalp massage?"

Babbitt's best thrill was in the shampoo. The barber made his hair creamy with thick soap, then (as Babbitt bent over the bowl, muffled in towels) drenched it with hot water which prickled along his scalp, and at last ran the water ice-cold. At the shock, the sudden burning cold on his skull, Babbitt's heart thumped, his chest heaved, and his spine was an electric wire. It was a sensation which broke the monotony of life. He looked grandly about the shop as he sat up. The barber obsequiously rubbed his wet hair and bound it in a towel as in a turban, so that Babbitt resembled a plump pink calif on an ingenious and adjustable throne. The barber begged (in the manner of one who was a good fellow yet was overwhelmed by the splendors of the calif), "How about a little Eldorado Oil Rub, sir? Very beneficial to the scalp, sir. Didn't I give you one the last time?"

He hadn't, but Babbitt agreed, "Well, all right."

With quaking eagerness he saw that his manicure girl was free.

"I don't know, I guess I'll have a manicure after all," he droned, and excitedly watched her coming, dark-haired, smiling, tender, little. The manicuring would have to be finished at her table, and he would be able to talk to her without the barber listening. He waited contentedly, not trying to peep at her, while she filed his nails and the barber shaved him and smeared on his burning cheeks all the interesting mixtures which the pleasant minds of barbers have devised through the revolving ages. When the barber was done and he sat opposite the girl at her table, he admired the marble slab of it, admired the sunken set bowl with its tiny silver taps, and admired himself for being able to frequent so costly a place. When she withdrew his wet hand from the bowl, it was so sensitive from the warm soapy water that he was abnormally aware of the clasp of her firm little paw. He delighted in the pinkness and glossiness of her nails. Her hands seemed to him more adorable than Mrs. Judique's thin fingers, and more elegant. He had a certain ecstasy in the pain when she gnawed at the cuticle of his nails with a sharp knife. He struggled not to look at the outline of her young bosom and her shoulders, the more apparent under a film of pink chiffon. He was conscious of her as an exquisite thing, and when he tried to impress his personality on her he spoke as awkwardly as a country boy at his first party:

"Well, kinda hot to be working to-day."

"Oh, yes, it is hot. You cut your own nails, last time, didn't you!"

"Ye-es, guess I must 've."

"You always ought to go to a manicure."

"Yes, maybe that's so. I—"

"There's nothing looks so nice as nails that are looked after good. I always think that's the best way to spot a real gent. There was an auto salesman in here yesterday that claimed you could always tell a fellow's class by the car he drove, but I says to him, 'Don't be silly,' I says; 'the wisenheimers grab a look at a fellow's nails when they want to tell if he's a tin-horn or a real gent!' "

"Yes, maybe there's something to that. Course, that is— with a pretty kiddy like you, a man can't help coming to get his mitts done."

"Yeh, I may be a kid, but I'm a wise bird, and I know nice folks when I see um—I can read character at a glance—and I'd never talk so frank with a fellow if I couldn't see he was a nice fellow."

She smiled. Her eyes seemed to him as gentle as April pools. With great seriousness he informed himself that "there were some roughnecks who would think that just because a girl was a manicure girl and maybe not awful well educated, she was no good, but as for him, he was a democrat, and understood people," and he stood by the assertion that this was a fine girl, a good girl—but not too uncomfortably good. He inquired in a voice quick with sympathy:

"I suppose you have a lot of fellows who try to get fresh with you."

"Say, gee, do I! Say, listen, there's some of these cigar-store sports that think because a girl's working in a barber shop, they can get away with anything. The things they saaaaaay! But, believe me, I know how to hop those birds! I just give um the north and south and ask um, 'Say, who do you think you're talking to?' and they fade away like love's young nightmare and oh, don't you want a box of nail-paste? It will keep the nails as shiny as when first mani-cured, harmless to apply and lasts for days."

"Sure, I'll try some. Say— Say, it's funny; I've been coming here ever since the shop opened and—" With arch surprise. "—I don't believe I know your name!"

"Don't you? My, that's funny! I don't know yours!"

"Now you quit kidding me! What's the nice little name?"

"Oh, it ain't so darn nice. I guess it's kind of kike. But my folks ain't kikes. My papa's papa was a nobleman in Poland, and there was a gentleman in here one day, he was kind of a count or something—"

"Kind of a no-account, I guess you mean!"

"Who's telling this, smarty? And he said he knew my papa's papa's folks in Poland and they had a dandy big house. Right on a lake!" Doubtfully, "Maybe you don't believe it?"

"Sure. No. Really. Sure I do. Why not? Don't think I'm kidding you, honey, but every time I've noticed you I've said to myself, 'That kid has Blue Blood in her veins!' "

"Did you, honest?"

"Honest I did. Well, well, come on—now we're friends— what's the darling little name?"

"Ida Putiak. It ain't so much-a-much of a name. I always say to Ma, I say, 'Ma, why didn't you name me Dolores, or something with some class to it?' "

"Well, now, I think it's a scrumptious name. Ida!"

"I bet I know *your* name!"

"Well, now, not necessarily. Of course— Oh, it isn't so specially well known."

"Aren't you Mr. Sondheim that travels for the Krackajack Kitchen Kutlery Ko.?"

"I am not! I'm Mr. Babbitt, the real-estate broker!"

"Oh, excuse me! Oh, of course. You mean here in Zenith."

"Yep." With the briskness of one whose feelings have been hurt.

"Oh, sure. I've read your ads. They're swell."

"Um, well— You might have read about my speeches."

"Course I have! I don't get much time to read but— I guess you think I'm an awfully silly little nit!"

"I think you're a little darling!"

"Well— There's one nice thing about this job. It gives a girl a chance to meet some awfully nice gentlemen and improve her mind with conversation, and you get so you can read a guy's character at the first glance."

"Look here, Ida; please don't think I'm getting fresh—" He was hotly reflecting that it would be humiliating to be rejected by this child, and dangerous to be accepted. If he took her to dinner, if he were seen by censorious friends— But he went on ardently: "Don't think I'm getting fresh if I suggest it would be nice for us to go out and have a little dinner together some evening."

"I don't know as I ought to but— My gentleman-friend's always wanting to take me out. But maybe I could to-night."

IV

There was no reason, he assured himself, why he shouldn't have a quiet dinner with a poor girl who would benefit by association with an educated and mature person like himself. But, lest some one see them and not understand, he would take her to Biddlemeier's Inn, on the outskirts of the city. They would have a pleasant drive, this hot lonely evening, and he might hold her hand—no, he wouldn't even do that. Ida was complaisant; her bare shoulders showed it only too clearly; but he'd be hanged if he'd make love to her merely because she expected it.

Then his car broke down; something had happened to the ignition. And he *had* to have the car this evening! Furiously he tested the spark-plugs, stared at the commutator. His angriest glower did not seem to stir the sulky car, and in disgrace it was hauled off to a garage. With a renewed thrill he thought of a taxicab. There was something at once wealthy and interestingly wicked about a taxicab.

But when he met her, on a corner two blocks from the Hotel Thornleigh, she said, "A taxi? Why, I thought you owned a car!"

"I do. Of course I do! But it's out of commission to-night."

"Oh," she remarked, as one who had heard that tale before.

All the way out to Biddlemeier's Inn he tried to talk as an old friend, but he could not pierce the wall of her words. With interminable indignation she narrated her retorts to "that fresh head-barber" and the drastic things she would do to him if he persisted in saying that she was "better at gassing than at hoof-paring."

At Biddlemeier's Inn they were unable to get anything to drink. The head-waiter refused to understand who George F. Babbitt was. They sat steaming before a vast mixed grill, and made conversation about baseball. When he tried to hold Ida's hand she said with bright friendliness, "Careful! That fresh waiter is rubbering." But they came out into a treacherous summer night, the air lazy and a little moon above transfigured maples.

"Let's drive some other place, where we can get a drink and dance!" he demanded.

"Sure, some other night. But I promised Ma I'd be home early to-night."

"Rats! It's too nice to go home."

"I'd just love to, but Ma would give me fits."

He was trembling. She was everything that was young and exquisite. He put his arm about her. She snuggled against his shoulder, unafraid, and he was triumphant. Then she ran down the steps of the Inn, singing, "Come on, Georgie, we'll have a nice drive and get cool."

It was a night of lovers. All along the highway into Zenith, under the low and gentle moon, motors were parked and dim figures were clasped in revery. He held out hungry hands to Ida, and when she patted them he was grateful. There was no sense of struggle and transition; he kissed her and simply she responded to his kiss, they two behind the stolid back of the chauffeur.

Her hat fell off, and she broke from his embrace to reach for it.

"Oh, let it be!" he implored.

"Huh? My hat? Not a chance!"

He waited till she had pinned it on, then his arm sank about her. She drew away from it, and said with maternal soothing, "Now, don't be a silly boy! Mustn't make lttle Mama scold! Just sit back, dearie, and see what a swell night it is. If you're a good boy, maybe I'll kiss you when we say nighty-night. Now give me a cigarette."

He was solicitous about lighting her cigarette and inquiring as to her comfort. Then he sat as far from her as possible. He was cold with failure. No one could have told Babbitt that he was a fool with more vigor, precision, and intelligence than he himself displayed. He reflected that from the standpoint of the Rev. Dr. John Jennison Drew he was a wicked man, and from the standpoint of Miss Ida Putiak, an old bore who had to be endured as the penalty attached to eating a large dinner.

"Dearie, you aren't going to go and get peevish, are you?"

She spoke pertly. He wanted to spank her. He brooded, "I don't have to take anything off this gutter-pup! Darn immigrant! Well, let's get it over as quick as we can, and sneak home and kick ourselves for the rest of the night."

He snorted, "Huh? Me peevish? Why, you baby, why should I be peevish! Now, listen, Ida; listen to Uncle George.

I want to put you wise about this scrapping with your head-barber all the time. I've had a lot of experience with employees, and let me tell you it doesn't pay to antagonize—"

At the drab wooden house in which she lived he said good-night briefly and amiably, but as the taxicab drove off he was praying "Oh, my God!"

chapter 25

HE awoke to stretch cheerfully as he listened to the sparrows, then to remember that everything was wrong; that he was determined to go astray, and not in the least enjoying the process. Why, he wondered, should he be in rebellion? What was it all about? "Why not be sensible; stop all this idiotic running around, and enjoy himself with his family, his business, the fellows at the club?" What was he getting out of rebellion? Misery and shame—the shame of being treated as an offensive small boy by a ragamuffin like Ida Putiak! And yet— Always he came back to "And yet." Whatever the misery, he could not regain contentment with a world which, once doubted, became absurd.

Only, he assured himself, he was "through with this chasing after girls."

By noontime he was not so sure even of that. If in Miss McGoun, Louetta Swanson, and Ida he had failed to find the lady kind and lovely, it did not prove that she did not exist. He was hunted by the ancient thought that somewhere must exist the not impossible she who would understand him, value him, and make him happy.

II

Mrs. Babbitt returned in August.

On her previous absences he had missed her reassuring buzz and of her arrival he had made a fête. Now, though he dared not hurt her by letting a hint of it appear in his letters, he was sorry that she was coming before he had found himself, and he was embarrassed by the need of meeting her and looking joyful.

He loitered down to the station; he studied the summer-resort posters, lest he have to speak to acquaintances and expose his uneasiness. But he was well trained. When the train clanked in he was out on the cement platform, peering into the chair-cars, and as he saw her in the line of passengers moving toward the vestibule he waved his hat. At the door he embraced her, and announced, "Well, well, well, well, by golly, you look fine, you look fine." Then he was aware of Tinka. Here was something, this child with her absurd little nose and lively eyes, that loved him, believed him great, and as he clasped her, lifted and held her till she squealed, he was for the moment come back to his old steady self.

Tinka sat beside him in the car, with one hand on the steering-wheel, pretending to help him drive, and he shouted back to his wife, "I'll bet the kid will be the best chuffer in the family! She holds the wheel like an old professional!"

All the while he was dreading the moment when he would be alone with his wife and she would patiently expect him to be ardent.

III

There was about the house an unofficial theory that he was to take his vacation alone, to spend a week or ten days in Catawba, but he was nagged by the memory that a year ago he had been with Paul in Maine. He saw himself returning; finding peace there, and the presence of Paul, in a life primitive and heroic. Like a shock came the thought that he actually could go. Only, he couldn't, really; he couldn't leave his business, and "Myra would think it sort of funny, his going way off there alone. Course he'd decided to do whatever he darned pleased, from now on, but still—to go way off to Maine!"

He went, after lengthy meditations.

With his wife, since it was inconceivable to explain that he was going to seek Paul's spirit in the wilderness, he frugally employed the lie prepared over a year ago and scarcely used at all. He said that he had to see a man in New York on business. He could not have explained even to himself why he drew from the bank several hundred dollars more than he needed, nor why he kissed Tinka so tenderly, and cried, "God bless you, baby!" From the train he waved to her till she was but a scarlet spot beside the brown bulkier presence of Mrs. Babbitt, at the end of a steel and cement aisle ending in vast barred gates. With melancholy he looked back at the last suburb of Zenith.

All the way north he pictured the Maine guides: simple and strong and daring, jolly as they played stud-poker in their unceiled shack, wise in woodcraft as they tramped the forest and shot the rapids. He particularly remembered Joe Paradise, half Yankee, half Indian. If he could but take up a backwoods claim with a man like Joe, work hard with his hands, be free and noisy in a flannel shirt, and never come back to this dull decency!

Or, like a trapper in a Northern Canada movie, plunge through the forest, make camp in the Rockies, a grim and wordless caveman! Why not? He *could* do it! There'd be enough money at home for the family to live on till Verona was married and Ted self-supporting. Old Henry T. would look out for them. Honestly! Why *not?* Really live—

He longed for it, admitted that he longed for it, then almost believed that he was going to do it. Whenever common sense snorted, "Nonsense! Folks don't run away from decent families and partners; just simply don't do it, that's all!" then Babbitt answered pleadingly, "Well, it wouldn't take any more nerve than for Paul to go to jail and—Lord, how I'd like to do it! Moccasins—six-gun—frontier town—gamblers —sleep under the stars—be a regular man, with he-men like Joe Paradise—gosh!"

So he came to Maine, again stood on the wharf before the camp-hotel, again spat heroically into the delicate and shivering water, while the pines rustled, the mountains glowed, and a trout leaped and fell in a sliding circle. He hurried to the guides' shack as to his real home, his real friends, long missed. They would be glad to see him. They would stand up and shout, "Why, here's Mr. Babbitt! He ain't one of these ordinary sports! He's a real guy!"

In their boarded and rather littered cabin the guides sat about the greasy table playing stud-poker with greasy cards: half a dozen wrinkled men in old trousers and easy old felt hats. They glanced up and nodded. Joe Paradise, the swart aging man with the big mustache, grunted, "How do. Back again?"

Silence, except for the clatter of chips.

Babbitt stood beside them, very lonely. He hinted, after a period of highly concentrated playing, "Guess I might take a hand, Joe."

"Sure. Sit in. How many chips you want? Let's see; you were here with your wife, last year, wa'n't you?" said Joe Paradise.

That was all of Babbitt's welcome to the old home.

He played for half an hour before he spoke again. His head was reeking with the smoke of pipes and cheap cigars, and he was weary of pairs and four-flushes, resentful of the way in which they ignored him. He flung at Joe:

"Working now?"

"Nope."

"Like to guide me for a few days?"

"Well, jus' soon. I ain't engaged till next week."

Only thus did Joe recognize the friendship Babbitt was offering him. Babbitt paid up his losses and left the shack rather childishly. Joe raised his head from the coils of smoke like a seal rising from surf, grunted, "I'll come 'round t'morrow," and dived down to his three aces.

Neither in his voiceless cabin, fragrant with planks of new-cut pine, nor along the lake, nor in the sunset clouds which presently eddied behind the lavender-misted mountains, could Babbitt find the spirit of Paul as a reassuring presence. He was so lonely that after supper he stopped to talk with an ancient old lady, a gasping and steadily discoursing old lady, by the stove in the hotel-office. He told her of Ted's presumable future triumphs in the State University and of Tinka's remarkable vocabulary till he was homesick for the home he had left forever.

Through the darkness, through that Northern pine-walled silence, he blundered down to the lake-front and found a canoe. There were no paddles in it but with a board, sitting awkwardly amidships and poking at the water rather than paddling, he made his way far out on the lake. The lights of the hotel and the cottages became yellow dots, a cluster of glow-worms at the base of Sachem Mountain. Larger and ever more imperturbable was the mountain in the star-filtered darkness, and the lake a limitless pavement of black marble. He was dwarfed and dumb and a little awed, but that insignificance freed him from the pomposities of being Mr. George F. Babbitt of Zenith; saddened and freed his heart. Now he was conscious of the presence of Paul, fancied him (rescued from prison, from Zilla and the brisk exactitudes of the

tar-roofing business) playing his violin at the end of the
canoe. He vowed, "I will go on! I'll never go back! Now that
Paul's out of it, I don't want to see any of those damn people
again! I was a fool to get sore because Joe Paradise didn't
jump up and hug me. He's one of these woodsmen; too wise
to go yelping and talking your arm off like a cityman. But
get him back in the mountains, out on the trail—! That's
real living!"

IV

Joe reported at Babbitt's cabin at nine the next morning. Babbitt greeted him as a fellow caveman:

"Well, Joe, how d' you feel about hitting the trail, and
getting away from these darn soft summerites and these
women and all?"

"All right, Mr. Babbitt."

"What do you say we go over to Box Car Pond—they tell
me the shack there isn't being used—and camp out?"

"Well, all right, Mr. Babbitt, but it's nearer to Skowtuit
Pond, and you can get just about as good fishing there."

"No, I want to get into the real wilds."

"Well, all right."

"We'll put the old packs on our backs and get into the
woods and really hike."

"I think maybe it would be easier to go by water, through
Lake Chogue. We can go all the way by motor boat—flat-
bottom boat with an Evinrude."

"No, sir! Bust up the quiet with a chugging motor? Not
on your life! You just throw a pair of socks in the old pack,
and tell 'em what you want for eats. I'll be ready soon 's
you are."

"Most of the sports go by boat, Mr. Babbitt. It's a long
walk."

"Look here, Joe: are you objecting to walking?"

"Oh, no, I guess I can do it. But I haven't tramped that
far for sixteen years. Most of the sports go by boat. But I can
do it if you say so—I guess." Joe walked away in sadness.

Babbitt had recovered from his touchy wrath before Joe
returned. He pictured him as warming up and telling the most
entertaining stories. But Joe had not yet warmed up when
they took the trail. He persistently kept behind Babbitt, and
however much his shoulders ached from the pack, however
sorely he panted, Babbitt could hear his guide panting equally.
But the trail was satisfying: a path brown with pine-needles

and rough with roots, among the balsams, the ferns, the sudden groves of white birch. He became credulous again, and rejoiced in sweating. When he stopped to rest he chuckled, "Guess we're hitting it up pretty good for a couple o' old birds, eh?"

"Uh-huh," admitted Joe.

"This is a mighty pretty place. Look, you can see the lake down through the trees. I tell you, Joe, you don't appreciate how lucky you are to live in woods like this, instead of a city with trolleys grinding and typewriters clacking and people bothering the life out of you all the time! I wish I knew the woods like you do. Say, what's the name of that little red flower?"

Rubbing his back, Joe regarded the flower resentfully. "Well, some folks call it one thing and some calls it another. I always just call it Pink Flower."

Babbitt blessedly ceased thinking as tramping turned into blind plodding. He was submerged in weariness. His plump legs seemed to go on by themselves, without guidance, and he mechanically wiped away the sweat which stung his eyes. He was too tired to be consciously glad as, after a sun-scourged mile of corduroy tote-road through a swamp where flies hovered over a hot waste of brush, they reached the cool shore of Box Car Pond. When he lifted the pack from his back he staggered from the change in balance, and for a moment could not stand erect. He lay beneath an ample-bosomed maple tree near the guest-shack, and joyously felt sleep running through his veins.

He awoke toward dusk, to find Joe efficiently cooking bacon and eggs and flapjacks for supper, and his admiration of the woodsman returned. He sat on a stump and felt virile.

"Joe, what would you do if you had a lot of money? Would you stick to guiding, or would you take a claim 'way back in the woods and be independent of people?"

For the first time Joe brightened. He chewed his cud a second, and bubbled, "I've often thought of that! If I had the money, I'd go down to Tinker's Falls and open a swell shoe store."

After supper Joe proposed a game of stud-poker but Babbitt refused with brevity, and Joe contentedly went to bed at eight. Babbitt sat on the stump, facing the dark pond, slapping mosquitos. Save the snoring guide, there was no other human being within ten miles. He was lonelier than he had ever been in his life. Then he was in Zenith.

He was worrying as to whether Miss McGoun wasn't paying too much for carbon paper. He was at once resenting and missing the persistent teasing at the Roughnecks' Table. He was wondering what Zilla Riesling was doing now. He was wondering whether, after the summer's maturity of being a garageman, Ted would "get busy" in the university. He was thinking of his wife. "If she would only—if she wouldn't be so darn satisfied with just settling down— No! I won't! I won't go back! I'll be fifty in three years. Sixty in thirteen years. I'm going to have some fun before it's too late. I don't care! I will!"

He thought of Ida Putiak, of Louetta Swanson, of that nice widow—what was her name?—Tanis Judique?—the one for whom he'd found the flat. He was enmeshed in imaginary conversations. Then:

"Gee, I can't seem to get away from thinking about folks!"

Thus it came to him merely to run away was folly, because he could never run away from himself.

That moment he started for Zenith. In this journey there was no appearance of flight, but he was fleeing, and four days afterward he was on the Zenith train. He knew that he was slinking back not because it was what he longed to do but because it was all he could do. He scanned again his discovery that he could never run away from Zenith and family and office, because in his own brain he bore the office and the family and every street and disquiet and illusion of Zenith.

"But I'm going to—oh, I'm going to start something!" he vowed, and he tried to make it valiant.

chapter 26

A S he walked through the train, looking for familiar faces, he saw only one person whom he knew, and that was Seneca Doane, the lawyer who, after the blessings of being in Babbitt's own class at college and of becoming a corporation-counsel, had turned crank, had headed farmer-labor tickets and fraternized with admitted socialists. Though he was in rebellion, naturally Babbitt did not care to be seen talking with such a fanatic, but in all the Pullmans he could find no other acquaintance, and reluctantly he halted. Seneca Doane was a slight, thin-haired man, rather like Chum Frink except that he hadn't Frink's grin. He was reading a book called "The Way of All Flesh." It looked religious to Babbitt, and he wondered if Doane could possibly have been converted and turned decent and patriotic.

"Why, hello, Doane," he said.

Doane looked up. His voice was curiously kind. "Oh! How do, Babbitt."

"Been away, eh?"

"Yes, I've been in Washington."

"Washington, eh? How's the old Government making out?"

"It's— Won't you sit down?"

"Thanks. Don't care if I do. Well, well! Been quite a while since I've had a good chance to talk to you, Doane. I was, uh— Sorry you didn't turn up at the last class-dinner."

"Oh—thanks."

"How's the unions coming? Going to run for mayor again?"

Doane seemed restless. He was fingering the pages of his book. He said "I might" as though it didn't mean anything in particular, and he smiled.

Babbitt liked that smile, and hunted for conversation: "Saw a bang-up cabaret in New York: the 'Good-Morning Cutie' bunch at the Hotel Minton."

"Yes, they're pretty girls. I danced there one evening."

"Oh. Like dancing?"

"Naturally. I like dancing and pretty women and good food better than anything else in the world. Most men do."

"But gosh, Doane, I thought you fellows wanted to take all the good eats and everything away from us."

"No. Not at all. What I'd like to see is the meetings of the Garment Workers held at the Ritz, with a dance afterward. Isn't that reasonable?"

"Yuh, might be good idea, all right. Well— Shame I haven't seen more of you, recent years. Oh, say, hope you haven't held it against me, my bucking you as mayor, going on the stump for Prout. You see, I'm an organization Republican, and I kind of felt—"

"There's no reason why you shouldn't fight me. I have no doubt you're good for the Organization. I remember—in college you were an unusually liberal, sensitive chap. I can still recall your saying to me that you were going to be a lawyer, and take the cases of the poor for nothing, and fight the rich. And I remember I said I was going to be one of the rich myself, and buy paintings and live at Newport. I'm sure you inspired us all."

"Well. . . . Well. . . . I've always aimed to be liberal." Babbitt was enormously shy and proud and self-conscious; he tried to look like the boy he had been a quarter-century ago, and he shone upon his old friend Seneca Doane as he rumbled, "Trouble with a lot of these fellows, even the live wires and some of 'em that think they're forward-looking, is they aren't broad-minded and liberal. Now, I always believe in giving the other fellow a chance, and listening to his ideas."

"That's fine."

"Tell you how I figure it: A little opposition is good for all of us, so a fellow, especially if he's a business man and engaged in doing the work of the world, ought to be liberal."

"Yes—"

"I always say a fellow ought to have Vision and Ideals. I guess some of the fellows in my business think I'm pretty visionary, but I just let 'em think what they want to and go right on—same as you do. . . . By golly, this is nice to have a chance to sit and visit and kind of, you might say, brush up on our ideals."

"But of course we visionaries do rather get beaten. Doesn't it bother you?"

"Not a bit! Nobody can dictate to me what I think!"

"You're the man I want to help me. I want you to talk to some of the business men and try to make them a little more liberal in their attitude toward poor Beecher Ingram."

"Ingram? But, why, he's this nut preacher that got kicked out of the Congregationalist Church, isn't he, and preaches free love and sedition?"

This, Doane explained, was indeed the general conception of Beecher Ingram. but he himself saw Beecher Ingram as a priest of the brotherhood of man, of which Babbitt was notoriously an upholder. So would Babbitt keep his acquaintances from hounding Ingram and his forlorn little church?

"You bet! I'll call down any of the boys I hear getting funny about Ingram," Babbitt said affectionately to his dear friend Doane.

Doane warmed up and became reminiscent. He spoke of student days in Germany, of lobbying for single tax in Washington, of international labor conferences. He mentioned his friends, Lord Wycombe, Colonel Wedgwood, Professor Piccoli. Babbitt had always supposed that Doane associated only with I. W. W., but now he nodded gravely, as one who knew Lord Wycombes by the score, and he got in two references to Sir Gerald Doak. He felt daring and idealistic and cosmopolitan.

Suddenly, in his new spiritual grandeur, he was sorry for Zilla Riesling, and understood her as these ordinary fellows at the Boosters' Club never could.

II

Five hours after he had arrived in Zenith and told his wife how hot it was in New York, he went to call on Zilla. He was buzzing with ideas and forgiveness. He'd get Paul released; he'd do things, vague but highly benevolent things, for Zilla; he'd be as generous as his friend Seneca Doane.

He had not seen Zilla since Paul had shot her, and he still pictured her as buxom, high-colored, lively, and a little blowsy. As he drove up to her boarding-house, in a depressing back street below the wholesale district, he stopped in discomfort. At an upper window, leaning on her elbow, was a woman with the features of Zilla, but she was bloodless and aged, like a yellowed wad of old paper crumpled into wrinkles. Where Zilla had bounced and jiggled, this woman was dreadfully still.

He waited half an hour before she came into the boarding-house parlor. Fifty times he opened the book of photographs of the Chicago World's Fair of 1893, fifty times he looked at the picture of the Court of Honor.

He was startled to find Zilla in the room. She wore a black streaky gown which she had tried to brighten with a girdle of crimson ribbon. The ribbon had been torn and patiently mended. He noted this carefully, because he did not wish to look at her shoulders. One shoulder was lower than the other; one arm she carried in contorted fashion, as though it were paralyzed; and behind a high collar of cheap lace there a gouge in the anemic neck which had once been shining and softly plump.

"Yes?" she said.

"Well, well, old Zilla! By golly, it's good to see you again!"

"He can send his messages through a lawyer."

"Why, rats, Zilla, I didn't come just because of him. Came as an old friend."

"You waited long enough!"

"Well, you know how it is. Figured you wouldn't want to see a friend of his for quite some time and— Sit down, honey! Let's be sensible. We've all of us done a bunch of things that we hadn't ought to, but maybe we can sort of start over again. Honest, Zilla, I'd like to do something to make you both happy. Know what I thought to-day? Mind you, Paul doesn't know a thing about this— doesn't know I was going to come see you. I got to thinking: Zilla's a fine big-hearted woman, and she'll understand that, uh, Paul's had his lesson now. Why wouldn't it be a fine idea if you asked the governor to pardon him? Believe he would, if it came from you. No! Wait! Just think how good you'd feel if you were generous."

"Yes, I wish to be generous." She was sitting primly, speaking icily. "For that reason I wish to keep him in prison, as an example to evil-doers. I've gotten religion, George, since the terrible thing that man did to me. Sometimes I used to be unkind, and I wished for worldly pleasures, for dancing and the theater. But when I was in the hospital the pastor of the Pentecostal Communion Faith used to come to see me, and he showed me, right from the prophecies written in the Word of God, that the Day of Judgment is coming and all the members of the older churches are going straight to eternal damnation, because they only do lip-service and swallow the world, the flesh, and the devil—"

For fifteen wild minutes she talked, pouring out admonitions to flee the wrath to come, and her face flushed, her dead voice recaptured something of the shrill energy of the old Zilla. She wound up with a furious:

"It's the blessing of God himself that Paul should be in prison now, and torn and humbled by punishment, so that he may yet save his soul, and so other wicked men, these horrible chasers after women and lust, may have an example."

Babbitt had itched and twisted. As in church he dared not move during the sermon so now he felt that he must seem attentive, though her screeching denunciations flew past him like carrion birds.

He sought to be calm and brotherly:

"Yes, I know, Zilla. But gosh, it certainly is the essence of religion to be charitable, isn't it? Let me tell you how I figure it: What we need in the world is liberalism, liberality, if we're going to get anywhere. I've always believed in being broad-minded and liberal—"

"You? Liberal?" It was very much the old Zilla. "Why, George Babbitt, you're about as broad-minded and liberal as a razor-blade!"

"Oh, I am, am I! Well, just let me tell you, just—let—me—tell—you, I'm as by golly liberal as you are religious, anyway! *You religious!*"

"I am so! Our pastor says I sustain him in the faith!"

"I'll bet you do! With Paul's money! But just to show you how liberal I am, I'm going to send a check for ten bucks to this Beecher Ingram, because a lot of fellows are saying the poor cuss preaches sedition and free love, and they're trying to run him out of town."

"And they're right! They ought to run him out of town! Why, he preaches—if you can call it preaching—in a theater, in the House of Satan! You don't know what it is to find God, to find peace, to behold the snares that the devil spreads out for our feet. Oh, I'm so glad to see the mysterious purposes of God in having Paul harm me and stop my wickedness—and Paul's getting his, good and plenty, for the cruel things he did to me, and I hope he *dies* in prison!"

Babbitt was up, hat in hand, growling, "Well, if that's what you call being at peace, for heaven's sake just warn me before you go to war, will you?"

III

Vast is the power of cities to reclaim the wanderer. More than mountains or the shore-devouring sea, a city retains its character, imperturbable, cynical, holding behind apparent changes its essential purpose. Though Babbitt had deserted his family and dwelt with Joe Paradise in the wilderness, though he had become a liberal, though he had been quite sure, on the night before he reached Zenith, that neither he nor the city would be the same again, ten days after his return he could not believe that he had ever been away. Nor was it at all evident to his acquaintances that there was a new George F. Babbitt, save that he was more irritable under the incessant chaffing at the Athletic Club, and once, when Vergil Gunch observed that Seneca Doane ought to be hanged, Babbitt snorted, "Oh, rats, he's not so bad."

At home he grunted "Eh?" across the newspaper to his commentatory wife, and was delighted by Tinka's new red tam o'shanter, and announced, "No class to that corrugated iron garage. Have to build me a nice frame one."

Verona and Kenneth Escott appeared really to be engaged. In his newspaper Escott had conducted a pure-food crusade against commission-houses. As a result he had been given an excellent job in a commission-house, and he was making a salary on which he could marry, and denouncing irresponsible reporters who wrote stories criticizing commission-houses without knowing what they were talking about.

This September Ted had entered the State University as a freshman in the College of Arts and Sciences. The university was at Mohalis, only fifteen miles from Zenith, and Ted often came down for the week-end. Babbitt was worried. Ted was "going in for" everything but books. He had tried to "make" the football team as a light half-back, he was looking forward to the basket-ball season, he was on the committee for the Freshman Hop, and (as a Zenithite, an aristocrat among the yokels) he was being "rushed" by two fraternities. But of his studies Babbitt could learn nothing save a mumbled, "Oh, gosh, these old stiffs of teachers just give you a lot of junk about literature and economics."

One week-end Ted proposed. "Say, Dad, why can't I transfer over from the College to the School of Engineering and take mechanical engineering? You always holler that I never study, but honest, I would study there."

"No, the Engineering School hasn't got the standing the College has," fretted Babbitt.

"I'd like to know how it hasn't! The Engineers can play on any of the teams!"

There was much explanation of the "dollars-and-cents value of being known as a college man when you go into the law," and a truly oratorical account of the lawyer's life. Before he was through with it, Babbitt had Ted a United States Senator.

Among the great lawyers whom he mentioned was Seneca Doane.

"But, gee whiz," Ted marveled, "I thought you always said this Doane was a reg'lar nut!"

"That's no way to speak of a great man! Doane's always been a good friend of mine—fact I helped him in college—I started him out and you might say inspired him. Just because he's sympathetic with the aims of Labor, a lot of chumps that lack liberality and broad-mindedness think he's a crank, but let me tell you there's mighty few of 'em that rake in the fees he does, and he's a friend of some of the strongest, most conservative men in the world—like Lord Wycombe, this, uh, this big English nobleman that's so well known. And you now, which would you rather do: be in with a lot of greasy mechanics and laboring-men, or chum up to a real fellow like Lord Wycombe, and get invited to his house for parties?"

"Well—gosh," sighed Ted.

The next week-end he came in joyously with, "Say, Dad, why couldn't I take mining engineering instead of the academic course? You talk about standing—maybe there isn't much in mechanical engineering, but the Miners, gee, they got seven out of eleven in the new elections to Nu Tau Tau!"

chapter 27

THE strike which turned Zenith into two belligerent camps, white and red, began late in September with a walk-out of telephone girls and linemen, in protest against a reduction of wages. The newly formed union of dairy-products workers went out, partly in sympathy and partly in demand for a forty-four hour week. They were followed by the truck-drivers' union. Industry was tied up, and the whole city was nervous with talk of a trolley strike, a printers' strike, a general strike. Furious citizens, trying to get telephones calls through strike-breaking girls, danced helplessly. Every truck that made its way from the factories to the freight-stations was guarded by a policeman, trying to look stoical beside the scab driver. A line of fifty trucks from the Zenith Steel and Machinery Company was attacked by strikers—rushing out from the sidewalk, pulling drivers from the seats, smashing carburetors and commutators, while telephone girls cheered from the walk, and small boys heaved bricks.

The National Guard was ordered out. Colonel Nixon, who

in private life was Mr. Caleb Nixon, secretary of the Pullmore Tractor Company, put on a long khaki coat and stalked through crowds, a .44 automatic in hand. Even Babbitt's friend, Clarence Drum the shoe merchant—a round and merry man who told stories at the Athletic Club, and who strangely resembled a Victorian pug-dog—was to be seen as a waddling but ferocious captain, with his belt tight about his comfortable little belly, and his round little mouth petulant as he piped to chattering groups on corners. "Move on there now! I can't have any of this loitering!"

Every newspaper in the city, save one, was against the strikers. When mobs raided the news-stands, at each was stationed a militiaman, a young, embarrassed citizen-soldier with eye-glasses, bookkeeper or grocery-clerk in private life, trying to look dangerous while small boys yelped, "Get onto de tin soldier!" and striking truck-drivers inquired tenderly, "Say, Joe, when I was fighting in France, was you in camp in the States or was you doing Swede exercises in the Y. M. C. A.? Be careful of that bayonet, now, or you'll cut yourself!"

There was no one in Zenith who talked of anything but the strike, and no one who did not take sides. You were either a courageous friend of Labor, or you were a fearless supporter of the Rights of Property; and in either case you were belligerent, and ready to disown any friend who did not hate the enemy.

A condensed-milk plant was set afire—each side charged it to the other—and the city was hysterical.

And Babbitt chose this time to be publicly liberal.

He belonged to the sound, sane, right-thinking wing, and at first he agreed that the Crooked Agitators ought to be shot. He was sorry when his friend, Seneca Doane, defended arrested strikers, and he thought of going to Doane and explaining about these agitators, but when he read a broadside alleging that even on their former wages the telephone girls had been hungry, he was troubled. "All lies and fake figures," he said, but in a doubtful croak.

For the Sunday after, the Chatham Road Presbyterian Church announced a sermon by Dr. John Jennison Drew on "How the Saviour Would End Strikes." Babbitt had been negligent about church-going lately, but he went to the service, hopeful that Dr. Drew really did have the information as to what the divine powers thought about strikes. Beside Babbitt in the large, curving, glossy, velvet-upholstered pew was Chum Frink.

Frink whispered, "Hope the doc gives the strikers hell! Ordinarily, I don't believe in a preacher butting into political matters—let him stick to straight religion and save souls, and not stir up a lot of discussion—but at a time like this, I do think he ought to stand right up and bawl out those plug-uglies to a fare-you-well!"

"Yes—well—" said Babbitt.

The Rev. Dr. Drew, his rustic bang flopping with the intensity of his poetic and sociologic ardor, trumpeted:

"During the untoward series of industrial dislocations which have—let us be courageous and admit it boldly—throttled the business life of our fair city these past days, there has been a great deal of loose talk about scientific prevention of scientific—*scientific!* Now, let me tell you that the most unscientific thing in the world is science! Take the attacks on the established fundamentals of the Christian creed which were so popular with the 'scientists' a generation ago. Oh, yes, they were mighty fellows, and great poo-bahs of criticism! They were going to destroy the church; they were going to prove the world was created and has been brought to its extraordinary level of morality and civilization by blind chance. Yet the church stands just as firmly to-day as ever, and the only answer a Christian pastor needs make to the long-haired opponents of his simple faith is just a pitying smile!

"And now these same 'scientists' want to replace the natural condition of free competition by crazy systems which, no matter by what high-sounding names they are called, are nothing but a despotic paternalism. Naturally, I'm not criticizing labor courts, injunctions against men proven to be striking unjustly, or those excellent unions in which the men and the boss get together. But I certainly am criticizing the systems in which the free and fluid motivation of independent labor is to be replaced by cooked-up wage-scales and minimum salaries and government commissions and labor federations and all that poppycock.

"What is not generally understood is that this whole industrial matter isn't a question of economics. It's essentially and only a matter of Love, and of the practical application of the Christian religion! Imagine a factory—instead of committees of workmen alienating the boss, the boss goes among them smiling, and they smile back, the elder brother and the younger. Brothers, that's what they must be, loving brothers, and then strikes would be as inconceivable as hatred in the home!"

It was at this point that Babbitt muttered, "Oh, rot!"

"Huh?" said Chum Frink.

"He doesn't know what he's talking about. It's just as clear as mud. It doesn't mean a darn thing."

"Maybe, but—"

Frink looked at him doubtfully, through all the service kept glancing at him doubtfully, till Babbitt was nervous.

II

The strikers had announced a parade for Tuesday morning, but Colonel Nixon had forbidden it, the newspapers said. When Babbitt drove west from his office at ten that morning, he saw a drove of shabby men heading toward the tangled, dirty district beyond Court House Square. He hated them, because they were poor, because they made him feel insecure. "Damn loafers! Wouldn't be common workmen if they had any pep," he complained. He wondered if there was going to be a riot. He drove toward the starting-point of the parade, a triangle of limp and faded grass known as Moore Street Park, and halted his car.

The park and streets were buzzing with strikers, young men in blue denim shirts, old men with caps. Through them, keeping them stirred like a boiling pot, moved the militiamen. Babbitt could hear the soldiers' monotonous orders: "Keep moving—move on, 'bo—keep your feet warm!" Babbitt admired their stolid good temper. The crowd shouted, "Tin soldiers," and "Dirty dogs—servants of the capitalists!" but the militiamen grinned and answered only, "Sure, that's right. Keep moving, Billy!"

Babbitt thrilled over the citizen-soldiers, hated the scoundrels who were obstructing the pleasant ways of prosperity, admired Colonel Nixon's striding contempt for the crowd; and as Captain Clarence Drum, that rather puffing shoe-dealer, came raging by, Babbitt respectfully clamored, "Great work, Captain! Don't let 'em march!" He watched the strikers filing from the park. Many of them bore posters with "They can't stop our peacefully walking." The militiamen tore away the posters, but the strikers fell in behind their leaders and straggled off, a thin unimpressive trickle between steel-glinting lines of soldiers. Babbitt saw with disappointment that there wasn't going to be any violence, nothing interesting at all. Then he gasped.

Among the marchers, beside a bulky young workman, was Seneca Doane, smiling, content. In front of him was Professor Brockbank, head of the history department in the State University, an old man and white-bearded, known to come from a distinguished Massachusetts family.

"Why, gosh," Babbitt marveled, "a swell like him in with the strikers? And good ole Senny Doane! They're fools to get mixed up with this bunch. They're parlor socialists! But they have got nerve. And nothing in it for them, not a cent! And—I don't know 's *all* the strikers look like such tough nuts. Look just about like anybody else to me!"

The militiamen were turning the parade down a side street.

"They got just as much right to march as anybody else! They own the streets as much as Clarence Drum or the American Legion does!" Babbitt grumbled. "Of course, they're—they're a bad element, but— Oh, rats!"

At the Athletic Club, Babbitt was silent during lunch, while the others fretted, "I don't know what the world's coming to," or solaced their spirits with "kidding."

Captain Clarence Drum came swinging by, splendid in khaki.

"How's it going, Captain?" inquired Vergil Gunch.

"Oh, we got 'em stopped. We worked 'em off on side streets and separated 'em and they got discouraged and went home."

"Fine work. No violence."

"Fine work nothing!" groaned Mr. Drum. "If I had my way, there'd be a whole lot of violence, and I'd start it, and then the whole thing would be over. I don't believe in standing back and wet-nursing these fellows and letting the disturbances drag on. I tell you these strikers are nothing in God's world but a lot of bomb-throwing socialists and thugs, and the only way to handle 'em is with a club! That's what I'd do; beat up the whole lot of 'em!"

Babbitt heard himself saying, "Oh, rats, Clarence, they look just about like you and me, and I certainly didn't notice any bombs."

Drum complained, "Oh, you didn't, eh? Well, maybe you'd like to take charge of the strike! Just tell Colonel Nixon what innocents the strikers are! He'd be glad to hear about it!" Drum strode on, while all the table stared at Babbitt.

"What's the idea? Do you want us to give those hell-hounds love and kisses, or what?" said Orville Jones.

"Do you defend a lot hoodlums that are trying to take the bread and butter away from our families?" raged Professor Pumphrey.

Vergil Gunch intimidatingly said nothing. He put on sternness like a mask; his jaw was hard, his bristly short hair seemed cruel, his silence was a ferocious thunder. While the others assured Babbitt that they must have misunderstood him, Gunch looked as though he had understood only too well. Like a robed judge he listened to Babbitt's stammering:

"No, sure; course they're a bunch of toughs. But I just mean— Strikes me it's bad policy to talk about clubbing 'em. Cabe Nixon doesn't. He's got the fine Italian hand. And that's why he's colonel. Clarence Drum is jealous of him."

"Well," said Professor Pumphrey, "you hurt Clarence's feelings, George. He's been out there all morning getting hot and dusty, and no wonder he wants to beat the tar out of those sons of guns!"

Gunch said nothing, and watched; and Babbitt knew that he was being watched.

III

As he was leaving the club Babbitt heard Chum Frink protesting to Gunch, "—don't know what's got into him. Last Sunday Doc Drew preached a corking sermon about decency in business and Babbitt kicked about that, too. Near 's I can figure out—"

Babbitt was vaguely frightened.

IV

He saw a crowd listening to a man who was talking from the rostrum of a kitchen-chair. He stopped his car. From newspaper pictures he knew that the speaker must be the notorious freelance preacher, Beecher Ingram, of whom Seneca Doane had spoken. Ingram was a gaunt man with flamboyant hair, weather-beaten cheeks, and worried eyes. He was pleading:

"—if those telephone girls can hold out, living on one meal a day, doing their own washing, starving and smiling, you big hulking men ought to be able—"

Babbitt saw that from the sidewalk Vergil Gunch was watching him. In vague disquiet he started the car and mechanically drove on, while Gunch's hostile eyes seemed to follow him all the way.

V

"There's a lot of these fellows," Babbitt was complaining to his wife, "that think if workmen go on strike they're a regular bunch of fiends. Now, of course, it's a fight between sound business and the destructive element, and we got to lick the stuffin's out of 'em when they challenge us, but dog-goned if I see why we can't fight like gentlemen and not go calling 'em dirty dogs and saying they ought to be shot down."

"Why, George," she said placidly, "I thought you always insisted that all strikers ought to be put in jail."

"I never did! Well, I mean— Some of 'em, of course. Irresponsible leaders. But I mean a fellow ought to be broad-minded and liberal about things like—"

"But dearie, I thought you always said these so-called 'liberal' people were the worst of—"

"Rats! Woman never can understand the different definitions of a word. Depends on how you mean it. And it don't pay to be too cocksure about anything. Now, these strikers: Honest, they're not such bad people. Just foolish. They don't understand the complications of merchandizing and profit, the way we business men do, but sometimes I think they're about like the rest of us, and no more hogs for wages than we are for profits."

"George! If people were to hear you talk like that—of course I *know* you; I remember what a wild crazy boy you were; I know you don't mean a word you say—but if people that didn't understand you were to hear you talking, they'd think you were a regular socialist!"

"What do I care what anybody thinks? And let me tell you right now—I want you to distinctly understand I never was a wild crazy kid, and when I say a thing, I mean it, and I stand by it and— Honest, do you think people would think I was too liberal if I just said the strikers were decent?"

"Of course they would. But don't worry, dear; I know you don't mean a word of it. Time to trot up to bed now. Have you enough covers for to-night?"

On the sleeping-porch he puzzled, "She doesn't understand me. Hardly understand myself. Why can't I take things easy, way I used to?

"Wish I could go out to Senny Doane's house and talk things over with him. No! Suppose Verg Gunch saw me going in there!

"Wish I knew some really smart woman, and nice, that would see what I'm trying to get at, and let me talk to her and— I wonder if Myra's right? Could the fellows think I've gone nutty just because I'm broad-minded and liberal? Way Verg looked at me—"

chapter 28

MISS McGoun came into his private office at three in the afternoon with "Lissen, Mr. Babbitt; there's a Mrs. Judique on the 'phone—wants to see about some repairs, and the salesmen are all out. Want to talk to her?"

"All right."

The voice of Tanis Judique was clear and pleasant. The black cylinder of the telephone-receiver seemed to hold a tiny animated image of her: lustrous eyes, delicate nose, gentle chin.

"This is Mrs. Judique. Do you remember me? You drove me up here to the Cavendish Apartments and helped me find such a nice flat."

"Sure! Bet I remember! What can I do for you?"

"Why, it's just a little— I don't know that I ought to bother you, but the janitor doesn't seem to be able to fix it. You know my flat is on the top floor, and with these autumn rains the roof is beginning to leak, and I'd be awfully glad if—"

"Sure! I'll come up and take a look at it." Nervously, "When do you expect to be in?"

"Why, I'm in every morning."

"Be in this afternoon, in an hour or so?"

"Ye-es. Perhaps I could give you a cup of tea. I think I ought to, after all your trouble."

"Fine! I'll run up there soon as I can get away."

He meditated, "Now there's a woman that's got refinement, savvy, *class!* 'After all your trouble—give you a cup of tea.' She'd appreciate a fellow. I'm a fool, but I'm not such a bad cuss, get to know me. And not so much a fool as they think!"

The great strike was over, the strikers beaten. Except that Vergil Gunch seemed less cordial, there were no visible effects of Babbitt's treachery to the clan. The oppressive fear of criticism was gone, but a diffident loneliness remained. Now he was so exhilarated that, to prove he wasn't, he droned about the office for fifteen minutes, looking at blue-prints, explaining to Miss McGoun that this Mrs. Scott wanted more money for her house—had raised the asking-price—raised it from seven thousand to eighty-five hundred—would Miss Mc-Goun be sure and put it down on the card—Mrs. Scott's house—raise. When he had thus established himself as a person unemotional and interested only in business, he saun-tered out. He took a particularly long time to start his car; he kicked the tires, dusted the glass of the speedometer, and tightened the screws holding the wind-shield spot-light.

He drove happily off toward the Bellevue district, conscious of the presence of Mrs. Judique as of a brilliant light on the horizon. The maple leaves had fallen and they lined the gut-ters of the asphalted streets. It was a day of pale gold and faded green, tranquil and lingering. Babbitt was aware of the meditative day, and of the barrenness of Bellevue—blocks of wooden houses, garages, little shops, weedy lots. "Needs pep-ping up; needs the touch that people like Mrs. Judique could give a place," he ruminated, as he rattled through the long, crude, airy streets. The wind rose, enlivening, keen, and in a blaze of well-being he came to the flat of Tanis Judique.

She was wearing, when she flutteringly admitted him, a frock of black chiffon cut modestly round at the base of her pretty throat. She seemed to him immensely sophisticated. He glanced at the cretonnes and colored prints in her living-room, and gurgled, "Gosh, you've fixed the place nice! Takes a clever woman to know how to make a home, all right!"

"You really like it? I'm so glad! But you've neglected me, scandalously. You promised to come some time and learn to dance."

Rather unsteadily, "Oh, but you didn't mean it seriously!"

"Perhaps not. But you might have tried!"

"Well, here I've come for my lesson, and you might just as well prepare to have me stay for supper!"

They both laughed in a manner which indicated that of course he didn't mean it.

"But first I guess I better look at that leak."

She climbed with him to the flat roof of the apartment-house—a detached world of slatted wooden walks, clothes-lines, water-tank in a penthouse. He poked at things with his toe, and sought to impress her by being learned about copper gutters, the desirability of passing plumbing pipes through a lead collar and sleeve and flashing them with cop-per, and the advantages of cedar over boiler-iron for roof-tanks.

"You have to know so much, in real estate!" she admired.

He promised that the roof should be repaired within two days. "Do you mind my 'phoning from your apartment?" he asked.

"Heavens, no!"

He stood a moment at the coping, looking over a land of hard little bungalows with abnormally large porches, and new apartment-houses, small, but brave with variegated brick walls and terra-cotta trimmings. Beyond them was a hill with a gouge of yellow clay like a vast wound. Behind every apartment-house, beside each dwelling, were small garages. It was a world of good little people, comfortable, industrious, credulous.

In the autumnal light the flat newness was mellowed, and the air was a sun-tinted pool.

"Golly, it's one fine afternoon. You get a great view here, right up Tanner's Hill," said Babbitt.

"Yes, isn't it nice and open."

"So darn few people appreciate a View."

"Don't you go raising my rent on that account! Oh, that was naughty of me! I was just teasing. Seriously though, there are so few who respond—who react to Views. I mean —they haven't any feeling of poetry and beauty."

"That's a fact, they haven't," he breathed, admiring her slenderness and the absorbed, airy way in which she looked toward the hill, chin lifted, lips smiling. "Well, guess I'd better telephone the plumbers, so they'll get on the job first thing in the morning."

When he had telephoned, making it conspicuously authori-tative and gruff and masculine, he looked doubtful, and sighed, "S'pose I'd better be—"

"Oh, you must have that cup of tea first!"

"Well, it would go pretty good, at that."

It was luxurious to loll in a deep green rep chair, his legs thrust out before him, to glance at the black Chinese telephone stand and the colored photograph of Mount Vernon which he had always liked so much, while in the tiny kitchen—so near—Mrs. Judique sang "My Creole Queen." In an intolerable sweetness, a contentment so deep that he was wistfully discontented, he saw magnolias by moonlight and heard plantation darkies crooning to the banjo. He wanted to be near her, on pretense of helping her, yet he wanted to remain in this still ecstasy. Languidly he remained.

When she bustled in with the tea he smiled up at her. "This is awfully nice!" For the first time, he was not fencing; he was quietly and securely friendly; and friendly and quiet was her answer: "It's nice to have you here. You were so kind, helping me to find this little home."

They agreed that the weather would soon turn cold. They agreed that prohibition was prohibitive. They agreed that art in the home was cultural. They agreed about everything. They even became bold. They hinted that these modern young girls, well, honestly, their short skirts were short. They were proud to find that they were not shocked by such frank speaking. Tanis ventured, "I know you'll understand—I mean—I don't quite know how to say it, but I do think that girls who pretend they're bad by the way they dress really never go any farther. They give away the fact that they haven't the instincts of a womanly woman."

Remembering Ida Putiak, the manicure girl, and how ill she had used him, Babbitt agreed with enthusiasm; remembering how ill all the world had used him, he told of Paul Riesling, of Zilla, of Seneca Doane, of the strike:

"See how it was? Course I was as anxious to have those beggars licked to a standstill as anybody else, but gosh, no reason for not seeing their side. For a fellow's own sake, he's got to be broad-minded and liberal, don't you think so?"

"Oh, I do!" Sitting on the hard little couch, she clasped her hands beside her, leaned toward him, absorbed him; and in a glorious state of being appreciated he proclaimed:

"So I up and said to the fellows at the club, 'Look here,' I—"

"Do you belong to the Union Club? I think it's—"

"No; the Athletic. Tell you: Course they're always asking me to join the Union, but I always say, 'No, sir! Nothing doing!" I don't mind the expense but I can't stand all the old fogies."

"Oh, yes, that's so. But tell me: what did you say to them?"

"Oh, you don't want to hear it. I'm probably boring you to death with my troubles! You wouldn't hardly think I was an old duffer; I sound like a kid!"

"Oh, you're a boy yet. I mean—you can't be a day over forty-five."

"Well, I'm not—much. But by golly I begin to feel middle-aged sometimes; all these responsibilities and all."

"Oh, I know!" Her voice caressed him; it cloaked him like warm silk. "And I feel lonely, so lonely, some days, Mr. Babbitt."

"We're a sad pair of birds! But I think we're pretty darn nice!"

"Yes, I think we're lots nicer than most people I know!" They smiled. "But please tell me what you said at the Club."

"Well, it was like this: Course Seneca Doane is a friend of mine—they can say what they want to, they can call him anything they please, but what most folks here don't know is that Senny is the bosom pal of some of the biggest statesmen in the world—Lord Wycombe, frinstance—you know, this big British nobleman. My friend Sir Gerald Doak told me the Lord Wycombe is one of the biggest guns in England —well, Doak or somebody tole me."

"Oh! Do you know Sir Gerald? The one that was here, at the McKelveys'?"

"Know him? Well, say, I know him just well enough so we call each other George and Jerry, and we got so pickled together in Chicago—"

"That must have been fun. But—" She shook a finger at him. "—I can't have you getting pickled! I'll have to take you in hand!"

"Wish you would! . . . Well, zize saying: You see I happen to know what a big noise Senny Doane is outside of Zenith, but of course a prophet hasn't got any honor in his own country, and Senny, darn his old hide, he's so blame modest that he never lets folks know the kind of an outfit he travels with when he goes abroad. Well, during the strike Clarence Drum comes pee-rading up to our table, all dolled up fit to kill in his nice lil cap'n's uniform, and somebody says to him, 'Busting the strike, Clarence?'

"Well, he swells up like a pouter-pigeon and he hollers,

so 's you could hear him way up in the reading-room, 'Yes, sure; I told the strike-leaders where they got off, and so they went home.'

" 'Well,' I says to him, 'glad there wasn't any violence.'

" 'Yes,' he says, 'but if I hadn't kept my eye skinned there would 've been. All those fellows had bombs in their pockets. They're reg'lar anarchists.'

" 'Oh, rats, Clarence,' I says. 'I looked 'em all over carefully, and they didn't have any more bombs 'n a rabbit,' I says. 'Course,' I says, 'they're foolish, but they're a good deal like you and me, after all.'

"And then Vergil Gunch or somebody—no, it was Chum Frink—you know, this famous poet—great pal of mine—he says to me, 'Look here,' he says, 'do you mean to say you advocate these strikes?' Well, I was so disgusted with a fellow whose mind worked that way that I swear, I had a good mind to not explain at all—just ignore him—"

"Oh, that's so wise!" said Mrs. Judique.

"—but finally I explains to him: 'If you'd done as much as I have on Chamber of Commerce committees and all,' I says, 'then you'd have the right to talk! But same time,' I says, 'I believe in treating your opponent like a gentleman!' Well, sir, that held 'em! Frink—Chum I always call him—he didn't have another word to say. But at that, I guess some of 'em kind o' thought I was too liberal. What do you think?"

"Oh, you were so wise. And courageous! I love a man to have the courage of his convictions!"

"But do you think it was a good stunt? After all, some of these fellows are so darn cautious and narrow-minded that they're prejudiced against a fellow that talks right out in meeting."

"What do you care? In the long run they're bound to respect a man who makes them think, and with your reputation for oratory you—"

"What do you know about my reputation for oratory?"

"Oh, I'm not going to tell you everything I know! But seriously, you don't realize what a famous man you are."

"Well— Though I haven't done much orating this fall. Too kind of bothered by this Paul Riesling business, I guess. But— Do you know, you're the first person that's really understood what I was getting at, Tanis— Listen to me, will you! Fat nerve I've got, calling you Tanis!"

"Oh, do! And shall I call you George? Don't you think

it's awfully nice when two people have so much—what shall
I call it?—so much analysis that they can discard all these
stupid conventions and understand each other and become
acquainted right away, like ships that pass in the night?"

"I certainly do! I certainly do!"

He was no longer quiescent in his chair; he wandered
about the room, he dropped on the couch beside her. But
as he awkwardly stretched his hand toward her fragile, immaculate fingers, she said brightly, "Do give me a cigarette.
Would you think poor Tanis was dreadfully naughty if she
smoked?"

"Lord, no! I like it!"

He had often and weightily pondered flappers smoking in
Zenith restaurants, but he knew only one woman who smoked
—Mrs. Sam Doppelbrau, his flighty neighbor. He ceremoni-
ously lighted Tanis's cigarette, looked for a place to deposit
the burnt match, and dropped it into his pocket.

"I'm sure you want a cigar, you poor man!" she crooned.

"Do you mind one?"

"Oh, no! I love the smell of a good cigar; so nice and—
so nice and like a man. You'll find an ash-tray in my bedroom, on the table beside the bed, if you don't mind getting it."

He was embarrassed by her bedroom: the broad couch
with a cover of violet silk, mauve curtains striped with gold,
Chinese Chippendale bureau, and an amazing row of slippers, with ribbon-wound shoe-trees, and primrose stockings
lying across them. His manner of bringing the ash-tray had
just the right note of easy friendliness, he felt. "A boob like
Verg Gunch would try to get funny about seeing her bedroom, but I take it casually." He was not casual afterward.
The contentment of companionship was gone, and he was
restless with desire to touch her hand. But whenever he
turned toward her, the cigarette was in his way. It was a
shield between them. He waited till she should have finished,
but as he rejoiced at her quick crushing of its light on the
ash-tray she said, "Don't you want to give me another
cigarette?" and hopelessly he saw the screen of pale smoke
and her graceful tilted hand again between them. He was
not merely curious now to find out whether she would let
him hold her hand (all in the purest friendship, naturally),
but agonized with need of it.

On the surface appeared none of all this fretful drama.
They were talking cheerfully of motors, of trips to California,

of Chum Frink. Once he said delicately, "I do hate these guys—I hate these people that invite themselves to meals, but I seem to have a feeling I'm going to have supper with the lovely Mrs. Tanis Judique to-night. But I suppose you probably have seven dates already."

"Well, I was thinking some of going to the movies. Yes, I really think I ought to get out and get some fresh air."

She did not encourage him to stay, but never did she discourage him. He considered, "I better take a sneak! She *will* let me stay—there *is* something doing—and I mustn't get mixed up with—I mustn't—I've got to beat it." Then, "No, it's too late now."

Suddenly, at seven, brushing her cigarette away, brusquely taking her hand:

"Tanis! Stop teasing me! You know we— Here we are, a couple of lonely birds, and we're awful happy together. Anyway I am! Never been so happy! Do let me stay! I'll gallop down to the delicatessen and buy some stuff—cold chicken maybe—or cold turkey—and we can have a nice little supper, and afterwards, if you want to chase me out, I'll be good and go like a lamb."

"Well—yes—it would be nice," she said.

Nor did she withdraw her hand. He squeezed it, trembling, and blundered toward his coat. At the delicatessen he bought preposterous stores of food, chosen on the principle of expensiveness. From the drug store across the street he telephoned to his wife, "Got to get a fellow to sign a lease before he leaves town on the midnight. Won't be home till late. Don't wait up for me. Kiss Tinka good-night." He expectantly lumbered back to the flat.

"Oh, you bad thing, to buy so much food!" was her greeting, and her voice was gay, her smile acceptant.

He helped her in the tiny white kitchen; he washed the lettuce, he opened the olive bottle. She ordered him to set the table, and as he trotted into the living-room, as he hunted through the buffet for knives and forks, he felt utterly at home.

"Now the only other thing," he announced, "is what you're going to wear. I can't decide whether you're to put on your swellest evening gown, or let your hair down and put on short skirts and make-believe you're a little girl."

"I'm going to dine just as I am, in this old chiffon rag, and if you can't stand poor Tanis that way, you can go to the club for dinner!"

"Stand you!" He patted her shoulder. "Child, you're the brainiest and the loveliest and finest woman I've ever met! Come now, Lady Wycombe, if you'll take the Duke of Zenith's arm, we will proambulate in to the magnolious feed!"

"Oh, you do say the funniest, nicest things!"

When they had finished the picnic supper he thrust his head out of the window and reported, "It's turned awful chilly, and I think it's going to rain. You don't want to go to the movies."

"Well—"

"I wish we had a fireplace! I wish it was raining like all get-out to-night, and we were in a funny little old-fashioned cottage, and the trees thrashing like everything outside, and a great big log fire and—I'll tell you! Let's draw this couch up to the radiator, and stretch our feet out, and pretend it's a wood-fire."

"Oh, I think that's pathetic! You big child!"

But they did draw up to the radiator, and propped their feet against it—his clumsy black shoes, her patent-leather slippers. In the dimness they talked of themselves; of how lonely she was, how bewildered he, and how wonderful that they had found each other. As they fell silent the room was stiller than a country lane. There was no sound from the street save the whir of motor-tires, the rumble of a distant freight-train. Self-contained was the room, warm, secure, insulated from the harassing world.

He was absorbed by a rapture in which all fear and doubting were smoothed away; and when he reached home, at dawn, the rapture had mellowed to contentment serene and full of memories.

chapter 29

THE assurance of Tanis Judique's friendship fortified Babbitt's self-approval. At the Athletic Club he became experimental. Though Vergil Gunch was silent, the others at the Roughnecks' Table came to accept Babbitt as having, for no visible reason, "turned crank." They argued windily with him, and he was cocky, and enjoyed the spectacle of his interesting martyrdom. He even praised Seneca Doane. Professor Pumphrey said that was carrying a joke too far; but Babbitt argued, "No! Fact! I tell you he's got one of the keenest intellects in the country. Why, Lord Wycombe said that—"

"Oh, who the hell is Lord Wycombe? What you always lugging him in for? You been touting him for the last six weeks!" protested Orville Jones.

"George ordered him from Sears-Roebuck. You can get those English high-muckamucks by mail for two bucks apiece," suggested Sidney Finkelstein.

"That's all right now! Lord Wycombe, he's one of the biggest intellects in English political life. As I was saying: Of course I'm conservative myself, but I appreciate a guy like Senny Doane because—"

Vergil Gunch interrupted harshly, "I wonder if you are so conservative? I find I can manage to run my own business without any skunks and reds like Doane in it!"

The grimness of Gunch's voice, the hardness of his jaw, disconcerted Babbitt, but he recovered and went on till they looked bored, then irritated, then as doubtful as Gunch.

II

He thought of Tanis always. With a stir he remembered her every aspect. His arms yearned for her. "I've found

her! I've dreamed of her all these years and now I've found
her!" he exulted. He met her at the movies in the morning;
he drove out to her flat in the late afternoon or on evenings
when he was believed to be at the Elks. He knew her financial affairs and advised her about them, while she lamented
her feminine ignorance, and praised his masterfulness, and
proved to know much more about bonds than he did. They
had remembrances, and laughter over old times. Once they
quarreled, and he raged that she was as "bossy" as his wife
and far more whining when he was inattentive. But that
passed safely.

Their high hour was a tramp on a ringing December afternoon, through snow-drifted meadows down to the icy Chaloosa
River. She was exotic in an astrachan cap and a short beaver
coat; she slid on the ice and shouted, and he panted after
her, rotund with laughter. . . . Myra Babbitt never slid on
the ice.

He was afraid that they would be seen together. In Zenith
it is impossible to lunch with a neighbor's wife without the
fact being known, before nightfall, in every house in your
circle. But Tanis was beautifully discreet. However appeal-
ingly she might turn to him when they were alone, she was
gravely detached when they were abroad, and he hoped that
she would be taken for a client. Orville Jones once saw them
emerging from a movie theater, and Babbitt bumbled, "Let
me make you 'quainted with Mrs. Judique. Now here's a lady
who knows the right broker to come to, Orvy!" Mr. Jones,
though he was a man censorious of morals and of laundry
machinery, seemed satisfied.

His predominant fear—not from any especial fondness for
her but from the habit of propriety—was that his wife would
learn of the affair. He was certain that she knew nothing
specific about Tanis, but he was also certain that she suspected
something indefinite. For years she had been bored by anything more affectionate than a farewell kiss, yet she was hurt
by any slackening in his irritable periodic interest, and now
he had no interest; rather, a revulsion. He was completely
faithful—to Tanis. He was distressed by the sight of his
wife's slack plumpness, by her puffs and billows of flesh, by
the tattered petticoat which she was always meaning and always forgetting to throw away. But he was aware that she,
so long attuned to him, caught all his repulsions. He elaborately, heavily, jocularly tried to check them. He couldn't.

They had a tolerable Christmas. Kenneth Escott was there,

admittedly engaged to Verona. Mrs. Babbitt was tearful
and called Kenneth her new son. Babbitt was worried about
Ted, because he had ceased complaining of the State University and become suspiciously acquiescent. He wondered what
the boy was planning, and was too shy to ask. Himself,
Babbitt slipped away on Christmas afternoon to take his
present, a silver cigarette-box, to Tanis. When he returned
Mrs. Babbitt asked, much too innocently, "Did you go out
for a little fresh air?"

"Yes, just lil drive," he mumbled.

After New Year's his wife proposed, "I heard from my sister to-day, George. She isn't well. I think perhaps I ought to
go stay with her for a few weeks."

Now, Mrs. Babbitt was not accustomed to leave home during the winter except on violently demanding occasions,
and only the summer before, she had been gone for weeks.
Nor was Babbitt one of the detachable husbands who take
separations casually. He liked to have her there; she looked after his clothes; she knew how his steak ought to be cooked;
and her clucking made him feel secure. But he could not
drum up even a dutiful "Oh, she doesn't really need you,
does she?" While he tried to look regretful, while he felt that
his wife was watching him, he was filled with exultant
visions of Tanis.

"Do you think I'd better go?" she said sharply.

"You've got to decide, honey; I can't."

She turned away, sighing, and his forehead was damp.

Till she went, four days later, she was curiously still, he
cumbrously affectionate. Her train left at noon. As he saw
it grow small beyond the train-shed he longed to hurry to
Tanis.

"No, by golly, I won't do that!" he vowed. "I won't go
near her for a week!"

But he was at her flat at four.

III

He who had once controlled or seemed to control his
life in a progress unimpassioned but diligent and sane was
for that fortnight borne on a current of desire and very bad
whisky and all the complications of new acquaintances, those
furious new intimates who demand so much more attention
than old friends. Each morning he gloomily recognized his
idiocies of the evening before. With his head throbbing, his

tongue and lips stinging from cigarettes, he incredulously counted the number of drinks he had taken, and groaned, "I got to quit!" He had ceased saying, "I *will* quit!" for however resolute he might be at dawn, he could not, for a single evening, check his drift.

He had met Tanis's friends; he had, with the ardent haste of the Midnight People, who drink and dance and rattle and are ever afraid to be silent, been adopted as a member of her group, which they called "The Bunch." He first met them after a day when he had worked particularly hard and when he hoped to be quiet with Tanis and slowly sip her admiration.

From down the hall he could hear shrieks and the grind of a phonograph. As Tanis opened the door he saw fantastic figures dancing in a haze of cigarette smoke. The tables and chairs were against the wall.

"Oh, isn't this dandy!" she gabbled at him. "Carrie Nork had the loveliest idea. She decided it was time for a party, and she 'phoned the Bunch and told 'em to gather round. . . . George, this is Carrie."

"Carrie" was, in the less desirable aspects of both, at once matronly and spinsterish. She was perhaps forty; her hair was an unconvincing ash-blond; and if her chest was flat, her hips were ponderous. She greeted Babbitt with a giggling "Welcome to our little midst! Tanis says you're a real sport."

He was apparently expected to dance, to be boyish and gay with Carrie, and he did his unforgiving best. He towed her about the room, bumping into other couples, into the radiator, into chair-legs cunningly ambushed. As he danced he surveyed the rest of the Bunch: A thin young woman who looked capable, conceited, and sarcastic. Another woman whom he could never quite remember. Three overdressed and slightly effeminate young men—soda-fountain clerks, or at least born for that profession. A man of his own age, immovable, self-satisfied, resentful of Babbitt's presence.

When he had finished his dutiful dance Tanis took him aside and begged, "Dear, wouldn't you like to do something for me? I'm all out of booze, and the Bunch want to celebrate. Couldn't you just skip down to Healey Hanson's and get some?"

"Sure," he said, trying not to sound sullen.

"I'll tell you: I'll get Minnie Sonntag to drive down with you." Tanis was pointing to the thin, sarcastic young woman. Miss Sonntag greeted him with an astringent "How d'you do, Mr. Babbitt. Tanis tells me you're a very prominent man, and I'm honored by being allowed to drive with you. Of course I'm not accustomed to associating with society people like you, so I don't know how to act in such exalted circles!"

Thus Miss Sonntag talked all the way down to Healey Hanson's. To her jibes he wanted to reply "Oh, go to the devil!" but he never quite nerved himself to that reasonable comment. He was resenting the existence of the whole Bunch. He had heard Tanis speak of "darling Carrie" and "Min Sonntag—she's so clever—you'll adore her," but they had never been real to him. He had pictured Tanis as living in a rose-tinted vacuum, waiting for him, free of all the complications of a Floral Heights.

When they returned he had to endure the patronage of the young soda-clerks. They were as damply friendly as Miss Sonntag was dryly hostile. They called him "Old Georgie" and shouted, "Come on now, sport; shake a leg" . . . boys in belted coats, pimply boys, as young as Ted and as flabby as chorus-men, but powerful to dance and to mind the phonograph and smoke cigarettes and patronize Tanis. He tried to be one of them; he cried "Good work, Pete!" but his voice creaked.

Tanis apparently enjoyed the companionship of the dancing darlings; she bridled to their bland flirtation and casually kissed them at the end of each dance. Babbitt hated her, for the moment. He saw her as middle-aged. He studied the wrinkles in the softness of her throat, the slack flesh beneath her chin. The taut muscles of her youth were loose and drooping. Between dances she sat in the largest chair, waving her cigarette, summoning her callow admirers to come and talk to her. ("She think she's a blooming queen!" growled Babbitt.) She chanted to Miss Sonntag, "Isn't my little studio sweet?" ("Studio, rats! It's a plain old-maid-and-chow-dog flat! Oh, God, I wish I was home! I wonder if I can't make a getaway now?")

His vision grew blurred, however, as he applied himself to Healey Hanson's raw but vigorous whisky. He blended with the Bunch. He began to rejoice that Carrie Nork and Pete, the most nearly intelligent of the nimble youths, seemed to like him; and it was enormously important to win over the surly older man, who proved to be a railway clerk named Fulton Bemis.

The conversation of the Bunch was exclamatory, high-colored, full of references to people whom Babbitt did not know. Apparently they thought very comfortably of themselves. They were the Bunch, wise and beautiful and amusing; they were Bohemians and urbanites, accustomed to all the luxuries of Zenith: dance-halls, movie-theaters, and road-houses; and in a cynical superiority to people who were "slow" or "tightwad" they cackled:

"Oh, Pete, did I tell you what that dub of a cashier said when I came in late yesterday? Oh, it was per-fect-ly price-less!"

"Oh, but wasn't T. D. stewed! Say, he was simply ossi-fied! What did Gladys say to him?"

"Think of the nerve of Bob Bickerstaff trying to get us to come to his house! Say, the nerve of him! Can you beat it for nerve? Some nerve I call it!"

"Did you notice how Dotty was dancing? Gee, wasn't she the limit!"

Babbitt was to be heard sonorously agreeing with the once-hated Miss Minnie Sonntag that persons who let a night go by without dancing to jazz music were crabs, pikers, and poor fish; and he roared "You bet!" when Mrs. Carrie Nork gurgled, "Don't you love to sit on the floor? It's so Bohemian!" He began to think extremely well of the Bunch. When he mentioned his friends Sir Gerald Doak, Lord Wy-combe, William Washington Eathorne, and Chum Frink, he was proud of their condescending interest. He got so thor-oughly into the jocund spirit that he didn't much mind see-ing Tanis drooping against the shoulder of the youngest and milkiest of the young men, and he himself desired to hold Carrie Nork's pulpy hand, and dropped it only because Tanis looked angry.

When he went home, at two, he was fully a member of the Bunch, and all the week thereafter he was bound by the exceedingly straitened conventions, the exceedingly wearing demands, of their life of pleasure and freedom. He had to go to their parties; he was involved in the agitation when every-body telephoned to everybody else that she hadn't meant what she'd said when she'd said that, and anyway, why was Pete going around saying she'd said it?

Never was a Family more insistent on learning one anoth-er's movements than were the Bunch. All of them volubly knew, or indignantly desired to know, where all the others had been every minute of the week. Babbitt found himself explaining to Carrie or Fulton Bemis just what he had been doing that he should not have joined them till ten o'clock,

and apologizing for having gone to dinner with a business
acquaintance.

Every member of the Bunch was expected to telephone to
every other member at least once a week. "Why haven't you
called me up?" Babbitt was asked accusingly, not only by
Tanis and Carrie but presently by new ancient friends, Jennie
and Capitolina and Toots.

If for a moment he had seen Tanis as withering and sentimental, he lost that impression at Carrie Nork's dance.
Mrs. Nork had a large house and a small husband. To her
party came all of the Bunch, perhaps thirty-five of them when
they were completely mobilized. Babbitt, under the name of
"Old Georgie," was now a pioneer of the Bunch, since each
month it changed half its membership and he who could recall the prehistoric days of a fortnight ago, before Mrs. Ab-
solom, the food-demonstrator, had gone to Indianapolis, and
Mac had "got sore at" Minnie, was a venerable leader and
able to condescend to new Petes and Minnies and Gladyses.

At Carrie's, Tanis did not have to work at being hostess.
She was dignified and sure, a clear fine figure in the black
chiffon frock he had always loved; and in the wider spaces
of that ugly house Babbitt was able to sit quietly with her.
He repented of his first revulsion, mooned at her feet, and
happily drove her home. Next day he bought a violent yellow
tie, to make himself young for her. He knew, a little sadly,
that he could not make himself beautiful; he beheld himself
as heavy, hinting of fatness, but he danced, he dressed, he
chattered, to be as young as she was . . . as young as she
seemed to be.

IV

As all converts, whether to a religion, love, or gardening,
find as by magic that though hitherto these hobbies have not
seemed to exist, now the whole world is filled with their fury,
so, once he was converted to dissipation, Babbitt discovered
agreeable opportunities for it everywhere.

He had a new view of his sporting neighbor, Sam Doppelbrau. The Doppelbraus were respectable people, industrious
people, prosperous people, whose ideal of happiness was an
eternal cabaret. Their life was dominated by suburban
bacchanalia of alcohol, nicotine, gasoline, and kisses. They
and their set worked capably all the week, and all week
looked forward to Saturday night, when they would, as they

expressed it, "throw a party;" and the thrown party grew noisier and noisier up to Sunday dawn, and usually included an extremely rapid motor expedition to nowhere in particular.

One evening When Tanis was at the theater, Babbitt found himself being lively with the Doppelbraus, pledging friendship with men whom he had for years privily denounced to Mrs. Babbitt as a "rotten bunch of tin-horns that I wouldn't go out with, not if they were the last people on earth." That evening he had sulkily come home and poked about in front of the house, chipping off the walk the ice-clots, like fossil footprints, made by the steps of passers-by during the recent snow. Howard Littlefield came up snuffling.

"Still a widower, George?"

"Yump. Cold again to-night."

"What do you hear from the wife?"

"She's feeling fine, but her sister is still pretty sick."

"Say, better come in and have dinner with us to-night, George."

"Oh—oh, thanks. Have to go out."

Suddenly he could not endure Littlefield's recitals of the more interesting statistics about totally uninteresting problems. He scraped at the walk and grunted.

Sam Doppelbrau appeared.

"Evenin', Babbitt. Working hard?"

"Yuh, lil exercise."

"Cold enough for you to-night?"

"Well, just about."

"Still a widower?"

"Uh-huh."

"Say, Babbitt, while she's away— I know you don't care much for booze-fights, but the Missus and I'd be awfully glad if you could come in some night. Think you could stand a good cocktail for once?"

"Stand it? Young fella, I bet old Uncle George can mix the best cocktail in these United States!"

"Hurray! That's the way to talk! Look here: There's some folks coming to the house to-night, Louetta Swanson and some other live ones, and I'm going to open up a bottle of pre-war gin, and maybe we'll dance a while. Why don't you drop in and jazz it up a little, just for a change?"

"Well— What time they coming?"

He was at Sam Doppelbrau's at nine. It was the third time he had entered the house. By ten he was calling Mr. Doppelbrau "Sam, old hoss."

At eleven they all drove out to the Old Farm Inn. Babbitt sat in the back of Doppelbrau's car with Louetta Swanson. Once he had timorously tried to make love to her. Now he did not try; he merely made love; and Louetta dropped her head on his shoulder, told him what a nagger Eddie was, and accepted Babbitt as a decent and well-trained libertine.

With the assistance of Tanis's Bunch, the Doppelbraus, and other companions in forgetfulness, there was not an evening for two weeks when he did not return home late and shaky. With his other faculties blurred he yet had the motorist's gift of being able to drive when he could scarce walk; of slowing down at corners and allowing for approaching cars. He came wambling into the house. If Verona and Kenneth Escott were about, he got past them with a hasty greeting, horribly aware of their level young glances, and hid himself up-stairs. He found when he came into the warm house that he was hazier than he had believed. His head whirled. He dared not lie down. He tried to soak out the alcohol in a hot bath. For the moment his head was clearer but when he moved about the bathroom his calculations of distance were wrong, so that he dragged down the towels, and knocked over the soap-dish with a clatter which, he feared, would betray him to the children. Chilly in his dressing-gown he tried to read the evening paper. He could follow every word; he seemed to take in the sense of things; but a minute afterward he could not have told what he had been reading. When he went to bed his brain flew in circles, and he hastily sat up, struggling for self-control. At last he was able to lie still, feeling only a little sick and dizzy—and enormously ashamed. To hide his "condition" from his own children! To have danced and shouted with people whom he despised! To have said foolish things, sung idiotic songs, tried to kiss silly girls! Incredulously he remembered that he had by his roaring familiarity with them laid himself open to the patronizing of youths whom he would have kicked out of his office; that by dancing too ardently he had exposed himself to rebukes from the rattiest of withering women. As it came relentlessly back to him he snarled, "I hate myself! God how I hate myself!" But, he raged, "I'm through! No more! Had enough, plenty!"

He was even surer about it the morning after, when he was trying to be grave and paternal with his daughters at breakfast. At noontime he was less sure. He did not deny that he had been a fool; he saw it almost as clearly as at midnight; but anything, he struggled, was better than going back to a life of barren heartiness. At four he wanted a drink. He kept a whisky flask in his desk now, and after two minutes of battle he had his drink. Three drinks later he began to see the Bunch as tender and amusing friends, and by six he was with them . . . and the tale was to be told all over.

Each morning his head ached a little less. A bad head for drinks had been his safeguard, but the safeguard was crumbling. Presently he could be drunk at dawn, yet not feel particularly wretched in his conscience—or in his stomach—when he awoke at eight. No regret, no desire to escape the toil of keeping up with the arduous merriment of the Bunch, was so great as his feeling of social inferiority when he failed to keep up. To be the "livest" of them was as much his ambition now as it had been to excel at making money, at playing golf, at motor-driving, at oratory, at climbing to the McKelvey set. But occasionally he failed.

He found that Pete and the other young men considered the Bunch too austerely polite and the Carrie who merely kissed behind doors too embarrassingly monogamic. As Babbitt sneaked from Floral Heights down to the Bunch, so the young gallants sneaked from the proprieties of the Bunch off to "times" with bouncing young women whom they picked up in department stores and at hotel coatrooms. Once Babbitt tried to accompany them. There was a motor car, a bottle of whisky, and for him a grubby shrieking cash-girl from Parcher and Stein's. He sat beside her and worried. He was apparently expected to "jolly her along," but when she sang out, "Hey, leggo, quit crushing me cootie-garage," he did not quite know how to go on. They sat in the back room of a saloon, and Babbitt had a headache, was confused by their new slang, looked at them benevolently, wanted to go home, and had a drink—a good many drinks.

Two evenings after, Fulton Bemis, the surly older man of the Bunch, took Babbitt aside and grunted, "Look here, it's none of my business, and God knows I always lap up my share of the hootch, but don't you think you better watch yourself? You're one of these enthusiastic chumps that always overdo things. D' you realize you're throwing in the booze as fast as you can, and you eat one cigarette right after another? Better cut it out for a while."

Babbitt tearfully said that good old Fult was a prince, and yes, he certainly would cut it out, and thereafter he lighted a cigarette and took a drink and had a terrific quarrel with

Tanis when she caught him being affectionate with Carrie Nork.

Next morning he hated himself that he should have sunk into a position where a fifteenth-rater like Fulton Bemis could rebuke him. He perceived that, since he was making love to every woman possible, Tanis was no longer his one pure star, and he wondered whether she had ever been anything more to him than A Woman. And if Bemis had spoken to him, were other people talking about him? He suspiciously watched the men at the Athletic Club that noon. It seemed to him that they were uneasy. They had been talking about him then? He was angry. He became belligerent. He not only defended Seneca Doane but even made fun of the Y. M. C. A. Vergil Gunch was rather brief in his answers.

Afterward Babbitt was not angry. He was afraid. He did not go to the next lunch of the Boosters' Club but hid in a cheap restaurant, and, while he munched a ham-and-egg sandwich and sipped coffee from a cup on the arm of his chair, he worried.

Four days later, when the Bunch were having one of their best parties, Babbitt drove them to the skating-rink which had been laid out on the Chaloosa River. After a thaw the streets had frozen in smooth ice. Down those wide endless streets the wind rattled between the rows of wooden houses, and the whole Bellevue district seemed a frontier town. Even with skid chains on all four wheels, Babbitt was afraid of sliding, and when he came to the long slide of a hill he crawled down, both brakes on. Slewing round a corner came a less cautious car. It skidded, it almost raked them with its rear fenders. In relief at their escape the Bunch—Tanis, Minnie Sonntag, Pete, Fulton Bemis—shouted "Oh, baby," and waved their hands to the agitated other driver. Then Babbitt saw Professor Pumphrey laboriously crawling up hill, afoot, staring owlishly at the revelers. He was sure that Pumphrey recognized him and saw Tanis kiss him as she crowed, "You're such a good driver!"

At lunch next day he probed Pumphrey with "Out last night with my brother and some friends of his. Gosh, what driving! Slippery 's glass. Thought I saw you hiking up the Bellevue Avenue Hill."

"No, I wasn't!—I didn't see you," said Pumphrey, hastily, rather guiltily.

Perhaps two days afterward Babbitt took Tanis to lunch at the Hotel Thornleigh. She who had seemed well content to wait for him at her flat had begun to hint with melancholy smiles that he must think but little of her if he never introduced her to his friends, if he was unwilling to be seen with her except at the movies. He thought of taking her to the "ladies' annex" of the Athletic Club, but that was too dangerous. He would have to introduce her and, oh, people might misunderstand and— He compromised on the Thornleigh.

She was unusually smart, all in black: small black tricorne hat, short black caracul coat, loose and swinging, and austere high-necked black velvet frock at a time when most street costumes were like evening gowns. Perhaps she was too smart. Every one in the gold and oak restaurant of the Thornleigh was staring at her as Babbitt followed her to a table. He uneasily hoped that the head-waiter would give them a discreet place behind a pillar, but they were stationed on the center aisle. Tanis seemed not to notice her admirers; she smiled at Babbitt with a lavish "Oh, isn't this nice! What a peppy-looking orchestra!" Babbitt had difficulty in being lavish in return, for two tables away he saw Vergil Gunch. All through the meal Gunch watched them, while Babbitt watched himself being watched and lugubriously tried to keep from spoiling Tanis's gaiety. "I felt like a spree to-day," she rippled. "I love the Thornleigh, don't you? It's so live and yet so—so refined."

He made talk about the Thornleigh, the service, the food, the people he recognized in the restaurant, all but Vergil Gunch. There did not seem to be anything else to talk of. He smiled conscientiously at her fluttering jests; he agreed with her that Minnie Sonntag was "so hard to get along with," and young Pete "such a silly lazy kid, really just no good at all." But he himself had nothing to say. He considered telling her his worries about Gunch, but—"oh, gosh, it was too much work to go into the whole thing and explain about Verg and everything."

He was relieved when he put Tanis on a trolley; he was cheerful in the familiar simplicities of his office.

At four o'clock Vergil Gunch called on him.

Babbitt was agitated, but Gunch began in a friendly way:

"How's the boy? Say, some of us are getting up a scheme we'd kind of like to have you come in on."

"Fine, Verg. Shoot."

"You know during the war we had the Undesirable Element, the Reds and walking delegates and just the plain common grouches, dead to rights, and so did we for quite a

while after the war, but folks forget about the danger and
that gives these cranks a chance to begin working under-
ground again, especially a lot of these parlor socialists. Well,
it's up to the folks that do a little sound thinking to make a
conscious effort to keep bucking these fellows. Some guy back
East has organized a society called the Good Citizens' League
for just that purpose. Of course the Chamber of Commerce
and the American Legion and so on do a fine work in keeping
the decent people in the saddle, but they're devoted to so
many other causes that they can't attend to this one problem
properly. But the Good Citizens' League, the G. C. L., they
stick right to it. Oh, the G. C. L. has to have some other
ostensible purposes—frinstance here in Zenith I think it ought
to support the park-extension project and the City Planning
Committee—and then, too, it should have a social aspect,
being made up of the best people—have dances and so on,
especially as one of the best ways it can put the kibosh on
cranks is to apply this social boycott business to folks big
enough so you can't reach 'em otherwise. Then if that don't
work, the G. C. L. can finally send a little delegation around
to inform folks that get too flip that they got to conform
to decent standards and quit shooting off their mouths so
free. Don't it sound like the organization could do a great
work? We've already got some of the strongest men in town,
and of course we want you in. How about it?"

Babbitt was uncomfortable. He felt a compulsion back to
all the standards he had so vaguely yet so desperately been
fleeing. He fumbled:

"I suppose you'd especially light on fellows like Seneca
Doane and try to make 'em—"

"You bet your sweet life we would! Look here, old Georgie:
I've never for one moment believed you meant it when you've
defended Doane, and the strikers and so on, at the Club. I
knew you were simply kidding those poor galoots like Sid
Finkelstein. . . . At least I certainly hope you were kidding!"

"Oh, well—sure— Course you might say—" Babbitt was
conscious of how feeble he sounded, conscious of Gunch's
mature and relentless eye. "Gosh, you know where I stand!
I'm no labor agitator! I'm a business man, first, last, and all
the time! But—but honestly, I don't think Doane means so
badly, and you got to remember he's an old friend of mine."

"George, when it comes right down to a struggle between
decency and the security of our homes on the one hand, and
red ruin and those lazy dogs plotting for free beer on the

other, you got to give up even old friendships. 'He that is not with me is against me.' "

"Ye-es, I suppose—"

"How about it? Going to join us in the Good Citizens' League?"

"I'll have to think it over, Verg."

"All right, just as you say." Babbitt was relieved to be let off so easily, but Gunch went on: "George, I don't know what's come over you; none of us do; and we've talked a lot about you. For a while we figured out you'd been upset by what happened to poor Riesling, and we forgave you for any fool things you said, but that's old stuff now, George, and we can't make out what's got into you. Personally, I've always defended you, but I must say it's getting too much for me. All the boys at the Athletic Club and the Boosters' are sore, the way you go on deliberately touting Doane and his bunch of hell-hounds, and talking about being liberal—which means being wishy-washy—and even saying this preacher guy Ingram isn't a professional free-love artist. And then the way you been carrying on personally! Joe Pumphrey says he saw you out the other night with a gang of totties, all stewed to the gills, and here to-day coming right into the Thornleigh with a—well, she may be all right and a perfect lady, but she certainly did look like a pretty gay skirt for a fellow with his wife out of town to be taking to lunch. Didn't look well. What the devil has come over you, George?"

"Strikes me there's a lot of fellows that know more about my personal business than I do myself!"

"Now don't go getting sore at me because I come out flat-footed like a friend and say what I think instead of tattling behind your back, the way a whole lot of 'em do. I tell you, George, you got a position in the community, and the community expects you to live up to it. And— Better think over joining the Good Citizens' League. See you about it later."

He was gone.

That evening Babbitt dined alone. He saw all the Clan of Good Fellows peering through the restaurant window, spying on him. Fear sat beside him, and he told himself that to-night he would not go to Tanis's flat; and he did not go . . . till late.

chapter 30

THE summer before, Mrs. Babbitt's letters had crackled with desire to return to Zenith. Now they said nothing of returning, but a wistful "I suppose everything is going on all right without me" among her dry chronicles of weather and sicknesses hinted to Babbitt that he hadn't been very urgent about her coming. He worried it:

"If she were here, and I went on raising cain like I been doing, she'd have a fit. I got to get hold of myself. I got to learn to play around and yet not make a fool of myself. I can do it, too, if folks like Verg Gunch 'll let me alone, and Myra 'll stay away. But—poor kid, she sounds lonely. Lord, I don't want to hurt her!"

Impulsively he wrote that they missed her, and her next letter said happily that she was coming home.

He persuaded himself that he was eager to see her. He bought roses for the house, he ordered squab for dinner, he had the car cleaned and polished. All the way home from the station with her he was adequate in his accounts of Ted's success in basket-ball at the university, but before they reached Floral Heights there was nothing more to say, and already he felt the force of her stolidity, wondered whether he could remain a good husband and still sneak out of the house this evening for half an hour with the Bunch. When he had housed the car he blundered upstairs, into the familiar talcum-scented warmth of her presence, blaring, "Help you unpack your bag?"

"No, I can do it."

Slowly she turned, holding up a small box, and slowly she said, "I brought you a present, just a new cigar-case. I don't know if you'd care to have it—"

She was the lonely girl, the brown appealing Myra Thomp-

son, whom he had married, and he almost wept for pity as he
kissed her and besought, "Oh, honey, honey, *care* to have it?
Of course I do! I'm awful proud you brought it to me. And
I needed a new case badly."

He wondered how he would get rid of the case he had
bought the week before.

"And you really are glad to see me back?"

"Why, you poor kiddy, what you been worrying about?"

"Well, you didn't seem to miss me very much."

By the time he had finished his stint of lying they were
firmly bound again. By ten that evening it seemed improbable
that she had ever been away. There was but one difference:
the problem of remaining a respectable husband, a Floral
Heights husband, yet seeing Tanis and the Bunch with frequency. He had promised to telephone to Tanis that evening,
and now it was melodramatically impossible. He prowled
about the telephone, impulsively thrusting out a hand to lift
the receiver, but never quite daring to risk it. Nor could he
find a reason for slipping down to the drug store on Smith
Street, with its telephone-booth. He was laden with responsibility till he threw it off with the speculation: "Why the
deuce should I fret so about not being able to 'phone Tanis?
She can get along without me. I don't owe her anything. She's
a fine girl, but I've given her just as much as she has me.
. . . Oh, damn these women and the way they get you all
tied up in complications!"

II

For a week he was attentive to his wife, took her to the
theater, to dinner at the Littlefields'; then the old weary dodging and shifting began, and at least two evenings a week he
spent with the Bunch. He still made pretense of going to the
Elks and to committee-meetings but less and less did he
trouble to have his excuses interesting, less and less did she
affect to believe them. He was certain that she knew he was
associating with what Floral Heights called "a sporty crowd,"
yet neither of them acknowledged it. In matrimonial geog-
raphy the distance between the first mute recognition of a
break and the admission thereof is as great as the distance
between the first naïve faith and the first doubting.

As he began to drift away he also began to see her as a
human being, to like and dislike her instead of accepting her
as a comparatively movable part of the furniture, and he com-

passionated that husband-and-wife relation which, in twenty-five years of married life, had become a separate and real entity. He recalled their high lights; the summer vacation in Virginia meadows under the blue wall of the mountains; their motor tour through Ohio, and the exploration of Cleveland, Cincinnati, and Columbus; the birth of Verona; their building of this new house, planned to comfort them through a happy old age—chokingly they had said that it might be the last home either of them would ever have. Yet his most softening remembrance of these dear moments did not keep him from barking at dinner, "Yep, going out f' few hours. Don't sit up for me."

He did not dare now to come home drunk, and though he rejoiced in his return to high morality and spoke with gravity to Pete and Fulton Bemis about their drinking, he prickled at Myra's unexpressed criticisms and sulkily meditated that a "fellow couldn't ever learn to handle himself if he was always bossed by a lot of women."

He no longer wondered if Tanis wasn't a bit worn and sentimental. In contrast to the complacent Myra he saw her as swift and air-borne and radiant, a fire-spirit tenderly stooping to the hearth, and however pitifully he brooded on his wife, he longed to be with Tanis.

Then Mrs. Babbitt tore the decent cloak from her unhappiness and the astounded male discovered that she was having a small determined rebellion of her own.

III

They were beside the fireless fire-place, in the evening.

"Georgie," she said, "you haven't given me the list of your household expenses while I was away."

"No, I — Haven't made it out yet." Very affably: "Gosh, we must try to keep down expenses this year."

"That's so. I don't know where all the money goes to. I try to economize, but it just seems to evaporate."

"I suppose I oughtn't to spend so much on cigars. Don't know but what I'll cut down my smoking, maybe cut it out entirely. I was thinking of a good way to do it, the other day: start on these cubeb cigarettes, and they'd kind of disgust me with smoking."

"Oh, I do wish you would! It isn't that I care, but honestly, George, it is so bad for you to smoke so much. Don't you think you could reduce the amount? And George—

I notice now, when you come home from these lodges and all, that sometimes you smell of whisky. Dearie, you know I don't worry so much about the moral side of it, but you have a weak stomach and you can't stand all this drinking."

"Weak stomach, hell! I guess I can carry my booze about as well as most folks!"

"Well, I do think you ought to be careful. Don't you see, dear, I don't want you to get sick."

"Sick, rats! I'm not a baby! I guess I ain't going to get sick just because maybe once a week I shoot a highball! That's the trouble with women. They always exaggerate so."

"George, I don't think you ought to talk that way when I'm just speaking for your own good."

"I know, but gosh all fishhooks, that's the trouble with women! They're always criticizing and commenting and bringing things up, and then they say it's 'for your own good'!"

"Why, George, that's not a nice way to talk, to answer me so short."

"Well, I didn't mean to answer short, but gosh, talking as if I was a kindergarten brat, not able to tote one highball without calling for the St. Mary's ambulance! A fine idea you must have of me!"

"Oh, it isn't that; it's just—I don't want to see you get sick and— My, I didn't know it was so late! Don't forget to give me those household accounts for the time while I was away."

"Oh, thunder, what's the use of taking the trouble to make 'em out now? Let's just skip 'em for that period."

"Why, George Babbitt, in all the years we've been married we've never failed to keep a complete account of every penny we've spent!"

"No. Maybe that's the trouble with us."

"What in the world do you mean?"

"Oh, I don't mean anything, only— Sometimes I get so darn sick and tired of all this routine and the accounting at the office and expenses at home and fussing and stewing and fretting and wearing myself out worrying over a lot of junk that doesn't really mean a doggone thing, and being so careful and— Good Lord, what do you think I'm made for? I could have been a darn good orator, and here I fuss and fret and worry—"

"Don't you suppose I ever get tired of fussing? I get so bored with ordering three meals a day, three hundred and sixty-five days a year, and ruining my eyes over that horrid sewing-machine, and looking after your clothes and Rone's and Ted's and Tinka's and everybody's, and the laundry, and darning socks, and going down to the Piggly Wiggly to market, and bringing my basket home to save money on the cash-and-carry and—*everything!*"

"Well, gosh," with a certain astonishment, "I suppose maybe you do! But talk about— Here I have to be in the office every single day, while you can go out all afternoon and see folks and visit with the neighbors and do any blinkin' thing you want to!"

"Yes, and a fine lot of good that does me! Just talking over the same old things with the same old crowd, while you have all sorts of interesting people coming in to see you at the office."

"Interesting! Cranky old dames that want to know why I haven't rented their dear precious homes for about seven times their value, and bunch of old crabs panning the everlasting daylights out of me because they don't receive every cent of their rentals by three P.M. on the second of the month! Sure! Interesting! Just as interesting as the small pox!"

"Now, George, I will not have you shouting at me that way!"

"Well, it gets my goat the way women figure out that a man doesn't do a darn thing but sit on his chair and have lovey-dovey conferences with a lot of classy dames and give 'em the glad eye!"

"I guess you manage to give them a glad enough eye when they do come in."

"What do you mean? Mean I'm chasing flappers?"

"I should hope not—at your age!"

"Now you look here! You may not believe it— Of course all you see is fat little Georgie Babbitt. Sure! Handy man around the house! Fixes the furnace when the furnace-man doesn't show up, and pays the bills, but dull, awful dull! Well, you may not believe it, but there's some women that think Old George Babbitt isn't such a bad scout! They think he's not so bad-looking, not so bad that it hurts anyway, and he's got a pretty good line of guff, and some even think he shakes a darn wicked Walkover at dancing!"

"Yes." She spoke slowly. "I haven't much doubt that when I'm away you manage to find people who properly appreciate you."

"Well, I just mean——" he protested, with a sound of denial. Then he was angered into semi-honesty. "You bet I do! I find plenty of folks, and doggone nice ones, that don't think I'm a weak-stomached baby!"

"That's exactly what I was saying! You can run around with anybody you please, but I'm supposed to sit here and wait for you. You have the chance to get all sorts of culture and everything, and I just stay home——"

"Well, gosh almighty, there's nothing to prevent your reading books and going to lectures and all that junk, is there?"

"George, I *told* you, I won't have you shouting at me like that! I don't know what's come over you. You never used to speak to me in this cranky way."

"I didn't mean to sound cranky, but gosh, it certainly makes me sore to get the blame because you don't keep up with things."

"I'm going to! Will you help me?"

"Sure. Anything I can do to help you in the culture-grabbing line—yours to oblige, G. F. Babbitt."

"Very well then, I want you to go to Mrs. Mudge's New Thought meeting with me, next Sunday afternoon."

"Mrs. Who's which?"

"Mrs Opal Emerson Mudge. The field-lecturer for the American New Thought League. She's going to speak on 'Cultivating the Sun Spirit' before the League of the Higher Illumination, at the Thornleigh."

"Oh, punk! New Thought! Hashed thought with a poached egg! 'Cultivating the——' It sounds like 'Why is a mouse when it spins?' That's a fine spiel for a good Presbyterian to be going to, when you can hear Doc Drew!"

"Reverend Drew is a scholar and a pulpit orator and all that, but he hasn't got the Inner Ferment, as Mrs. Mudge calls it; he hasn't any inspiration for the New Era. Women need inspiration now. So I want you to come, as you promised."

IV

The Zenith branch of the League of the Higher Illumination met in the smaller ballroom at the Hotel Thornleigh, a refined apartment with pale green walls and plaster wreaths of roses, refined parquet flooring, and ultra-refined frail gilt chairs. Here were gathered sixty-five women and ten men. Most of the men slouched in their chairs and wriggled, while their wives sat rigidly at attention, but two of them—red-necked, meaty men—were as respectably devout as their wives. They were newly rich contractors who, having bought houses, motors, hand-painted pictures, and gentlemanliness, were now buying a refined ready-made philosophy. It had been a tossup with them whether to buy New Thought, Christian Science, or a good standard high-church model of Episcopalianism.

In the flesh, Mrs. Opal Emerson Mudge fell somewhat short of a prophetic aspect. She was pony-built and plump, with the face of a haughty Pekingese, a button of a nose, and arms so short that, despite her most indignant endeavors, she could not clasp her hands in front of her as she sat on the platform waiting. Her frock of taffeta and green velvet, with three strings of glass beads, and large folding eye-glasses dangling from a black ribbon, was a triumph of refinement.

Mrs. Mudge was introduced by the president of the League of the Higher Illumination, an oldish young woman with a yearning voice, white spats, and a mustache. She said that Mrs. Mudge would now make it plain to the simplest intellect how the Sun Spirit could be cultivated, and they who had been thinking about cultivating one would do well to treasure Mrs. Mudge's words, because even Zenith (and everybody knew that Zenith stood in the van of spiritual and New Thought progress) didn't often have the opportunity to sit at the feet of such an inspiring Optimist and Metaphysical Seer as Mrs. Opal Emerson Mudge, who had lived the Life of Wider Usefulness through Concentration, and in the Silence found those Secrets of Mental Control and the Inner Key which were immediately going to transform and bring Peace, Power, and Prosperity to the unhappy nations; and so, friends, would they for this precious gem-studded hour forget the Illusions of the Seeming Real, and in the actualization of the deep-lying Veritas pass, along with Mrs. Opal Emerson Mudge, to the Realm Beautiful.

If Mrs. Mudge was rather pudgier than one would like one's swamis, yogis, seers, and initiates, yet her voice had the real professional note. It was refined and optimistic; it was overpoweringly calm; it flowed on relentlessly, without one comma, till Babbitt was hypnotized. Her favorite word was "always," which she pronounced ollllle-ways. Her principal gesture was a pontifical but thoroughly ladylike blessing with two stubby fingers.

She explained about this matter of Spiritual Saturation:
"There are those—"

Of "those" she made a linked sweetness long drawn out;
a far-off delicate call in a twilight minor. It chastely rebuked
the restless husbands, yet brought them a message of healing.

"There are those who have seen the rim and outer seeming
of the Logos there are those who have glimpsed and in enthusiasm possessed themselves of some segment and portion
of the Logos there are those who thus flicked but not pene-
trated and radioactivated by the Dynamis go always to and
fro assertative that they possess and are possessed of the
Logos and the Metaphysikos but this word I bring you this
concept I enlarge that those that are not utter are not even
inceptive and that holiness is in its definitive essence always
always always whole-iness and—"

It proved that the Essence of the Sun Spirit was Truth, but
its Aura and Effluxion were Cheerfulness:

"Face always the day with the dawn-laugh with the enthusiasm of the initiate who perceives that all works together
in the revolutions of the Wheel and who answers the stric-
tures of the Soured Souls of the Destructionists with a Glad
Affirmation—"

It went on for about an hour and seven minutes.

At the end Mrs. Mudge spoke with more vigor and punc-
tuation:

"Now let me suggest to all of you the advantages of the
Theosophical and Pantheistic Oriental Reading Circle, which
I represent. Our object is to unite all the manifestations of
the New Era into one cohesive whole—New Thought, Christian Science, Theosophy, Vedanta, Bahaism, and the other
sparks from the one New Light. The subscription is but ten
dollars a year, and for this mere pittance the members receive not only the monthly magazine, *Pearls of Healing*,
but the privilege of sending right to the president, our revered
Mother Dobbs, any questions regarding spiritual progress,
matrimonial problems, health and well-being questions, financial difficulties, and—"

They listened to her with adoring attention. They looked
genteel. They looked ironed-out. They coughed politely, and
crossed their legs with quietness, and in expensive linen hand-
kerchiefs they blew their noses with a delicacy altogether
optimistic and refined.

As for Babbitt, he sat and suffered.

When they were blessedly out in the air again, when they

drove home through a wind smelling of snow and honest sun, he dared not speak. They had been too near to quarreling, these days. Mrs. Babbitt forced it:

"Did you enjoy Mrs. Mudge's talk?"

"Well I— What did you get out of it?"

"Oh, it starts a person thinking. It gets you out of a routine of ordinary thoughts."

"Well, I'll hand it to Opal she isn't ordinary, but gosh— Honest, did that stuff mean anything to you?"

"Of course I'm not trained in metaphysics, and there was lots I couldn't quite grasp, but I did feel it was inspiring. And she speaks so readily. I do think you ought to have got something out of it."

"Well, I didn't! I swear, I was simply astonished, the way those women lapped it up! Why the dickens they want to put in their time listening to all that blaa when they—"

"It's certainly better for them than going to roadhouses and smoking and drinking!"

"I don't know whether it is or not! Personally I don't see a whole lot of difference. In both cases they're trying to get away from themselves—most everybody is, these days, I guess. And I'd certainly get a whole lot more out of hoofing it in a good lively dance, even in some dive, than sitting looking as if my collar was too tight, and feeling too scared to spit, and listening to Opal chewing her words."

"I'm sure you do! You're very fond of dives. No doubt you saw a lot of them while I was away!"

"Look here! You been doing a hell of a lot of insinuating and hinting around lately, as if I were leading a double life or something, and I'm damn sick of it, and I don't want to hear anything more about it!"

"Why, George Babbitt! Do you realize what you're saying? Why, George, in all our years together you've never talked to me like that!"

"It's about time then!"

"Lately you've been getting worse and worse, and now, finally, you're cursing and swearing at me and shouting at me, and your voice so ugly and hateful— I just shudder!"

"Oh, rats, quit exaggerating! I wasn't shouting, or swearing either."

"I wish you could hear your own voice! Maybe you don't realize how it sounds. But even so— You never used to talk like that. You simply *couldn't* talk this way if something dreadful hadn't happened to you."

His mind was hard. With amazement he found that he wasn't particularly sorry. It was only with an effort that he made himself more agreeable: "Well, gosh, I didn't mean to get sore."

"George, do you realize that we can't go on like this, getting farther and farther apart, and you ruder and ruder to me? I just don't know what's going to happen."

He had a moment's pity for her bewilderment; he thought of how many deep and tender things would be hurt if they really "couldn't go on like this." But his pity was impersonal, and he was wondering, "Wouldn't it maybe be a good thing if— Not a divorce and all that, o' course, but kind of a little more independence?"

While she looked at him pleadingly he drove on in a dreadful silence.

chapter 31

WHEN he was away from her, while he kicked about the garage and swept the snow off the running-board and examined a cracked hose-connection, he repented, he was alarmed and astonished that he could have flared out at his wife, and thought fondly how much more lasting she was than the flighty Bunch. He went in to mumble that he was "sorry, didn't mean to be grouchy," and to inquire as to her interest in movies. But in the darkness of the movie theater he brooded that he'd "gone and tied himself up to Myra all over again." He had some satisfaction in taking it out on Tanis Judique. "Hang Tanis anyway! Why'd she gone and got him into these mix-ups and made him all jumpy and nervous and cranky? Too many complications! Cut 'em out!"

He wanted peace. For ten days he did not see Tanis nor telephone to her, and instantly she put upon him the compulsion which he hated. When he had stayed away from her

for five days, hourly taking pride in his resoluteness and
hourly picturing how greatly Tanis must miss him, Miss
McGoun reported, "Mrs. Judique on the 'phone. Like t' speak
t' you 'bout some repairs."

Tanis was quick and quiet:

"Mr. Babbitt? Oh, George, this is Tanis. I haven't seen
you for weeks—days, anyway. You aren't sick, are you?"

"No, just been terribly rushed. I, uh, I think there'll be a
big revival of building this year. Got to, uh, got to work
hard."

"Of course, my man! I want you to. You know I'm terribly ambitious for you; much more than I am for myself. I
just don't want you to forget poor Tanis. Will you call me
up soon?"

"Sure! Sure! You bet!"

"Please do. I sha'n't call you again."

He meditated, "Poor kid! . . . But gosh, she oughtn't to
'phone me at the office. . . . She's a wonder—sympathy—
'ambitious for me.' . . . But gosh, I won't be made and compelled to call her up till I get ready. Darn these women, the
way they make demands! It'll be one long old time before
I see her! . . . But gosh, I'd like to see her to-night—sweet
little thing. . . . Oh, cut that, son! Now you've broken
away, be wise!"

She did not telephone again, nor he, but after five more
days she wrote to him:

> Have I offended you? You must know, dear, I didn't mean
> to. I'm so lonely and I need somebody to cheer me up. Why
> didn't you come to the nice party we had at Carrie's last
> evening I remember she invited you. Can't you come
> around here to-morrow Thur evening? I shall be alone and
> hope to see you.

His reflections were numerous:

"Doggone it, why can't she let me alone? Why can't women
ever learn a fellow hates to be bulldozed? And they always
take advantage of you by yelling how lonely they are.

"Now that isn't nice of you, young fella. She's a fine,
square, straight girl, and she does get lonely. She writes a
swell hand. Nice-looking stationery. Plain. Refined. I
guess I'll have to go see her. Well, thank God, I got till
to-morrow night free of her, anyway.

"She's nice but— Hang it, I won't be *made* to do things!

I'm not married to her. No, nor by golly going to be!
"Oh, rats, I suppose I better go see her."

II

Thursday, the to-morrow of Tanis's note, was full of emotional crises. At the Roughnecks' Table at the club, Verg
Gunch talked of the Good Citizens' League and (it seemed to
Babbitt) deliberately left him out of the invitations to join.
Old Mat Penniman, the general utility man at Babbitt's office,
had Troubles, and came in to groan about them: his oldest
boy was "no good," his wife was sick, and he had quarreled
with his borther-in-law. Conrad Lyte also had Troubles,
and since Lyte was one of his best clients, Babbitt had to
listen to them. Mr. Lyte, it appeared, was suffering from a
peculiarly interesting neuralgia, and the garage had over-
charged him. When Babbitt came home, everybody had Troubles: his wife was simultaneously thinking about discharging
the impudent new maid, and worried lest the maid leave; and
Tinka desired to denounce her teacher.

"Oh, quit fussing!" Babbitt fussed. "You never hear me
whining about my Troubles, and yet if you had to run a real-
estate office— Why, to-day I found Miss Bannigan was two
days behind with her accounts, and I pinched my finger in
my desk, and Lyte was in and just as unreasonable as ever."

He was so vexed that after dinner, when it was time for a
tactful escape to Tanis, he merely grumped to his wife, "Got
to go out. Be back by eleven, should think."

"Oh! You're going out again?"

"Again! What do you mean 'again'! Haven't hardly been
out of the house for a week!"

"Are you—are you going to the Elks?"

"Nope. Got to see some people."

Though this time he heard his own voice and knew that it
was curt, though she was looking at him with wide-eyed re-
proach, he stumped into the hall, jerked on his ulster and
fur-lined gloves, and went out to start the car.

He was relieved to find Tanis cheerful, unreproachful, and
brilliant in a frock of brown net over gold tissue. "You
poor man, having to come out on a night like this! It's terribly cold. Don't you think a small highball would be nice?"

"Now, by golly, there's a woman with savvy! I think we
could more or less stand a highball if it wasn't too long a
one—not over a foot tall!"

He kissed her with careless heartiness, he forgot the compulsion of her demands, he stretched in a large chair and felt that he had beautifully come home. He was suddenly loquacious; he told her what a noble and misunderstood man he was, and how superior to Pete, Fulton Bemis, and the other men of their acquaintance; and she, bending forward, chin in charming hand, brightly agreed. But when he forced himself to ask, "Well, honey, how's things with *you*," she took his duty-question seriously, and he discovered that she too had Troubles:

"Oh, all right but— I did get so angry with Carrie. She told Minnie that I told her that Minnie was an awful tightwad, and Minnie told me Carrie had told her, and of course I told her I hadn't said anything of the kind, and then Carrie found Minnie had told me, and she was simply furious because Minnie had told me, and of course I was just boiling because Carrie had told her I'd told her, and then we all met up at Fulton's—his wife is away—thank heavens!—oh, there's the dandiest floor in his house to dance on—and we were all of us simply furious at each other and— Oh, I do hate that kind of a mix-up, don't you? I mean—it's so lacking in refinement, but— And Mother wants to come and stay with me for a whole month, and of course I do love her, I suppose I do, but honestly, she'll cramp my style something dreadful—she never can learn not to comment, and she always wants to know where I'm going when I go out evenings, and if I lie to her she always spies around and ferrets around and finds out where I've been, and then she looks like Patience on a Monument till I could just scream. And oh, *I must* tell you— You know I *never* talk about myself; I just hate people who do, don't you? But— I feel so stupid to-night, and I know I must be boring you with all this but— What would you do about Mother?"

He gave her facile masculine advice. She was to put off her mother's stay. She was to tell Carrie to go to the deuce. For these valuable revelations she thanked him, and they ambled into the familiar gossip of the Bunch. Of what a sentimental fool was Carrie. Of what a lazy brat was Pete. Of how nice Fulton Bemis could be—"course lots of people think he's a regular old grouch when they meet him because he doesn't give 'em the glad hand the first crack out of the box, but when they get to know him, he's a corker."

But as they had gone conscientiously through each of these analyses before, the conversation staggered. Babbitt tried to be intellectual and deal with General Topics. Babbitt tried to thoroughly sound things about Disarmament, and broad-mindedness and liberalism; but it seemed to him that General Topics interested Tanis only when she could apply them to Pete, Carrie, or themselves. He was distressingly conscious of their silence. He tried to stir her into chattering again, but silence rose like a gray presence and hovered between them.

"I, uh—" he labored. "It strikes me—it strikes me that unemployment is lessening."

"Maybe Pete will get a decent job, then."

Silence.

Desperately he essayed, "What's the trouble, old honey? You seem kind of quiet to-night."

"Am I? Oh, I'm not. But—do you really care whether I am or not?"

"Care? Sure! Course I do!"

"Do you really?" She swooped on him, sat on the arm of his chair.

He hated the emotional drain of having to appear fond of her. He stroked her hand, smiled up at her dutifully, and sank back.

"George, I wonder if you really like me at all?"

"Course I do, silly."

"Do you really, precious? Do you care a bit?"

"Why certainly! You don't suppose I'd be here if I didn't!"

"Now see here, young man, I won't have you speaking to me in that huffy way!"

"I didn't mean to sound huffy. I just—" In injured and rather childish tones: "Gosh almighty, it makes me tired the way everybody says I sound huffy when I just talk natural! Do they expect me to sing it or something?"

"Who do you mean by 'everybody'? How many other ladies have you been consoling?"

"Look here now, I won't have this hinting!"

Humbly: "I know, dear. I was only teasing. I know it didn't mean to talk huffy—it was just tired. Forgive bad Tanis. But say you love me, say it!"

"I love you. . . . Course I do."

"Yes, you do!" cynically. "Oh, darling, I don't mean to be rude but— I get so lonely. I feel so useless. Nobody needs me, nothing I can do for anybody. And you know, dear, I'm so active—I could be if there was something to do. And I *am* young, aren't I! I'm not an old thing! I'm not old and stupid, am I?"

He had to assure her. She stroked his hair; and he had to look pleased under that touch, the more demanding in its beguiling softness. He was impatient. He wanted to flee out to a hard, sure, unemotional man-world. Through her delicate and caressing fingers she may have caught something of his shrugging distaste. She left him—he was for the moment buoyantly relieved—she dragged a footstool to his feet and sat looking beseechingly up at him. But as in many men the cringing of a dog, the flinching of a frightened child, rouse not pity but a surprised and jerky cruelty, so her humility only annoyed him. And he saw her now as middle-aged, as beginning to be old. Even while he detested his own thoughts, they rode him. She was old, he winced. Old! He noted how the soft flesh was creasing into webby folds beneath her chin, below her eyes, at the base of her wrists. A patch of her throat had a minute roughness like the crumbs from a rubber eraser. Old! She was younger in years than himself, yet it was sickening to have her yearning up at him with rolling great eyes—as if, he shuddered, his own aunt were making love to him.

He fretted inwardly, "I'm through with this asinine fooling around. I'm going to cut her out. She's a darn decent nice woman, and I don't want to hurt her, but it'll hurt a lot less to cut her right out, like a good clean surgical operation."

He was on his feet. He was speaking urgently. By every rule of self-esteem, he had to prove to her, and to himself, that it was her fault.

"I suppose maybe I'm kind of out of sorts to-night, but honest, honey, when I stayed away for a while to catch up on work and everything and figure out where I was at, you ought to have been cannier and waited till I came back. Can't you see, dear, when you *made* me come, I—being about an average bull-headed chump—my tendency was to resist? Listen, dear, I'm going now——"

"Not for a while, precious! No!"

"Yep. Right now. And then sometime we'll see about the future."

"What do you mean, dear, 'about the future'? Have I done something I oughtn't to? Oh, I'm so dreadfully sorry!"

He resolutely put his hands behind him. "Not a thing, God bless you, not a thing. You're as good as they make 'em. But it's just— Good Lord, do you realize I've got things to do in the world? I've got a business to attend to and, you might not believe it, but I've got a wife and kids that I'm awful fond of!" Then only during the murder he was committing was he able to feel nobly virtuous. "I want us to be friends but, gosh, I can't go on this way feeling I *got* to come up here every so often—"

"Oh, darling, darling, and I've always told you, so carefully, that you were absolutely free. I just wanted you to come around when you were tired and wanted to talk to me, or when you could enjoy our parties—"

She was so reasonable, she was so gently right! It took him an hour to make his escape, with nothing settled and everything horribly settled. In a barren freedom of icy Northern wind he sighed, "Thank God that's over! Poor Tanis, poor darling decent Tanis! But it is over. Absolute! I'm free!"

chapter 32

HIS wife was up when he came in. "Did you have a good time?" she sniffed.

"I did not. I had a rotten time! Anything else I got to explain?"

"George, how can you speak like— Oh, I don't know what's come over you!"

"Good Lord, there's nothing come over me! Why do you look for trouble all the time?" He was warning himself, "Careful! Stop being so disagreeable. Course she feels it, being left alone here all evening." But he forgot his warning as she went on:

"Why do you go out and see all sorts of strange people? I suppose you'll say you've been to another committee-meeting this evening!"

"Nope. I've been calling on a woman. We sat by the fire

and kidded each other and had a whale of a good time, if
you want to know!"

"Well— From the way you say it, I suppose it's my fault
you went there! I probably sent you!"

"You did!"

"Well, upon my word—"

"You hate 'strange people' as you call 'em. If you had your
way, I'd be as much of an old stick-in-the-mud as Howard
Littlefield. You never want to have anybody with any git
to 'em at the house; you want a bunch of old stiffs that sit
around and gas about the weather. You're doing your level
best to make me old. Well, let me tell you, I'm not going
to have—"

Overwhelmed she bent to his unprecedented tirade, and in
answer she mourned:

"Oh, dearest, I don't think that's true. I don't mean to
make you old, I know. Perhaps you're partly right. Perhaps
I am slow about getting acquainted with new people. But
when you think of all the dear good times we have, and the
supper-parties and the movies and all—"

With true masculine wiles he not only convinced himself
that she had injured him but, by the loudness of his voice and
the brutality of his attack, he convinced her also, and presently he had her apologizing for his having spent the evening
with Tanis. He went up to bed well pleased, not only the
master but the martyr of the household. For a distasteful
moment after he had lain down he wondered if he had been altogether just. "Ought to be ashamed, bullying her. Maybe
there is her side to things. Maybe she hasn't had such a
bloomin' hectic time herself. But I don't care! Good for her
to get waked up a little. And I'm going to keep free. Of
her and Tanis and the fellows at the club and everybody. I'm
going to run my own life!"

II

In this mood he was particularly objectionable at the Boosters' Club lunch next day. They were addressed by a congressman who had just returned from an exhaustive three-months
study of the finances, ethnology, political systems, linguistic
divisions, mineral resources, and agriculture of Germany,
France, Great Britain, Italy, Austria, Czechoslovakia, Jugo-
slavia, and Bulgaria. He told them all about those subjects,
together with three funny stories about European misconcep-

tions of America and some spirited words on the necessity of keeping ignorant foreigners out of America.

"Say, that was a mighty informative talk. Real he-stuff," said Sidney Finkelstein.

But the disaffected Babbitt grumbled, "Four-flusher! Bunch of hot air! And what's the matter with the immigrants? Gosh, they aren't all ignorant, and I got a hunch we're all descended from immigrants ourselves."

"Oh, you make me tired!" said Mr. Finkelstein.

Babbitt was aware that Dr. A. I. Dilling was sternly listening from across the table. Dr. Dilling was one of the most important men in the Boosters'. He was not a physician but a surgeon, a more romantic and sounding occupation. He was an intense large man with a boiling of black hair and a thick black mustache. The newspapers often chronicled his operations; he was professor of surgery in the State University; he went to dinner at the very best houses on Royal Ridge; and he was said to be worth several hundred thousand dollars. It was dismaying to Babbitt to have such a person glower at him. He hastily praised the congressman's wit, to Sidney Finkelstein, but for Dr. Dilling's benefit.

III

That afternoon three men shouldered into Babbitt's office with the air of a Vigilante committee in frontier days. They were large, resolute, big-jawed men, and they were all high lords in the land of Zenith—Dr. Dilling the surgeon, Charles McKelvey the contractor, and, most dismaying of all, the white-bearded Colonel Rutherford Snow, owner of the *Advocate-Times*. In their whelming presence Babbitt felt small and insignificant.

"Well, well, great pleasure, have chairs, what c'n I do for you?" he babbled.

They neither sat nor offered observations on the weather.

"Babbitt," said Colonel Snow, "we've come from the Good Citizens' League. We've decided we want you to join. Vergil Gunch says you don't care to, but I think we can show you a new light. The League is going to combine with the Chamber of Commerce in a campaign for the Open Shop, so it's time for you to put your name down."

In his embarrassment Babbitt could not recall his reasons for not wishing to join the League, if indeed he had ever definitely known them, but he was passionately certain that he did not wish to join, and at the thought of their forcing him he felt a stirring of anger against even these princes of commerce.

"Sorry, Colonel, have to think it over a little," he mumbled.

McKelvey snarled, "That means you're not going to join, George?"

Something black and unfamiliar and ferocious spoke from Babbitt: "Now, you look here, Charley! I'm damned if I'm going to be bullied into joining anything, not even by you plutes!"

"We're not bullying anybody," Dr. Dilling began, but Colonel Snow thrust him aside with, "Certainly we are! We don't mind a little bullying, if it's necessary. Babbitt, the G.C.L. has been talking about you a good deal. You're supposed to be a sensible, clean, responsible man; you always have been; but here lately, for God knows what reason, I hear from all sorts of sources that you're running around with a loose crowd, and what's a whole lot worse, you've actually been advocating and supporting some of the most dangerous elements in town, like this fellow Doane."

"Colonel, that strikes me as my private business."

"Possibly, but we want to have an understanding. You've stood in, you and your father-in-law, with some of the most substantial and forward-looking interests in town, like my friends of the Street Traction Company, and my papers have given you a lot of boosts. Well, you can't expect the decent citizens to go on aiding you if you intend to side with precisely the people who are trying to undermine us."

Babbitt was frightened, but he had an agonized instinct that if he yielded in this he would yield in everything. He protested:

"You're exaggerating, Colonel. I believe in being broad-minded and liberal, but, of course, I'm just as much agin the cranks and blatherskites and labor unions and so on as you are. But fact is, I belong to so many organizations now that I can't do 'em justice, and I want to think it over before I decide about coming into the G.C.L."

Colonel Snow condescended, "Oh, no, I'm not exaggerating! Why the doctor here heard you cussing out and defaming one of the finest types of Republican congressmen, just this noon! And you have entirely the wrong idea about 'thinking over joining.' We're not begging you to join the G.C.L.—we're permitting you to join. I'm not sure, my boy, but what if you put if off it'll be too late. I'm not sure we'll want you then. Better think quick—better think quick!"

The three Vigilantes, formidable in their righteousness, stared at him in a taut silence. Babbitt waited through. He thought nothing at all, he merely waited, while in his echoing head buzzed, "I don't want to join—I don't want to join—I don't want to."

"All right. Sorry for you!" said Colonel Snow, and the three men abruptly turned their beefy backs.

IV

As Babbitt went out to his car that evening he saw Vergil Gunch coming down the block. He raised his hand in salutation, but Gunch ignored it and crossed the street. He was certain that Gunch had seen him. He drove home in sharp discomfort.

His wife attacked at once: "Georgie dear, Muriel Frink was in this afternoon, and she says that Chum says the committee of this Good Citizens' League especially asked you to join and you wouldn't. Don't you think it would be better? You know all the nicest people belong, and the League stands for—"

"I know what the League stands for! It stands for the suppression of free speech and free thought and everything else! I don't propose to be bullied and rushed into joining anything, and it isn't a question of whether it's a good league or a bad league or what the hell kind of a league it is; it's just a question of my refusing to be told I got to—"

"But dear, if you don't join, people might criticize you."

"Let 'em criticize!"

"But I mean *nice* people!"

"Rats, I— Matter of fact, this whole League is just a fad. It's like all these other organizations that start off with such a rush and let on they're going to change the whole works and pretty soon they peter out and everybody forgets all about 'em!"

"But if it's *the* fad now, don't you think you—"

"No, I don't! Oh, Myra, please quit nagging me about it. I'm sick of hearing about the confounded G.C.L. I almost wish I'd joined it when Verg first came around, and got it over. And maybe I'd 've come in to-day if the committee hadn't tried to bullyrag me, but, by God, as long as I'm a free-born independent American cit—"

"Now, George, you're talking exactly like the German furnace-man."

"Oh, I am, am I! Then, I won't talk at all!"

He longed, that evening, to see Tanis Judique, to be strengthened by her sympathy. When all the family were upstairs he got as far as telephoning to her apartment-house, but he was agitated about it and when the janitor answered he blurted, "Nev' mind—I'll call later," and hung up the receiver.

V

If Babbitt had not been certain about Vergil Gunch's avoiding him, there could be little doubt about William Washington Eathorne, next morning. When Babbitt was driving down to the office he overtook Eathorne's car, with the great banker sitting in anemic solemnity behind his chauffeur. Babbitt waved and cried, "Mornin'!" Eathorne looked at him deliberately, hesitated, and gave him a nod more contemptuous than a direct cut.

Babbitt's partner and father-in-law came in at ten:

"George, what's this I hear about some song and dance you gave Colonel Snow about not wanting to join the G.C.L.? What the dickens you trying to do? Wreck the firm? You don't suppose these Big Guns will stand your bucking them and springing all this 'liberal' poppycock you been getting off lately, do you?"

"Oh, rats, Henry T., you been reading bum fiction. There ain't any such a thing as these plots to keep folks from being liberal. This is a free country. A man can do anything he wants to."

"Course th' ain't any plots. Who said they was? Only if folks get an idea you're scatter-brained and unstable, you don't suppose they'll want to do business with you, do you? One little rumor about your being a crank would do more to ruin this business than all the plots and stuff that these fool storywriters could think up in a month of Sundays."

That afternoon, when the old reliable Conrad Lyte, the merry miser, Conrad Lyte, appeared, and Babbitt suggested his buying a parcel of land in the new residential section of Dorchester, Lyte said hastily, too hastily, "No, no, don't want to go into anything new just now."

A week later Babbitt learned, through Henry Thompson, that the officials of the Street Traction Company were planning another real-estate coup, and that Sanders, Torrey and Wing, not the Babbitt-Thompson Company, were to handle it for them.

"I figure that Jake Offutt is kind of leery about the way folks are talking about you. Of course Jake is a rock-ribbed old die-hard, and he probably advised the Traction fellows to get some other broker. George, you got to do something!" trembled Thompson.

And, in a rush, Babbitt agreed. All nonsense the way people misjudged him, but still— He determined to join the Good Citizens' League the next time he was asked, and in furious resignation he waited. He wasn't asked. They ignored him. He did not have the courage to go to the League and beg in, and he took refuge in a shaky boast that he had "gotten away with bucking the whole city. Nobody could dictate to *him* how he was going to think and act!"

He was jarred as by nothing else when the paragon of stenographers, Miss McGoun, suddenly left him, though her reasons were excellent—she needed a rest, her sister was sick, she might not do any more work for six months. He was uncomfortable with her successor, Miss Havstad. What Miss Havstad's given name was, no one in the office ever knew. It seemed improbable that she had a given name, a lover, a powder-puff, or a digestion. She was so impersonal, this slight, pale, industrious Swede, that it was vulgar to think of her as going to an ordinary home to eat hash. She was a perfectly oiled and enameled machine, and she ought, each evening, to have been dusted off and shut in her desk beside her too-slim, too-frail pencil points. She took dictation swiftly, her typing was perfect, but Babbitt became jumpy when he tried to work with her. She made him feel puffy, and at his best-beloved daily jokes she looked gently inquiring. He longed for Miss McGoun's return, and thought of writing to her.

Then he heard that Miss McGoun had, a week after leaving him, gone over to his dangerous competitors, Sanders, Torrey and Wing.

He was not merely annoyed; he was frightened. "Why did she quit, then?" he worried. "Did she have a hunch my business is going on the rocks? And it was Sanders got the Street Traction deal. Rats—sinking ship!"

Gray fear loomed always by him now. He watched Fritz Weilinger, the young salesman, and wondered if he too would leave. Daily he fancied slights. He noted that he was not asked to speak at the annual Chamber of Commerce dinner. When Orville Jones gave a large poker party and he was not invited, he was certain that he had been snubbed. He was afraid to go to lunch at the Athletic Club, and afraid not to go. He believed that he was spied on; that when he left the table they whispered about him. Everywhere he heard the rustling whispers: in the offices of clients, in the bank when he made a deposit, in his own office, in his own home. Interminably he wondered what They were saying of him. All day long in imaginary conversations he caught them marveling, "Babbitt? Why, say, he's a regular anarchist! You got to admire the fellow for his nerve, the way he turned liberal and, by golly, just absolutely runs his life to suit himself, but say, he's dangerous, that's what he is, and he's got to be shown up."

He was so twitchy that when he rounded a corner and chanced on two acquaintances talking—whispering—his heart leaped, and he stalked by like an embarrassed schoolboy. When he saw his neighbors Howard Littlefield and Orville Jones together, he peered at them, went indoors to escape their spying, and was miserably certain that they had been whispering—plotting—whispering.

Through all his fear ran defiance. He felt stubborn. Sometimes he decided that he had been a very devil of a fellow, as bold as Seneca Doane; sometimes he planned to call on Doane and tell him what a revolutionist he was, and never got beyond the planning. But just as often, when he heard the soft whispers enveloping him he wailed, "Good Lord, what have I done? Just played with the Bunch, and called down Clarence Drum about being such a high-and-mighty sodger. Never catch *me* criticizing people and trying to make them accept *my* ideas!"

He could not stand the strain. Before long he admitted that he would like to flee back to the security of conformity, provided there was a decent and creditable way to return. But, stubbornly, he would not be forced back; he would not, he swore, "eat dirt."

Only in spirited engagements with his wife did these turbulent fears rise to the surface. She complained that he seemed nervous, that she couldn't understand why he did not want to "drop in at the Littlefields'" for the evening. He tried, but he could not express to her the nebulous facts of his rebellion and punishment. And, with Paul and Tanis lost, he had no one to whom he could talk. "Good Lord, Tinka is

the only real friend I have, these days," he sighed, and he
clung to the child, played floor-games with her all evening.

He considered going to see Paul in prison, but, though he
had a pale curt note from him every week, he thought of
Paul as dead. It was Tanis for whom he was longing.

"I thought I was so smart and independent, cutting Tanis
out, and I need her, Lord how I need her!" he raged. "Myra
simply can't understand. All she sees in life is getting along
by being just like other folks. But Tanis, she'd tell me I
was all right."

Then he broke, and one evening, late, he did run to Tanis.
He had not dared to hope for it, but she was in, and alone.
Only she wasn't Tanis. She was a courteous, brow-lifting,
ice-armored woman who looked like Tanis. She said, "Yes,
George, what is it?" in even and uninterested tones, and he
crept away, whipped.

His first comfort was from Ted and Eunice Littlefield.

They danced in one evening when Ted was home from the
university, and Ted chuckled, "What's this I hear from Euny,
dad? She says her dad says you raised Cain by boosting
old Seneca Doane. Hot dog! Give 'em fits! Stir 'em up! This
old burg is asleep!" Eunice plumped down on Babbitt's lap,
kissed him, nestled her bobbed hair against his chin, and
crowed, "I think you're lots nicer than Howard. Why is it,"
confidentially, "that Howard is such an old grouch? The man
has a good heart, and honestly, he's awfully bright, but he
never will learn to step on the gas, after all the training I've
given him. Don't you think we could do something with him,
dearest?"

"Why, Eunice, that isn't a nice way to speak of your papa,"
Babbitt observed, in the best Floral Heights manner, but
he was happy for the first time in weeks. He pictured himself
as the veteran liberal strengthened by the loyalty of the young
generation. They went out to rifle the ice-box. Babbitt gloated,
"If your mother caught us at this, we'd certainly get our
come-uppance!" and Eunice became maternal, scrambled a
terrifying number of eggs for them, kissed Babbitt on the
ear, and in the voice of a brooding abbess marveled, "It
beats the devil why feminists like me still go on nursing these
men!"

Thus stimulated, Babbitt was reckless when he encountered
Sheldon Smeeth, educational director of the Y.M.C.A. and
choir-leader of the Chatham Road Church. With one of his
damp hands Smeeth imprisoned Babbitt's thick paw while he

chanted, "Brother Babbitt, we haven't seen you at church
very often lately. I know you're busy with a multitude of
details, but you mustn't forget your dear friends at the old
church home."

Babbitt shook off the affectionate clasp—Sheldy liked to
hold hands for a long time—and snarled, "Well, I guess you
fellows can run the show without me. Sorry, Smeeth; got to
beat it. G'day."

But afterward he winced, "If that white worm had the
nerve to try to drag me back to the Old Church Home, then
the holy outfit must have been doing a lot of talking about me,
too."

He heard them whispering—whispering—Dr. John Jennison
Drew, Cholmondeley Frink, even William Washington Eathorne. The independence seeped out of him and he walked
the streets alone, afraid of men's cynical eyes and the incessant hiss of whispering.

chapter 33

HE tried to explain to his wife, as they prepared for bed,
how objectionable was Sheldon Smeeth, but all her answer was, "He has such a beautiful voice—so spiritual. I
don't think you ought to speak of him like that just because
you can't appreciate music!" He saw her then as a stranger;
he stared bleakly at this plump and fussy woman with the
broad bare arms, and wondered how she had ever come here.

In his chilly cot, turning from aching side to side, he pondered of Tanis. "He'd been a fool to lose her. He had to
have somebody he could really talk to. He'd—oh, he'd *bust*
if he went on stewing about things by himself. And Myra,
useless to expect her to understand. Well, rats, no use dodging
the issue. Darn shame for two married people to drift apart
after all these years; darn rotten shame; but nothing could

bring them together now, as long as he refused to let Zenith
bully him into taking orders—and he was by golly not going
to let anybody bully him into anything, or wheedle him or
coax him either!"

He woke at three, roused by a passing motor, and struggled
out of bed for a drink of water. As he passed through the
bedroom he heard his wife groan. His resentment was night-
blurred; he was solicitous in inquiring, "What's the trouble,
hon?"

"I've got—such a pain down here in my side—oh, it's
just—it tears at me."

"Bad indigestion? Shall I get you some bicarb?"

"Don't think—that would help. I felt funny last evening
and yesterday, and then—oh!—it passed away and I got to
sleep and— That auto woke me up."

Her voice was laboring like a ship in a storm. He was
alarmed.

"I better call the doctor."

"No, no! It'll go away. But maybe you might get me an
ice-bag."

He stalked to the bathroom for the ice-bag, down to the
kitchen for ice. He felt dramatic in this late-night expedition,
but as he gouged the chunk of ice with the dagger-like pick he
was cool, steady, mature; and the old friendliness was in his
voice as he patted the ice-bag into place on her groin, rum-
bling, "There, there, that'll be better now." He retired to bed,
but he did not sleep. He heard her groan again. Instantly he
was up, soothing her, "Still pretty bad, honey?"

"Yes, it just gripes me, and I can't get to sleep."

Her voice was faint. He knew her dread of doctors' ver-
dicts and he did not inform her, but he creaked down-stairs,
telephoned to Dr. Earl Patten, and waited, shivering, trying
with fuzzy eyes to read a magazine, till he heard the doctor's
car.

The doctor was youngish and professionally breezy. He
came in as though it were sunny noontime. "Well, George,
little trouble, eh? How is she now?" he said busily as, with
tremendous and rather irritating cheerfulness, he tossed his
coat on a chair and warmed his hands at a radiator. He took
charge of the house. Babbitt felt ousted and unimportant
as he followed the doctor up to the bedroom, and it was the
doctor who chuckled, "Oh, just little stomach-ache" when
Verona peeped through her door, begging, "What is it, Dad,
what is it?"

To Mrs. Babbitt the doctor said with amiable belligerence, after his examination, "Kind of a bad old pain, eh? I'll give you something to make you sleep, and I think you'll feel better in the morning. I'll come in right after breakfast." But to Babbitt, lying in wait in the lower hall, the doctor sighed, "I don't like the feeling there in her belly. There's some rigidity and some inflammation. She's never had her appendix out, has she? Um. Well, no use worrying. I'll be here first thing in the morning, and meantime she'll get some rest. I've given her a hypo. Good night."

Then was Babbitt caught up in the black tempest.

Instantly all the indignations which had been dominating him and the spiritual dramas through which he had struggled became pallid and absurd before the ancient and overwhelming realities, the standard and traditional realities, of sickness and menacing death, the long night, and the thousand steadfast implications of married life. He crept back to her. As she drowsed away in the tropic languor of morphia, he sat on the edge of her bed, holding her hand, and for the first time in many weeks her hand abode trustfully in his.

He draped himself grotesquely in his toweling bathrobe and a pink and white couch-cover, and sat lumpishly in a wing-chair. The bedroom was uncanny in its half-light, which turned the curtains to lurking robbers, the dressing-table to a turreted castle. It smelled of cosmetics, of linen, of sleep. He napped and woke, napped and woke, a hundred times. He heard her move and sigh in slumber; he wondered if there wasn't some officious brisk thing he could do for her, and before he could quite form the thought he was asleep, racked and aching. The night was infinite. When dawn came and the waiting seemed at an end, he fell asleep, and was vexed to have been caught off his guard, to have been aroused by Verona's entrance and her agitated "Oh, what is it, Dad?"

His wife was awake, her face sallow and lifeless in the morning light, but now he did not compare her with Tanis; she was not merely A Woman, to be contrasted with other women, but his own self, and though he might criticize her and nag her, it was only as he might criticize and nag himself, interestedly, unpatronizingly, without the expectation of changing—or any real desire to change—the eternal essence.

With Verona he sounded fatherly again, and firm. He consoled Tinka, who satisfactorily pointed the excitement of the hour by wailing. He ordered early breakfast, and wanted to look at the newspaper, and felt somehow heroic and useful in not looking at it. But there were still crawling and totally unheroic hours of waiting before Dr. Patten returned.

"Don't see much change," said Patten. "I'll be back about eleven, and if you don't mind, I think I'll bring in some other world-famous pill-pedler for consultation, just to be on the safe side. Now George, there's nothing you can do. I'll have Verona keep the ice-bag filled—might as well leave that on, I guess—and you, you better beat it to the office instead of standing around her looking as if you were the patient. The nerve of husbands! Lot more neurotic than the women! They always have to horn in and get all the credit for feeling bad when their wives are ailing. Now have another nice cup of coffee and git!"

Under this derision Babbitt became more matter-of-fact. He drove to the office, tried to dictate letters, tried to telephone and, before the call was answered, forgot to whom he was telephoning. At a quarter after ten he returned home. As he left the down-town traffic and sped up the car, his face was as grimly creased as the mask of tragedy.

His wife greeted him with surprise. "Why did you come back, dear? I think I feel a little better. I told Verona to skip off to her office. Was it wicked of me to go and get sick?"

He knew that she wanted petting, and she got it, joyously. They were curiously happy when he heard Dr. Patten's car in front. He looked out of the window. He was frightened. With Patten was an impatient man with turbulent black hair and a hussar mustache—Dr. A. I. Dilling, the surgeon. Babbitt sputtered with anxiety, tried to conceal it, and hurried down to the door.

Dr. Patten was profusely casual: "Don't want to worry you, old man, but I thought it might be a good stunt to have Dr. Dilling examine her." He gestured toward Dilling as toward a master.

Dilling nodded in his curtest manner and strode up-stairs. Babbitt tramped the living-room in agony. Except for his wife's confinements there had never been a major operation in the family, and to him surgery was at once a miracle and an abomination of fear. But when Dilling and Patten came down again he knew that everything was all right, and he wanted to laugh, for the two doctors were exactly like the bearded physicians in a musical comedy, both of them rubbing their hands and looking foolishly sagacious.

Dr. Dilling spoke:

"I'm sorry, old man, but it's acute appendicitis. We ought to operate. Of course you must decide, but there's no question as to what has to be done."

Babbitt did not get all the force of it. He mumbled, "Well, I suppose we could get her ready in a couple o' days. Probably Ted ought to come down from the university, just in case anything happened."

Dr. Dilling growled, "Nope. If you don't want peritonitis to set in, we'll have to operate right away. I must advise it strongly. If you say go ahead, I'll 'phone for the St. Mary's ambulance at once, and we'll have her on the table in three-quarters of an hour."

"I—I— Of course, I suppose you know what— But great God, man, I can't get her clothes ready and everything in two seconds, you know! And in her state, so wrought-up and weak—"

"Just throw her hair-brush and comb and tooth-brush in a bag; that's all she'll need for a day or two," said Dr. Dilling, and went to the telephone.

Babbitt galloped desperately up-stairs. He sent the frightened Tinka out of the room. He said gaily to his wife, "Well, old thing, the doc thinks maybe we better have a little operation and get it over. Just take a few minutes—not half as serious as a confinement—and you'll be all right in a jiffy."

She gripped his hand till the fingers ached. She said patiently, like a cowed child, "I'm afraid—to go into the dark, all alone!" Maturity was wiped from her eyes; they were pleading and terrified. "Will you stay with me? Darling, you don't have to go to the office now, do you? Could you just go down to the hospital with me? Could you come see me this evening—if everything's all right? You won't have to go out this evening, will you?"

He was on his knees by the bed. While she feebly ruffled his hair, he sobbed, he kissed the lawn of her sleeve, and swore, "Old honey, I love you more than anything in the world! I've kind of been worried by business and everything, but that's all over now, and I'm back again."

"Are you really? George, I was thinking, lying here, maybe it would be a good thing if I just *went*. I was wondering if anybody really needed me. Or wanted me. I was wondering what was the use of my living. I've been getting so stupid and ugly—"

"Why, you old humbug! Fishing for compliments when I ought to be packing your bag! Me, sure, I'm young and handsome and a regular village cut-up and—" He could not go on. He sobbed again; and in muttered incoherencies they found each other.

As he packed, his brain was curiously clear and swift. He'd have no more wild evenings, he realized. He admitted that he would regret them. A little grimly he perceived that this had been his last despairing fling before the paralyzed contentment of middle-age. Well, and he grinned impishly, "it was one doggone good party while it lasted!" And—how much was the operation going to cost? "I ought to have fought that out with Dilling. But no, damn it, I don't care how much it costs!"

The motor ambulance was at the door. Even in his grief the Babbitt who admired all technical excellences was interested in the kindly skill with which the attendants slid Mrs. Babbitt upon a stretcher and carried her down-stairs. The ambulance was a huge, suave, varnished, white thing. Mrs. Babbitt moaned, "It frightens me. It's just like a hearse, just like being put in a hearse. I want you to stay with me."

"I'll be right up front with the driver," Babbitt promised.

"No, I want you to stay inside with me." To the attendants: "Can't he be inside?"

"Sure, ma'am, you bet. There's a fine little camp-stool in there," the older attendant said, with professional pride.

He sat beside her in that traveling cabin with its cot, its stool, its active little electric radiator, and its quite unexplained calendar, displaying a girl eating cherries, and the name of an enterprising grocer. But as he flung out his hand in hopeless cheerfulness it touched the radiator, and he squealed:

"Ouch! Jesus!"

"Why, George Babbitt, I won't have you cursing and swearing and blaspheming!"

"I know, awful sorry but— Gosh all fish-hooks, look how I burned my hand! Gee whiz, it hurts! It hurts like the mischief! Why, that damn radiator is hot as—it's hot as —it's hotter 'n the hinges of Hades! Look! You can see the mark!"

So, as they drove up to St. Mary's Hospital, with the nurses already laying out the instruments for an operation to save her life, it was she who consoled him and kissed the place to make it well, and though he tried to be gruff and mature, he yielded to her and was glad to be babied.

The ambulance whirled under the hooded carriage-entrance of the hospital, and instantly he was reduced to a zero in the nightmare succession of cork-floored halls, endless doors open on old women sitting up in bed, an elevator, the anesthetizing room, a young interne comtemptuous of husbands. He was permitted to kiss his wife; he saw a thin dark nurse fit the cone over her mouth and nose; he stiffened at a sweet and treacherous odor; then he was driven out, and on a high stool in a laboratory he sat dazed, longing to see her once again, to insist that he had always loved her, had never for a second loved anybody else or looked at anybody else. In the laboratory he was conscious only of a decayed object preserved in a bottle of yellowing alcohol. It made him very sick, but he could not take his eyes from it. He was more aware of it than of waiting. His mind floated in abeyance, coming back always to that horrible bottle. To escape it he opened the door to the right, hoping to find a sane and business-like office. He realized that he was looking into the operating-room; in one glance he took in Dr. Dilling, strange in white gown and bandaged head, bending over the steel table with its screws and wheels, then nurses holding basins and cotton sponges, and a swathed thing, just a lifeless chin and a mound of white in the midst of which was a square of sallow flesh with a gash a little bloody at the edges, protruding from the gash a cluster of forceps like clinging parasites.

He shut the door with haste. It may be that his frightened repentance of the night and morning had not eaten in, but this dehumanizing interment of her who had been so pathetically human shook him utterly, and as he crouched again on the high stool in the laboratory he swore faith to his wife . . . to Zenith . . . to business efficiency . . . to the Boosters' Club . . . to every faith of the Clan of Good Fellows.

Then a nurse was soothing. "All over! Perfect success! She'll come out fine! She'll be out from under the anesthetic soon, and you can see her."

He found her on a curious tilted bed, her face an unwholesome yellow but her purple lips moving slightly. Then only did he really believe that she was alive. She was muttering. He bent, and heard her sighing, "Hard get real maple syrup for pancakes." He laughed inexhaustibly; he beamed on the nurse and proudly confided, "Think of her talking about maple syrup! By golly, I'm going to go and order a hundred gallons of it, right from Vermont!"

II

She was out of the hospital in seventeen days. He went
to see her each afternoon, and in their long talks they drifted
back to intimacy. Once he hinted something of his relations
to Tanis and the Bunch, and she was inflated by the view that
a Wicked Woman had captivated her poor George.

If once he had doubted his neighbors and the supreme charm
of the Good Fellows, he was convinced now. You didn't, he
noted, "see Seneca Doane coming around with any flowers or
dropping in to chat with the Missus," but Mrs. Howard Littlefield brought to the hospital her priceless wine jelly (flavored
with real wine); Orville Jones spent hours in picking out the
kind of novels Mrs. Babbitt liked—nice love stories about
New York millionaires and Wyoming cowpunchers; Louetta
Swanson knitted a pink bed-jacket; Sidney Finkelstein and
his merry brown-eyed flapper of a wife selected the prettiest
nightgown in all the stock of Parcher and Stein.

All his friends ceased whispering about him, suspecting
him. At the Athletic Club they asked after her daily. Club
members whose names he did not know stopped him to inquire, "How's your good lady getting on?" Babbitt felt that he
was swinging from bleak uplands down into the rich warm
air of a valley pleasant with cottages.

One noon Vergil Gunch suggested, "You planning to be at
the hospital about six? The wife and I thought we'd drop in."
They did drop in. Gunch was so humorous that Mrs. Babbitt said he must "stop making her laugh because honestly it
was hurting her incision." As they passed down the hall
Gunch demanded amiably, "George, old scout, you were
soreheaded about something, here a while back. I don't know
why, and it's none of my business. But you seem to be feeling all hunky-dory again, and why don't you come join us
in the Good Citizens' League, old man? We have some corking
times together, and we need your advice."

Then did Babbitt, almost tearful with joy at being coaxed
instead of bullied, at being permitted to stop fighting, at being able to desert without injuring his opinion of himself,
cease utterly to be a domestic revolutionist. He patted
Gunch's shoulder, and next day he became a member of the
Good Citizens' League.

Within two weeks no one in the League was more violent

regarding the wickedness of Seneca Doane, the crimes of labor unions, the perils of immigration, and the delights of golf, morality, and bank-accounts than was George F. Babbitt.

chapter 34

THE Good Citizens' League had spread through the country, but nowhere was it so effective and well esteemed as in cities of the type of Zenith, commercial cities of a few hundred thousand inhabitants, most of which—though not all—lay inland, against a background of cornfields and mines and of small towns which depended upon them for mortgage-loans, table-manners, art, social philosophy and millinery.

To the League belonged most of the prosperous citizens of Zenith. They were not all of the kind who called themselves "Regular Guys." Besides these hearty fellows, these salesmen of prosperity, there were the aristocrats, that is, the men who were richer or had been rich for more generations: the presidents of banks and of factories, the land-owners, the corporation lawyers, the fashionable doctors, and the few young-old men who worked not at all but, reluctantly remaining in Zenith, collected luster-ware and first editions as though they were back in Paris. All of them agreed that the working-classes must be kept in their place; and all of them perceived that American Democracy did not imply any equality of wealth, but did demand a wholesome sameness of thought, dress, painting, morals, and vocabulary.

In this they were like the ruling-class of any other country, particularly of Great Britain, but they differed in being more vigorous and in actually trying to produce the accepted standards which all classes, everywhere, desire, but usually despair of realizing.

The longest struggle of the Good Citizens' League was

against the Open Shop—which was secretly a struggle against all union labor. Accompanying it was an Americanization Movement, with evening classes in English and history and economics, and daily articles in the newspapers, so that newly arrived foreigners might learn that the true-blue and one hundred per cent. American way of settling labor-troubles was for workmen to trust and love their employers.

The League was more than generous in approving other organizations which agreed with its aims. It helped the Y.M. C.A. to raise a two-hundred-thousand-dollar fund for a new building. Babbitt, Vergil Gunch, Sidney Finkelstein, and even Charles McKelvey told the spectators at movie theaters how great an influence for manly Christianity the "good old Y." had been in their own lives; and the hoar and might Colonel Rutherford Snow, owner of the *Advocate-Times*, was photographed clasping the hand of Sheldon Smeeth of the Y.M. C.A. It is true that afterward, when Smeeth lisped, "You must come to one of our prayer-meetings," the ferocious Colonel bellowed, "What the hell would I do that for? I've got a bar of my own," but this did not appear in the public prints.

The League was of value to the American Legion at a time when certain of the lesser and looser newspapers were criticizing that organization of veterans of the Great War. One evening a number of young men raided the Zenith Socialist Headquarters, burned its records, beat the office staff, and agreeably dumped desks out of the window. All of the newspapers save the *Advocate-Times* and the *Evening Advocate* attributed this valuable but perhaps hasty direct-action to the American Legion. Then a flying squadron from the Good Citizens' League called on the unfair papers and explained that no ex-soldier could possibly do such a thing, and the editors saw the light, and retained their advertising. When Zenith's lone Conscientious Objector came home from prison and was righteously run out of town, the newspapers referred to the perpetrators as an "unidentified mob."

II

In all the activities and triumphs of the Good Citizens' League Babbitt took part, and completely won back to self-respect, placidity, and the affection of his friends. But he began to protest, "Gosh, I've done my share in cleanng up the city. I want to tend to business. Think I'll just kind of slacken up on this G.C.L. stuff now."

He had returned to the church as he had returned to the Boosters' Club. He had even endured the lavish greeting which Sheldon Smeeth gave him. He was worried lest during his late discontent he had imperiled his salvation. He was not quite sure there was a Heaven to be attained, but Dr. John Jennison Drew said there was, and Babbitt was not going to take a chance.

One evening when he was walking past Dr. Drew's parsonage he impulsively went in and found the pastor in his study.

"Jus' minute—getting 'phone call," said Dr. Drew in business-like tones, then, aggressively, to the telephone: "'Lo—'lo! This Berkey and Hannis? Reverend Drew speaking. Where the dickens is the proof for next Sunday's calendar? Huh? Y' ought to have it here. Well, I can't help it if they're *all* sick! I got to have it to-night. Get an A.D.T. boy and shoot it up here quick."

He turned, without slackening his briskness. "Well, Brother Babbitt, what c'n I do for you?"

"I just wanted to ask— Tell you how it is, dominie: Here a while ago I guess I got kind of slack. Took a few drinks and so on. What I wanted to ask is: How is it if a fellow cuts that all out and comes back to his senses? Does it sort of, well, you might say, does it score against him in the long run?"

The Reverend Dr. Drew was suddenly interested. "And, uh, brother—the other things, too? Women?"

"No, practically, you might say, practically not at all."

"Don't hesitate to tell me, brother! That's what I'm here for. Been going on joy-rides? Squeezing girls in cars?" The reverend eyes glistened.

"No—no—"

"Well, I'll tell you. I've got a deputation from the Don't Make Prohibition a Joke Association coming to see me in a quarter of an hour, and one from the Anti-Birth-Control Union at a quarter of ten." He busily glanced at his watch. "But I can take five minutes off and pray with you. Kneel right down by your chair, brother. Don't be ashamed to seek the guidance of God."

Babbitt's scalp itched and he longed to flee, but Dr. Drew had already flopped down beside his desk-chair and his voice had changed from rasping efficiency to an unctuous familiarity with sin and with the Almighty. Babbitt also knelt, while Drew gloated:

"O Lord, thou seest our brother here, who has been led astray by manifold temptations. O Heavenly Father, make his heart to be pure, as pure as a little child's. Oh, let him know again the joy of a manly courage to abstain from evil—"

Sheldon Smeeth came frolicking into the study. At the sight of the two men he smirked, forgivingly patted Babbitt on the shoulder, and knelt beside him, his arm about him, while he authorized Dr. Drew's imprecations with moans of "Yes, Lord! Help our brother, Lord!"

Though he was trying to keep his eyes closed, Babbitt squinted between his fingers and saw the pastor glance at his watch as he concluded with a triumphant, "And let him never be afraid to come to Us for counsel and tender care, and let him know that the church can lead him as a little lamb."

Dr. Drew sprang up, rolled his eyes in the general direction of Heaven, chucked his watch into his pocket, and demanded, "Has the deputation come yet, Sheldy?"

"Yep, right outside," Sheldy answered, with equal liveliness; then, caressingly, to Babbitt, "Brother, if it would help, I'd love to go into the next room and pray with you while Dr. Drew is receiving the brothers from the Don't Make Prohibition a Joke Association."

"No—no thanks—can't take the time!" yelped Babbitt, rushing toward the door.

Thereafter he was often seen at the Chatham Road Presbyterian Church, but it is recorded that he avoided shaking hands with the pastor at the door.

III

If his moral fiber had been so weakened by rebellion that he was not quite dependable in the more rigorous campaigns of the Good Citizens' League nor quite appreciative of the church, yet there was no doubt of the joy with which Babbitt returned to the pleasures of his home and of the Athletic Club, the Boosters, the Elks.

Verona and Kenneth Escott were eventually and hesitatingly married. For the wedding Babbitt was dressed as carefully as was Verona; he was crammed into the morning coat he wore to teas thrice a year; and with a certain relief, after Verona and Kenneth had driven away in a limousine, he returned to the house, removed the morning coat, sat with his aching feet up on the davenport, and reflected that his wife and he could have the living-room to themselves now, and not have to listen to Verona and Kenneth worrying, in a cultured collegiate manner, about minimum wages and the Drama League.

But even this sinking into peace was less consoling than his return to being one of the best-loved men in the Boosters' Club.

IV

President Willis Ijams began that Boosters' Club luncheon by standing quiet and staring at them so unhappily that they feared he was about to announce the death of a Brother Booster. He spoke slowly then, and gravely:

"Boys, I have something shocking to reveal to you; something terrible about one of our own members."

Several Boosters, including Babbitt, looked disconcerted.

"A knight of the grip, a trusted friend of mine, recently made a trip up-state, and in a certain town, where a certain Booster spent his boyhood, he found out something which can no longer be concealed. In fact, he discovered the inward nature of a man whom we have accepted as a Real Guy and as one of us. Gentlemen, I cannot trust my voice to say it, so I have written it down."

He uncovered a large blackboard and on it, in huge capitals, was the legend:

George Follansbee Babbitt—oh you Folly!

The Boosters cheered, they laughed, they wept, they threw rolls at Babbitt, they cried, "Speech, speech! Oh you Folly!"

President Ijams continued:

"That, gentlemen, is the awful thing Georgie Babbitt has been concealing all these years, when we thought he was just plain George F. Now I want you to tell us, taking it in turn, what you've always supposed the F. stood for."

Flivver, they suggested, and Frog-face and Flathead and Farinaceous and Freezone and Flapdoodle and Foghorn. By the joviality of their insults Babbitt knew that he had been taken back to their hearts, and happily he rose.

"Boys, I've got to admit it. I've never worn a wrist-watch, or parted my name in the middle, but I will confess to 'Follansbee.' My only justification is that my old dad—though otherwise he was perfectly sane, and packed an awful wallop when it came to trimming the City Fellers at checkers—named me after the family doc, old Dr. Ambrose Follansbee. I apologize, boys. In my next what-d'you-call-it I'll see to it that I get named something really practical—something that sounds swell and yet is good and virile—something, in fact, like that grand old name so familiar to every household— that bold and almost overpowering name, Willis Jimjams Ijams!"

He knew by the cheer that he was secure again and popular; he knew that he would no more endanger his security and popularity by straying from the Clan of Good Fellows.

v

Henry Thompson dashed into the office, clamoring, "George! Big news! Jake Offutt says the Traction Bunch are dissatisfied with the way Sanders, Torrey and Wing handled their last deal, and they're willing to dicker with us!"

Babbitt was pleased in the realization that the last scar of his rebellion was healed, yet as he drove home he was annoyed by such background thoughts as had never weakened him in his days of belligerent conformity. He discovered that he actually did not consider the Traction group quite honest. "Well, he'd carry out one more deal for them, but as soon as it was practicable, maybe as soon as Old Henry Thompson died, he'd break away from all association from them. He was forty-eight; in twelve years he'd be sixty; he wanted to leave a clean business to his grandchildren. Course there was a lot of money in negotiating for the Traction people, and a fellow had to look at things in a practical way, only—" He wriggled uncomfortably. He wanted to tell the Traction group what he thought of them. "Oh, he couldn't do it, not now. If he offended them this second time, they would crush him. But—"

He was conscious that his line of progress seemed confused. He wondered what he would do with his future. He was still young; was he through with all adventuring? He felt that he had been trapped into the very net from which he had with such fury escaped and, supremest jest of all, been made to rejoice in the trapping.

"They've licked me; licked me to a finish!" he whimpered.

The house was peaceful, that evening, and he enjoyed a game of pinochle with his wife. He indignantly told the Tempter that he was content to do things in the good old-fashioned way. The day after, he went to see the purchasing-agent of the Street Traction Company and they made plans for the secret purchase of lots along the Evanston Road. But as he drove to his office he struggled, "I'm going to run things and figure out things to suit myself—when I retire."

VI

Ted had come down from the University for the week-end. Though he no longer spoke of mechanical engineering and though he was reticent about his opinion of his instructors, he seemed no more reconciled to college, and his chief interest was his wireless telephone set.

On Saturday evening he took Eunice Littlefield to a dance at Devon Woods. Babbitt had a glimpse of her, bouncing in the seat of the car, brilliant in a scarlet cloak over a frock of thinnest creamy silk. They two had not returned when the Babbitts went to bed, at half-past eleven. At a blurred indefinite time of late night Babbbitt was awakened by the ring of the telephone and gloomily crawled down-stairs. Howard Littlefield was speaking:

"George, Euny isn't back yet. Is Ted?"

"No—at least his door is open—"

"They ought to be home. Eunice said the dance would be over at midnight. What's the name of those people where they're going?"

"Why, gosh, tell the truth, I don't know, Howard. It's some classmate of Ted's, out in Devon Woods. Don't see what we can do. Wait, I'll skip up and ask Myra if she knows their name."

Babbitt turned on the light in Ted's room. It was a brown boyish room; disordered dresser, worn books, a high-school pennant, photographs of basket-ball teams and baseball teams. Ted was decidedly not there.

Mrs. Babbitt, awakened, irritably observed that she certainly did not know the name of Ted's host, that it was late, that Howard Littlefield was but little better than a born fool, and that she was sleepy. But she remained awake and worrying while Babbitt, on the sleeping-porch, struggled back into sleep through the incessant soft rain of her remarks. It was after dawn when he was aroused by her shaking him and calling "George! George!" in something like horror.

"Wha— wha—what is it?"

"Come here quick and see. Be quiet!"

She led him down the hall to the door of Ted's room and pushed it gently open. On the worn brown rug he saw a froth of rose-colored chiffon lingerie; on the sedate Morris chair a girl's silver slipper. And on the pillows were two sleepy heads—Ted's and Eunice's.

Ted woke to grin, and to mutter with unconvincing defiance, "Good morning! Let me introduce my wife—Mrs. Theodore Roosevelt Eunice Littlefield Babbitt, Esquiress."

"Good God!" from Babbitt, and from his wife a long wailing, "You've gone and—"

"We got married last evening. Wife! Sit up and say a pretty good morning to mother-in-law."

But Eunice hid her shoulders and her charming wild hair under the pillow.

By nine o'clock the assembly which was gathered about Ted and Eunice in the living-room included Mr. and Mrs. George Babbitt, Dr. and Mrs. Howard Littlefield, Mr. and Mrs. Kenneth Escott, Mr. and Mrs. Henry T. Thompson, and Tinka Babbitt, who was the only pleased member of the inquisition.

A crackling shower of phrases filled the room:

"At their age—" "Ought to be annulled—" "Never heard of such a thing in—" "Fault of both of them and—" "Keep it out of the papers—" "Ought to be packed off to school—" "Do something about it at once, and what I say is—" "Damn good old-fashioned spanking—"

Worst of them all was Verona. "*Ted!* Some way *must* be found to make you under*stand* how dreadfully *serious* this is, instead of standing *around* with that silly foolish *smile* on your face!"

He began to revolt. "Gee whittakers, Rone, you got married yourself, didn't you?"

"That's entirely different."

"You bet it is! They didn't have to work on Eu and me with a chain and tackle to get us to hold hands!"

"Now, young man, we'll have no more flippancy," old Henry Thompson ordered. "You listen to me."

"You listen to Grandfather!" said Verona.

"Yes, listen to your Grandfather!" said Mrs. Babbitt.

"Ted, you listen to Mr. Thompson!" said Howard Littlefield.

"Oh, for the love o' Mike, I am listening!" Ted shouted. "But you look here, all of you! I'm getting sick and tired of being the corpse in this post mortem! If you want to kill somebody, go kill the preacher that married us! Why, he stung me five dollars, and all the money I had in the world was six dollars and two bits. I'm getting just about enough of being hollered at!"

A new voice, booming, authoritative, dominated the room. It was Babbitt. "Yuh, there's too darn many putting in their oar! Rone, you dry up. Howard and I are still pretty strong, and able to do our own cussing. Ted, come into the dining-room and we'll talk this over."

In the dining-room, the door firmly closed, Babbitt walked to his son, put both hands on his shoulders. "You're more or less right. They all talk too much. Now what do you plan to do, old man?"

"Gosh, dad, are you really going to be human?"

"Well, I— Remember one time you called us 'the Babbitt men' and said we ought to stick together? I want to. I don't pretend to think this isn't serious. The way the cards are stacked against a young fellow to-day, I can't say I approve of early marriages. But you couldn't have married a better girl than Eunice; and way I figure it, Littlefield is darn lucky to get a Babbitt for a son-in-law! But what do you plan to do? Course you could go right ahead with the U., and when you'd finished—"

"Dad, I can't stand it any more. Maybe it's all right for some fellows. Maybe I'll want to go back some day. But me, I want to get into mechanics. I think I'd get to be a good inventor. There's a fellow that would give me twenty dollars a week in a factory right now."

"Well—" Babbitt crossed the floor, slowly, ponderously, seeming a little old. "I've always wanted you to have a college degree." He meditatively stamped across the floor again. "But I've never— Now, for heaven's sake, don't repeat this to your mother, or she'd remove what little hair I've got left, but practically, I've never done a single thing I've wanted to in my whole life! I don't know 's I've accomplished anything except just get along. I figure out I've made about a quarter of an inch out of a possible hundred rods. Well, maybe you'll carry things on further. I don't know. But I do get a kind of sneaking pleasure out of the fact that you knew what you wanted to do and did it. Well, those folks in there will try to bully you, and tame you down. Tell 'em to go to the devil! I'll back you. Take your factory job, if you want to. Don't be scared of the family. No, nor all of Zenith. Nor of yourself, the way I've been. Go ahead, old man! The world is yours!"

Arms about each other's shoulders, the Babbitt men marched into the living-room and faced the swooping family.

AFTERWORD

Before Sinclair Lewis finished *Main Street* (1920), he was already working up the materials for his next novel, *Babbitt* (1922). Toward the end of *Main Street*, the Commercial Club of Gopher Prairie opens a "campaign of boosting" the town with a view to bringing in new industries. This campaign is put into the hands of one "Honest Jim" Blausser, a newcomer who speculates in land and is known as "a Hustler." The banquet given in his honor is an occasion for

> . . . oratorical references to Pep, Punch, Go, Vigor, Enterprise, Red Blood, He-Men, Fair Women, God's Country, James J. Hill, the Blue Sky, the Green Fields, the Bountiful Harvest, Increasing Population, Fair Return on Investments, Alien Agitators Who Threaten the Security of Our Institutions, the Hearthstone the Foundation of the State, Senator Knute Nelson, One Hundred Per Cent. Americanism, and Pointing with Pride.

Here are all the clichés of our commercial culture, the rasping rhetoric of American business enterprise at its crudest middle-class level. This is the world of George F. Babbitt.

The difference is that the scene has been moved from a small town like Sauk Centre, Minnesota (the campaign of boosting came to nothing in Gopher Prairie) to a medium-sized city like Cincinnati, Ohio, and a hundred others, where business enterprise at this middle level not only thrives but to which it gives the chief cultural characteristics. *Main Street* ends in 1920, and appropriately, since this novel is a kind of elegy to the decade just ending. *Babbitt* begins in 1920, and quite as appropriately, since it is a satiric prelude to a decade of dizzying and often mindless economic expansion. *Babbitt* is the epic of our "boom" years, and it remains today as the major documentation in literature of American business culture in general.

Documentation is the proper word, for in some ways *Babbitt* is hardly a novel at all. The structure of the book, if examined closely, proves to be quite fantastic. A year after its publication, when asked about its origins, Lewis said that all he could remember was that the original name of the protagonist was Pumphrey and that "I planned to make the whole novel 24 hours in his life, from alarm clock to alarm clock. The rest came more or less unconsciously." The name Pumphrey remained in a minor character—"Professor Joseph K. Pumphrey, owner of the Riteway Business College and instructor in Public Speaking, Business English, Scenario Writing, and Commercial Law"—and the original structural conception remains in the first seven chapters, in which we do indeed follow Babbitt from dreaming sleep to dreaming sleep. But that is only one fourth of the whole novel.

The remainder, twenty-seven chapters, did not come about, it is quite clear, "unconsciously." They are, rather, a highly conscious, indeed systematic, series of set pieces, each with its own topic, and all together giving us a punctilious analysis of the sociology of American commercial culture, of American middle-class life. Over halfway through the book, mingling with these set pieces, the first of three "plots" begins.

Chapters Eight and Nine, given over to a dinner party at the Babbitts' house, have as their topic Domestic Manners. The next two chapters are concerned with Marriage, Pullman Car Culture, and Relaxation. Chapter Twelve is about Leisure Time: baseball, golf, the movies, bridge, motoring. Chapter Thirteen takes up the phenomenon of the annual Trade Association Convention and, since it ends in a brothel, what for lack of a better word one must call Sin. Chapter Fourteen has to do with Political and Professional Oratory, and Fifteen, with Social Stratification. Sixteen and Seventeen devote themselves to Religion, and Eighteen, to Family Relations. Putting aside for the moment the three separate "plots" (the first of which begins in Chapter Nineteen), we may observe that topics that remain to be treated are the weekly Service Club Lunch, the Bachelor, the Barber Shop, Labor Relations, the Speakeasy, and "Crank" Religion. It is a very thorough canvassing of an entire milieu, and its nearly anthropological intention is made evident in such a sentence as "Now this was the manner of obtaining alcohol under the reign of righteousness and prohibition," the sentence which introduces Babbitt's visit to a bootlegger.

The ordering of these pieces is almost as aimless as the canvass is complete. They could be ordered in almost any other arrangement, and that is because there is no real plot, or connected march of events from the beginning to the end, which would necessarily have determined their order. Their fragmentariness is in part overcome by the fact that Babbitt moves through all of them in the course of his rising discontent—his rebellion, his retreat and resignation. Each of these three moods, in turn, centers in a more or less separate narrative. The first develops after Babbitt's one real friend, Paul Riesling, shoots his wife and is given a three-year prison sentence. It is this event that suddenly makes Babbitt feel that his life is empty and that all his bustling activities are meaningless. It is in this mood that he decides to be "liberal" (although he hardly understands what the word means) and thus declare his independence from the clan of his business associates. Paul Riesling disappears pretty much from the novel, but now Babbitt meets a new friend, Mrs. Tanis Judique, an adventuress with whom, in the absence of Mrs. Babbitt, he begins a love affair. This open break with the professed moral code of the middle class is the dramatization of his revolt from the values of his business culture. He tries to forget his discontent and the insecurity and fear from which he is immediately suffering by drink and debauchery with "the Bunch," a miscellaneous group of trivial and tawdry persons who are Tanis Judique's friends. These pleasures pall, and presently he breaks off his friendship with Tanis, and now she disappears from the novel. In the meantime, Vergil Gunch and other of Babbitt's associates are forming the Good Citizens' League, an anti-labor vigilante organization, and they attempt to coerce Babbitt into joining them. In his mood of stubborn discontent, he resists their efforts and suffers alarming social and economic injuries as a result, and it is only his wife's happily coincidental emergency operation that enables him to scuttle into that organization and back into the old security of the Boosters' Club and the business order of Zenith. Perfectly safe again, he recognizes at the end of the book that he has never in his life really done anything that he wanted to, and he hopes for a fuller, more independent life for his not very promising son, Theodore Roosevelt Babbitt. But he cannot define for himself anything real that he ever did want to do except what in fact he had always done.

It is Babbitt's tragedy that he can never be anything but Babbitt, and this he learns well before the end of the book:

That moment he started for Zenith. In his journey there was no appearance of flight, but he was fleeing, and four days afterward he was on the Zenith train. He knew that he was slinking back not because it was what he longed to do but because it was all he could do. He scanned again his discovery that he could never run away from Zenith and family and office, because in his own brain he bore the office and the family and every street and disquiet and illusion of Zenith.

He can never be anything but Babbitt even though he has a glimmering recognition of what it is about being Babbitt that he does not always like:

> He was conscious of life, and a little sad. With no Vergil Gunches before whom to set his face in resolute optimism, he beheld, and half admitted that he beheld, his way of life as incredibly mechanical. Mechanical business—a brisk selling of badly built houses. Mechanical religion—a dry, hard church, shut off from the real life of the streets, inhumanly respectable as a top-hat. Mechanical golf and dinner-parties and bridge and conversation. Save with Paul Riesling, mechanical friendships—back-slapping and jocular, never daring to essay the test of quietness.

The terror and loneliness that he feels in his brief taste of freedom (and that freedom itself consists largely of a very "mechanical" bit of adultery) arise from the fact that when he is free he is nothing at all. His only self is the self that exists only within the circle of conformity.

Since the publication of *Babbitt*, everyone has learned that conformity is the great price that our predominantly commercial culture exacts of American life. But when *Babbitt* was published, this was its revelation to Americans, and this was likewise how the novel differed from all novels about business that had been published before it.

American literature had a rich if brief tradition of the business novel. James, Howells, Norris, London, Phillips, Herrick, Sinclair, Wharton, Dreiser, Poole, Tarkington—all these writers had been centrally concerned with the businessman, and after James and Howells, only Tarkington was to find in him any of the old, perdurable American virtues. Business was synonymous with ethical corruption; the world of business was savagely competitive, brutally aggressive, murderous. The motivation of the businessman was power, money, social prestige—in that order. But the businessman in all this fiction was the tycoon, the powerful manufacturer, the vast speculator, the fabulous financier, the monarch of enormous enterprises, the arch-individual responsible only to himself. And his concern was with production.

After the First World War, the tycoon may still have been the most colorful and dramatic figure in the business myth, but he was no longer by any means the characteristic figure, and *Babbitt* discovers the difference. This is the world of the little businessman, and more particularly, of the middleman. If his morals are no better, his defections are anything but spectacular. A little cheating in a deal, a little lie to one's wife, a little fornication that one pretends did not occur. Not in the least resembling the autocratic individualist, he is always the compromising conformist. No producer himself, his success depends on public relations. He does not rule; he "joins" to be safe. He boosts and boasts with his fellows, sings and cheers and prays with the throng, derides all differences, denounces all dissent—and all to climb with the crowd. With the supremacy of public relations, he abolishes human relations. And finally, therefore, he abolishes his own humanity.

All this Sinclair Lewis's novel gave back to a culture that was just becoming aware that it could not tolerate what it had made of itself. And his novel did it with a difference. The older novels, generally speaking, were solemn or grandly melodramatic denunciations of monstrous figures of aggressive evil. *Babbitt* was raucously satirical of a crowd of ninnies and buffoons who, if they were malicious and mean, were also ridiculous. And yet, along with all that, *Babbitt* was pathetic. How could it possibly have failed? It did not. It was one of the greatest international successes in all publishing history.

The European response was unadulterated delight: This was the way—crass, materialistic, complacent, chauvinistic— that Europe had always known America to be, and now an American had made the confession to the world. In the United States the response was, understandably, more mixed. Among those who were either unimpressed or outraged, there was, however, small complaint on the score of the deficiencies of *Babbitt* as a novel. No one, for example, observed the slack structure, or the repetitiousness of point in the long series of sociological demonstrations. Edith Wharton, in her letter of congratulation to Lewis, did observe that he seemed to depend on an excess of slang, on nearly endless imitation of midwestern garrulity; but this did not bother others. Had

anyone complained, for example, that in his use of public
addresses of one sort or another, Lewis's pleasure in mimicry
threatened to carry him far beyond the demands of his
fiction, it might have been pointed out that here is a very
integral part of his satire. Elocution is an old American in-
stitution, and a windy, mindless rhetoric has been of its
essence. Lewis's use of elocution adds a swelling note to the
already loud *blat-blat* of the public voice that roars and
clacks throughout the novel, and if Lewis lets Babbitt admire
Chan Mott because he "can make a good talk even when he
hasn't got a doggone thing to say," he is also making an
observation on the empty and noisy restlessness of American
life.

There are other faults. Lewis had a tendency to reduce his
irony to the most mechanical formulas, as when he immediately juxtaposes the disaster of the Babbitts' dinner for
the McKelveys with the disaster of the Overbrooks' dinner
for the Babbitts, or when, in Chapter Eighteen, he juxtaposes
Ted Babbitt's complaints about his father with the father's
similar complaints about his daughter. Ted's grumblings end
as follows:

". . . just keep sitting there—sitting there every night—not
wanting to go anywhere—not wanting to do anything—
thinking us kids are crazy—sitting there—Lord!"

Babbitt's conclusions are identical:

". . . Sitting there—sitting there—night after night—not
wanting to do anything—thinking I'm crazy because I like
to go out and play a fist of cards—sitting there—gosh!"

Such aesthetic crudities were overlooked by readers who
delighted once more in Lewis's detail-crowded canvas, in his
faithful observation of social and material surfaces, in his
stream of reportorial lingo. These were, of course, his virtues. How perfect is a detail such as this, descriptive of a
real-estate speculator: "Below his eyes were semicircular hollows, as though silver dollars had been pressed against them
and had left an imprint." Lewis had developed, too, a kind
of rhetorical flourish of style that he had probably learned
from Dickens, his favorite novelist: "His shoes were black
laced boots, good boots, honest boots, standard boots, extraordinarily uninteresting boots," and neat rhetorical turns
such as these: "He announced that he would be enchanted

to have Ted left out of things, and hurried in to be polite, lest Ted be left out of things," and "Babbitt loved his mother, and sometimes he rather liked her . . ."

Most readers of *Babbitt* found more to praise in the writing than to condemn. As for those who were unsatisfied, it was not the writing, nor even Lewis's satiric exposure of American commercial culture in itself that disturbed them, but rather their failure to find in the novel anything beyond this grossness. With George Santayana, who was otherwise impressed by the novel, they saw "no suggestion of the direction . . . in which salvation may come." In Babbitt they saw only the exemplification of Mencken's "boob," who was not capable of being saved, and in the novel at large they saw no one else who was, and Sinclair Lewis seemed to them, like Mencken, to be without "spiritual gifts." The world that Lewis drew was a damned world, as closed to escape as a circle in Hell, "our native *Inferno* of the mechanized hinterland." And not, many readers inferred, of the hinterland alone. This spectacle was supposed to be America. The complaint was to say of Lewis, in effect, what Lewis had himself said of Babbitt, that he was "without a canon [of value] which would enable him to speak with authority."

The question seems to be a double one: Can even the doubting Babbitt conceive of the qualities that make a man as well as a businessman, that create a society as well as a mere association of "joiners"; and, can Sinclair Lewis?

Babbitt is obsessed with a love of *things*. "He had enormous and poetic admiration, though very little understanding, of all mechanical devices. They were his symbols of truth and beauty." In his discontent, he has vague glimmerings of a freer and a fuller life than a world of things will permit, but outside his world of things, as we have seen, he is lost and a cipher. His identity has been imposed upon him by that world of things.

Just as he was an Elk, a Booster, and a member of the Chamber of Commerce, just as the priests of the Presbyterian Church determined his every religious belief and the senators who controlled the Republican Party decided in little smoky rooms in Washington what he should think about disarmament, tariff, and Germany, so did the large national advertisers fix the surface of his life, fix what he believed to be his individuality. These standard advertised wares— toothpastes, socks, tires, cameras, instantaneous hot-water heaters—were his symbols and proofs of excellence; at first the signs, then the substitutes, for joy and passion and wisdom.

Truth, beauty, excellence, joy, passion, and wisdom—these are all the qualities that Zenith lacks and all the qualities that Zenith, if it is to be humane, needs. This the novel makes plain enough. How to find them? There is only one way, and that is through the cultivation of a true individuality, but how to cultivate a true individuality George F. Babbitt assuredly does not know, since he has no sense of what it is.

And Sinclair Lewis? Are we justified in asking that a writer be not only the diagnostician but the healer, too? I think not. It has been a commonplace to say of Lewis that he was himself too much a George F. Babbitt to lift his sights to values beyond Babbitt's own. In many ways the charge is just. But he is different from Babbitt in one supreme way: He *observed* him, and Babbitt had not been observed before; thus he *created* him; and Babbitt endures in our literature as in life, where Sinclair Lewis enabled all of us to see him for the first and for an enduring time. If this is to say, with Joseph Wood Krutch, that Lewis "reported a range of grotesque vulgarity which but for him would have left no record of itself because no one else could have adequately reported it," is that not to say quite enough for any writer? The drift of our commercial culture in the forty years since *Babbitt* suggests that Lewis did little to alter it, perhaps; but he was the first novelist to tell us explicitly into what stupid, and finally devastating, social damnation we were drifting. Have we landed?

Mark Schorer
University of California

SELECTED BIBLIOGRAPHY

Other Works by Sinclair Lewis

Our Mr. Wrenn, 1914   Novel
The Job, 1917   Novel
Free Air, 1919   Novel
Main Street, 1920   Novel (Signet CE875)
Arrowsmith, 1925   Novel (Signet CW809)
Elmer Gantry, 1927   Novel (Signet CY509)
The Man Who Knew Coolidge, 1928   Novel
Dodsworth, 1929   Novel (Play with Sidney Howard, 1934) (Signet CY594)
Nobel Prize Acceptance Speech, 1930
Ann Vickers, 1933   Novel
It Can't Happen Here, 1935   Novel (Play, with John C. Moffit, 1936) (Signet W6616)
Selected Short Stories, 1935
Cass Timberlane, 1945   Novel
Kingsblood Royal, 1947   Novel
The God-Seeker, 1949   Novel
World So Wide, 1951   Novel

Selected Biography and Criticism

The definitive biography of Sinclair Lewis is Mark Schorer's *Sinclair Lewis: An American Life*. New York: McGraw-Hill Book Company, 1961. Mr. Schorer has also written the Afterwords to the Signet Classic editions of *Main Street* and *Arrowsmith*; and the Introduction to *Lewis at Zenith:* (*Main Street, Babbitt, Arrowsmith*). New York: Harcourt, Brace & World, Inc., 1961. A collection of criticism of Sinclair Lewis edited by Mr. Schorer will be published in 1962 in the *Twentieth Century Views* Series. New York: Prentice-Hall, Inc.

Geismar, Maxwell D. *The Last of the Provincials: The American Novel, 1915-1925*. Boston: Houghton Mifflin Company, 1947; London: Secker & Warburg, Ltd., 1948.
Kazin, Alfred. "The New Realism: Sherwood Anderson and Sinclair Lewis," in *On Native Grounds: An Interpretation of Modern American Prose Literature*. New York: Reynal & Hitchcock, 1942; London: Jonathan Cape; Ltd., 1943.
Lewis, Grace Hegger. *With Love from Gracie: Sinclair Lewis, 1912-1925*. New York: Harcourt, Brace & Company, 1955.
Lippmann, Walter. "Sinclair Lewis," in *Men of Destiny*. New York: The Macmillan Company, 1927.
Maule, Harry E. and others (eds.). *The Man from Main Street: Selected Essays and Other Writings, 1904-1950*. New York: Random House, 1953.
Parrington, V. L. *Main Currents in American Thought*. Vol. 3. New York: Harcourt, Brace & Company, 1930, pp. 360-369.
Smith, Harrison (ed.). *From Main Street to Stockholm: Letters of Sinclair Lewis, 1919-1930*. New York: Harcourt, Brace & Company, 1952.
Van Doren, Carl. "Sinclair Lewis," in *The American Novel, 1789-1939*. New York: The Macmillan Company, 1921; rev. 1940.
West, Rebecca. "Sinclair Lewis Introduces Elmer Gantry" in *The Strange Necessity*. Garden City, L. I.: Doubleday, Doran & Company, 1928; London: Jonathan Cape, Ltd., 1931.
Whipple, T. K. "Sinclair Lewis," in *Spokesmen: Modern Writers and American Life*. New York: D. Appleton-Century Company, Inc., 1928.